Cognitive Development

For Phyll

Cognitive Development

An Information Processing Approach

John McShane

Basil Blackwell

First published 1991

Basil Blackwell Ltd
108 Cowley Road, Oxford, OX4 1JF, UK

Basil Blackwell, Inc.
3 Cambridge Center
Cambridge, Massachusetts 02142, USA

British Library Cataloguing in Publication Data

A CIP catalogue record for this book is available from the British Library

Library of Congress Cataloging in Publication Data

McShane, John
   Cognitive development: an information processing approach/John McShane.
      p.   cm.
   Includes bibliographical references and index.
   ISBN 0–631–17018–9 (hard): ISBN 0–631–17019–7 (pbk.)
      1. Cognition in children.   2. Human information processing in children.   I. Title.
   BF723.C5M37   1991
   155.4′13–dc20   90–35932
                                                                                                                    CIP

Typeset in 10 on 12 pt Plantin
by Photo·graphics, Honiton, Devon
Printed in Great Britain by T. J. Press Ltd, Padstow, Cornwall

Contents

Acknowledgements

The author and publishers are grateful for permission to reproduce the following material:

Figure 1.2 from *The Perception of the Visual World* by J.J. Gibson. © 1950 by Houghton Mifflin Company. Used with permission. **Table 1.1** from 'Three aspects of cognitive psychology' by R.S. Siegler, *Cognitive Psychology*, 4, p. 486. © 1976 by Academic Press. **Figure 2.3** from 'Infant pattern vision' by M.S. Banks and P. Salapatek, *Journal of Experimental Child Psychology*, 31. © 1981 by Academic Press. **Figure 2.4** from 'Visual scanning of triangles by the human newborn' by P. Salapatek and W. Kessen, *Journal of Experimental Child Psychology*, 3, p. 511. © 1966 by Academic Press. **Figure 2.5** from 'Infants' discrimination of internal and external pattern elements' by A.E. Milewski, *Journal of Experimental Child Psychology*, 22, p. 233. © 1976 by Academic Press. **Figure 2.9** from 'The co-ordination of visual and tactual input in infancy' by T.G.R. Bower et al, *Perception and Psychophysics*, 8. © 1970 by the Psychonomic Society, Inc. Used with permission. **Figure 2.10** Figure 4–1 from *Sensation and Perception*, Second Edition, by Stanley Coren, Clare Porac, and Lawrence M. Ward. © 1984 by Harcourt Brace Jovanovich, Inc., reprinted with permission of the publisher. **Figure 2.12** from *Neonate Cognition* edited by J. Mehler and R. Fox, p. 203. © 1985 by Laurence Erlbaum Associates Inc. Used with permission. **Figure 4.2** from 'Abstraction and the process of recognition' by M.I. Posner in *The Psychology of Learning and Motivation*, vol. 3, p. 63, edited by G.H. Bower and J.T. Spence. © 1976 by Academic Press. **Figure 4.4** from 'The nature and structure of infant form categories' by P.C. Bomba and E.R. Siqueland, *Journal of Experimental Child Psychology*, 35, p. 302. ©

Preface

In the late 1970s I began to teach courses and conduct research on cognitive development at St Andrews University. The more I learnt, the more dissatisfied I became with the state of the subject. Piaget had provided the dominant framework for research on cognitive development but his theory was increasingly under challenge. Theoretical constructs derived from information processing were beginning to influence cognitive developmental theory as were arguments about the necessity for innate cognitive structures derived from linguistics. Together with Dave Morrison and Steve Whittaker, I began to search for a satisfactory theoretical framework for cognitive development. We read and discussed a wide range of papers, which improved our erudition no end, but failed to lead us to a satisfactory theoretical stance. We broadly concluded that human cognition should be modelled as an information processing system, rather than the structural system proposed by Piaget. However, the parts that attracted us did not seem to add up to a whole. One important reason for our dissatisfaction was that most of the research on cognitive development only addressed the issue of the changes in cognitive functioning with age, without addressing the issue of the mechanisms that are responsible for change.

In 1981 I moved to the London School of Economics and continued research and teaching on cognitive development. Over the next few years I continued to pursue the search for a coherent framework for this work with Steve Whittaker, Julie Dockrell, and Sue Michie. In 1985 I was awarded a six-month fellowship by the Nuffield Foundation to prepare a monograph on mechanisms of cognitive change, which I had now concluded was an issue being seriously neglected by cognitive developmental theory. As I worked on that issue, I found it impossible to separate it from the great bulk of literature that documented cognitive change. Thus, I began to put together a more comprehensive review of the area of cognitive development, from which this book eventually took shape. During this phase I had many valuable discussions with Tony Simon and especially with Julie Dockrell, who read and commented upon many drafts and has caused the text to be better than it would otherwise have been.

I am grateful to the many students and colleagues who have helped my thinking through their questioning over the years. I am grateful to the Nuffield Foundation for their support. In producing this book, I have had excellent secretarial assistance from Pat Christopher, Ida McConnell, and Vanessa Cragoe. My thanks to them. Above all, my thanks to Julie, Steve, Tony, Dave, and Sue for the stimulating discussions, which made the enterprise possible and enjoyable.

1

What is Cognitive Development?

Some Historical Points

The Origin of the Scientific Study of Children

There have always been theories about cognitive development (Borstelmann, 1983). However, the scientific study of children's thought did not begin until the end of the nineteenth century and owed its origin to a variety of educational, medical, and social factors (Sears, 1975). One of the earliest proponents of the scientific study of children was G. Stanley Hall (1844–1924). Hall was the first American student to study at Leipzig with Wilhelm Wundt (1832–1920), often regarded as the founding father of modern psychology. Hall returned to America in 1880 bringing with him the 'questionnaire method' with which he was to investigate 'the contents of children's minds'. Hall asked children straightforward questions such as 'Have you ever seen a cow?' and 'Where are your ribs?' and scored the percentage correct for different groups of children (Cairns, 1983). Although Hall attempted to introduce a scientific approach to research with children, his methods were far from rigorous and his interpretation of data wildly speculative by today's standards. Hall's importance lies in the fact that he organized and promoted the study of child development by scientific means. He played a more general significant role in helping to establish psychology as a scientific discipline. He was the first president of the American Psychological Association, the first person to be named to a chair of psychology in the United States, the founder and the first editor of the *American Journal of Psychology*, and the founder and first editor of the *Pedagogical Seminary*, a journal devoted to child studies (Cairns, 1983).

In Europe, Alfred Binet (1857–1911) was among the pioneers of experimental studies with children. Binet's interest in psychology seems to have derived from independent reading. His early career in psychology was devoted to the study of hypnotism and its effects but he quickly extended his range of interests to cover the memory feats of chess masters, the psychology of aesthetics, suggestibility, the nervous system of invertebrates, perception in children (e.g., Binet, 1890) and memory development (e.g., Binet and Henri, 1894; see also Thieman and Brewer, 1978). Binet also founded and edited *l'Année Psychologique*. However, it is as the joint inventor, with Theodore Simon, of the first intelligence test that Binet is best remembered (Binet and Simon, 1905; 1908). Binet and Simon's tests were designed to differentiate among children so that those who were backward and might benefit from special education could be identified. From this practical concern grew a psychological innovation that has had a major impact on the assessment of children's cognitive abilities.

Although Hall and Binet were influential in determining how children were studied in the early part of this century, neither made a significant contribution to our theoretical understanding of the child's mind. Binet was, with good cause, sceptical of the theorists of his day. He was dedicated to the exploration of empirical facts. Hall, however, was not shy of theory. Although his early work was largely descriptive, he later began to apply Haeckel's dictum that 'ontogeny recapitulates phylogeny' as a universal explanation for development. This led to some exceedingly bizarre pronouncements, especially about adolescence (Cairns, 1983). Hall's theoretical interpretations probably hindered rather than advanced the study of developmental processes.

The first major modern developmental theorist was James Mark Baldwin (1861–1934). Baldwin made theoretical contributions to three areas: cognitive development, the social and cognitive foundations of personality, and the relations between behavioural ontogeny and behavioural phylogeny. Where Hall and Binet had founded journals to report the results of empirical studies, Baldwin co-founded and co-edited (with James McKeen Cattell) two journals largely concerned with theory: *Psychological Review*, and *Psychological Bulletin*.

In 1895 Baldwin published his major work on cognitive development *Mental Development in the Child and the Race*. (In this context 'race' means 'species'.) In this text Baldwin argued that development begins with reflexes and then progresses through a series of stages. These begin with a sensorimotor stage, progress to a symbolic or ideational stage, and then through prelogical, logical and hyperlogical stages. Baldwin was not only concerned with charting the course of development but also with the mechanisms that moved the child from stage to stage. Given his interest in biological adaptation Baldwin emphasized the adaptation of the child to the environment through 'accommodation' and through 'oppositions' and 'assimilation'. Baldwin also invented the concept of a feedback mechanism through which the infant learns to repeat movements that have had pleasurable effects. He called this mechanism a 'circular action'. These circular actions gave rise to mental representations of the environment, which Baldwin termed 'schemes'.

In outline Baldwin's theory of development is, as we shall see, very similar to that of Jean Piaget. Piaget acknowledged the influence of Baldwin on his own thinking. There are, however, considerable differences in the detail of the two theories. Although Baldwin's theory has a contemporary ring, when presented as selectively as it has been here, it would be a mistake to over-interpret its contemporary relevance.

Further contributions from Baldwin were prevented by his being forced to resign from his professorship at Johns Hopkins University in 1909 due to a personal scandal. The same fate was to befall John B. Watson at Johns Hopkins in 1920. To paraphrase Oscar Wilde: to lose one professor may be regarded as a misfortune; to lose two looks like carelessness.

The theoretical understanding of cognition, as proposed by Baldwin, failed to flourish in America. However, in Europe, Jean Piaget (1896–1980), who was much influenced by Baldwin's research, began a programme of research that was to have a profound effect on how we think about the child's mind. In the United States itself, the behaviourist movement began to assert its dominance over method and theory. John B. Watson (1878–1958) was the founding father of behaviourism. The tradition to which he gave rise was to be the dominant force in psychology from the 1920s to the 1960s. The attempt to explain behaviour in terms of mental processes was replaced by explanations in terms of laws of learning that concentrated exclusively on the functional relations between environmental stimuli and behavioural responses. Watson, for example, was convinced that the conditioning methods of behaviourism could be applied successfully to children's learning. To test the validity of these ideas Watson and Rayner (1920) attempted to condition a fear response in Albert, a 9-month-old baby, to a previously neutral stimulus – a white rat. It is a moot point now how successful the experiment actually was (Harris, 1979) but it became a focal point of the claim by Watson and others that conditioning was the key to understanding development. For 40 years after Watson, that belief had considerable appeal among psychologists committed to a rigorous scientific approach to human behaviour. Theories of cognitive development were not seriously entertained again until the 1960s. At that time two forces began to shape modern theories of cognitive development. The first was a growing interest in the work and ideas of Piaget. Flavell (1963) brought this interest to a focus in an important exposition of Piaget's theory. The second force was the rise of information processing theories of cognition. Initially, information processing theories were applied exclusively to the study of adult cognition. However, there has been an increasing attempt to apply an information processing analysis to the study of cognitive development.

Piaget's Theory

Piaget has had a greater influence on how cognitive development is viewed and studied than any other theorist. Piaget links the past and the present in more ways than one. There is an indirect link between Binet and Piaget. In 1920, Piaget came to Paris from Switzerland, already armed with a doctorate in biology, to study psychology. While in Paris, Piaget began work, in the laboratory that Binet had founded, on the standardization of a new intelligence test. Piaget's task was to determine pass–fail age norms for the questions on the test. On his own initiative, Piaget began to investigate why children failed the questions they did. He did this by asking probing questions designed to uncover the reasoning strategies employed by the child. This method was based on psychiatric interviewing techniques Piaget had previously learnt in Zurich. The method was to become the hallmark of Piaget's investigative technique. Piaget called it *the clinical method*.

From his questioning, Piaget noticed that the difference between children who passed and failed particular items was not simply that some children knew more than others, but rather that children who failed seemed to employ a different reasoning strategy from children who passed. He set out to investigate the nature of these developmental differences. It was to become his life's work.

Piaget's initial investigations led to five books (1923/1926; 1924/1926; 1926/1929; 1927/1930; 1932/1932)* that investigated various aspects of cognitive functioning in preschool and school-aged children. The theoretical interpretation offered by Piaget during this early phase of his work were couched largely in terms of the child's peculiar consciousness. Thus, the child's language was said to be 'egocentric' because the child does not take into account the need to adapt speech to the listener's point of view; thought was 'animistic' because the child attributed animate characteristics to inanimate objects such as the moon and the wind.

In the introduction to his first book, *The Language and Thought of The*

* Here, and elsewhere, the first date is the year of the original publication and the second the year it first appeared in English translation. The first date should be used to locate the work in the list of references.

Child, Piaget acknowledges the influence of Baldwin, among others on his thinking. With Baldwin, Piaget shared the assumption that children begin life with an undifferentiated sense of self and other. It is only gradually, and as a result of contact with the world, that children learn to distinguish their own thoughts and judgements both as private to themselves and not available to others unless there is explicit communication. This development represents a shift from an egocentric to a non-egocentric mode of thinking.

The early phase of Piaget's work can be separated from his later work. The later work began during the 1930s when Piaget made detailed observations of his own three infants and published the results in three volumes (Piaget, 1936a/1952; 1936b/1955; 1945/1951). These volumes represent the beginning of what might today be called 'Piaget's theory'. They differ from the earlier volumes in that Piaget now begins to articulate a theory of cognition cast in terms of cognitive structures. The major difference is that where previously there was an *ad hoc* collection of theoretical constructs to suit the phenomenon studied, there now begins to emerge a view of cognition as a system working according to general principles. These principles are very similar to those proposed by Baldwin. The theory is a stage theory. Cognition begins with reflexes, then moves through a sensorimotor stage, the end of which is marked by the emergence of symbolic thought. There then follows a preoperational stage, a concrete operational stage, and a formal operational stage. There is a close similarity here to Baldwin's prelogical, logical, and hyperlogical stages. The debt to Baldwin does not end there. The major mechanism of development is one of adaptation to the environment by means of assimilation and accommodation; and 'circular reactions' are a major means of learning during infancy.

Subsequent to his work on infancy Piaget and a variety of co-workers, most notably Barbel Inhelder, began to explore the development of various aspects of logical thought in the child. In 1941 Piaget and Inhelder published *Le Développement des Quantités Physiques chez l'Enfant*, which reported research on conservation, among other things. Piaget and Inhelder showed that young children fail to understand that when, for example, water is poured from one container into a taller narrower container, the amount of liquid remains the same. (Most children think the amount in the taller glass is greater.) Other volumes on number (Piaget, 1941/1952) time (1946a/1969), movement and speed (1946b/1970) and many other topics followed. In these volumes Piaget attempted to document the way in which a child's thinking about the world changes with development. These aspects of Piaget's theory will be discussed in more detail later.

The Information Processing Approach

The second force to have shaped contemporary theories of cognitive development is an approach that was not the product of any one particular person. The information processing approach has its roots in disciplines that were concerned with the study of information in the period following the Second World War, notably, communications theory (Shannon, 1948); the theory of computation (Turing, 1936); artificial intelligence (Newell, Shaw and Simon, 1958) and linguistics (Chomsky, 1957). The story of its origins has been well told by Gardner (1985) and by Lachman, Lachman, and Butterfield (1979).

The information processing approach to the study of cognition contains ideas borrowed from all these sources. From communications theory came the concept of information as something that could be coded and transmitted through a channel. It was proposed that the cognitive system could be modelled as a series of channels that carried information, processes that changed the information at critical points in its passage through the channels, and stores that retained information. Broadbent's (1958) analysis of attention was very strongly influenced by communications theory, and in its turn strongly influenced the shape of cognitive theories.

Where communications theory provided a model of how information might be transmitted and manipulated through the cognitive system, the theory of computation provided a way of thinking about what a system that manipulated information could and could not do, in principle. The most influential work was that of Turing (1936) who showed that any series of specific steps that led to the solution of a logical or mathematical problem could be accomplished also by a 'machine' with only a small number of properties and capabilities. The term 'machine' is in quotes because what Turing described were the principles by which a machine could accomplish its computations. The phrase 'Turing machine' is now used to describe these principles. Turing's work was important in that it showed that complex problems could be solved by a mechanical procedure. (This, in fact, is one of the major results of mathematical logic of the twentieth century.) This result suggested that the complex thought processes of the human mind might also be treated in a mechanical way (see e.g., Newell, 1980a; Pylyshyn, 1984). The key to a successful model of thought along these lines is to specify the precise steps (*an effective procedure*, as it is called) that are involved in processing precisely specified units of information. This metatheoretical assumption is one of the central assumptions of information processing theories of cognition and serves to distinguish the approach from other approaches to the study of cognition.

Artificial intelligence provides a link between the formal results of computability theory and cognitive psychology. The classic reference is Newell and Simon (1972). They proposed that the human mind can be regarded as a symbol-manipulating system and its workings simulated by computer programs that store, manipulate, and transform these symbols. Whether or not cognitive psychologists wish to use the technique of simulation, they generally subscribe to the assumptions articulated by Newell and Simon. A further influence of their approach is that the manipulation and transformation of information by the cognitive system is accomplished by the operation of rules. The view that human thought should be understood as the result of applying rules to information is a further central metatheoretical assumption of information processing theories and one that is intimately linked with the notion of an effective procedure discussed above. These central assumptions were reinforced by convergent developments in linguistics.

Linguistics has influenced the information processing approach in two important ways. Firstly, linguists have proposed detailed rule-based models of the basic units and processes involved in generating the sentences of a language (e.g., Chomsky, 1957; 1965). Since language is a fundamental human cognitive activity these models have held considerable interest as proposals about the type of computational machinery necessary to generate language. Secondly, linguists, most notably Noam Chomsky, have engaged directly in the debate about how the human cognitive system should be conceptualized. One of Chomsky's major contributions to this debate was his contention (Chomsky, 1965) that a child could not learn language unless he or she had a considerable innate knowledge of the structure of language. More recently, Chomsky has been central in arguing that the cognitive system should not be viewed as one general system with one set of principles but as a series of largely self-contained cognitive modules, each obeying principles of operation specific to itself (Chomsky, 1980).

The information processing approach to the study of cognition is an attempt to specify the processes that operate to extract information from the sources of environmental stimulation available to us. These processes are specified functionally rather than neurologically; very often they are specified as rules. The dynamic operation of the system is often depicted by a flow-chart that shows the sequence of the steps involved in processing some particular type of input (see Newell (1980b) for a discussion of flow-charts in information processing theories). Figure 1.1 is an example of the steps that might be involved in performing the addition of two or more numbers. Although, to adults, the task is simple, it is surprising

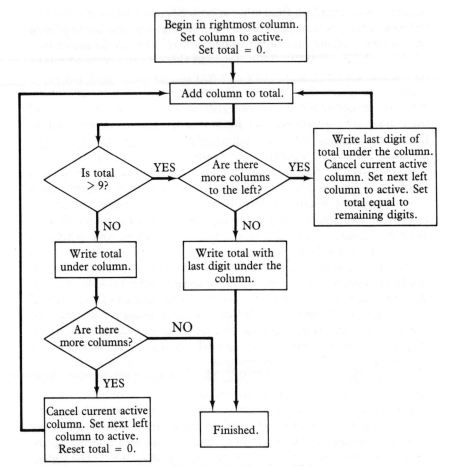

Figure 1.1 *An algorithm for addition.*

on analysis the number of steps that are actually involved in performing the task. Figure 1.1 shows the steps that are necessary in order to be able to add any arbitrarily complex set of numbers. Figure 1.1 simply represents the control procedure necessary to carry out addition successfully – it assumes that the person is actually able to add two numbers. Let us take as a concrete example the addition sum

    474
    <u>562</u>

Figure 1.1 instructs us to begin in the rightmost column and to attend

only to this column ('set column to active'). The running total is 0 before we start. This may seem unnecessary at this stage but later in the process the running total may not be zero when we begin to add the numbers in a column. This will occur when, for example, we carry a number from one column to the next. To the running total we add the numbers in the column and obtain 6. Since this total is less than 9 we follow the left hand path in figure 1.1 and simply write the total under the column. As there are more columns we now focus attention on the next column to the left, making it the active column and resetting the total to 0 before we begin to add the numbers in this column.

Adding the numbers in the second column gives a total of 13. This is greater than 9 so we follow a different path in figure 1.1. We first check whether or not there are more columns to the left. Since there are we must add these but first we must give a total for the present column. In order to do that we must decompose 13 into units we can carry forward to the next column and units we leave as the total for the present column. Since every column is ten times bigger than the previous one, every 10 can be carried forward as a unit of 1. We do not, however, need to reason like this every time we carry out addition, although this is the logic of the process. We simply need a procedure that captures this logic. (We could even learn the procedure without understanding the logic.) A simple procedure is provided in figure 1.1 in the right-hand box. We simply write the last digit of the total under the column and carry the remaining digits forward. In this case we write 3 and carry 1 forward to the next column. This time when we start to add the column the total is 1, and when we add the remaining numbers to this we obtain 10. This total is greater than 9 so we again follow the same path that we took for the previous column. However, since there are no more columns to be added, we can write down the 10 as the sum of the column. The answer is thus 1036.

The detailed analysis of the processes involved in performing a task as simple as the addition of two numbers is typical of information processing theories. This analysis reveals what the cognitive system must be able to do in order to perform a task effectively. It is evident that, even in simple tasks, a great deal of cognitive activity is involved. Psychological theories of cognition must discover what this activity is. It should be emphasized that the steps shown in figure 1.1 are not a psychological account of addition. Figure 1.1 shows the logical structure of the task. People who can add will have procedures that conform to this logical structure, although the actual procedures may differ in minor ways. (For example one could dispense with the notion of total and handle carrying from one column to another by writing the number carried as an additional number to the column.) Figure 1.1 is also incomplete as a psychological account. It does not deal with how the addition of numbers in a column is performed, nor does it discuss the resources of memory that are necessary to carry out the task. These issues are also of considerable importance to an overall theory of information processing. Ultimately, a theory of cognitive development must deal in an integrated way with the resources of the cognitive system, the way it selects the information to which it will attend, and the way it manipulates the information attended to.

Background to Contemporary Theories

The modern era of cognitive development began in the 1960s when American researchers began to conduct experimental investigations of the results reported by Piaget. The early investigations were largely attempts to replicate Piaget's results using standard experimental procedures. The replication studies were largely successful. Gradually, the emphasis shifted to testing the further implications of Piaget's theory. A massive amount of research has now been conducted within the Piagetian paradigm using the tasks he invented to probe the reasoning processes of children. This research has helped to refine our understanding of the developmental process. However, not all the results could be easily accommodated within Piaget's theoretical framework. As researchers sought new theoretical interpretations they came to rely more and more on ideas borrowed from the information processing approach. These ideas have helped to give a more exact specification of what information is relevant to performance on a particular task and on how information is stored and manipulated by the child. However, information processing cannot be regarded as an alternative theory to Piaget's theory. At present, information processing is an approach taken by different theorists who derive their theoretical constructs from a common loosely related framework. It is possible, of course, to construct theories within the information processing framework but it would be a mistake to assume that there is a single grand theory of information processing.

Information processing theories of cognitive development have addressed two central issues. There has been considerable attention paid to the nature of the information processing system itself, its basic organization and the basic processes that drive it. There has also been considerable attention to the study of how the information processing system can be modelled for complex tasks such as mathematical reasoning and reading. Before discussing further the outline of theories of cognitive development, it would be useful to stand back from the theories and consider what issues a theory of cognitive development could reasonably be expected to address.

What and *How*: A First Pass

It is commonly agreed that there are two fundamental questions that a theory of cognitive development should answer: *what develops?* and *how does development occur?* The answer to the first question is obvious at one level: what develops is the child's ability to think, talk, read, do mathematics and so forth. However, a theory of cognitive development needs to supply more than this answer. Behind the development of these abilities there lies a cognitive system; the question *what develops?* concerns the nature of this cognitive system and the nature of the changes that it undergoes over time. The answer to *how does development occur?* requires an account of the mechanisms responsible for changes in the cognitive system. I shall call these questions the *what* and the *how* of development. Theories of cognitive development have paid unequal attention to these issues. *What* has been intensively studied, while *how* has been relatively neglected. There are complex historical reasons for this state of affairs. Without attempting to explain the situation, the following observations can be made. From a practical point of view it is easier to study *what* than *how*, as will become evident. From a theoretical point of view it could be argued that it is necessary to understand what is developing before explaining how that development is occurring. However, there has not been a notable move from a stage of investigating what develops to a succeeding stage of investigating how development occurs. This is a state of affairs that must be borne in mind in discussing theories of cognitive development.

Different theories of cognitive development will postulate different types of cognitive system and thus different answers to *what* and *how*. However, all theories must address these two issues. Before considering how the cognitive system might be conceptualized, it is worth considering, in outline, the general requirements imposed on a theory of cognitive development.

To study development is to study change over time. Suppose we were to obtain data on how two groups of children, with a two-year age difference between the groups, perform on some cognitive task – say, solving a set of arithmetical problems. We should expect the older group to perform better than the younger group because we should expect them to have a better knowledge of arithmetical procedures. The first job of a theory of cognitive development is to account for the differences between the groups as a function of differences in the cognitive abilities of children at different stages of development. If this can be done, then the theory can claim to have addressed the issue of *what develops?* for the task and the period studied.

I shall call such theories Level I theories. Level I theories provide an explanatory account of age-related differences in cognitive abilities on some specific task of theoretical interest between time t_1 and a later time t_2.

To be a satisfactory theory of the *what* of cognitive development for the domain of arithmetic, our candidate theory would have to address a larger range of facts. It would first of all have to account for known facts about arithmetical reasoning across the complete span of development. In addition to this it would have to withstand further tests of its theoretical assumptions. Should it continue to survive we might begin to feel confident that we have one component – the *what* component – for the theory of cognitive development for arithmetic. I shall call this type of theory a Level II theory. Level II theories have generality across tasks. They are theories about a domain of cognition. For a Level II theory to be successful it must be possible to derive task-specific accounts of behaviour (i.e. Level I theories) from the general principles of the Level II theory.

It might seem natural now to propose a Level III theory, which is general across domains, in the same way that Level II theories are general across tasks. There may well be such a theory, but it is not a possibility accepted by all. The basic issue at stake is whether the different domains of cognition such as mathematical reasoning, language, perception, and so forth all use some common core set of cognitive principles or whether each domain has its own specific principles. The latter view has come to be known as the modular theory of cognition (Chomsky, 1980; Fodor, 1983). It proposes that the cognitive system consists of separate but co-operating modules. Each module handles a specific type of information according to principles specific to that module. If this view is true then there is not likely to be a general theory of cognition, in the sense of a common set of principles for handling information across all domains. However, this simply shifts the nature of a Level III theory from the articulation of a set of general, domain-independent principles for information processing to the articulation of how cognitive modules interact. Whatever type of Level II theory is proposed, whether modular or non-modular, the Level III theory must be a statement of the basic principles of organization of the cognitive system. In general, these principles will represent the basic innate processes by which the cognitive system will extract and modify information from the environment. Such a set of principles is often referred to as *the architecture of cognition*.

A complete answer to *what* and *how* would begin with the fundamental architecture with which the child is innately equipped and explain how this architecture interacts with environmental stimulation to yield changing mental representations. Such an answer does not exist at present. However, the framework of different levels of theoretical construction is a useful one in which to view empirical research. There has, for example, been considerable interest in recent years in what innate abilities the child has. This research can be seen as an attempt to specify the basic components of the architecture of cognition. The task remains, however, of providing a plausible overall theory of the architecture.

The great bulk of developmental research has separated the question of *what* develops from the question of *how* development occurs. Most accounts of what develops are either Level II or Level I theories in that they concentrate on one domain of cognitive development or one task within a domain. The most popular method of research is to compare children of different ages performing the same task and to explain the differences in performance that are invariably observed as due to differences in the mental representations of the task and the procedures available to manipulate those representations. This would seem to be a perfectly reasonable method of theory construction except that it is often left unexplained how the child progresses from one set of mental representations and procedures to a more advanced set of mental representations and procedures.

Explaining how development occurs is considerably more difficult than explaining what develops. Part of the difficulty lies in the methods available to the investigator. Studying what develops can be done by observing children at different points in development. The standard technique of comparing groups of children as they perform a task once (or at most a few times) effectively gives one a series of snapshots frozen in time. For some developments, these points may be well-spaced in periods of months, or even years. Between any two observation points, change is probably a slow gradual process that does not lend itself easily to standard techniques of investigation. Thus, the data on how development occurs are much more sparse than the data on what develops.

Studying the Cognitive System

The Cognitive System as an Information Processing System

How can the development of a cognitive system be studied? We certainly cannot observe the system directly; we can only observe its behavioural output. This means that we must find ways of using behavioural output to make and test inferences about the underlying cognitive system that produced the output. In this section we shall begin to consider what a cognitive system is and how it can be studied.

The human brain receives and processes vast amounts of information. The brain itself is a structure of tightly-packed neurons – there are estimated to be 10^{12} neurons in the brain with massive interconnections among the neurons. A single central cortical neuron may have as many as 90,000 connections to other neurons (Kuffler, Nicholls and Martin, 1984). In order to understand how the brain functions when processing information it is necessary to abstract from the individual neurons and to consider the broader pattern of the brain's functional organization. Although it is possible, in principle, to approach this information processing from the neurophysiological end, there is still relative ignorance about how the brain's neuronal network accomplishes information processing. Accordingly, study of the brain's information processing has proceeded in relative isolation from neurophysiological data.

When the effects of the brain's processing of information can be observed as behavioural measures, it is possible to make inferences about what the functional organization of the brain must be like in order for behaviour to be as observed. The inferred functional organization of the brain is referred to as the cognitive system. The relations between the neurophysiological organization of the brain and its functional organization as postulated in cognitive theories is still not well understood (see Churchland (1986) for a recent detailed consideration of the issues). Accordingly, neurophysiological considerations do not play a very large role in cognitive theories. Cognitive theories attempt to provide structural and functional accounts of cognitive activity on its own terms.

The basic jobs of a cognitive system are to receive, process, store, and retrieve information. The information in question covers a wide range; from basic perceptual information through the myriad forms of information about everyday events to the information contained in complex symbolic expressions. Any environmental event that can be detected by an organism's senses is a potential source of information.

So far, the terms 'information' and 'cognitive system' have been used without specifying precisely what these terms denote. It is part of the task of this book to explore the detailed proposals that have been made about the organization of the cognitive system and the way in which its selection of information changes during the period of development. However, there are some general points that can be made at this stage.

The cognitive system has evolved to detect and interpret information about the environment that we inhabit. What aspects of the environment convey information to an organism? How is it that we see objects in space and hear speech when our perceptual systems have evolved to detect such things as wavelengths and intensities of light and sound? There are two types of answer to this question in contemporary theories of cognition. One is the answer provided by information processing theories and the other is the answer provided by theories of direct perception.

The general answer of information processing theories to how we see and hear is that we do so as the result of computations performed on representations of the input that our senses receive. This is the major theoretical commitment of information processing theories. To deliver on this commitment requires that the input itself and the computations performed on it be specified precisely. In recent years, most notably in the area of vision, there has been impressive progress towards detailed solutions to how sensory input is processed to yield our common experience of perceiving objects located in space (Marr, 1982).

Is Information Processing Necessary?

J. J. Gibson (1966, 1979) rejects the view that we see and hear as a result of computations. He argued that organisms could directly perceive information from the structure of the stimulation in the environment. According to Gibson the light that strikes our eyes and the sounds that strike our ears are highly informative and do not require extensive processing. An organism can simply 'pick up' the information. What then is the information that can be picked up? According to Gibson organisms can detect higher-order invariant properties of ratios and relations in the flow of stimulation. These invariants constitute information about the environment and are directly available to an organism without needing to be processed. As one example consider figure 1.2. The texture in this figure forms a gradient and this texture gradient is a clue to distance and depth. If the visual system can pick up information about texture gradients then it can perceive depth directly.

Gibson (1966, 1979) described various other higher-order invariants that, he argued, conveyed information directly. But he went beyond demonstrating that there are higher-order invariants to argue that all the information that an organism needed could be directly perceived and that the processing of information was unnecessary. Gibson is here making two distinct claims that have not always been separated in discussions of direct perception. The first is that information about objects may be carried by higher-order invariants in the stimulation that impinges on an organism. This is Gibson's theory of 'ecological optics'. The second is that this information can be detected directly without the need to process the input. This is Gibson's theory of 'direct perception'. The two claims

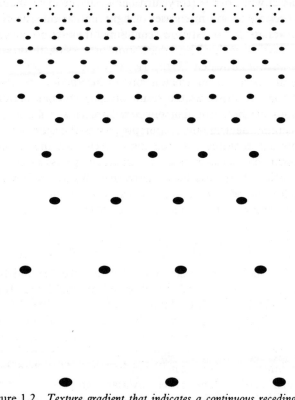

Figure 1.2   *Texture gradient that indicates a continuous receding space.*
Source: Gibson 1950

are partially independent; the first could be true quite independently of the second, although the reverse could not be the case.

Ullman (1980) has argued that there is a wealth of computational and psychophysical evidence to show that perceptual information is broken down into simpler units. The force of this argument is that if, in fact, we know that much of perception is computational, it is pointless to posit theories that attempt to exclude these computational processes from consideration. A different line of attack has been used against Gibson's theory by Fodor and Pylyshyn (1981). They argue that Gibson has failed to specify what would count as an invariant in his theory of direct perception. Hence, there is no principled way to constrain the concept of an invariant. This would not be a serious problem if Gibson's aim were to search for plausible invariants and then test how the information they specify is detected by an organism, since this strategy leaves the theory of perception open; it may turn out to be direct or indirect. But Gibson has proposed a stronger case: that perception consists of directly detecting invariants in the environment. Since there is no constraint on what is to count as an invariant there is no way of testing this theory properly.

Although the theory of direct perception is opposed to an information processing approach, Gibson's emphasis on the importance of analysing the information available from higher-order invariants in the environment is perfectly compatible with an information processing approach. Specifying which features of the environment convey information to an organism is an important part of an information processing theory. Nobody has done more than Gibson to enrich the analysis of the environment. As Ullman (1980: pp. 380–1) remarks:

> The crucial point is to appreciate the distinct role of "ecological optics" and information processing in the theory of visual perception . . . Processing models do not dispense with the information–content analysis. But the converse is also true: the fact that reliable information exists in the light array does not entail that processing is unnecessary. The role of the processing is not to create information, but to extract it, integrate it, make it explicit and usable.

In order to extract, integrate, and use information, the cognitive system must develop ways of representing the available information. As has been previously pointed out a representation is an encoding of selective information about an external event; it does not encode all the possible information available. What gets selected for encoding is a function of the organism's present interests and abilities. It is a commonplace observation that children of different ages extract different information from the same stimulus event. Therefore, part of what develops will be the ability to form increasingly complex representations of stimulus input. It would be decidedly odd to find a theory of cognitive development that did not espouse this principle. Theories will differ however, in their view of the representations that are necessary in order to account for particular behaviours.

Methodological Perspectives

In this section we shall discuss in more detail techniques of research that help to cast light on cognitive development. It is not the aim of this section to provide a survey of methodological techniques but rather to draw attention to the diversity of ways in which insight can be gained into the cognitive system.

The Experimental Method

The standard technique of research in psychology is the experimental method. Research on cognitive development is no exception. The experimental method is at its strongest in investigating the effect that a particular variable or set of variables has on the performance of some given task. For example, age is a variable that has been much studied in cognitive development. A straightforward experiment on some aspect of cognitive development might take the form of comparing the performance of, say, 5-, 7-, and 9-year-olds on some task selected for its theoretical interest. Everybody, of course, expects that the performance of the three groups will differ – the major interest is the way in which performance differs and whether it is consistent with theoretical predictions. A well-designed experiment can have a crucial effect in strengthening or weakening support for a theoretical position.

A second advantage of the experimental method is that years of practice with the method have led to the development of a wide variety of experimental techniques and response measures. Many of these techniques and measures can be used successfully with children whose willing participation as experimental subjects cannot be guaranteed. This applies particularly to the study of infancy. During the last quarter of a century there has been explosive growth in research on the perceptual and cognitive abilities of infants. This research has utilized techniques such as habituation and response measures such as orientation or eye movements. The skilful use of these techniques has revolutionized our views about the cognitive competence of infants – a competence that is all too invisible to the naked eye.

The experimental method however, has its limitations. Although it is well-suited to answering questions about what develops, given a reasonable theory to test, it is not well-suited to answering question about how development occurs. In studies of cognitive development the experimental method relies primarily on gathering cross-sectional samples of data at different points in time. By its nature, this method cannot answer questions about the processes responsible for the developmental changes observed between groups of different age. In fact, the very use of age as an independent variable in developmental research has been criticized by Wohlwill (1970; 1973).

The great strength and popularity of the experimental method has resulted in a large neglect of study and theory about how development occurs. It might seem that the method could be adapted to study processes by, for example, testing a group of children at regular intervals during development. Regrettably, this avenue is much more limited than it may seem. Probably the vast majority of theoretically interesting experimental tasks will display either a large practice effect or the development of task-specific strategies if used repeatedly, thus vitiating their usefulness for studying developmental processes.

Quasi-Experiments

It is frequently assumed that different environmental conditions have a causal effect on some aspect of cognitive development. For example, a researcher might have a hypothesis that a particular method of teaching reading is better than other methods. In order to test the hypothesis the researcher may use a set of measures to compare groups of children that have been taught using different methods. Such a procedure is akin to the experimental method but it differs from it in one important respect: the experimenter has not randomly assigned subjects to the different conditions. Hence, these experiments are called quasi-experiments (Cook and Campbell, 1979). In many situations where the effect of different environmental conditions on development is being tested, quasi-experiments are the best that can be achieved. It is often impossible, for reasons of practicality and ethics, deliberately to manipulate the environment to observe its effect on development. Nevertheless, there are many situations where it seems that it should be possible to compare two or more natural groups with each other. Under appropriate conditions such comparisons can legitimately be made, even though a randomized experiment has not been carried out (see Cook and Campbell, 1979).

The Observational Method

As already remarked the experimental method is of limited use when repeated data collection is required. There is a method, however, that is suited to repeated use over time; that is the observational method. This method differs from the experimental method in that the researcher does not usually manipulate any variables to observe their effect on performance. Rather, he or she records natural behaviour, as it occurs. The method is suited to some types of development but not to all. It is time-consuming, requiring a one-to-one (and sometimes a two-to-one or more) ratio between researcher and subject. This inevitably means that data can only be collected on a small sample of subjects. Observation is only the first step of the research: the observations must be turned into data for analysis, usually by coding the behaviour observed (and this of course requires a coding scheme with its attendant requirements of validity and reliability). This is enormously time-consuming by comparison with the rate of data collection in the laboratory. The method is therefore used sparingly, but it has advantages in some situations. It has been used with considerable success in the study of language development. It is interesting to consider the reasons for its successful application in this area. Much of the developmental study of early language development has been concerned with establishing the extent and the scope of the child's system. This is not a question to which the experimental method can be readily applied, although there are other issues of early language development to which it is readily applicable. However, the observational method is well-suited to this question because the scope of an early language system is reasonably apparent from its natural use. Talking is also a behaviour that occurs in plentiful quantity and so a good return of data can be expected from observations. Language also has the advantage of apparently having a reasonably universal pattern of development of the system and therefore observation of a small number of children will provide sufficient data to test hypotheses and to make theoretical inferences. In the limiting case, data on a single child's development can be collected. Some exceedingly useful data have been collected in just this way, usually by a parent observer. The most famous example is Leopold's (1939–49) four-volume study of his daughter. Lewis (1936) and Bloom (1973) are other notable examples.

The observational method does, however, have major limitations, most of which relate to the lack of control that the observer has over the data. The input cannot be manipulated to observe its effects on output in an observation. If the observer is interested in a particular type of data, there is no guarantee that these data will occur with adequate frequency for meaningful analysis. Although the observational method can be used repeatedly over time with the same child, it shares with the experimental method the fact that it is most suited to answering questions about the *what* of development. The method has not been used to address the *how* of development. Nor does it seem particularly suited to addressing this issue.

Simulations of Cognitive Processing

The major problem about addressing the how of development is that development is a slow gradual process. Over a time span of a year or two there are impressive changes in a child's abilities. Over a time span of days or weeks there is usually little to see. This does not mean that development is not occurring, but that its pace is too slow to observe over short time spans. The developmental processes that control this slow pace are therefore going to be that much more difficult to study.

One possible approach to the study of developmental processes is to back off from any attempt at direct study and instead to simulate the process, or some aspects of it. Simulation is not a technique that is often employed to study development. It requires that the processes that control development and the representations on which these processes act be precisely specified. The processes are then implemented as a computer program in an attempt to simulate development. The program is provided with input similar to what a child would receive. The test of the simulation is whether the program uses the input data to produce the same output as a child would produce. If the program can do so for a range of data, then it is likely that it is using processes analogous to those used by the child. In recent years there have been a number of attempts made to create such programs. Potentially, such attempts offer a new way of studying how development occurs and also of testing the detailed assumptions of a developmental model. Examples of this approach can be found in Wallace, Klahr and Bluff (1987) and in Rumelhart and McClelland (1986). The approach is, as yet, relatively untried, and it remains to be seen whether or not it can provide significant advantages over more traditional methods. Recently, simulation studies have been much to the fore in cognition generally as a result of attempts to create neural network simulations of cognitive activity. These developments will be discussed in chapter 9.

Piaget's Theory of Cognitive Development

Piaget's theory is the product of a lifetime's work, during which he investigated a large range of issues concerned with cognitive development and revised and refined his theoretical views. There is no one text in which the whole theory is presented but Piaget (1970) is a useful summary of the main points. In terms of our questions about *what* and *how* the theory falls neatly into two components because Piaget presents quite different accounts of what develops and of how development proceeds. In answer to *what develops?* Piaget presents a stage theory of development. There are four major stages of cognitive development in Piaget's theory: the sensorimotor, the preoperational, the concrete operational, and the formal operational. Each stage is characterized by a particular type of cognitive structure. Cognitive structures play a key role in Piaget's theory.

They constitute the abstract organizational principles that Piaget believes underlie and control thought.

It is important to emphasize the very abstract nature of cognitive structures. Cognitive structures are not tangible nor directly observable in any way. Cognitive structures constitute organizational principles that are inferred from the various behaviours that can be measured. Cognitive structures are Piaget's particular theoretical answer to the general question that all cognitive theories ask: if behaviours X, Y, and Z can be observed then what type of cognitive system would we need to postulate in order to account for these behaviours? In very general terms, this is the standard question that leads to the construction of a cognitive theory and the postulation of hypothetical cognitive structures. This is a common method of theory construction in science. For example, atomic theory is not based on the direct observation of electrons, protons, neutrons, and their subatomic relatives. Rather these concepts represent the inferred structure of matter; and inference is based on the observable effects of these elements. In the same way the cognitive structures proposed by Piaget are the inferred organization of the human cognitive system.

How can cognitive structures be characterized? Piaget turns to the mathematical theory of groups for his characterization of the organizational principles of thought. Group theory is a branch of abstract algebra that is widely used in the analysis of a variety of structures. The basis of group theory is a set of laws about how elements combine. A simple example is the law of associativity, which states that $a + b = b + a$; that is, the order of combination of the elements of the group is irrelevant. Piaget argues that the principles of thought during the concrete operational stage of development can be characterized by a group theory, and during the formal operational stage by related but more complex logico-mathematical structures.

We are now in a position to return to Piaget's notion of stages. He argues that cognitive structures of the type outlined above have a pervasive effect on thought during long spans of development. Within a particular stage there is, of course, a more fine-grained developmental progression to be observed. However, it is not this finer grain on which Piaget typically focuses but on the more global issue of stages. As a first approximation we can state that a stage is characterized by the controlling presence, across all aspects of thought, of a particular structure.

The first of Piaget's stages is the sensorimotor stage, which lasts from birth until about 2 years of age. During this stage the child lacks true thoughts; behaviour is organized as a function of some sensory or motor effect that it has. These effects are precisely described by a sequence of six substages. During this stage the child moves from having only innate reflexes at the beginning to being able to represent mentally the external world at the end. Between reflexes and 'true representations' lie schemata. Schemata are the non-symbolic organizational structures through which the child's interactions with the world are mediated during the sensorimotor stage (just as interactions are mediated by cognitive structures during later stages). Schemata arise from the actions the child performs on the world. Thus, Piaget writes of a schema for looking, a schema for grasping, a schema for imitating. Schemata eventually develop into mental representations when the child begins to store information about the world and use that information as the basis of later behaviour. The ability to represent reality mentally is the beginning of thought proper, according to Piaget, and it marks the transition to the preoperational stage of development.

The preoperational stage lasts from 2 years until 6 or 7. It can be characterized in two somewhat different ways. In his early work, before he had developed his structuralist theory of cognition, Piaget described the child's thought during this period as being governed by principles such as egocentrism, animism and other similar constructs. Once he had proposed his structuralist theory, Piaget characterized the preoperational child as lacking the cognitive structures possessed by the concrete operational child. The absence of these structures explains, in part, the behaviours Piaget had previously described as egocentric and animistic.

The concrete operational stage lasts from 6 or 7 years until about 12 or 13. During this stage the child's cognitive structures can be characterized by group theory. Piaget argues that the same general principles can be discerned in a wide range of behaviours. One of the best-known achievements of this stage is that of conservation. In a typical conservation experiment a child is asked to judge whether or not two quantities are the same – such as the two quantities of liquid shown in figure 1.3. Once the child's agreement has been obtained the liquid is poured from the short container into the taller, thinner container and the child is asked if the amounts are still the same. A preoperational child will typically judge the taller, thinner container to contain more, while a concrete operational child will judge the amounts still to be the same. The ability to reason in this way reflects the development of a principle of conservation; a principle that Piaget believes to be fundamental to thought. We shall return to the conservation issue in chapter 6.

The formal operational stage begins at about 12 or 13 years. It marks a movement from an ability to think and reason about concrete visible events to an ability to think hypothetically; to entertain what-if possibilities about the world. The cognitive structures of this stage can be characterized by four rules for manipulating the content of thought: identity,

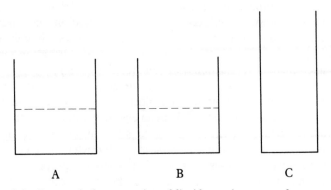

Figure 1.3 *In a typical conservation of liquid experiment, equal amounts of water are poured into glasses A and B and the child's agreement is secured that the amounts are equal. The water from either glass A or B is then poured into glass C, in which it will rise to a greater height, and the child is again asked if the amounts are equal.*

negation, reciprocity, and correlativity (the INRC group) and by 16 'binary operations' that are, effectively, laws of reasoning.

Having outlined Piaget's stage-theory of development in relation to our question *what* develops, we shall turn to his account of *how* development proceeds.

There are two, somewhat different, accounts of how development proceeds to be found in Piaget. One occurs in his early works published during the 1920s and focuses on the role of peer interaction in cognitive change. It is a theme to which recent Genevan research has returned (e.g., Perret-Clermont, 1980) but it is not a theme that Piaget himself pursued vigorously. In his study of the sensorimotor development of his own children during the 1930s Piaget introduced the constructs 'assimilation' and 'accommodation'. Assimilation and accommodation thereafter were the major mechanisms of cognitive change. Unlike cognitive structures, which change during development, assimilation and accommodation are unchanging processes. They are the fundamental mechanisms of change postulated by Piaget. It is through their action that cognitive structures change. Assimilation and accommodation operate continuously to control the detection of information by the cognitive system. Assimilation is a mechanism whereby existing cognitive structures dictate what information is selected from the environment. Here, Piaget is making a point made by Baldwin (1895) and Bartlett (1932) among others: that we interpret the world to fit existing knowledge structures. Accommodation is the reverse of assimilation: it is a mechanism whereby an existing cognitive structure is adjusted slightly because it cannot completely process the information available in the environment. Piaget argued that both mechanisms operate together so that the environment is always interpreted in the light of existing cognitive structures (assimilation) but these structures are themselves modified by the structure of the environment (accommodation). Assimilation and accommodation are slow continuous mechanisms whereby the novel is assimilated to the known but the structure of the known is not left untouched by its encounter with the novel.

The concepts of assimilation and accommodation derive from biology. Piaget began his life as a biologist and he always strove to interpret his structural model of cognition as the product of biological adaptation. He begins his discussion of his first work on infancy (Piaget 1936a/1952) with a chapter entitled 'The Biological Problem of Intelligence' and in this he argues that intelligence is the result of evolutionary adaptation and that adaptation is an equilibrium between assimilation and accommodation (p. 18). Having set up this argument, Piaget proceeds to use the concepts of assimilation and accommodation in his analysis of infant behaviour by interpreting particular instances of behaviour through these concepts. The concepts are much in evidence in Piaget's other two works on infancy (Piaget 1936b/1955; 1945/1951) but only fleeting reference is made to them in the great body of work that he carried out in the 1940s and the 1950s, on the development of concepts of such things as number, space, time, geometry, and logic. Eventually, he returned to the issues of the relation between biology and intelligence in a book entitled *Biology and Knowledge* (Piaget, 1967a/1971).

Piaget's theory of cognitive development provides the background for much of contemporary cognitive development for a number of reasons. The first and foremost reason is that he produced a large range of acute observations of children's cognitive abilities. These observations were often surprising, often the product of simple but ingenious experiments. Even for those who do not agree with Piaget's theory, the phenomena he observed have often been the starting point of an alternative interpretation. When theories of cognition became popular in Anglo-American psychology, following the demise of the behaviourist paradigm, it was to the replication of Piaget's results and the discussion of his ideas that many developmental psychologists first turned. Many of Piaget's tasks continue to be popular in the experimental literature on cognitive development even if the aim is to provide an alternative to Piaget's interpretation of performance on the task. A second reason for the continuing centrality of Piaget's theory is the range and scope of the theory. Whether or not one accepts what he proposed, he made a serious and sustained attempt to produce an integrated theory of cognitive development, one that answered both the what and the how of development. Moreover, Piaget's theory makes general links with evolutionary issues on the one hand, and with the perennial debates in philosophy and psychology between empiricist and rationalist theories of the mind. The scope of this effort has to be admired.

Piaget saw himself as steering a course between the defects of empiricist and rationalist theories of knowledge. Empiricist theories of knowledge argue that all knowledge derives from our experience of the world. Modern empiricist theories owe their origins to the writings of the British empiricist philosophers of the seventeenth and eighteenth centuries: Locke (1632–1704), Berkeley (1685–1753), and Hume (1711–76). Locke (1690) put it thus:

> Let us then suppose the mind to be, as we say, white paper, void of all characters, without any ideas:- How comes it to be furnished? Whence comes it by that vast store which the busy and boundless fancy of man has painted on it with an almost endless variety? Whence has it all the materials of reason and knowledge? To this I answer, in one word, from EXPERI-ENCE. In that all our knowledge is founded; and from that it ultimately derives itself. (Book II, Ch.1, Sec.2)

Twentieth-century empiricist theories might change the language slightly but the view would be essentially the same. By contrast, rationalist theories emphasized the role of innate principles of reason in interpreting experience. At approximately the same period as the British Empiricists, continental philosophers such as Descartes (1596–1650), Spinoza (1634–77), and Leibniz (1646–1716) were also attempting to understand the capabilities of the human mind. They were less impressed by the role of experience and more impressed by mental capabilities that did not seem to them reasonably to derive from experience. In various ways they argued for innate reasoning principles.

An attempt to synthesize the empirical basis of knowledge with innate principles of reasoning was made by Kant (1724–1804). Kant accepted that knowledge was heavily influenced by experience but he argued that knowledge was never 'raw' but was always mediated by the mind. Kant proposed a number of a priori mental categories that are, in effect, innate principles for interpreting experience.

Piaget's middle course between empiricism and rationalism argues that the mind does impose a grid on experience. However, this grid is not an innate endowment but is constructed out of experience. This constructivist theory of knowledge arose out of Piaget's attempt to understand cognition as an evolutionary phenomenon. Experience builds new cognitive structures but only through the schemes established up to the present, through which experience is interpreted. Over time the schemes transform themselves to create more powerful systems of mental representation. Thus, Piaget argues that cognitive structures are not innate.

However, new arguments for innateness have been advanced by Chomsky in recent years (Chomsky, 1965; 1968; 1980). The issues raised by Chomsky are, inevitably, not ones that Piaget confronted when he first constructed his theory. Chomsky's arguments, although not directed against Piaget specifically, have served to undermine the constructivist theory of mind espoused by Piaget. We shall examine the issues raised by both innatist theories of mind and by the information processing framework in the following sections.

Despite Piaget's stature, theories of cognitive development are now beginning to emerge from his shadow. During the 1960s and 1970s Piaget's agenda dominated much of the content of cognitive development. However, Piaget's agenda left much untouched. He had little to say about how language develops or about reading. These issues are of considerable practical and theoretical significance for cognitive development. In recent years they have received their due attention, and must be considered a central part of any course on cognitive development. While we are putting these issues in perspective it is worth stating also that some of the phenomena studied by Piaget, such as object permanence and conservation, have been the subject of an amount of study and investigation that is almost certainly out of all proportion to their significance to a theory of cognitive development. Needless to say, Piaget can hardly be blamed for this state of affairs.

The Information Processing Approach

It is useful, at this point to distinguish between *frameworks*, *theories*, and *models*. A framework is a general set of assumptions and constructs that are shared by particular theories. The framework is itself only loosely organized; the relations among constructs are not well-specified. Within a framework some subset of the framework's constructs can be tied together by further specific constructs to form a predictive theory for some domain. Such theories are Level II theories as described previously. A model is either the application of a theory to a specific phenomenon or a theory whose range of application is a single phenomenon. Models are equivalent to Level I theories as described previously.

Information processing is best viewed as a framework within which particular theories are constructed. The framework provides the general principles for particular theories. Information processing theories divide the cognitive system into components and explore the way in which these components transform and manipulate information. The memory system is an example of a high-level component, which will be discussed in chapter 5. A second characteristic of information processing theories is an emphasis on the codes or representations used to store information. The final encoding of some piece of information after it has been processed may be quite different from the environmental input. An obvious example is that of doing mental arithmetic in which only the final total is encoded, with the input being discarded by the information processing system once it has been used to add to the running total. A more subtle example is the processing of language input, which will be discussed in chapter 7.

Besides an emphasis on the fundamental components and operations of the cognitive system, information processing theories have been much concerned with studying the difference between a skilled expert and a novice performing some task. As a person learns a skill, he or she acquires and stores increasingly complex knowledge about that skill. There is a considerable difference in the knowledge that an expert and a novice possess and this difference will affect such factors as how a task is approached and what information is sought (Chi, Glaser and Rees, 1982). Children can be regarded as universal novices on tasks. The information processing framework provides some useful techniques for studying development from novice to expert state, as children learn to perform a task.

Knowledge is not the only thing that distinguishes experts from novices; the expert usually has available a variety of problem-solving strategies not available to the novice. The acquisition of strategies is thus another major facet of information processing theories. Finally, the co-ordination and control of performance is an issue of crucial significance for any theory that explains performance as resulting from the assembly of subcomponent skills.

Information processing theorists have long since adopted a divide-and-conquer approach to the cognitive system. This means that the majority of theories within the information processing framework are either Level II theories that apply to a domain of behaviour such as language, or mathematical reasoning, or Level I theories that apply to some particular task. There are some exceptions to this, notably Anderson's (1983) attempt to specify general properties of a cognitive architecture, but the prevailing trend is for theories to address a domain of behaviour.

It can be argued that the attempt to create domain-specific theories is a sensible tactic, given the complexity of the phenomenon with which we are dealing. Progress in science is often achieved by concentrating on specific rather than on general issues. The absence of a grand unifying theory is not always a barrier. When dealing with the human cognitive system the further issue arises of whether the system itself has a modular organization in the sense that, at least for some domains, there are processes and representations that are dedicated to the analysis of information within that domain and have no application outside the domain. If there are modular systems contained within the cognitive system then obviously they are best theorized about by Level II theories. This still leaves the issue of how the overall system achieves modular integration to be handled by a Level III theory. These might best be regarded as separate issues, calling for separate theoretical treatment.

The issue has just been raised of whether there could be a theoretically motivated fragmentation of the cognitive system. Arguments have been advanced in favour of this (Chomsky, 1980; Fodor, 1983). However, in practice, the fragmentation of information processing theories is often less than theoretically motivated. There are many Level I theories that address a phenomenon, or range of phenomena, in a way entirely consistent with the information processing framework, but which are not easily extendable into more general Level II theories. This has been commented upon and discussed within the framework itself (Neisser, 1976; Newell, 1973).

Within the information-processing framework there are two basic types of research on cognitive development. The first type concerns the development of the information processing system itself. Studies of basic perceptual processes or memory processes are examples of this type of research. The vast majority of these studies address the question of what develops in the basic information processing system. The (perhaps surprising) answer advocated by many researchers is that the basic components do not develop at all; they are innate. What does develop, it seems, are the control processes that manipulate information. To take an example, the strategies used by adults to process information in short-term or working memory are likely to be very different from the strategies used by children. Thus, the general answer to *what develops?* provided by research into memory development is that strategies for encoding and manipulating information develop. A corollary of this is that the type of information stored in long-term memory will change as strategies develop. Given the same memory task, for example, a 4-year-old and a 10-year-old child are likely to use different encoding strategies and thus show different recall.

The second type of research within the information processing framework focuses on performance on particular tasks. Task performance in information processing theories is usually regarded as the result of children applying computational rules to a task. A rule is a procedure or strategy that the child uses to respond to particular conditions in the environment. Very frequently rules are stated as an 'if-then' condition –

action pair. This means that if certain conditions pertain the rule specifies that a certain action should be carried out. A properly specified rule-based account of performance on a task should explain the errors that children make in addition to their correct choices. An example of this approach will be discussed below when Siegler's (1976) analysis of performance on the balance scale task will be contrasted with the analysis of Inhelder and Piaget (1955/1958). An area in which rule-based accounts of behaviour have predominated is in the study of grammatical development, which will be considered in chapter 7.

One major difference between information processing theories and Piagetian theory is the attempt by many information processing theories to provide a more detailed account of the reasoning process used by children on a Piagetian task. Perhaps the best way to illustrate the differences in both research methods and theory is to contrast a Piagetian and an information processing account of the same phenomenon. One of the best examples is the balance-scale problem, which has been investigated by Inhelder and Piaget (1955/1958) and by Siegler (1976) among others.

A balance scale is shown in figure 1.4. To the scale can be added weights at varying distances from the fulcrum. Each weight has a turning moment about the fulcrum, which is given by the product of the weight and the distance from the fulcrum, W x D. The scale balances if the sum of W x D on one side equals the sum of W x D on the other; otherwise the scale tilts in the direction of the side that has the greater torque.

The balance scale problem is an interesting one, both because it represents fundamental mathematical principles and because it admits of problems of varying complexity. The simplest problems can be solved by children as young as 5 years; the most difficult continue to baffle children well into their teens.

Inhelder and Piaget (1955/1958) propose three major stages of solving the balance scale problem. These stages correspond, more or less, to the preoperational, the concrete operational, and the formal operational stages of Piaget's general theory. In Stage I children below about 5 years initially

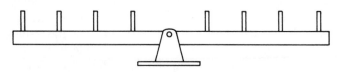

Figure 1.4   *A balance scale. Weights are placed on the pegs.*

fail to solve the problem. Between 5 and 8 years children begin to understand that weight is needed on both sides to achieve a balance but this understanding is not based on systematic principles.

During Stage II children initially treat the addition and equalization of weights in a systematic way but the co-ordination between weights and distances 'goes no further than intuitive regulations' (Inhelder and Piaget, 1955/1958: p. 169). Later (at about 10 years or so) this co-ordination is achieved as a qualitative principle. However, the child has not yet grasped the quantitative law that governs the balance scale.

During Stage III (from about 13 years onwards) the child begins to discover the principles that underlie the balance scale. The qualitative understanding achieved during Stage II provides the basis for the prin-cipled understanding of Stage III. The basis of these principles is the INRC group, which Piaget believes to be the general basis of formal operational thought.

Inhelder and Piaget used the clinical method, mentioned previously, in their investigation of reasoning about the balance scale. The method was designed to be maximally sensitive to the child's approach to a problem and to capture the individual style of the child's reasoning. Using the clinical method, an investigator probes a child as a function of the responses provided. The method of analysis and of reporting is to present typical protocols of the child's reasoning at a particular stage of development. The following examples illustrate this. In these examples the alphabetical series A, B, C, etc. represents increasing weight and the number series 1, 2, 3, etc. represents increasing distance.

NEM (7;4) discovers empirically that C on the left at a distance of 10 balances E on the right at a distance of 5. We ask him to place C on the right and E on the left, but he does not succeed in inverting the distance relationship. After the experiment, he exclaimed 'Ah! You have to do the same thing as before but in the opposite way!' (Inhelder and Piaget, 1955/1958: p. 170)

FIS (10;7) sees that P does not balance F "because it's heavy: that one [F] is too light." – "What should be done?" – "Move it forward [he moves P toward the axis and attains equilibrium]. "I had to pull it back from 16 holes [arbitrary] to see if it would lower twice [arbitrary] the weight." – "What do you mean by that?" – "It raises the weight." – "And if you put it back over there?" [moves P away]. – "It would make the other one go up." – "And if you put it at the end?" [P]. – "It would go up still more" [F], etc. Conclusion: When you have two unequal weights "you move up the heaviest" [toward the median axis]. But FIS does not measure the lengths even for the relations of 1 to 2. (Inhelder and Piaget, 1955/1958: p. 171)

Siegler's (1976) research on the balance scale problem differs methodologically from Piaget's. Siegler used a balance scale that was fixed so that it could not move when weights were placed on it. The child's task was to predict which, if either, side would go down when particular combinations of weights were placed on the scale. Siegler studied children with ages ranging from 5 years to 17 years. All children in an experiment were tested on the same problem.

Siegler found that children used one of four rules in solving the balance scale problem and that the rules formed an ordered series. Children following Rule I considered only weight in predicting balance; no account was taken of distance. Children following Rule II did consider distance, but only when the weights were equal. Thus, a weight of three units at three units of distance from the fulcrum would be judged to tip the balance against a weight of three units at two units of distance from the fulcrum. Rule III represents a slight improvement over Rule II in that both weight and distance are always considered but when the cues are discrepant the child does not know how to resolve the conflict and will guess. A discrepant cue arises when the weights are greater on one side but the distance is greater on the other. In this situation the only sure solution is to calculate the torque. This is what children following Rule IV do.

Siegler found that the rules proposed provided a good account of the children's performance on the task. Out of 120 children, 107 could be classified as using one of the four rules. Of particular interest are the results of the conflict tasks. These tasks can be arranged so that either the side with greater weight or the side with greater distance will tip the scale. Because younger children base their judgements entirely on weight, they should always predict that the side with greater weight will tip. This is what Siegler found. However, what would one predict for Stage III children? These children know that both weight and distance are relevant but they do not know how to resolve the conflict. Siegler predicted that Rule III children would perform at chance level on conflict tasks, with 33 per cent predicting balance, 33 per cent predicting that the side with greater weight would tip, and 33 per cent predicting the side with the weights at greater distance would tip. Table 1.1 shows the complete set of predictions for the various problems as a function of the rule being used. The results conformed to the general pattern predicted.

Comparison of the Piagetian and the information processing approach to the balance scale problem brings out a number of points. First, there are large methodological differences in the approaches. Inhelder and Piaget did not use a controlled technique of investigation and their data are anecdotal. The data are obviously intended to be taken as representative, but no formal statistical procedures are used to demonstrate their representativeness. By contrast Siegler's method was controlled and systematic and the data were subjected to conventional statistical analysis.

Second, Inhelder and Piaget's account explains improvement with age as a result of the development of logical principles (as specified by the INRC group). Their analysis revolves around the extent to which the protocols cast light on the emergence of an INRC group. It is worth stressing that the INRC group is not *tested* as an explanatory account by Inhelder and Piaget; rather it provides a framework within which explanations are to be couched. Siegler's information processing account also provides an interpretive account of developmental progression of the balance scale problem (in terms of rules) but he then proceeds to test this account against performance under controlled conditions. This is a much more preferable scientific approach.

A further feature of the information processing account is that it makes specific predictions about error patterns and about the representational basis of these patterns. This last feature is one of the most important elements introduced by information processing theories. A theory of cognitive development should be able to predict how a child will perform on a particular task at a given stage of development as a function of the child's representation of the task. This means that it is not sufficient to predict only the representational basis of correct responses and then account for incorrect responses as resulting from the absence of an appropriate representational structure. Both correct and incorrect responses derive from representations of the task that the child is asked to perform. Explaining the representational basis of incorrect responses is just as important as explaining the representational basis of correct responses. A theory of cognitive development cannot claim to be complete until both correct and incorrect responses alike are predictable and can be explained in terms of the child's representation of the task.

Siegler's answer to *what develops?* is that rules of problem-solving develop. How does this development occur? Siegler (1976) did not address this question directly. However, in a later paper, Siegler (1984) proposed that new rules develop as a result of changes in the features of the problem that are encoded. The fundamental postulate of Siegler's proposal is that the cognitive system monitors more features of the environment than the rules use and continuously seeks new features to monitor. As long as a rule produces satisfactory outcomes, it continues to be used. When a

Table 1.1 Predictions for percentage of correct answers and error patterns on posttest for children using different rules.

Problem type	Rules				Predicted developmental trend
	I	II	III	IV	
Balance	100	100	100	100	No change: all children at high level
Weight	100	100	100	100	No change: all children at high level
Distance	0 (Should say 'balance')	100	100	100	Dramatic improvement with age

Conflict–weight	100	100	33 (Chance responding)	100	Decline with age. Possible upturn in oldest group
Conflict–distance	0 (Should say 'right down')	0 (Should say 'right down')	33 (Chance responding)	100	Improvement with age
Conflict–balance	0 (Should say 'right down')	0 (Should say 'right down')	33 (Chance responding)	100	Improvement with age

Source: Siegler 1986

rule yields unacceptable outcomes all features that are being monitored are considered for inclusion in new rules. New rules are formed according to a principle of simplicity: try unidimensional rules before conjunctive ones, conjunctive before disjunctive, disjunctive before biconditional, and so on. Siegler considers that younger children have a strong preference for unidimensional rules due, in part, to having had fewer opportunities to reject these rules, but also fewer opportunities to monitor a wide range of features for possible inclusion in new rules.

Further experiments reported by Siegler (1976) serve to clarify his proposals about the mechanisms of change. When 5- and 8-year-olds, who were both Rule I users, were provided with feedback (by showing what actually happened to the balance scale after the child had made his or her prediction) the 8-year-olds but not the 5-year-olds advanced from Rule I to Rule III. In a further experiment 5- and 8-year-old children were shown a balance scale configuration of weights on pegs, which was then removed, and the children were asked to reproduce the configuration. The 5-year-olds reproduced the weights accurately but not their distance from the fulcrum. The 8-year-olds reproduced both features accurately. Nevertheless, both groups predominantly used Rule I. These results serve to underscore two points about Siegler's proposal about mechanisms of change. Firstly, a feature may be monitored but not incorporated into a rule for making predictions. Secondly, if a feature is being monitored it is relatively easy to cause an advance in the rule being used through feedback; if it is not being monitored it is impossible.

Kessen (1984) has pointed out that the notion of development implies an end-point towards which the system in development moves. For contemporary theories of cognitive development (but not for behaviourism, for example) there is an expectation that children will systematically approach some common end-state. On balance scale tasks, the expectation is that children will acquire more sophisticated rules. A more potent example is the expectation that all children will become mature language users. These expectations imply that there are some guiding principles to the way a cognitive system changes. The system is not simply buffeted about by environmental input but rather selects, represents, and operates upon that input in a progressive, law-like and universal way. What principles guide development so that the end-point is reached? Increasingly, in recent years, the answer has been that development is constrained by innate principles of cognitive functioning. We turn now to a consideration of these.

Innateness and Development

Empirical and Logical Approaches to Innateness

The issue of what is innate and what is learned has long been of concern to developmental psychology. Historically, innateness and learning have been treated as alternatives, with such questions debated as whether some aspect of perception was innate (in the sense that the capacity was evident in an animal deprived of relevant experience) or whether it could be attributed to learning. Many have pointed out that the either/or type of question about innateness and learning is not a profitable approach: both factors contribute to development. The question should be: in what ways do they contribute? Despite this insight, there has been relatively little progress within developmental psychology on producing theories that integrate innateness and learning. The reason for this may be that there has been an excessive tendency to treat innateness and learning as variables to be manipulated in an experiment rather than as constructs to be theorized about. Even as variables, they were usually badly treated, with innateness being regarded as the presence of an ability in the absence of experience and learning being its opposite: the failure of an ability to develop when experience is withheld. Such findings have not, on the whole, greatly enhanced our understanding of the developmental process.

In recent years the issue has been tackled from a completely different angle: logical analysis of whether or not an ability is learnable. This approach derives, in large part, from the work of Chomsky (1965). He argued that language was not learnable given only the input available to a child and conventional mechanisms of learning. Since children obviously do learn a language, Chomsky concluded that they must be supported in this by some innate 'language acquisition device'. Chomsky did not specify exactly what this was; simply that it had to exist to account for the fact that language was learnt. The particular features of a language acquisition device could be worked out alongside a theory of the grammar of language. The details of these issues will be discussed further below and in chapter 7.

Logical analysis of what must be innate in order for the cognitive system to develop as it does is an increasingly important part of contemporary theorizing about cognitive development. There is no question but that human beings are born with a brain that is predisposed to interact with the world in particular ways. In the sections below these predispositions will be discussed with reference to cognitive processes and structures. The assumptions about innateness made by behaviourist and

Piagetian theories will be outlined briefly to provide a contrast with contemporary views.

Processes

All theories of behaviour make some assumptions about innateness and, thus, about the architecture of cognition, even though the issue has not always been explicitly addressed when the theory sets out its assumptions. In particular, all theories assume that the mechanisms of learning or development are themselves invariant, and are innate endowments of the organism. Behaviourist theories attribute all of behaviour to learned responses. Such a theory presumes an organism that is disposed to learn; an organism that is innately endowed with the ability to associate a stimulus with a response. While the association between a particular S and a particular R is learned, behaviourists do not argue that organisms learn how to make associations; associations are part of the organism's innate repertoire. Similarly the ability to discriminate among stimuli and to generalize across stimuli are innate even though the basis of particular discriminations and generalizations may have to be learned.

For Piaget's constructivist theory the mechanisms of assimilation and accommodation are innate and unchanging mechanisms. Piaget is quite explicit on this issue. He sees these mechanisms as evolution's answer to adaptation to the environment (Piaget, 1967a/1971). These mechanisms support changing cognitive structures.

The information processing framework also postulates a variety of innate mechanisms for learning and development. Many developmental theorists within the information processing framework have borrowed Piaget's constructs of assimilation and accommodation. However, the major mechanism of learning presumed by information processing theories is induction (Holland, Holyoak, Nisbett and Thagard, 1986). Induction is the formulation of general laws from particular cases as for example:

> I have seen lots of white swans.
> I have never seen any other colour of swan.
> Therefore, all swans are white.

This reasoning is an impeccable piece of induction, although it is not logically valid. Philosophers have been much preoccupied by the fact that it is not logically valid. However, from a psychological viewpoint it is the mechanism itself that is of interest, not its logical status. Clearly, much human knowledge is based on much less than certainty. Bertrand

Russell (1912: p. 38) concluded that the inductive process itself is 'incapable of being *proved* by an appeal to experience' but went on to argue that 'we must either accept the inductive principle on the ground of its intrinsic evidence, or forgo all justification of our expectations about the future'. Any theory that postulates rule learning needs a mechanism for deriving rules from environmental regularities and induction serves this purpose admirably. The importance of induction is that it permits extrapolation from particular instances and provides a rule-based framework for cognitive processing. An example of what is commonly regarded as inductive learning is the child's derivation of the linguistic rule 'add -*ed* to the verb stem to form the past tense'. Initially children learn past tense forms on a word-by-word basis and thereby acquire the correct past tense form for both regular and irregular verbs (e.g., *walked* and *took*). However, as more verbs are learnt the child notices that the majority of verbs form the past tense by adding -*ed* to the verb root. This results in an inductive generalization that all verbs form the past tense by adding -*ed* to the root. Application of this rule results in an overregularization of previously correct forms, so that *taked* will now replace *took*. The phenomenon will be discussed in more detail in chapter 7. Here, the major point is to illustrate that an inductive inference can have powerful effects on the child's cognitive representations.

There seems to be general agreement that the basic cognitive mechanisms of change are innate evolutionary products and are not themselves subject to developmental change. The content to which they apply does, of course, change with changing cognitive representations. Associations formed late in development may have a considerably more complex representational structure than associations formed in the first few days of life. Similarly, induction may produce relatively simple rules in early development but more complex rules in later development. The difference in complexity in both cases lies in the representation not in the mechanism that produced it.

Structure

For classical behaviourists the structure of cognition was an associative chain of 'mediating responses'. As the content of associations was entirely the product of learning, the structure of cognition was thus entirely the product of learning.

For Piaget the structure of cognition was also a developmental product. However, Piaget thought that cognition was more than a copy of environmental associations, and he thought that it developed but was not necessarily learned (Piaget, 1964). The Piagetian view is that through the processes of assimilation and accommodation new cognitive structures emerge. Piaget argued that reflexes were the initial innate structures from which all other structures eventually develop.

Information processing theories have a much more complex theory of the structure of cognition than either behaviourist or Piagetian theories. According to information processing theories, the cognitive system consists of a variety of interacting components. At a very general level, the major components are memory and attention. These components have various processes associated with them that transform and encode the input received. The system also has components that control the processing of information in accordance with the organism's goals and plans.

Behaviourist, Piagetian, and many Information Processing theories regard the content of cognition as a developmental product. This seems an entirely reasonable position. Evolution could not possibly have prepared us for the particular information content that we receive. Content is a function of the particular environment that we inhabit – be it desert, or forest, or city; of our particular culture; and of our particular experience within an environment and a culture.

At one level this analysis is true but it fails to do justice to the fact that regardless of the variation in content there are certain requirements placed by evolution on how content is processed. For example, different inputs must be treated as functionally similar by an organism in order for behaviour to be adaptive. This requires an innate ability to treat input in a categorical fashion. If an organism could not treat some stimuli as functionally equivalent to others, there would be no possibility of learning from experience because every encounter with the world would be unique. As we shall see in chapter 2, the empirical evidence is completely in accord with this line of reasoning.

Categorization is only one among a variety of structures imposed on information. During the course of development the child acquires a variety of increasingly complex organizational structures. The most notable example of this is human language. It has been a matter of considerable debate in recent years to what extent the structure of language (and of other cognitive representations) is learnt and to what extent it is innate. The issue was first raised by Chomsky (1959, 1965) and it has not yet been completely resolved. We shall return to this issue in chapter 7.

What and *How*: A Second Pass

The question of how development occurs can be approached in several ways. Firstly, it is necessary to identify the learning mechanisms possessed by the cognitive system. Secondly, it is necessary to describe how these mechanisms act over time. Thirdly, there is the issue of how the environment in which a child learns, affects development. The first two issues are central to a theory of cognitive development; the third is most relevant to issues of individual differences.

The nature of learning mechanisms postulated by a theory is very largely dependent on its view of what develops. It is easiest to illustrate this by example. In some behaviourist theories of development (e.g., Bijou and Baer, 1961) what develops is a series of discriminative responses to environmental stimuli. Such a theory places no more demands on learning than that a child be capable of associating a stimulus and a response. Thus, the answer to how development occurs is by forming new associations or refining old ones. By contrast Piaget's theory of development regards the child as engaged in a continuous attempt to construct a theory of the world, while, at the same time, interpreting the world in the light of the child's current theory. Such a theory requires a give and take between the child's existing theory and new information, otherwise the system would never progress. Piaget accordingly postulates mechanisms of assimilation and accommodation as the primary learning mechanisms. Assimilation is the process by which new information is interpreted in the light of existing cognitive structures; accommodation is the process by which cognitive structures change in the light of new information.

Information processing theories place great emphasis on changes in the child's representation of the world. Accordingly, mechanisms of change are needed that shift the child from one representation of a task to another, more sophisticated representation of that task. The mechanisms of change proposed will vary as a function of the relation between the representations. Flavell (1972) discusses some of the varieties of representational change from an information processing perspective. However, it is noteworthy that the issue of how change occurs has rarely been given serious theoretical discussion within the information processing framework.

As one further example consider Chomsky's (1965) view of language development. Chomsky argued that what develops during language development is a system of rules for a particular language. These rules are derived from a system of abstract grammatical rules shared by all languages. He argued further that this system could not be learnt from the environment by any conventional learning procedure. Nevertheless it must he possible for children to acquire these rules because children evidently do learn a language. Consequently, Chomsky proposed that, in some sense, general rules of language were innate although obviously the grammar and vocabulary of a particular language must be a product of interaction between environmental input and innate general rules. This interaction is conducted through the mechanism of testing hypotheses (derived from the innate general rules) about the structure of the particular language the child hears.

It is evident from the three theoretical sketches that there is a strong inter-dependency between the what and the how of development. Chomsky is the most notable example here because he was led to question whether conventional accounts of how development proceeds could adequately explain the acquisition of the rules of grammar. Finding a negative answer Chomsky then proposed a greater role for biological inheritance than was common in theories of development. We shall return to the issue of innateness and biological inheritance in due course. For now, it can be remarked that the basic mechanisms of development postulated by most, if not all, theories are regarded as the product of evolution rather than of development. That is to say, the child is assumed to have an innate ability to make associations, or to engage in assimilation and accommodation. These mechanisms do not themselves require a developmental explanation within a theory of cognitive development.

How do mechanisms act over time to produce change? In a behaviourist theory associations are strengthened or weakened over time as a function of the child's history of reinforcement. In a Piagetian account of cognitive development the mechanisms of assimilation and accommodation serve as a filter between cognitive structures and new information. They act continually over time to modify existing cognitive structures. For Chomsky the major mechanism at the child's disposal is hypothesis-testing about the particular structure that language might have. The hypotheses to be tested are generated from the child's innate knowledge of the general rules of language. By continuous hypothesis testing the child gradually arrives at the correct particular structure of the language that he or she hears.

Theories of cognition emphasize the creation and manipulation of representations of the environment. Cognitive development is, to a large extent, the development of the ability to create increasingly complex and sophisticated representations of the environment. The next two chapters will examine the origins of mental representations.

2

Perceptual Development in Infancy

Method and Interpretation

Writing in 1890, William James declared: 'The baby, assailed by eyes, ears, nose, skin and entrails at once, feels it all one great blooming buzzing confusion' (p. 488). Until comparatively recently this was the generally accepted view of infant perception. However, research during the past quarter century has changed the way we think about mental organization in the infant. Prior to this there was little or no evidence to challenge James's assertion. For example, in a review of studies of perceptual development by Wohlwill (1960) less than 10 per cent of the studies reported findings on infants below 2 years. It is instructive to consider why the view represented by James prevailed for so long and why the tide has now begun to turn. Part of the reason why the James view prevailed is that experimenters did not think it worth looking for perceptual abilities in infants. Even those who did were hampered by the methods that they adopted. Hochberg (1962: p. 323) could comment 'the human infant displays insufficient behaviour co-ordination to permit its study to give us very much useful information'.

The infant is not a particularly easy organism to study. For one thing infants do not spend long periods awake and alert and when they are awake they are likely to be involved for much of that time in feeding. Clifton and Nelson (1976) observed that except for feeding situations the average alert period in newborns was five minutes, with over 90 per cent of alert periods lasting less than ten minutes. This makes such an infant difficult to study and it also, of course, imposes a major limitation on the infant's ability to attend to, process and store information about the environment. In addition to this there is the methodological problem of choosing an appropriate response variable to measure. As infants do not talk, verbal responses are ruled out – and verbal responses of one sort or another are by far the most common type of response measure in experimental studies with adults and older children. Thus, a way has to be found to circumvent the limited communication that can exist between experimenter and infant in order to discover what the infant's cognitive capabilities are. This often demands considerable experimental ingenuity. We shall encounter some of that ingenuity in the following pages.

A large part of the progress in infancy research is due to methodological advances in designing tasks that will be of sufficient interest to attract an infant's attention but are at the same time sufficiently controlled to allow the experimenter to draw conclusions about the infant's abilities. During the past 25 years behavioural measures such as an infant's preference for which of two stimuli to attend to (*spontaneous visual preference*), the waning of attention to a repeated presentation of a stimulus (*habituation*) and subsequent recovery of attention when a new stimulus is presented (*dishabituation*) have been widely used in a variety of ingenious studies with infants. The success of these methods is due to the fact that they exploit a natural part of the infant's everyday behaviour: attention to stimuli in the environment. This means that even during the short periods when a neonate is awake and alert, it is possible to gather very useful data by using measures of attention. Previous investigators were hampered by their attempts to apply techniques that require greater amounts of time than the infant will give. For example, although conditioning techniques have been used successfully to study infant abilities, the techniques are often difficult to apply because of the time it may take to establish a conditioned response. In general, conditioning an infant to respond to stimuli is much more difficult than presenting stimuli and monitoring how the infant attends.

The spontaneous visual preference technique was introduced by Fantz (1958, 1961). It consists simply of presenting two stimuli to an infant, usually spaced to left and right in the visual field. The experimenter measures which of the stimuli the infant prefers to look at. In order to ensure that what is being measured is not simply a preference to look to left or right, the positions of the stimuli must be randomized across experimental trials. If the infant reliably prefers one stimulus to another, this tells us that the infant can discriminate the stimuli and it also tells us about the visual preferences of infants. The technique has its limitations: the absence of a preference for one or the other stimulus does not tell us that the infant cannot discriminate between the stimuli; the infant could find both equally interesting or equally boring. This raises the important issue of how stimuli should be chosen in studying preferences. In many of the experiments that have used the technique of visual preference, stimuli have been selected on the basis of the experimenter's intuitions about their appropriateness for studying a particular perceptual dimension. However, it is also possible to apply scaling techniques to the results of preference data to verify that the stimuli used are, in fact, arranged along a perceptual dimension (Thomas, 1973).

An alternative technique of measuring attention that has proved particularly valuable in the study of infancy is habituation. The technique is more complex methodologically than the spontaneous visual preference technique but it is also more general in that it is not restricted to a single behaviour and can be used with all sense modalities. The basic phenomenon captured by habituation is that we adapt to the familiar and attend to the novel. The phenomenon was discovered by Pavlov (1927) who noticed that when a novel stimulus is presented to any organism, the first response is what Pavlov called 'an orienting reflex' in which the animal turns towards and attends to the stimulus. There is an identifiable pattern of physiological activity which will be discussed below. With repeated presentations of the stimulus the animal's attention declines to zero. This decline is called habituation. An everyday example of habituation is the fact that we do not notice a clock ticking or a fan humming in the background.

The attention of an habituated animal can easily be regained by presenting a stimulus different from the stimulus to which the animal is habituated. A new 'orienting reflex' will then occur or, in modern terminology, dishabituation will occur.

The habituation technique is a very useful way of testing a wide variety of abilities in infants. It has been used to study learning, memory, perceptual discrimination, and categorization. The technique is suitable for the study, in any sense modality, of issues that can be operationalized in terms of differential patterns of discrimination and generalization. In a typical habituation experiment a stimulus is presented and some measure of attention to it is recorded. Initially the infant will attend readily to the stimulus but with repeated presentation attention will wane. Following either a fixed number of trials or the attainment of some criterial level of responding the post-habituation trials commence. These will contain presentations of the novel stimulus, sometimes mixed with further presentations of the familiar stimulus. The level of attentiveness to these stimuli is measured. Increases in attentiveness to the novel stimuli indicate that the infant has discriminated the difference between the familiar and the novel stimuli. A failure to increase attentiveness indicates either a failure to discriminate between the novel and the familiar or general fatigue. It is possible to test for fatigue by presenting, during the post-habituation trials, some additional stimuli that the infant is known to be capable of discriminating from the stimulus used in the habituation trials. A succinct and accessible review of the more detailed methodology of the habituation technique may be found in Olson and Sherman (1983).

Behavioural measures of attention such as spontaneous visual preference and habituation are concerned with the selection of information from the environment. There is another sense of attention that is concerned with an organism's level of arousal. This is also of relevance in the study of infants. Changes in level of arousal indicate changes in the processing of environmental information. When an organism detects novel or significant environmental events a number of changes are triggered by the autonomic nervous system, which include changes in heart rate, sweat gland activity, pupil dilation and EEG activity. These changes can be monitored and used as indirect measures of the detection and selection of information in the environment. Heart rate has been the most common measure of arousal used in the study of infants. Heart rate can either accelerate or decelerate from a baseline. Graham and Clifton (1966) argued that deceleration is associated with orienting or behavioural attention, whereas acceleration is associated with a defensive or fear reaction. Although there has been some dispute over the directional claims advanced by Graham and Clifton (see Olson and Sherman, 1983), the changes in heart rate, whether up or down, form a useful measure of attentiveness in infants. Like habituation measures, heart rate can be used to measure changes of attention to stimuli in any sense modality.

Scientific investigation of any phenomenon crucially depends on having suitable methods available. The recent advances in our understanding of infants are largely the result of the ingenious application of the methods outlined above. The improvements in techniques of research have resulted in a total re-evaluation of the mental world of the infant. Considerable evidence has now accumulated on the psychological abilities of the human infant. With this evidence to hand it is now possible to begin to address proposals about the innate architecture of cognition with empirical evidence. It is also possible to begin to unravel the ways in which the architecture provides the foundation for the infant's representation of the environment. During the earliest months of infancy the infant's information processing is limited by constraints on sensory, perceptual, and attentional processes. Nevertheless, during these months it is possible to detect many of the abilities that are the foundations for later cognitive development. Studying the perceptual abilities of the infant allows us to begin to address, from an empirical standpoint, questions about what might constitute the basic components of an information processing system, and how an infant uses these components to learn and remember about the environment.

There are two general issues of interpretation that will recur in relation to empirical evidence. The first derives from the fact that different methods may yield different measures of an ability. For example, as we shall see below, different techniques of measuring visual acuity in infants give slightly different estimates of the infant's acuity. The problem can be more serious than this. In chapter 3, for example, we shall encounter different methods of measuring whether or not infants believe that an out-of-sight object continues to exist (*object permanence*). One method uses the way infants search for a hidden object as its measure; another uses measures of perceptual behaviour when infants track moving objects. The two methods give very different estimates of the age at which infants possess object permanence. Both cannot be right. But it is not obvious from the evidence which, if either, is correct. Evidence has to be interpreted for what it reveals about the cognitive system. Interpretation is by no means a straightforward affair. In the object permanence example the different response criteria make very different demands on the infant. In such cases the line of inference from the different methods to the cognitive system must be carefully examined.

A second issue that arises is how to interpret different results using the same method. Some of the more startling results about infant abilities have failed to be replicated. This has often been attributed to differences (sometimes slight) in the methodological techniques employed by the different experiments. While these differences do sometimes explain different results they are not always the explanation. Some researchers are much more willing than others to detect evidence of some particular ability in the infant's behaviour. This difference is largely due to an inherent problem in the study of infants: it is genuinely difficult, at times, to know whether the infant has behaved in a particular way. This is particularly the case where an experimenter has to code the infant's response without the aid of any parametric measure.

A further issue of interpretation is the significance attributed to a result. Even when a result itself is not in dispute, its theoretical significance frequently is. This, however, is a familiar issue in science, and is not peculiar to research on infancy. It simply means that competing theories are seeking to explain a result by postulating different processes or mechanisms. In infancy research issues of interpretation of this sort are probably no more nor less common than in any other area of psychology.

Basic Visual Processes

One of the most impressive advances in our understanding of infants in the past quarter century has been in the area of vision. With considerable methodological ingenuity, researchers have begun to construct a detailed account of how the infant's visual system functions. Much of this work has focused on basic perceptual processes – that is to say, it has explored one or other component of vision, such as accommodation, acuity, and contrast sensitivity. In order to study these phenomena with maximum vigour, researchers have, of necessity, used stimuli that are not likely to be encountered outside the laboratory. These stimuli are particularly suited to obtaining reliable measures of the process in which the researcher is interested. Such studies are an important part of understanding perceptual development but they are not sufficient in themselves. The visual system is a complex system of interacting components that has evolved to extract information from the environment we inhabit. But what information is it designed to extract? Marr (1982) has argued that the primary purposes of vision are to recognize and identify objects and their spatial layout. Marr's own analysis of the visual system reveals what a complex task this is. At present our knowledge of how the visual system accomplishes its evolutionary role is far from complete. The absence of a precise model of how the adult visual system works makes it difficult to know which are the more important issues that should be pursued in studying the development of vision. Nevertheless, in addition to attempting to understand the basic individual processes of the visual system, developmental studies need also address the issue of how, within the constraints imposed by the visual system, an infant processes information about the environment.

Visual Accommodation

One of the most basic visual mechanisms is the ability of the eye to bring objects at different distances into focus. This is done by changing the curvature of the lens. It is an automatic response of the mature eye and is called visual accommodation. Figure 2.1 shows the structure of the human eye, for reference purposes.

Haynes, White and Held (1965) were the first to study visual accommodation in infants experimentally. They presented a small target at varying distances from infants ranging in age from six days to four months. While the infant was fixating the target the experimenter studied the eye with a retinoscope – an instrument that enables the observer to look into the eye and examine the lens. It is possible from the measurements obtained to calculate at what distance the eye is focused. This can be compared with the distance the object is placed from the infant. Haynes et al. found that below 1 month of age there was no accommodation. Thereafter accommodation improved until, by 4 months, it was near adult level.

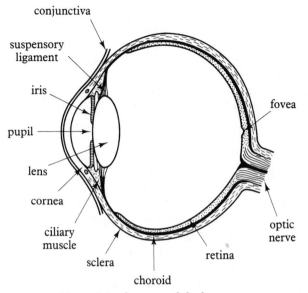

conjunctiva

suspensory
ligament

iris

pupil

lens

cornea

ciliary
muscle

sclera

choroid

fovea

optic
nerve

retina

Figure 2.1 *Structure of the human eye.*

More recent evidence has suggested that the technique used by Haynes et al. may have underestimated the abilities of young infants. Haynes et al. used a small patterned shield as the target stimulus. This may not have been an ideal stimulus on which to test young infants because poor visual acuity and contrast sensitivity (see below) may have impeded accommodation. Using the same retinoscopic technique Banks (1980) tested accommodation to a large high-contrast checkerboard pattern. Banks found superior accommodation at all ages but especially at 1 month.

One disadvantage of the retinoscopic technique is that it requires that the infant fixate the target during the interval that the measurement is being made. This makes it insensitive to rapid looks at and accommodations to a target. Braddick, Atkinson, French and Howland (1979) used an alternative technique of photorefraction in which a light is shone into the eye and the reflections are photographed. Attention to the target is only required for the instant the photograph is taken. Braddick et al. tested infants ranging in age from 1 day to 12 months at two stimulus distances, 75 and 150 cm. Below 10 days old infants accommodated better to the 75 cm target. Above this age they accommodated consistently to both targets.

The results of recent studies of visual accommodation suggest that Haynes et al. (1965) underestimated the capacity of the infant's eye to accommodate. Nevertheless, accommodation is far from perfect at birth but it does improve considerably in the first few months of life. This may have more to do with changes in other aspects of perceptual processing that affect accommodation than with changes in the motor ability to accommodate (Banks and Salapatek, 1983). Even if the lens of the eye accommodates to cast a sharp image on the retina, this is to no avail if the rest of the visual system cannot take advantage of it.

Visual Acuity

Acuity is a measure of how well patterns are perceived. Visual acuity is usually measured by showing patterns that consist of a grating of black and white vertical stripes as shown in figure 2.2. The thickness of the stripes is gradually reduced until the pattern can no longer be detected and simply looks a uniform grey. The finest grating that can be resolved is taken as the measure of acuity.

Fantz, Ordy and Udelf (1962) used the phenomenon of *optokinetic nystagmus* (OKN) to measure acuity in infants from 4 days to 6 months. OKN is an involuntary response that occurs when a subject looks at a repetitive moving pattern. It consists of slow rhythmic tracking followed by rapid refixation. Fantz et al. presented infants with moving gratings of stripes and gradually reduced the thickness of the stripes until OKN ceased. When OKN ceases, it means that the infant can no longer detect the pattern. Acuity in the infants varied from about 1/30th the adult sensitivity at 2 weeks (i.e. the stripes had to be 30 times wider than for

Figure 2.2   *Examples of gratings used to test visual acuity.*

adults to be seen as separate) to about 1/10th the adult sensitivity at 6 months.

Other measures of acuity have yielded similar results. Allen (1978) used the visual preference technique to measure acuity from 2 weeks to 6 months. The infants were shown two stimuli of equal size, luminance, and hue. One stimulus was a high contrast grating pattern while the other was unpatterned. Since infants are known to prefer patterned to unpatterned stimuli, they should look more at the patterned stimulus until the stripes are too close to be detected at which point there will be no difference in preference. Allen's results were similar to those reported by Fantz et al. (1962).

There is yet a third way of measuring acuity. Unfortunately it yields somewhat different results. The technique relies on measuring localized brain activity in the visual cortex in response to a changing visual stimulus. If bar gratings are presented briefly a characteristic waveform, called a *visually evoked potential* (VEP) can be recorded. Very fine out-of-focus gratings give no evoked response. Using VEP measurements Marg, Freeman, Peltzman and Goldstein (1976) found results that were similar to those of behavioural methods for infants below 6 weeks, but also found much more rapid improvement than the behavioural methods so that adult acuity was achieved by 6 months. Sokol (1978) obtained similar results to Marg et al. (1976).

At present it is not clear why behavioural and VEP measures of acuity do not agree completely. It may be that VEP measures a different mechanism from the behavioural measures. However, it is clear that acuity is poor in young infants and the question arises of why it is so poor and how it improves so rapidly. At present not enough is known to answer these questions precisely. One factor, however, that is likely to constrain the infant's acuity is the immaturity of the retina. The fovea of the infant's eye is not as densely packed with cones as the adult's eye is. The density of foveal cones increases gradually after birth (Abramov, Gordon, Hendrickson, Hainline, Dobson and La Bossiere, 1982). Banks and Salapatek (1983) suggest that this factor may largely be responsible for increases in acuity.

Contrast Sensitivity

Measurements of visual acuity reveal the finest discriminations the eye can make. However, in order to recognize objects in the world, we rarely have to make these discriminations. In addition, the degree of contrast in the real world is often much less than that in the typical stimuli used in measurements of acuity. Thus, it is not possible easily to predict from a single measure of acuity our ability to detect pattern information in everyday environments. A better index of this ability is the *contrast sensitivity function* (CSF) which represents the complete range of sensitivity. The CSF is a plot of the amount of contrast that is needed at different spatial frequencies between the light and dark stripes of a sine-wave grating in order for it to be just distinguishable from a uniform grey. Figure 2.3 shows the relation between contrast and spatial frequency together with a plot of a typical adult CSF.

Measures of the CSF in infants have revealed that young infants are sensitive to a lower range of spatial frequencies than adults and to a restricted range of contrasts (Atkinson, Braddick and Moar, 1977; Banks and Salapatek, 1978). What this means, in practice, is that the infant is sensitive initially to only a fraction of the information to which the adult is sensitive. However, there is a steady increase over the first six months in the infant's sensitivity (Pirchio, Spinelli, Fiorentini and Maffei, 1978).

What are the implications of the poor contrast sensitivity of infants for their ability to detect objects in the environment? Does the infant's poor contrast sensitivity mean that common objects cannot be distinguished from their background? Can the infant see faces, for example? Banks and Salapatek (1983) point out that the contours of many common objects and of faces will have contrasts high enough for the object to be detected by the infant. The fact that infants are more sensitive to low spatial frequencies means that they will be able to perceive near objects but will be poor at perceiving distant objects.

In summary, the available evidence indicates that the infant is capable of detecting information in the environment practically from birth. However, the range of information to which the infant is sensitive is limited. This range increases as the visual system matures during the early months of life. Given that infants are not alert for long periods in the earliest months of life it seems unlikely that the limits of the infant's visual system hinder or retard the ability to learn about the environment.

Pattern Vision

Pattern Preferences

Research on infants' pattern vision was initiated by Fantz (1958, 1961). Until Fantz began his research little was known about the ability of an infant to distinguish one pattern from another. Fantz was interested in determining whether the infant really experienced the world as 'one great blooming, buzzing confusion'. His way of tackling the problem was to test whether or not infants could differentiate visual stimuli on the

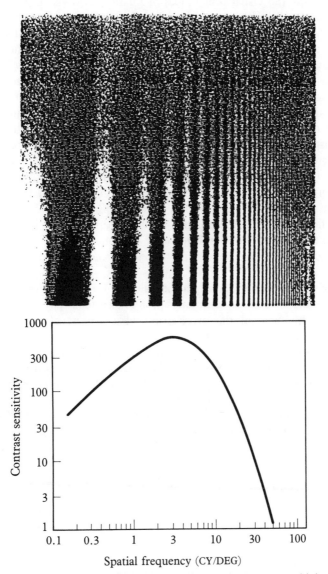

Figure 2.3 *A sine wave grating and a typical adult contrast sensitivity function (CSF). The upper part of the figure displays a sine wave grating in which spatial frequency increases from left to right and contrast increases from top to bottom. The lower part of the figure shows a typical adult CSF.*
Source: Banks & Salapatek, 1981.

basis of differences in form. Fantz devised an apparatus to investigate systematically the visual preferences of infants. Two visual patterns are placed about 10 inches above the eyes of an infant lying on his or her back. The apparatus allows the experimenter to observe the infant from directly above the patterns without being seen, and to record how often the infant looks at each pattern. The experimenter can tell where the infant is looking by observing the images of the objects mirrored in the infant's eyes. When the image of one of the objects is over the centre of the eye the infant is looking directly at it. If an infant looks significantly more at one pattern than the other, Fantz reasoned that the patterns had been discriminated on the basis of their form. This is the spontaneous visual preference technique, which was invented by Fantz. The experimental technique is ingeniously simple, exploits a natural behaviour of the infant, and provides a method of determining visual preferences. Using a variety of different stimuli Fantz (1958, 1961) found that from the earliest weeks of life infants show preferences for some stimuli over others. Fantz (1963) showed that even newborns display reliable preferences. Thus, the basic ability to detect and discriminate forms is innate.

Fantz's work opened the experimental door for research on infants. A large number of studies of infants' preferences followed. The question addressed by most of this work was: what aspects of visual stimuli determine infants' preferences?

One of the first stimulus dimensions to be investigated was the complexity of a pattern. Patterns can, of course, be complex in a variety of ways. The experiments on infant preferences kept complexity under operational control by manipulating the number of squares on a checkerboard. The more squares, the more complex. Hershenson (1964) presented newborn infants with a 6-inch square board that had either a 2x2, 4x4, or 12x12 pattern of squares. Hershenson found that newborns preferred the least complex pattern. Brennan, Ames and Moore (1966) presented patterns of 2x2, 8x8, or 24x24 squares and found that 3-week-old infants looked longest at the 2x2 patterns but 8-week-old infants looked longest at the 8x8 patterns and 14-week-old infants looked longest at the 24x24 patterns. Thus, an infant's preference for complexity would appear to be age-related, greater complexity being preferred as the infant matures.

However, other interpretations of the data described are possible. As the complexity of a pattern is increased other attributes of the pattern change also. It may be that the infant is responding to one of these attributes rather than to complexity. One attribute that has been proposed as an alternative determinant of the infant's responses is contour density.

For checkerboard patterns the amount of contour is obtained by adding the length of all the sides in the pattern. Contour density is obtained by dividing this sum by the area of the pattern. As the number of squares in a pattern of fixed size is increased the contour density will increase, as will the complexity. Karmel (1969) found that contour density was a better predictor of infant responses than complexity. He contrasted check patterns with random patterns and found that the pattern with more contour was preferred. However, subsequent research by Fantz, Fagan and Miranda (1975) and Greenberg and Blue (1975) showed that infant preferences were not due to contour alone. Both studies were designed to tease apart the effects of contour density and complexity. Greenberg and Blue separated complexity and contour density by using circles rather than squares. Fantz et al. used a pattern of black squares on a white background but the squares did not touch as in a checked pattern. With either method contour density can be manipulated by varying the size of the elements within the figure while maintaining the number of elements (and thus the complexity) constant. Likewise, contour density can be held constant and complexity manipulated. Greenberg and Blue found that both the dimensions of contour and number were important in determining attentional preference while Fantz et al. found a preference for large-sized elements in 1-month-olds but a preference for an increased number of elements (when contour was equal) at 2 months and older.

These results indicate that infant preferences are not simply a function of any one single stimulus dimension. However, as a first approximation there is a relation between an increase in complexity and increasing age. Recently, Banks and Ginsburg (1985) have proposed a model that relates the data on infant preferences to the changing capabilities of the infant's visual system. The model they propose uses the data on the infant's contrast sensitivity function and the fact that it is possible, following Fourier's theorem, to represent any two-dimensional pattern as a set of sine-wave gratings of various frequencies, and amplitudes. The first step of the model is to carry out a Fourier analysis of the pattern. This decomposes the pattern into a set of values for its various components. The CSF can now be used to 'filter' these components. Effectively, this is a simulation of what happens to the information as it passes through the infant's visual system. The result is that components of the stimulus to which an infant's visual system is sensitive are transmitted by the system and those to which the system is insensitive are attenuated. The filtered pattern is what is assumed to be available to 'decision centres' in the central nervous system. The model assumes that when different patterns are presented the decision centres will attend to the most salient of the filtered patterns. The salience of a pattern can be computed from the output of the filtered pattern. This model successfully predicts the results of a wide range of visual preference data for infants in the early months of life.

The Banks and Ginsburg model implies, as they put it, 'that infants' visual preferences are governed simply by a tendency to look at highly visible patterns' (p. 211). They argue that such a tendency has adaptive significance for the infant's visual development. They offer two reasons why this should be the case. The first is that such a looking strategy will aid the postnatal development of the visual cortex; looking strategies reflect an evolutionary strategy to provide stimulation for cortical development to proceed optimally. There is, as they point out, considerable evidence of the importance of particular types of visual experience for the normal development of the visual system in other species (Blakemore and Van Sluyters, 1975; Derrington and Fuchs, 1981; Pettigrew, 1974).

The second hypothesis emphasizes adaptive significance also, but in a different way. Banks and Ginsburg argue that the infant's looking strategies provide maximally useful information for the perception of objects. They point out that most objects are seen because of the contrast between their surface and the background. An infant preference for high-contrast contours would correspond to a tendency to fixate object boundaries. The sensitivity of the infant to low spatial frequencies will lead to the infant fixating near rather than far objects. This has adaptive significance in aiding the co-ordination of looking and acting. Young infants are very limited in their motor abilities and in the distances over which they can act (due to their immobility). A sensitivity to low spatial frequencies makes it possible for the infant to direct effective action towards objects that can be seen clearly.

The filtered patterns proposed by Banks and Ginsburg are the beginning rather than the end of an information processing account of pattern vision. Banks and Ginsburg hypothesize that these patterns are available to 'decision centres' in the brain. What might these 'decision centres' be? How might we translate from the metaphor of 'decision centres' to the components of an information processing account? It is in addressing questions such as this that studies using the habituation technique are particularly useful. If an infant habituates to a stimulus then this implies the presence of a functional system of recognition memory. Friedman and his associates have conducted a number of studies of habituation in neonates (Friedman, 1972a; 1972b; Friedman, Bruno and Vietze, 1974; Friedman and Carpenter, 1971). Friedman and Carpenter (1971) demonstrated habituation in infants between 1 and 3 days old. Friedman (1972a) demonstrated both habituation and recovery in a similar age group. He showed infants black and white checkerboards for 60 seconds and recorded how long the infant looked at the board. After several presentations interest declined significantly. When shown a smaller pattern the infants looked more at this than a control group who continued to view the original pattern. When this group too was shown the new smaller checkerboard pattern there was an increase in their looking. However, it is also important to point out many of the infants who began the experiment did not manage to complete it, and of those that did, not all habituated. This could be taken to suggest that the processes responsible for habituation are not very robust in very young infants. However, it must be remembered how exceedingly difficult it is to conduct experiments with such infants. An alternative explanation for failure to complete is that changes of state lead to the infant losing interest in the stimulus. More recently Slater, Morison and Rose (1982) have produced further evidence of habituation in newborns without the high drop-out rate experienced by Friedman.

At present, the habituation evidence suggests a functional system of recognition memory in new-born infants. However, the experiments do not reveal whether the infants retained the information over a longer period of time. At present there are no experiments that address this issue in newborns. The erratic state cycle of the newborn makes the issue particularly difficult to study.

During the early months of life the infant's state cycles become more regular and the periods of alertness increase considerably (Parmelee, 1974; Parmelee and Stern, 1972). This affords experimenters a better opportunity to study infants and it affords infants a better opportunity to learn. By 3 months it is possible to obtain habituation to a wide variety of stimuli (Olson and Sherman, 1983), thus showing a well-established recognition memory by this age. A number of studies have also addressed the issue of how well infants retain information.

The standard method of measuring retention of information is to ask subjects to recall or recognize stimuli presented some time previously. It is, of course, impossible to do this with infants. However, it is possible to approach retention in a more indirect manner. Let us assume that an infant has been habituated to a stimulus. The stimulus is then presented again some hours or days later. What should happen? We should expect habituation to occur again and we might also expect it to occur more quickly if there has been retention of the information gained on the earlier trial. If we were to find an increase in speed of habituation over repeated trials then this is evidence for retention of information over trials. It is also necessary to control for the fact that speed of habituation may be changing due to other factors. This can be done by presenting a variety of novel and familiar stimuli on each trial. Each stimulus should be novel for half the children and familiar for the other half to ensure that there are no effects due to the stimuli themselves.

Using the type of procedure just outlined Martin (1975) tested infants aged 2 months, 3.5 months, and 5 months over a two-day period. On the first day a geometric figure was shown six times for a period of 30 seconds. The figure was shown again on the second day. The infants looked at the figure less on the second day than they did on the first. The decline in looking also increased slightly with age, suggesting that the 5-month-old infants may have been more sure of the familiarity of the stimulus. Using a similar technique Cornell (1979) found recognition by 5- to 6-month-olds for intervals up to 48 hours. Fagan (1973) showed that 6-month-old infants recognize checkerboard patterns up to 48 hours after presentation of the original stimulus and black-and-white photographs of human faces for periods up to two weeks. A number of studies have also shown that infant visual memories are relatively robust and resistant to interference from intervening experience (Cohen, DeLoache and Pearl, 1977; Fagan, 1977; McCall, Kennedy and Dodds, 1977).

Visual Scanning

Thus far the infant's ability to detect information in the environment has been considered. However, as Gibson (1966, 1979) has emphasized, organisms do not passively wait for stimuli to impinge upon their senses; they actively seek information from the environment. None of the research discussed so far has revealed anything about the extent to which infants seek information. As usual, in research with infants, it is of prime importance to find a behavioural measure that can be linked with some confidence to the cognitive process in which we are interested. One measure that has been widely used in studying the more dynamic aspects of visual behaviour is eye movements. The technique involves recording on which elements of a pattern infants fixate. It is possible to do this by recording on video camera the reflections of infra-red light sources (which are invisible to the infant) off the cornea of the eye while the infant is looking at some stimulus. The corneal reflections can then be used to work out where the infant fixated the stimulus (Maurer, 1975). The technique is a high-tech version of the visual preference technique. It offers the experimenter much greater precision than gross preferences.

Salapatek and Kessen (1966) measured the eye fixations of newborns to a triangle. They found that fixations tended to cluster around one of the vertices of the triangle. Figure 2.4 shows some typical results. The fact that infants tend to fixate one vertex only was initially taken as indicating that infants are 'captured' by a visual stimulus. However, a

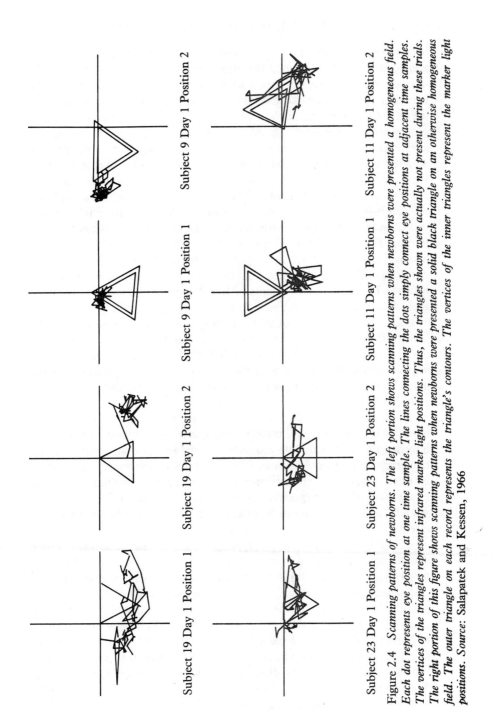

Subject 19 Day 1 Position 1   Subject 19 Day 1 Position 2   Subject 9 Day 1 Position 1   Subject 9 Day 1 Position 2

Subject 23 Day 1 Position 1   Subject 23 Day 1 Position 2   Subject 11 Day 1 Position 1   Subject 11 Day 1 Position 2

Figure 2.4   Scanning patterns of newborns. The left portion shows scanning patterns when newborns were presented a homogeneous field. Each dot represents eye position at one time sample. The lines connecting the dots simply connect eye positions at adjacent time samples. The vertices of the triangles represent infrared marker light positions. Thus, the triangles shown were actually not present during these trials. The right portion of this figure shows scanning patterns when newborns were presented a solid black triangle on an otherwise homogeneous field. The outer triangle on each record represents the triangle's contours. The vertices of the inner triangles represent the marker light positions. Source: Salapatek and Kessen, 1966

later experiment suggested that this conclusion is overly strong. Salapatek and Kessen (1973) examined the effects of repeated presentations of the triangles they had used in their earlier experiment. Although most of the neonates did not scan the triangles for more than a few minutes, a few subjects scanned for longer and over a more extensive area of the triangle. Nevertheless, extensive scanning is relatively rare in neonates. Leahy (1976) compared scanning in 1- and 3-month-olds. The 1-month-olds scanned much less extensively than the 3-month-olds. Salapatek (1975) reported consonant data for compound stimuli (stimuli that had both internal and external elements). The 1-month-olds typically did not fixate the internal elements, whereas the 2-month-olds did. Research on how infants scan more complex stimuli, such as faces, have produced similar findings (Hainline, 1978; Haith, Bergman and Moore, 1977; Maurer and Salapatek, 1976). All studies reported extensive scanning of the border of the face (the area of highest contrast) but little attention to the internal features by 1-month-old infants. After 2 months, fixations were much more likely to cluster around internal features, particularly the eyes.

There are several difficulties in the way of direct conclusions from the literature on visual scanning about how infants seek or process information. As Banks and Salapatek (1983) point out, most infant scanning experiments have not dealt with the relation between scanning and information processing. Most experiments have simply described how various stimulus variables affect eye movements. Some limited conclusions can be drawn, however. The pattern of looking by infants up to at least 1 month suggests that these infants must receive a very limited amount of information about stimulus properties. This, in any case, is what would be expected from the Banks and Ginsburg (1985) analysis of the relation between stimulus complexity and the contrast sensitivity function of the infant eye. The young infant is not equally capable of processing all stimuli. This is brought out by research on the so-called internal–external effect.

As has been reported above, young infants do not scan the internal components of complex stimuli (Salapatek, 1975). This led researchers to ask whether or not infants could discriminate changes in the internal components of a complex stimulus. Milewski (1976, 1978) presented stimuli that consisted of one geometric shape inside another as shown in figure 2.5. Milewski habituated 1- and 4-month old infants to the stimuli and then changed the shape of either the external figure, the internal figure, or both. The 4-month-old infants dishabituated to all the changes but the 1-month-olds only dishabituated when the shape of the external figure was changed. Milewski concluded that young infants only attend to the external elements of a complex stimulus. However, it may have

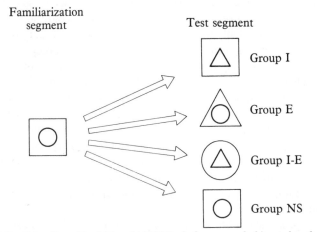

Figure 2.5   *Stimuli used by Milewski (1976). Infants were habituated to the stimulus on the left and tested for dishabituation on the stimuli on the right.*

been that the limits of the younger infants' visual system told against them in these experiments. Ganon and Swartz (1980) used internal elements known to be highly salient to young infants – a bull's eye or a checkerboard pattern. Under these conditions 1-month-old infants detected changes in both the internal and external figure. Thus, it would seem that young infants do process 'complex' stimulus information – providing, of course, that their visual system is capable of detecting the information.

The picture that emerges from research on infant scanning is one of a gradual development from highly constrained scanning during the first month to fairly detailed scanning of complex stimuli by 3 months. The more limited scanning of the younger infants is almost certainly due to the constraints imposed by the immaturity of the visual system itself. By 3 or 4 months, however, the infant is capable of reasonably detailed scanning, which affords the opportunity for more effective encoding of stimuli and thus more effective learning.

Perception of Depth

As previously remarked, Marr (1982) has argued that vision has two primary functions: the recognition of objects in the environment and the determination of their spatial layout. The basic visual processes that have been discussed can be seen as some of the component inputs to object recognition. From the evidence reviewed it would seem that the visual system is reasonably well-adapted to a primitive recognition of objects. In this section we shall discuss the second primary function of vision identified by Marr: determination of spatial layout. Perception of depth is crucial to determining spatial layout. The obvious question now to ask is how well the visual system is adapted to the perception of depth.

Before considering the developmental evidence it is worth remembering why depth perception is an important issue for a theory of vision. The retinal image of objects, which is the first level at which perceptual information is registered, is two-dimensional. Thus, the image itself cannot be a source of any direct information about depth. Somehow the visual system must supplement the information available from the retinal image so that depth can be perceived. This supplement comes from three main sources: monocular cues, binocular cues, and kinetic cues. Evolution has been profligate with the ability to detect depth because different cues provide reliable information in different situations. As Banks and Salapatek (1983) point out, this raises the non-trivial problem of how the visual system interprets and integrates depth information from different sources that may be in conflict.

Monocular cues include such things as texture gradients, linear perspective and familiar size. Binocular cues arise from the fact that each eye receives slightly different information about an object, resulting in a slight discrepancy between the two retinal images, called *binocular parallax*. Kinetic cues arise from the fact that perception by an organism is not the result of a single momentary stimulus leading to a single retinal image but is a process that occurs over time. Over time either the observer or the objects being viewed may move, giving potential information about depth.

There are two basic approaches to the study of depth in infancy. The first is to put infants in situations that contain information about depth and to measure depth-appropriate behaviours. The second is to conduct discrimination or habituation experiments that manipulate one individual depth cue.

The Visual Cliff

A classic example of measuring depth-appropriate behaviours is the visual cliff experiments conducted by Gibson and Walk (1960; Walk and Gibson, 1961). The visual cliff is illustrated in figure 2.6. It consists of a sheet of thick glass supported above the floor. The glass surface is divided into two by a board laid across the middle of the glass. On one side of the board a checkerboard pattern is placed directly beneath the glass. This

Deep side   Shallow side

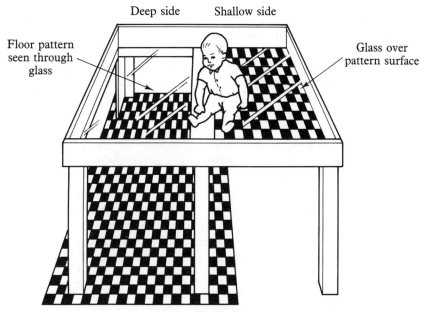

Figure 2.6 *Visual cliff apparatus.*

gives the glass the appearance of a solid surface. On the other side of the board a similar pattern is placed on the floor. This does not give a solid appearance; it creates a visual cliff. Gibson and Walk tested 36 infants aged 6 months upwards. Each infant was placed on the centre board and the mother called the infant from the deep side and the shallow side successively. The infants were extremely reluctant to venture onto the deep side (only three did so at all) but were quite willing to crawl on the shallow side. Many of the infants crawled away from the mother when she called from the deep side. Gibson and Walk concluded that infants can discriminate depth as soon as they can crawl.

A major limitation of the technique used by Gibson and Walk is that it is limited to studying infants who have the ability to crawl. Since depth perception is evident as soon as crawling, the technique cannot tell us about the origins of depth perception. There is also another issue that is unresolved: what information does the infant gain from being able to perceive depth? Why, for example, do infants refuse to crawl on to the deep side? Is it because they fear falling? Scarr and Salapatek (1970) measured fear reactions when infants were pulled in a trolley across the deep and shallow sides of the cliff. They found that only 20 per cent of infants 7 months old showed fear on the visual cliff. There was, however, an increase in fear with age until, by 13 months, it was evident in all infants tested. Campos, Langer and Krowitz (1970) measured heart-rate when 2-month-old infants were lowered onto the cliff. Heart-rate decreased when infants were lowered onto the deep side of the cliff but not onto the shallow side. A decrease in heart-rate is often taken to be an indicator of an increase in attention whereas an increase in heart-rate is often taken to indicate fear. Campos et al. concluded that the infants detected the drop but were not afraid of it. Schwartz, Campos and Baisel (1973) showed that the heart-rate of 5-month-old infants also decreased when they were lowered onto the visual cliff but the heart-rate of 9-month-olds increased. Campos, Hiatt, Ramsay, Henderson and Svejda (1978) showed that infants express fear on the visual cliff as a function of the time since they have begun crawling: the longer an infant has been crawling the more likely he or she is to show fear on the visual cliff. They argue that although young infants can perceive depth, it is only through experience with crawling that they learn to fear depth. However, there is evidence against this view. Rader, Bausano and Richards (1980) found that infants who began crawling late were more likely to avoid the visual cliff than infants of the same age who had begun to crawl early. This is exactly the opposite of what Campos et al. (1978) would predict because the latter group had more experience of crawling than the former. In a follow-up study Richards and Rader (1981) showed that age of onset of crawling predicted avoidance, whereas age of testing and amount of crawling experience did not. Rader et al. (1980) propose that avoidance is determined by an innate visuomotor program that specifies support and that matures at about the time that crawling begins. However, early crawlers do not have access to this program (because it has not matured) and use tactile information to guide their locomotion. For these infants crawling continues to be guided by tactual information. For late crawlers the visuomotor program suppresses crawling over the visual cliff. These infants, however, show no fear of the cliff until some months later. Fear of depth, presumably, is learnt through experience.

None of the studies discussed so far reveal the mechanisms by which depth might be processed by infants. In order to determine to which depth cues infants are sensitive it is necessary to control the cues to depth to which the infant has access. As mentioned previously the three major types of cue are monocular, binocular, and kinetic.

Monocular Depth Cues

Monocular depth cues are cues that can be picked up by one eye. Some, such as motion parallax, require motion of the observer's head, while others require motion by the object (these will both be treated under 'Kinetic Depth Cues'). In addition to these, there are some depth cues that can be derived purely from the static pattern of an object in space. These include texture gradient (textures become finer with increasing distance), interposition (far objects are partly occluded by nearer objects that are in the same line of sight), linear perspective (size decreases with increasing distance) and some others such as relative and familiar size. Yonas, Cleaves and Pettersen (1978) used the trapezoidal window developed by Ames (1951), shown in figure 2.7, to investigate whether infants would use a linear perspective cue to guide their reaching. When adults view the window monocularly, they judge, incorrectly, that the larger side of the window is nearer. Yonas et al. found that when 7-month-old infants viewed the window monocularly, they reached more frequently to the near than the far side, even though the window was fronto-parallel. However, the 5-month-olds did not exhibit selective reaching to the near side. A follow-up study (Kaufmann, Maland and Yonas, 1981) revealed similar results. This suggests that a sensitivity to linear perspective may develop between 5 and 7 months. Other monocular cues may also develop during this period. Yonas, Pettersen and Granrud (1982) found that familiar size is an effective depth cue for 7-month-olds but not for 5-month-olds. Granrud, Yonas and Pettersen (1984) reported a similar result for relative size. Granrud and Yonas (1984) examined sensitivity to interposition and found that 7-month-olds used interposition cues to guide reaching but 5-month-olds did not.

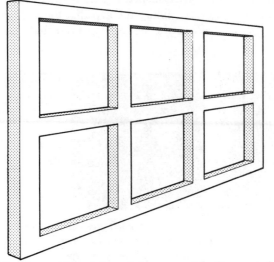

Figure 2.7   *Trapezoidal window of the type used by Yonas et al, (1978).*

The data on static depth information are remarkably consistent: 7-month-olds are sensitive to this information; 5-month-olds are not. Yonas and Granrud (1985) speculate that the results may be explained by the emergence of constraints (such as continuity of surfaces in space) for the interpretation of input by the visual system. Essentially, the speculation is that the perception of static depth information is a complex architectural principle inherent in the structure of the visual system that requires the establishment of more basic principles before it can manifest itself.

Binocular Depth Cues

When a person focuses on an object with both eyes, two slightly different retinal images result. The difference between the images is called *binocular disparity*. The brain fuses these images to produce one image that has depth. This process is called *stereopsis*. Fusion requires very precise convergence of the two eyes. Infants in the first few months of life are erratic in their ability to converge (Aslin, 1977). This might be expected to affect their ability to achieve stereopsis, if indeed they can do so at all. The two basic methods of conducting discrimination/habituation experiments and of attempting to elicit depth-appropriate behaviours have again been used in the study of infant stereopsis.

The random-dot stereogram developed by Julesz (1960) has been used in discrimination/habituation experiments. The basis of this technique is to create two identical random dot patterns of the type shown in figure 2.8 and then to shift a square-shaped region at the centre of one of the patterns slightly to one side, filling the gap that the shift creates with a new random pattern. When the images are presented one to each eye

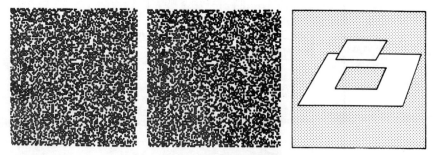

Figure 2.8   *The stereoscopic images on the left give rise to a panel floating above a background, represented on the right, when viewed through a stereoscope or with a prism held in front of one eye.*
Source: Julesz 1965.

through a stereoscope the area shifted creates an effect of binocular disparity. Adults report seeing the area shifted stand out against the background. The disparity introduced into a meaningless pattern of random dots is used by the visual system to organize the array into two separate depth planes of a figure against a background. A number of experiments have used random dot stereograms to assess the ability of infants to detect the disparity and, by inference, to achieve stereopsis (Atkinson and Braddick, 1976; Fox, Aslin, Shea and Dumais, 1980; Petrig, Julesz, Kropfl, Baumgartner and Anliker, 1981). Although none of the studies can be regarded as conclusive on its own (the notorious difficulties of conducting experiments with young infants make the data 'noisy'), Banks and Salapatek (1983) have collated the various results and concluded that they point to a consistent conclusion: the ability to detect disparity is evident in a small proportion of infants by 2 months and demonstrable in virtually all infants by 6 months. They also point out that the poor visual acuity of younger infants will often lead to poor quality retinal images that will make stereopsis accordingly more difficult.

Studies of disparity detection do not actually demonstrate that infants perceive depth. It is possible that the ability to perceive disparity may develop before the ability to detect depth. If depth-appropriate behaviours could be elicited to stereoscopic displays, this would constitute better evidence.

Bower, Broughton and Moore (1970b) tested the relation between stereoscopic vision and reaching using the apparatus shown in figure 2.9. A point source of light passes through two Polaroid filters to produce two shadows of the object on the screen. The infant views the shadows through Polaroid filters and only by stereopsis is it possible to see the image of a virtual object located between the screen and the infant. Bower et al. (1970a, 1970b) reported that infants within the first month of life reached for the virtual object when it was about 8 inches in front of them, thus indicating stereopsis at a previously unsuspected age. However, these data may not be reliable. Both Dodwell, Muir and DiFranco (1976) and Ruff and Halton (1978) have failed to replicate the result. Leaving the issue of stereopsis aside altogether, it is also open to question whether infants of this age can coordinate eye and hand movements. This issue will be discussed in the section on intersensory co-ordination. Reliable evidence of reaching for a virtual object has been produced by Gordon and Yonas (1976), Field (1977), and Bechtoldt and Hutz (1979) at 5 months.

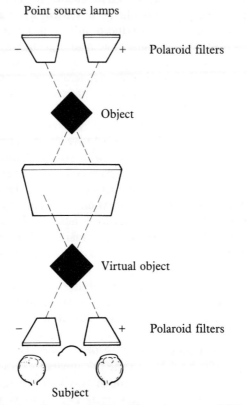

Figure 2.9 *Production of a virtual object. The point source of light passes through two Polaroid filters to produce two shadows of the object on the screen. The infant views shadows through Polaroid filters and only by stereopsis can see the image of a virtual object in front.*
Source: Bower et al. 1970.

Kinetic Depth Cues

Kinetic cues for depth are produced by changes in the retinal image over time. The simplest way to produce these changes is to move one's head. This results in the depth cue called *motion parallax*. Other cues result from the motion of an object itself. As an object moves the retinal image changes and this provides cues to depth. Object movement has been used to study infants' sensitivity to kinetic depth cues. The usual method of investigation is to observe an infant's defensive reactions as an object approaches apparently on a collision path with the infant. Bower, Broughton and Moore (1971b) studied infants' reaction to the approach of objects towards their faces. They reported that infants less than 3 weeks old made defensive responses that included a widening of the eyes, head retraction, and interposition of the hands between the face and object. One possible objection to this is that the infant is simply responding to displacement of air caused by the approaching object and not to the object itself. In order to test this Bower et al. repeated the experiment using a shadow-casting device that projects a shadow of solid object onto a screen. The shadow can be made to expand or contract, which, to adults, specifies the approach or withdrawal of an object respectively. In this condition avoidance behaviours were also observed although they were not as strong as in the real object condition. Using a shadow-caster also, Ball and Tronick (1971) reported that infants could discriminate between a shadow of an object that appeared to be headed directly at them (specified by a symmetrical optical expansion) and one that appeared to be headed for a miss (specified by an asymmetrical optical expansion).

However, the findings of these studies have been called into question by Yonas, Bechtold, Frankel, Gordon, McRoberts, Norcia and Sternfels (1977). Using a shadow-caster to manipulate hit-and-miss courses as well as a rising contour of a non-expanding form (which does not specify a collision) they found upward head rotation to both symmetrical expansion of the shadow and to the rising contour. In a second experiment, in which this contour was eliminated, Yonas et al. found that 1- to 2-month-old infants responded similarly to hit and to miss trials whereas 4- to 6-month-olds responded selectively to the hit trials. It would thus seem that by about 4 months of age infants are sensitive to kinetic depth cues. Whether or not they are sensitive before this age remains open to question.

Summary of Perception of Depth

As Yonas and Granrud (1985) point out, infants seem to become sensitive to depth information in the order kinetic, binocular, monocular. It may be that infants are sensitive to kinetic depth information earlier than the age of 3 to 4 months for which it has been demonstrated. The difficulty is in finding a behavioural response measure that would allow one to test this.

The experiments with the visual cliff show that the relation between the perception of depth, crawling, and the development of a fear response to heights is complex. The best available evidence suggests that infants' lack of willingness to crawl on the deep side of the visual cliff is not due to fear but to the maturation of visuomotor program. Fear of depth develops subsequently to this, presumably on the basis of experience of falling.

Perceptual Constancies

Thus far the emphasis has largely been on an analysis of how various components of the visual system develop. In this section the grain of analysis will be more molar and will consider some aspects of how the integrated visual system processes the information it receives from the environment.

As an organism moves about in its environment the retinal image associated with objects changes continually. In spite of this, we do not see a flux of changing sensations. We perceive stationary and moving objects that retain the same size and shape despite wide variations in the projected retinal image. This stability is called perceptual constancy. It is generally assumed that constancies result from the integration of different sources of perceptual information by the brain, although the precise mechanisms involved are not at present understood. There are two major types of visual constancy for objects: shape constancy and size constancy. An obvious question to ask now about an infant's perception of objects is when these constancies emerge.

The first evidence that infants possess shape constancy was provided by Bower (1966). Infants of 2 months were conditioned to respond with a head turn to a rectangle in a 45° orientation. After they had reached a criterial rate of response they were tested on four stimuli: (1) the rectangle in its original orientation; (2) the rectangle in a new orientation; (3) a trapezoidal figure in the same orientation as 2 projecting a retinal image identical to that produced by 1; and (4) the trapezoid in the same orientation as 1 projecting a novel retinal image. If infants of 2 months have shape constancy then they should generalize more to the rectangle in a new orientation than to the other stimuli. If, on the other hand, they do not have shape constancy then more generalization to the trapezoid projecting the same retinal image as the original rectangle might be expected. Bower's results indicate that the infants generalized most to real rectangular shapes. Further evidence for shape constancy using the habituation technique was provided by Day and McKenzie (1973; 1977) and by Caron, Caron and Carlson (1979). Day and McKenzie (1973) tested infants aged 1.5 to 4 months. One group of infants was shown a series of 20-second presentations of a cube in a constant orientation and, as might be expected, rapid habituation occurred. A second group was shown the cube in varying orientations. If the infants possess shape constancy then they should also habituate rapidly to these stimuli because cubes in different orientations will simply look like cubes, not a variety of novel stimuli. This indeed is what was found. However, it might be objected that the results are simply due to boredom or some other extraneous factor. Day and McKenzie countered such arguments by presenting a third group with a series of two-dimensional cut-outs, each of which produced the same retinal image as the cube in one of its orientations. In this situation no habituation occurred.

Shape constancy can even be demonstrated in newborns. Slater and Morison (1985) habituated newborn infants to a shape tilted at different angles. During the dishabituation trials the newborns were shown either the same shape at a different angle or a novel shape. The newborns showed a strong preference for the novel shape. Cumulatively, these experiments suggest that shape constancy is not a learned phenomenon but is an innate architectural principle of how the visual system works.

It should not be thought that because shape constancy is an innate architectural principle that no learning needs to take place about the encoding of shape information. As has been emphasized previously, architectural principles provide the foundations for learning; they do not replace it. In this context, Ruff (1978) has shown that infants do some-times have difficulty in encoding complex shapes. Infants aged 6 and 9 months old were presented with complex objects made up of combinations of cubes, blocks, spheres, and cylinders. After a series of familiarization trials, discrimination was tested with both familiar and novel shaped objects. Infants of 6 months did not recognize the familiar shapes as the same; infants of 9 months, on the other hand, did recognize the familiar shapes under some conditions. Thus, an innate ability for shape constancy in perceiving simple objects is the basis from which learning to encode information about complex stimuli begins, rather than the end of the story about the perception of shape.

The evidence in relation to size constancy is less clear. Bower (1966) also reported that when 2-month-old infants were conditioned to turn their heads in the presence of a 12-inch cube 3 feet away and then presented with generalization trials, generalization was greatest to a cube with the same true size at a different distance. However, McKenzie and Day (1972; 1976) and Day and McKenzie (1977), using the habituation technique, failed to find evidence of size constancy in infants up to 5 months old.

Later experiments by the same group changed this picture somewhat. McKenzie, Tootell and Day (1980) habituated infants aged 4, 6, and 8 months to a stimulus at a distance of 60 cm. On the dishabituation trials they presented the same stimulus either at the same distance or at half the distance together with a smaller stimulus at these two distances. The 6- and 8-month-old infants dishabituated to the smaller but not to the same size stimuli. The 4-month-old group showed a similar overall pattern but there was a great deal of variability among the group. In a later experiment Day and McKenzie (1981) found clear evidence for size constancy among 4-month-olds.

The data on size constancy are not as clear cut as the data on shape constancy. Size constancy is definitely present by 6 months, probably by 4 months, and possibly by 2 months. As is usual with research on infants, it is difficult to know whether a failure to find an ability at a given age is due to its genuine absence or due to its being masked by some extraneous factor in the experimental design. However, let us consider some reasons why size constancy may not be perceived by young infants in habituation experiments. The properties of an object that are usually considered relevant to size constancy are the size of the retinal image and apparent distance of the object. The apparent distance of an object is judged from depth cues. As Yonas and his associates have demonstrated, the static monocular depth cues are not evident in 5-month-old infants but are definitely evident in 7-month-olds. These may be cues on which size constancy crucially depends in habituation experiments with static displays. The depth cues to which infants are most sensitive – kinetic cues – may be of little use in detecting apparent distance in these experiments. Motion parallax, for example, is a major cue to the relative depth of two or more objects; habituation experiments present a single object at a time. It might be interesting to try habituating infants to an object presented against a salient background in order to increase the utility of kinetic cues, and then to conduct dishabituation trials with same and different sized objects at various distances.

In summary, perceptual constancies are evident in early infancy. Shape constancy, at least, seems to be an innate architectural principle of the visual system. At present, we do not know much in detail about the principle, nor, in detail, with what types of stimuli the visual system is capable of preserving shape constancy at birth and with what types it must supplement innate principles with learning. The data on size constancy are less clear in their implications for innate architectural principles.

Auditory Development

Auditory perception is the process that detects sounds in the environment. Sound originates from the motion or vibration of an object, which produces periodic waves of compressions (increased pressure) and rarefactions (decreased pressure) of the surrounding air. Sound waves are transmitted through the air in all directions, generally weakening as the distance from the source increases. Sound waves cause changes in pressure on the eardrum, which in turn causes the neural activity that results in hearing.

The auditory system is sensitive to two dimensions of a sound wave: frequency and amplitude (see figure 2.10). Frequency is the number of repetitions of the wave per second (measured in Hertz (Hz), where one Hz is one cycle per second) and amplitude is a measure of the pressure of the wave. The response of the auditory system to a sound stimulus is measured as a function of frequency and intensity, which is a measure closely related to amplitude. Intensity is the sound power transmitted through a given area in a sound field. The intensity of a sound is measured as a ratio of some reference sound and is expressed in decibels (dB). An adult can normally hear sound of an appropriate intensity from a very low frequency of about 60 Hz to about 16,000 Hz. Figure 2.11 shows that speech sounds are only a small portion of the audible sounds, between about 200 and 6,400 Hz.

Audition is the poor relation of the two major senses as far as research goes. Yet, the auditory modality is, if anything, psychologically more important than the visual modality. The auditory environment is pervasive; we may close our eyes and visual stimulation ceases but auditory stimulation never ceases completely, not even when we sleep. Auditory signals give us a variety of information including the direction and, to some extent, the distance of a sound. The auditory modality is also the sensory vehicle for language input, which is a prototypical information source for human beings, and for musical input. Aslin, Pisoni and Jusczyk (1983) list the following five reasons why, until recently, there has not been detailed study of auditory development:

1 The auditory system is devoid of unique behavioural responses, which makes the choice of a response measure problematic.
2 Many studies have failed to specify precisely the stimuli used, which has made replication of results difficult.
3 Until recently psychophysical methods have not been used, despite a long tradition of such methods when studying adults.
4 The auditory system has traditionally been less well understood than the visual system.
5 Researchers studying auditory development, by contrast with those studying visual development, have not had the benefit of analogies derived from animal research.

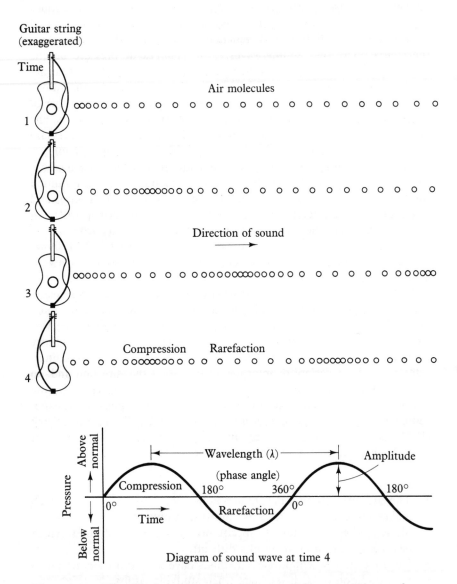

Figure 2.10 *The vibrating guitar string causes successive compressions and rare-factions of air molecules. The amplitude of the sound wave curve indicates a degree of compression or rarefraction of the air molecules. The wavelength represents a single cycle of the wave. The frequency is the number of cycles that pass a given point per second.*

Source: Coren et al., 1978.

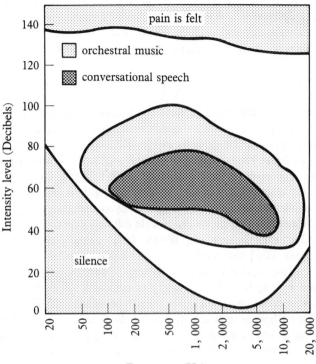

Figure 2.11   *The auditory area, showing how perception of sound is a function of both intensity and frequency of sound waves. The lower curve shows the minimal intensities required at each frequency in order to hear sound. Above the upper curve the intensities are so great that they produce a painful sensation. Between the two curves is the area of hearing. Also shown are the approximate areas of conversational speech and of orchestral music. (Frequency is measured on an octave scale).*
Source: Krech et al., 1969.

Although it is evident that the auditory system is well-developed at birth, there is much that remains to be discovered about its development. As Aslin et al. (1983) point out many of the functional properties of various structures in the adult auditory system are unknown at present, which makes the developmental status of these structures even less clear. However, in spite of this it is still possible to investigate the psychological functioning of the auditory system in infancy. As usual, the key to unlocking the study of infant auditory abilities is to find methods that yield reliable, replicable results. The methods that have been most frequently used are head-turning to the source of a sound, changes in heart-rate, electrophysiological measures of evoked neural responses, habituation, conditioning, and sucking for an auditory reward. For a detailed review of the various techniques see Aslin et al. (1983).

Auditory Sensitivity

There are many anecdotal reports of auditory function in the fetus – typically reports of a sudden movement by the fetus after a loud sound has been presented. In an early study, Bernard and Sontag (1947) recorded fetal heart rate changes to auditory stimuli. They found reliable heart-rate responses in the two months prior to birth. However, because there was a response latency of 10 to 15 seconds it is possible that the fetal response was in some way triggered by the mother's response to the sound. More recent studies seem to rule out this explanation. Grimwade, Walker, Bartlett, Gordon and Wood (1971) found that fetal responses were present when the mother was prevented from hearing the sound. The conclusion that the auditory system is functional prior to birth is reinforced by the fact that a variety of measures of auditory responses have been successfully used with premature infants (Aslin et al., 1983).

At present there is only a little known about the details of the auditory system and its environment prior to birth. Walker, Grimwade and Wood (1971) found that there was significant attenuation of frequencies above 1,000 Hz. (Adults are sensitive to sounds in the region 20 to 20,000 Hz.) However, auditory signals below 1,000 Hz are transmitted to the intrauterine environment with little attenuation (Querleu and Renard, 1981). These findings mean that the range of auditory stimulation to which a fetus is exposed will be more limited than the range in the extrauterine environment. This, undoubtedly, will affect the prenatal development of the auditory system.

The study of auditory function in neonates is complicated by the fact that behavioural response measures are difficult to obtain and negative evidence is very problematic to interpret. Whereas it is relatively easy to measure such things as preference for one of two stimuli in the visual modality, it is more difficult to do this in the auditory modality. This is due, in part, to the fact that there is no unique behavioural response that can be used as a measure of auditory sensitivity. Failure to provide a consistent response to auditory stimulation could be due to many factors besides failure to process the auditory signal (including indifference, inhibition, or habituation). In recent years some of these problems have been overcome to some extent by the use of electrophysiological responses rather than behavioural responses (see Hecox, 1984, for a review of techniques). The most common electrophysiological technique is to attach electrodes to the scalp and record the gross electrical activity of the brain in response to presentations of auditory stimuli. This technique has the advantage that it can be used to record auditory responses from infants who are asleep. This, in any case, is a desirable state for the infant to be in because variations in the state of the infant greatly affect the recording (Hecox, 1984). Electrophysiological techniques have been used to determine how loud a sound must be at a particular frequency in order for a cortical response to be evoked. The studies of neonates indicate that the auditory system is functional at birth but that the auditory threshold is higher in infants than in adults. The estimated amount of elevation of the infant's threshold – i.e. the extra amount of loudness that was necessary over the adult baseline before an infant responded to the sound varied in the initial studies. Taguchi, Picton, Orpin and Goodman (1969) reported elevated thresholds of up to 50 decibels (dB) whereas Engel and Young (1969) reported thresholds within 15 dB of adult norms. More recent studies, (Hecox and Galambos, 1974; Schulman-Galambos and Galambos, 1979), have supported the lower of these estimates. One practical advantage of having an agreed response level for neonates is that electrophysiological techniques can be used to screen for gross hearing loss. This is of considerable importance because hitherto hearing loss has been difficult to detect reliably in infants.

It can be reliably concluded from the preceding research that the auditory system is functional at and prior to birth and that infants have an elevated response threshold relative to adults. Although electrophysiological techniques have been used widely to study neonates, they have not been extensively used to study auditory sensitivity beyond the immediate neonatal period. There are relatively few studies of the development of auditory sensitivity in the period up to 6 months of age; after that period, the situation is somewhat better. Most of the research on older infants has used a reinforcement technique in order to overcome the infant's low level of motivation to respond to repeated presentations of an auditory stimulus. In a typical experiment the infant is required to turn his or her head in the direction of a sound in order to receive a visual reinforcement. This technique was originally introduced by Suzuki and Ogiba (1961). As infants appear to be willing to 'work' quite hard for visual reinforcement the technique can be used to present a wide variety of stimuli to a single infant and thus improve the efficiency of data collection with an age-group for whom data collection is not notably efficient. Use of head-turning as a behavioural response precludes the technique from being a reliable measure with infants below 5 or 6 months of age because of poor voluntary control of head movements. Using the head-turning technique

Trehub, Schneider and Endman (1980) compared auditory thresholds for infants aged 6, 12, and 18 months and adults. They found that adults showed a relatively flat threshold function for different frequencies of sound. At low frequencies infant thresholds were 15 to 25 dB above the adult thresholds but this difference decreased with increasing frequency. Thus, infants are more like adults in their threshold for high frequency sounds. Based on the differences between adults and infants, Trehub et al. concluded that there is (a later) developmental improvement in auditory sensitivity, especially in low-frequency sensitivity. A more recent study by Sinnott, Pisoni and Aslin (1983) has confirmed this broad conclusion.

In summary, although there is not anything like the detailed evidence available for the auditory modality as there is for the visual modality, it appears that the auditory system is well-developed at birth and is not greatly different in its sensitivity from the adult auditory system. The research discussed up to now has all been concerned with measuring this sensitivity in the human infant using either relatively pure sound stimuli or white noise. Although these stimuli are perfectly appropriate for establishing the basic sensitivity of the auditory system, they are not appropriate for establishing how *information* is detected by the auditory system. The primary source of information for the auditory system is speech. There is a considerable literature on how infants perceive speech, to which we will now turn.

Development of Speech Perception

Speech Perception by Infants

Of all the sources of auditory stimulation that infants receive, the human voice is the one that contains the richest potential for information. Newborn infants are sensitive to the human voice. Alegria and Noirot (1978) presented 1- to 7-day-old infants with a male voice through loud-speakers and found more head-turning towards the loudspeakers in the presence of speech sounds than in its absence. Butterfield and Siperstein (1972) reported that newborn infants can be conditioned to suck for the sound of folk songs but not for white noise. DeCasper and Fifer (1980) trained neonates at 3 days old or less to suck in one way to hear the mother's voice and in another to hear the voice of a stranger. The infants preferred to listen to the mother's voice, indicating that soon after birth infants can recognize the mother's voice and distinguish it from the voice of a stranger.

These studies reveal that the infant is sensitive to the human voice but they do not reveal anything about the auditory dimensions that determine this sensitivity. The speech stimulus to which the infants responded is an exceedingly complex stimulus. In adults it conveys communicative information in the content of the speech itself and also information about various other things including the speaker's mood, age, and sex. In order to determine to what it is that the infant responds in speech stimuli it is necessary to begin to decompose the stimulus itself into its various dimensions and examine infant responses to these dimensions. Although there is now a considerable amount of research on these issues, there is much that still remains to be explored. Research has to date addressed a variety of questions, including the ability of infants to distinguish between speech stimuli such as *pin* and *bin* that differ only in their initial consonant; the ability to treat different pronunciations of a stimulus as the same stimulus; and sensitivity to 'higher-order' units of speech such as intonation.

Much of the research on speech perception has used a method of investigation called *high amplitude sucking* (HAS). HAS is a measure of attention. The technique was developed by Siqueland and DeLucia (1969) who showed that infants will suck to obtain the visual stimulation of the projection of a slide. When used to study auditory perception, the technique takes advantage of the fact that the spontaneous behaviour of sucking can be brought under the control of an auditory stimulus. The presentation of an auditory stimulus is made contingent on some level of sucking by the infant. When a stimulus is first presented an infant will suck quite hard to hear the stimulus. With repeated presentations interest declines and so does the rate of sucking. Presentation of a new auditory stimulus leads to an increase in the rate of sucking, so long as the new stimulus can be discriminated from the old. The technique can thus be used to measure auditory discrimination with a no-change control group providing a comparative baseline for spontaneous changes in the rate of sucking.

One of the most striking findings using the HAS technique was reported by Eimas, Siqueland, Jusczyk and Vigorito (1971). They reported that infants distinguish between the letters *b* and *p* in exactly the same way as adults. In order to appreciate the significance of this result it is necessary to consider both how the human voice produces these sounds and how adults perceive the difference between the sounds.

The speech sounds *b* and *p* are produced by closing the lips, then opening them and releasing air. This is accompanied by a slight vibration of the vocal cords. In producing *b* the vocal cords begin to vibrate as soon as the air is released. For *p* a short latency occurs between the release of the air and the vibration of the vocal cords. The length of the latency between the release of air and the beginning of the vibrations is referred to as the *voice onset time* (VOT). It is possible, using synthetic speech sounds (i.e. sounds generated by a computer program) to vary the VOT of a stimulus all along the continuum from a *b* to a *p*. When this is done and subjects are asked to judge whether a *b* or a *p* has been produced, the judgement is not that there is a *b* at one end of the continuum and a *p* at the other, with one sound shading into the other in between, as might be expected. Up to a VOT of 10 msec, the sound is unanimously judged to be a *b*. After 40 msec the sound is unanimously judged to be a *p*. In between 10 and 40 msec individuals vary in their judgements but all judge the sound to be either a definite *b* or a definite *p*. There is no subjective sensation of a mixture of *b* and *p*. This phenomenon is called *categorical perception* because subjects perceive the sounds as definitely belonging to one category or the other, rather than being ranked on a continuum from *b* to *p*. Figure 2.12 shows how identification varies with VOT for adult speakers of English.

Eimas et al. showed that infants of 1 month perceive *b* and *p* in exactly the same way as adults. They habituated one-month-old infants to a variety of sounds with different VOTs. They found that the critical factor for dishabituation was not the absolute VOT difference between two stimuli but whether or not the stimuli were on the same or different sides of a boundary that occurred at about 20 msec VOT. Thus, two stimuli with VOTs of 10 and 40 msec respectively will be heard as different sounds and will cause dishabituation, whereas two stimuli at 40 and 70 msec, or even 40 and 100 msec VOTs will be heard as the same sound and will not cause dishabituation.

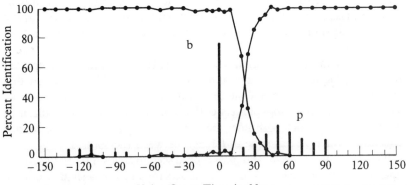

Figure 2.12 *Perception of* b *and* p *as a function of voice onset time (VOT). The vertical bars show the frequency distribution of VOT values.*
Source: Jusczyk, 1985.

The results of Eimas et al. (1971) were widely interpreted as evidence for an innate language processing mechanism in humans. However, voicing is only one of the contrasts that need to be discriminated in speech perception. Thus, it was important to determine whether the results reported by Eimas et al. (1971) were a peculiarity of the voicing contrast or a general feature of the ability of infants to discriminate speech stimuli. Since that initial study a variety of further studies have been undertaken to test the discrimination of the infant. In virtually every case infants have been shown to be able to discriminate the phonetic contrast prior to 12 months of age (see Aslin et al., 1983, for a review). Further, the ability to perceive contrasts is not limited to sounds that occur in the initial segment of syllables (Jusczyk, 1977; Jusczyk and Thompson, 1978). Of particular significance are some of the cross-cultural findings that appear to rule out the possibility that the discriminations are learnt.

Languages differ in the contrasts that convey differences of meaning, such as *bin* and *pin* do in English. In Spanish, for example, the VOT boundary for adult speakers is located at about 0 msec whereas in English it is located at +20 msec. Nevertheless, Lasky, Syrdal-Lasky and Klein (1975) showed that Guatemalan infants (of Spanish speaking parents) segmented the VOT continuum in the same way as the infants studied by Eimas et al. (1971). Further, they found no discrimination between VOT of −20 and +20, even though this is a boundary that is perceived by Spanish-speaking adults. Streeter (1976) reported a similar result for Kikuyu infants even though Kikuyu does not distinguish voiced from voiceless consonants (i.e. *bin* and *pin* would sound the same to an adult speaker of Kikuyu). Trehub (1976) presented infants from English-speaking homes with contrasts that occur in Czech and in French but not in English. She found that 1- to 4-month-old infants had no difficulty in discriminating the contrast.

These various studies demonstrate a wide range of discrimination of speech sounds by infants, mostly in the first few months of life. The discriminations do not seem to be the product of experience because infants were capable of discriminating contrasts not present in their native language. Can it be concluded, on the basis of this impressive body of evidence, that there is an innate language processing mechanism? It must have seemed that the answer was 'yes' until Kuhl and Miller (1975; 1978) tested chinchillas and Kuhl and Padden (1982; 1983) macaque monkeys. They found that these species were also capable of categorical perception. Thus, although the earlier findings from the research on infants clearly indicated that there was an innate basis to the infant's perception of speech this could no longer be interpreted as the result of a species-specific language processing mechanism. A possible alternative interpretation (Aslin et al., 1983) is that categorical auditory perception is a general auditory skill of older evolutionary origin than language and that language has evolved to fit the processing capacities of this general auditory capacity. If this is the case then the abilities of human infants are not a language-specific adaptation at all.

The research on categorical perception reveals that the infant's auditory system imposes discontinuities on acoustic stimuli that vary along a continuum; effectively, the continuum is reduced to a set of phonetic categories. Within a category the varying stimuli all have equivalent information value as indicated by the behavioural responses using the HAS technique. However, the conditions for testing for categorical perception of phonetic stimuli are highly restrictive; all non-criterial dimensions of the speech stimulus such as frequency, intensity, and duration are held constant and one critical dimension is varied. It is possible that infants exhibit categorical perception for one of two reasons: an inability to discriminate among the different stimuli or the detection of categorical equivalence among them. The first alternative reduces categorical perception by infants to an artifact: if an infant cannot detect the variation along the stimulus dimension that is the object of study then all stimuli will be equivalent; the infant will not have encoded different stimuli and then made a categorical judgement. The second alternative is precisely that the infant has encoded different stimuli but the cognitive system has some basis for treating these differences as less relevant than the similarities among the stimuli. This basis, whatever it might be, would be the explanation of an innate ability to treat the stimulus dimension in a categorical fashion. However, it is unclear at present either whether the infant's perceptions are genuinely categorical (the first alternative has not been ruled out), and, if they are categorical, what the basis of categorical perception is. It may be that there is some as yet unspecified acoustic invariant among within-category stimuli that is detected by the auditory system. At present there is disagreement among researchers about the mechanisms that are responsible for categorical perception with some arguing in favour of perceptual invariants (Stevens and Blumstein, 1981) and some against (Eimas, Miller and Jusczyk, 1987).

The two alternatives – inability to discriminate and recognition of category equivalence – are very different in their implications for our understanding of the development of information processing. The former simply reveals a constraint on the sensitivity of the auditory system to certain stimulus dimensions. The latter, on the other hand, reveals the existence of a genuine ability to treat detectably different stimuli as equivalent, which is the fundamental achievement of categorization (see chapter 4, Concepts and Words). As yet, there is no evidence of whether or not infants detect the differences among the stimuli they respond to in a categorical fashion. As ever, in research with infants the problem is one of finding an appropriate methodological technique with which to address the issue. With adults, it is possible to ask whether stimuli differ; with infants it is not. However, it is possible to determine whether infants will still make categorical judgements if variation is introduced along the range of parameters that are held constant in the categorical perception experiments. Effectively, this would be a test of whether stimuli that are subject to categorical perception are also subject to perceptual constancy. Recently, Kuhl (1979; 1983) has addressed this issue, using an operant conditioning technique. Infants were presented with within-category stimuli through a loudspeaker and trained to turn their heads only when a new stimulus category was presented. Head-turning at the appropriate time was reinforced with a visual display. The training was continued until infants met a criterion of nine out of ten category contrasts correct. They were then given transfer-of-learning trials to novel, discriminably different instances of the categories used in the training trials. If the infants respond in the same way to the novel stimuli as to the trained stimuli they can be said to show a genuine categorization ability for speech sounds.

Kuhl (1979) trained 6-month-old infants to discriminate the /a/ and /i/ vowels produced by a male speaker. Generalization of the discrimination was tested for novel stimuli produced by women and child speakers. The level of performance for all children was extremely high and for many it was near perfect. In a second study Kuhl (1983) extended this finding to a more difficult vowel contrast, that between the vowels in 'cot' and 'caught'. This distinction is more difficult because there is considerable overlap in the acoustic stimulus provided by these vowels. Nevertheless, 6-month-old infants readily learned the contrast and generalized it to novel stimuli on transfer of learning trials. Kuhl (1983) suggested that infants demonstrate vowel constancy, probably for all vowel categories in English.

The experiments by Kuhl (1979, 1983) used single vowel contrasts. Hillenbrand (1984) combined consonant and vowel syllables to produce the acoustic stimuli /ma/, /mi/, and /mu/ within one category and /na/, /ni/, and /nu/ within another. He trained a group of infants to discriminate one set of stimuli from the other by turning their heads only to stimuli from one set. A control group of infants received equal amounts of training but with the six stimuli randomly assigned to two categories. The experiment was designed to test whether infants would categorize together stimuli whose initial phonetic unit (the consonants) were the same but whose final phonetic unit (the vowels) were different. This experiment is of particular interest because when a consonant occurs in different phonetic contexts, the acoustic cues representing the consonant are altered significantly. There is considerable evidence from adults that context affects the perception of consonants (see Repp, 1983, for a review). Hillenbrand found that infants could easily learn the categorical distinction between /m/ and /n/, even when these consonants occurred in the neighbourhood of a vowel. By contrast, the infants for whom the same stimuli had been randomly arranged into two sets, failed to learn to distinguish the sets reliably.

Speech Perception and Language Development

The research on infant speech perception reveals that infants have considerable innate abilities to perceive a continuous input signal in a categorical manner. This constitutes another component of the architecture of cognition. The neural hardware has evolved to impose a pattern of categorical organization on continuous auditory input. This has often been seen as part of an innate language faculty, possessed only by humans (e.g. Fodor, 1983). However, categorical perception itself is not sufficient evidence to establish an innate language faculty. As Eimas et al. (1987) point out, the phenomenon occurs for non-speech auditory stimuli, for a variety of visual stimuli, and it occurs in non-human species. The import of these various findings is that categorical perception is not a mechanism specially evolved to process speech signals. At present, there is no convincing evidence that speech stimuli are processed any differently from other auditory stimuli. Further, as Jusczyk (1985) points out, if there is a special language faculty, it has not yet been explained how it distinguishes speech from non-speech inputs in the auditory signals it receives.

The relation between speech perception and language development is not yet well understood. It is unlikely that it will be simple or straightforward. The following section raises some of the issues involved and outlines some of the speculative suggestions that have been made.

Most of the research on infant speech perception concerns the perception of single phonetic units. However, it is not necessarily the case that units as small as this are extracted for the representation of language from the input received in everyday life. There are several lines of evidence that converge to suggest that the syllable rather than the phoneme may be the basic unit of language representation. First, the syllable rather than the phoneme seems to be the basic unit of information for the cognitive system. Eimas (1974, 1975) has shown that certain phonetic distinctions are not as well discriminated by adult informants when presented in isolation as when presented in a context that is perceived as a coherent syllable. Second, infants are differentially sensitive to certain types of syllabic configurations. Bertoncini and Mehler (1981) have shown that infants younger than two months are better able to discriminate speech patterns when the pattern has the linguistically permissible syllabic structure of consonant-vowel-consonant than when it has an impermissible consonant-consonant-consonant structure. Third, research into phonological development suggests that the initial phonological representations are in syllable-sized units (Menn, 1982). Fourth, and perhaps most important, the basis of segmentation into syllable-sized chunks may be readily available from another parameter of the auditory input: prosodic stress. It will, in any case, need to come from some such source, because there are no well-documented acoustic cues for syllable boundaries (Eimas et al., 1987). There is, moreover, evidence both that infants are highly attentive to the prosody of speech (Fernald and Simon, 1984) and that, in older children, the rate of acquisition of certain linguistic elements is highly correlated with the extent to which the elements appear in stressed positions in the input (Furrow, Nelson and Benedict, 1979; Newport, Gleitman and Gleitman, 1977).

Eimas et al. (1987) suggest that the initial stage of processing involves passing the unsegmented auditory inputs through an array of categorical processors. Each processor responds only to its own special input and no other. The effect of these processors will be to preserve phonetic constancy in the face of varying stimulus characteristics presented by different speakers and by the same speaker on different occasions. They also suggest that the output of a system of categorical processors are segmented into syllable-sized chunks. (This could be done on the basis of information provided by another parameter of the speech signal: prosodic stress.) It is these syllable-sized chunks that are available for representation at the lexical level of the linguistic system.   Let us assume that prosodic stress acts in conjunction with categorical perception of phonetic input to determine the syllabic units of representation for language. This formula brings together the linguistic environment and innate auditory organization. The innate auditory organization is predisposed to impose a categorical structure on a continuous stream of phonetic input. However, the speech input that the child receives comes with additional organizational properties of its own, one of which is prosodic stress. The interaction of these organizational factors will serve to create a unit of linguistic representation of syllabic size. This unit seems to be especially salient both to young infants (Bertoncini and Mehler, 1981) and to children learning language (Gleitman and Wanner, 1982). Thus, experience, in interaction with biological endowment serves to create the content of the syllabic units that are basic to language representation.

Experience is also important in fine-tuning the categorical perceptions of the child. Recall that English and Spanish, for example, have different boundaries for a voiced/voiceless distinction but that infants in both linguistic communities perceive the difference in the same place. In order for the children in the Spanish-speaking environment to acquire the adult version of their native language, the location of the voiced/voiceless distinction must be malleable by experience. Experience also has the effect of weakening the sensitivity of an infant to a contrast not heard in the native language. Werker and Tees (1984) found that two contrasts not present in English could be discriminated by infants at 6 months of age but not at 12 months. It seems most likely that the loss of sensitivity is due to the absence of the contrast in the speech input that the child hears.

Intersensory Co-ordination

Up to now the perceptual systems of vision and audition have been discussed in isolation from each other. In the infant's everyday world information is often available simultaneously from different modalities: for example, there is usually a face to look at and a voice to listen to. To what extent can infants integrate the information presented by different modalities? Does the sound of an object tell an infant where to look? Does an infant know that a particular face is always accompanied by a particular voice? Can an infant predict from information available in one modality what to expect in another sensory modality? For example, adults can predict, from seeing an object, various properties that are usually associated with other senses: what sound an object is likely to make if dropped; its tactile properties of hardness and whether it can be grasped.

Theoretical positions on intersensory co-ordination are various. Piaget (1936b/1955) argues that the various sensory modalities are separate at birth and become integrated during development. This is very much the traditional view. In recent years it has been challenged by theories that argue that the senses are co-ordinated at birth. Bower (1974), for example, argues that there is a primitive unity of the senses at birth and that the different senses are later differentiated from each other. Thus Bower reverses the argument: sensory integration does not develop; it is sensory differentiation that develops. At birth, according to Bower, there is one 'supramodal' sensory system. Bower advances two arguments for this. The first is that it is highly likely that in the course of evolution the different senses evolved as specialized developments of a supramodal perceptual system. Even if this were true, it is hardly a compelling argument when applied to the perceptual development of infants. There is very little, if any, reason to expect evolution necessarily to repeat itself in the infant's development. The second argument, or set of arguments, advanced by Bower is that there is evidence of intersensory co-ordination in infancy in the first few weeks of life, long before it is reasonable to expect that it could have been learnt. The evidence for this will be examined below.

Vision and Audition

The most basic type of intersensory co-ordination is when information in one modality provides directional information for the receptors in another modality. Wertheimer (1961) was the first to investigate the relation between the visual and the auditory modality at birth. He tested one infant, a few seconds old, by presenting clicks to the infant's right or left. Two independent observers recorded whether the infant turned his eyes in the direction of the sound. The results were positive suggesting not only that the infant could hear but that he could also orientate to the source of the sound stimulus. Subsequent experiments have reported different results. Butterworth and Castillo (1976) and McGurk, Turnure and Creighton (1977) both found that infants turned their eyes *away* from the source of a sound rather than towards it. It may be that in these experiments the infants were trying to avoid the sound stimuli, which were of greater intensity than the stimulus used by Wertheimer. If this interpretation is correct, then all three studies can be interpreted as showing an innate co-ordination between the auditory and visual modality. Several more recent studies (Alegria and Noirot, 1978; Clifton, Morrongiello, Kulig and Dowd, 1981; Crassini and Broerse, 1980; Mendelson and Haith, 1976; Muir and Field, 1979) have shown that infants in the first few days of life will reliably orient towards the source of sound. Muir and Field (1979) found that newborns reliably turned their heads towards the source of a sound but that there was a long response latency. In their study, 2- to 4-day-old infants were presented for 20 seconds with a tape-recorded sound from one of two loudspeakers located either side of the head. Control trials consisting of 20 seconds of silence were interspersed with experimental trials. The responses of the infants were videotaped and later scored by two independent observers, who were unaware of the type of trial or the location of the sound source. It was found that the infants reliably turned their heads towards the source of the sound.

The results of these studies provide good evidence that the basic ability to co-ordinate vision and audition is present at birth. However, the ability appears to decline temporarily after birth, for reasons that are not, at present, clear. Field, Muir, Pilon, Sinclair and Dodwell (1980) reported that orientation in 2-month-old infants occurred less often than in 1-month-olds or newborns. Muir, Abraham, Forbes and Harris (1979) reported longitudinal data on four infants tested repeatedly from birth to 4 months of age. Shortly after birth orientation was almost 100 per cent correct but thereafter began to decline until it reached a trough of 50 per cent correct during the period between 1.5 and 3 months. After that it recovered to 100 per cent correct by 4 months. Clifton et al. (1981) suggest that newborn orientation is a reflex response to crude binaural cues of stimulus intensity mediated by the midbrain, whereas the orientation of infants some months older is due to processing cues of stimulus onset carried out by the auditory cortex.

The experiments discussed above show that infants will orientate to the source of a sound. These experiments do not, however, tell us to what extent infants are capable of integrating information that emanates from a single source and is received by different modalities. The natural environment is full of sights and sounds that go together. By far the most frequent source of simultaneous auditory-visual information are the human beings with whom an infant interacts. They provide a rich source of co-ordinated information. How sensitive are infants to this? Can they, for example, detect violations of co-ordination? Such violations do not usually occur in the real world but they are easy enough to create in the laboratory. Studying them should tell us a good deal about the extent to which an infant is capable of integrating sensory information.

One of the first studies to manipulate the co-ordination of auditory and visual information was reported by Aronson and Rosenbloom (1971). Infants between 1 and 2 months old at first watched their mothers speaking to them through a window and heard her voice coming through loudspeakers on either side of the infant's head. With adults this arrangement results in the voice being heard as if it came from in front. As the infants listened to the voice it was suddenly switched (or dislocated) to one speaker only. The infants increased their rate of tongue protrusion when this occurred, which Aronson and Rosenbloom interpreted as a measure of distress at the dislocation between face and voice. The increase in tongue protrusions cannot be attributed to the shift alone because a control group, who could not see the mother and merely heard the voice changed from both sides to one, showed no increase in tongue protrusions.

The experimental procedure used by Aronson and Rosenbloom (1971) has been criticized by other researchers. McGurk and Lewis (1974) noted that the dislocation condition always followed a relatively long period (two to five minutes) of integrated voice and face and also that the longer an infant is in an experimental situation the more likely it is that the infant will become upset. They repeated the experiment but this time started and finished with an integrated voice, with the dislocation of the voice in between. The whole procedure was confined to two minutes. They failed to replicate the results of Aronson and Rosenbloom (1971). A further failure to replicate has been reported by Condry, Halton and Neisser (1977). It is not clear, however, how these results should be interpreted. The basic problem springs from the assumption of Aronson and Rosenbloom (1971) that dislocating the source of the sound would be stressful to the infants. There seems no particular reason why this should be the case, so the finding that it is not by subsequent research does not tell us very much.

Evidence for the integration of visual and auditory information has been provided by Spelke (1976). Infants aged 4 months had the opportunity to watch either of two films on screens placed side by side. In one film a woman played 'peekaboo' while in the other percussion instruments were played. The sounds appropriate to the films were played alternately through a speaker located centrally. When the sound-track was appropriate to peekaboo infants tended to watch that film and when it was appropriate to drumming, they tended to watch that. In later experiments using the same arrangement (Spelke, 1979; 1981) the infant's gaze was first centred by means of a flashing light and a short burst of one sound-track was then given. The infant's orientation to one film or the other was recorded. Infants reliably looked at the event specified by the sound (see also Bahrick, Walker and Neisser, 1981). These experiments suggest that by 4 months infants can integrate the information from the two modalities into a single unified experience.

Finally, there is evidence that infants can detect the absence of normal synchrony between visual and auditory information. Dodd (1979) read nursery rhymes to infants 10 to 16 weeks old, while maintaining eye contact. The sound was either in synchrony with Dodd's lip movements, as in normal speech, or out of synchrony, which was caused by creating a slight delay between her lip movements and her voice. The infants looked at her face more often when sound and lip movements were in synchrony than when they were not. This suggests that the detection of the lack of synchrony violated the infants' expectation that sound and lip movements should go together, causing them to look away.

Vision and Touch

Bower et al. (1970a, 1970b) have argued that vision and touch are integrated from birth. Bower et al. (1970b) observed how infants reached for objects placed at various locations. They reported that infants reached in the appropriate direction although their arm movements were not always sufficiently well-controlled to result in contact with the object. Bower et al (1970a) used a different technique to study the co-ordination of vision and reaching: presentation of a virtual object described previously in the discussion of stereopsis. Bower et al. claimed that infants reached for the virtual object. In order for this to have occurred the infants would have had to process binocular depth cues. However, the available evidence on stereoscopic vision suggests that infants in the first few weeks of life cannot process binocular depth cues. Therefore, it must be open to question if the behaviours recorded by Bower et al. constituted true reaching. Two other studies by Dodwell et al. (1976) and Ruff and Halton (1978) have failed to replicate the findings of Bower et al. They found many of the characteristics of mature reaching in young infants but little control over the reach itself. It would thus seem that there is some rudimentary eye–hand co-ordination in newborns but that infants are not capable of visually-guided movement as Bower et al. claimed.

In a further study Rader and Stern (1982) presented various objects and pictures of these objects to infants 5 to 8 inches in front of their faces and recorded their arm movements. They found no significant difference in the amount of reaching elicited by the objects as opposed to the pictures. This is of significance because Bower (1974; Bower et al., 1970a) has claimed that a neonatal reaching response is elicited by 3-dimensional objects but not by 2-dimensional pictures of objects. However, Rader and Stern did find that the amount of reaching increased to both 3-D and 2-D stimuli over a baseline rate. They also found that reaching declined over the age-range studied, which was 8 to 16 days. Rader and Stern suggest that patterned visual stimulation increases the probability of reaching-like behaviour, but the behaviour is not selective to graspable objects and thus is not true reaching. It has been suggested by von Hofsten (1982) that neonate reaching should be seen as attentional orientation towards an object rather than an attempt to grasp the object. He also reported rudimentary eye–hand co-ordination in infants 4 to 9 days old. Movements performed while the neonate fixated objects were aimed closer at the object than were other movements. In the best aimed of the reaches the hand slowed down as it approached the object. However, there was no evidence that the infants intended to grasp or manipulate the objects they reached for; von Hofsten suggests that the neonate has an ability to direct both hands and eyes towards an external event. The co-ordination works both from eye to hand and from hand to eye. Several cases were observed in which the infant accidentally touched the object and immediately afterwards turned his or her eyes towards it. The conclusion drawn by von Hofsten is that looking and reaching are part of the same orientation response in which 'the infant prepares himself or herself for the encounter with the external event by pointing his or her feelers toward it' (von Hofsten, 1982: p. 460).

Evidence from studies of slightly older infants supports the view that there is primitive coordination of eye and hand in infancy. Bruner and Koslowski (1972) studied infants between 8 and 22 weeks and found that although the infants were not able to perform a successful visually directed reach they were more likely to make grasping movements in the presence of an object of graspable size than when they were faced by an object too large to grasp. They were more likely to swipe at the larger than at smaller objects. Thus, although the infants could not execute a smooth reach, the components of the reach were adapted to the size of the object. By the age of 6 months looking and reaching have become co-ordinated (Rubenstein, 1976; Ruff, 1976).

The extent of intersensory co-ordination in the later part of the first year has been demonstrated by Bryant, Jones, Claxton and Perkins (1972). In their experiment an object that made a noise was placed in the infant's hand, but the infant was not allowed to see the object. This object was then offered together with another to the infants and they were forced to choose. Neither object had been seen before. Nevertheless the majority of infants chose the object that had previously made a noise – presumably to repeat the experience. The only basis on which they could have done this was by the cross-modal matching of the tactual and visual information. Similar results have been obtained with slightly older infants by Gottfried, Rose and Bridger (1977) and Rose, Gottfried and Bridger (1983). Gottfried et al. habituated 12-month-old infants with an object either by sight or by touch. The infants were then presented visually with the habituated object paired with a novel object. More attention was directed to the new object in both cross-modal and within-modal conditions. In the cross-modal condition infants had never seen either object before, which implies that information gathered in the tactual mode was available to the visual mode.

In summary, the available evidence on intersensory coordination does not support either an extreme differentiation or an extreme integration point of view. The information received by various senses is separately represented from birth, contrary to Bower's (1974) proposal. However, there is also an amount of intersensory mapping among the senses evident in the architecture of the cognitive system. Infants orientate to the source of a sound from birth, although their ability to do so accurately improves with experience. Once again, evolution has provided the basic neural wiring but left the fine tuning to the developmental process. This seems also to be the case for vision and touch. The two senses are co-ordinated from birth but the fine motor control of grasping a seen object develops with experience.

Perceptual Development and Information Processing

In the last quarter-century a variety of methodological techniques have been developed for or adapted to the study of the infant's perceptual abilities. These studies have changed dramatically our view of the infant from that of a passive organism ill-adapted to the environment to one of an organism endowed at birth with complex and highly developed perceptual systems. Most, if not all, of the basic mechanisms of perception are innate endowments of nature. Nature has provided the basic resources to receive and process information. In this section we shall consider the implications of the results discussed in this chapter for an information processing account of development.

At birth the infant has an immature but reasonably well-developed visual system and a functioning auditory system. These sensory systems provide the basis of the infant's interaction with the world. However, that interaction is limited by several factors. Primary among these is that the infant spends relatively small amounts of time awake and alert, thus restricting the opportunity to receive and organize input of information from the environment. There is, during the early months, considerable neural development and several investigators in the field of visual perception (Banks and Salapatek, 1981, 1983; Haith, 1980; Karmel and Maisel, 1975) have attempted to relate changes in behavioural preferences over the early months of life to basic maturational data. The general pattern of development in the early months is that infants change from visual attention dominated by very simple stimulus dimensions to visual attention responsive to a wider range of stimulus dimensions and become more actively exploratory of the visual world.

The result of these developments is a greater opportunity for learning about the informational content of visual stimulation. A large number of studies have shown that infants in the early months of life are capable of learning a variety of contingent relations among stimuli; to turn their heads to one stimulus but not another, to increase or decrease rate of sucking to control stimulus presentation (see Olson and Sherman (1983) for a review). By 3 months of age the infant can remember a learned contingent relation over a period of days and even weeks. Thus, by the age of 3 months the infant has begun to show, in elementary form, many of the recognizable psychological characteristics associated with long-term learning and remembering.

During the next few months the level of basic perceptual functioning begins to approach adult levels. This means that the information transmitted by the sensory receptors to the central cognitive processes becomes of increasingly good quality. The infant's ability to use such information in learning and remembering is enhanced by the increasing regularity of sleep/wake cycles and the increasing length of periods of continuous alertness. The emergence of these regular sleep patterns is sometimes regarded as a result of physiological maturation of the brain (Berg and Berg, 1979). Reaching and grasping become active exploratory behaviours after 3 months; objects can now be both looked at and manipulated. By the age of 6 months looking and reaching have become coordinated (Rubenstein, 1976; Ruff, 1976). This is undoubtedly a significant development in the infant's interaction with the environment and the information it contains. Olson and Sherman (1983) suggest that the infant's increasing knowledge base begins to play a role in the way information is processed. They cite in support of this the results of Fagan (1972). He showed that infants of 6 months could discriminate a familiar face from a novel face when both were right side up. However, when he presented the same face upside down for the same familiarization period, infants of the same age could not discriminate this from a novel upside-down face. Olson and Sherman attribute this difference to ease of encoding the right-side-up face due to the infant's developing knowledge base of faces. The knowledge base facilitates rapid extraction of information from the environment and its relatively rapid encoding and storage. Retention of information over long periods is now evident. Fagan (1973) reported excellent recognition memory for intervals up to 14 days.

The first six months of life result in the development of an exploring, socially responsive infant capable of learning and recognition, who displays an active interest in the environment. The first evidence of a representational capacity is provided by the infant's recognition memory. The presence of recognition memory in young infants shows that information is stored by the infant and that the cognitive system makes use of this stored information during the processing of subsequent information. It must be assumed that these processes constitute one of the primitive innate organizational structures of the information processing system. From a very early age (from birth perhaps but subject to the

constraints of basic perceptual processes) the human infant shows recogni-
tory abilities and from these abilities we may infer that the infant has
represented and stored information obtained from the environment. However, we must be careful not to exaggerate the infant's abilities. The type
of events to which recognition has been demonstrated are limited to
objects in a very simple form. There is no evidence yet that complex
events are represented and stored, nor that represented information is
manipulated. In the next chapter the issue of representation will be
considered in more detail.

3

The Origins of Representations

Representations and Information Processing

Information begins as a stimulus in the environment that is detected by the organism's perceptual receptors and is then processed by the cognitive system. During this processing certain features of the stimulus will receive attention and be retained. Other features will be ignored and discarded. The features retained may be transformed in various ways. At this point we are not particularly concerned with the details of how information is selected and transformed, merely with the fact that it happens. In some cases the final information encoded and stored by the cognitive system may be quite unlike the environmental stimulus that acted as input to the cognitive system. Nevertheless, there is a lawful relation of representation between what is encoded and the stimulus that initiated the encoding; the information encoded is a representation of the stimulus input. How information is represented depends very much on the processes that act upon it, because processes transform the input in various ways. Processes can be thought of as acquired procedures for manipulating information (see chapter 1). The infant will have had little opportunity to acquire procedures through experience. This means that, initially, representations are very much a function of innate architectural mechanisms. As development proceeds, additional learnt procedures for processing information will come to play a more significant role than they do initially.

A representation is, essentially, something that stands for something else. This, as Palmer (1978) points out, implies the existence of two related but functionally separate worlds; the represented world and the representing world. The representing world need not model all aspects of the represented world; in fact the essence of a representation is that

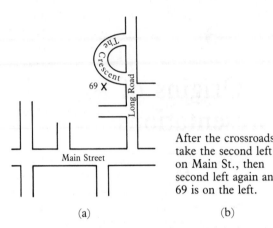
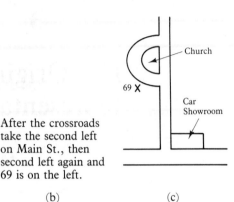

After the crossroads
take the second left
on Main St., then
second left again and
69 is on the left.

(a)   (b)   (c)

Figure 3.1

it is *not* a faithful picture of that which is represented but that it accurately
denotes some aspect of what it represents. Figure 3.1(a) shows a map of
the type that might be used by one person giving directions to another.
In this case it is likely to represent the spatial relations accurately but
unlikely to do so for distance. The same information can be represented
in other ways also as in (b), while (c) provides an alternative set of cues
to (a). In all cases the represented world is the same but the representing
world presents a selective amount of the information available in the
represented world. A representation is, essentially, a stylized picture of
the represented world.

The key elements of the representational relations depicted in figure
3.1 are that the representing world is different from the represented
world and that, because of this, the representing world contains a selection
of the potential information present in the represented world. Obviously,
the manner in which this selection is done is of extreme importance, not
least because once a particular representation has been constructed, it
will contain only certain information.

This chapter will be mainly concerned with the origin of the child's
capacity to create internal representations of the environment. In particular, it will address the issue of how representations of the environment
arise. As has been remarked, a representation is not an exact copy of the
features of the environment but is some stylized economical version of

the environment. Mental representations are selective symbolic encodings of the external environment. It must be part of a theory of cognitive development to explain the origins of mental representations. Representations cannot be observed directly; they must be inferred from the behaviour of the child. Thus, the methodology of the investigative procedure and the inferences that the methodology warrants will be issues of critical significance in discussing infant representations. Methodology and scientific inference are always, of course, issues of significance, but they assume particular importance in discussing the origins of representations because the theories that will be discussed differ radically in what they attribute to the infant.

Obviously, representations cannot develop out of nothing; they must be explained with reference to some initial state of the cognitive system that is capable of creating from the environmental input the variety of representational systems the adult possesses. Developmental theorists do not agree on what is the initial state of the cognitive system. In fact, the initial state is an issue of major fundamental disagreement. At one extreme there are those who argue that the infant's initial state is one of a complete lack of mental organization. This has been the dominant view until comparatively recently. It is evident in Locke's *tabula rasa* view of the human mind and in William James's view that the infant's mind is one of 'blooming, buzzing confusion'. At the other extreme are innatist theories of cognition that argue that the infant's initial state is one in which there is already a rich representational structure, predisposed to interpret experience in certain ways. Somewhere between these extremes lies Piaget's theory. Piaget recognized the need for an innate endowment to make adaptive behaviour a possibility. To this extent his thinking is like that of an innatist theorist. However, unlike innatist theorists, he considered that the infant had only a limited repertoire of innate behaviours; the rest had to be acquired through experience. This balance would seem to push Piaget more towards the empiricist than the innatist end of the spectrum. However, here again Piaget had something different to offer. Experience is the stimulus for development in Piaget's theory but what develops is not simply a copy of what is experienced but a set of cognitive structures with which to interpret experience (see chapter 1). Out of experience the child constructs a cognitive system, beginning from a few innate reflexes. This view is often called a *constructivist* view of development to set it apart both from empiricism and innatism. One of the most important constructions of the early years of life is a system for mentally representing objects and events.

Piaget's Theory of Sensorimotor Development

Piaget's view of development is one in which the newborn infant enters the world with a limited repertoire of hereditary behaviour patterns. During the first two years of life the child builds on these hereditary endowments and acquires a variety of more complex behavioural patterns for interacting with and manipulating the immediate environment. These are *schemes*, which are meant to convey the presence of organization but the absence of a mental component in that organization. The label 'sensorimotor' reveals the level at which Piaget believes the organization of behaviour exists. As a practical example of the difference between a scheme and a mental representation consider a 1-year-old infant playing with a ball that rolls out of reach. The infant cannot first think about how the ball might be retrieved but can activate a motor scheme, such as crawling, that may lead to the successful recovery of the ball. The key aspects of a scheme are that it involves motor activity on the part of the infant and that it refers to some basic organizational structure that underlies particular actions – in the example above the organizational structure would be the motor program for crawling. But schemes are limited in that they apply only to objects that are immediately present. They can never be used to imagine or think about objects and situations that are not present. In the example above, if the ball rolls just out of reach, but also out of sight, the infant will not crawl to where the object vanished and search for it. The infant cannot reason about what to do because he or she does not possess any mental symbols with which to represent the absent ball.

Piaget's proposal about the world of the infant is an extremely radical one. He postulates a way of experiencing the world for infant that is very different from the way we normally experience the world. Mandler (1983: pp. 424–5) has captured the flavour well:

> According to Piaget, the sensorimotor child before Stage 6 (18 to 24 months) does not have a capacity for representation in the true sense, but only sensorimotor intelligence. Knowledge about the world consists only of perceptions and actions; objects are only understood through the child's own actions and perceptual schemata. It is a most un-Proustian life, not thought, only lived. Sensorimotor schemata (or, in our sense, representation as knowledge) enable a child to walk a straight line but not to think about a line in its absence, to recognize his or her mother but not to think about her when she is gone. It is a world very difficult for us to conceive, accustomed as we are to spend much of our time ruminating about the past and anticipating the future. Nevertheless, this is the state that Piaget

posits for the child before $1\frac{1}{2}$, that is, an ability to recognize objects and events but an inability to recall them in their absence. Because of this inability, this lack of concepts of things and symbols to represent them, Piaget does not consider the sensorimotor child's knowledge to be 'mental representation'; to be mental means to be thought and the sensorimotor child cannot think. Note that lack of thought in this view does not merely mean that the child is still missing the ability to reason or make deductive inferences; it means that the child cannot even remember what he or she did a few minutes ago, what his room looks like or what she had for lunch, except accidentally in the course of carrying out actions relevant to these past perceptions and activities. What is missing, according to Piaget, is both a system of concepts and a mobile, flexible symbol system capable of pointing to, or referring to, those concepts.

The missing element of representation identified by Mandler serves both to define the sensorimotor stage by its absence and to mark the beginning of the end of that stage when it first appears. The move out of the sensorimotor stage begins with the development of mental symbols that can represent objects and events in their absence.

Piaget uses the term 'representation' in two different senses that he calls broad and narrow. In the broad sense representation is identical with thought. In the narrow sense representation is the relation between a symbol and its external referent. Piaget (1936a/1952: p. 243) remarks: 'Representation in the narrow sense is the capacity to evoke by a sign or a symbolic image an absent object or an event not yet carried out.'

Before considering Piaget's views on the development of representation in more detail it will be useful to obtain a general overview of the sensorimotor period. Piaget divides the period into six substages and he discusses the development of representation, as manifested particularly in imitation and play, within the framework of these substages. Table 3.1 presents a synopsis of the six substages.

The initial point of departure for Piaget's theory is a small set of innate reflexes, such as sucking and grasping, which are present at birth. Initially these reflexes are the limits of the infant's knowledge of the world and everything with which the infant comes into contact can be 'known' only in so far as it triggers a reflex, otherwise it is not known at all. Thus, Piaget's view of the innate architecture of cognition is that it consists only of reflexes and mechanisms of assimilation and accommodation. The rest is constructed; the child, while learning about the world, constructs the cognitive system with which to interpret the world.

Reflexes constitute the first of six substages of sensorimotor development. However, some reflex behaviours are repeated by the infant because of the desirable or reinforcing consequences of the behaviour itself. This

Table 3.1 *Piaget's substages of sensorimotor development.*

Substage	Age (months)	Dominant Scheme	Major Developments
I	0–1	Reflex	Sucking, grasping
II	1–4	Primary circular reactions	Adaptations of reflexes to external environment; systematic protrusion of tongue; sucking of thumb; beginning of eye–hand co-ordination
III	4–8	Secondary circular reactions	Beginning of intentional means-end behaviour; increased co-ordination of looking and grasping; search for partially hidden objects
IV	8–12	Co-ordination of secondary schemes	Widespread flexible combination of previously separate schemes; search for hidden objects; emergence of ability to predict one external event from another
V	12–18	Tertiary circular reactions	Discovery of new means through experimentation with means-end behaviours
VI	18–24	Mental representations	Symbolic representation of external events; invention of new means through mental combinations

repetition has a fundamentally different origin from the reflex itself: it is not innately triggered but voluntarily engaged in. This behaviour constitutes the second substage of sensorimotor development, the stage of primary circular reactions. Learning, in the conventional sense, first occurs during this substage, and this leads Piaget to conclude that sensorimotor schemes are first established during this substage. A scheme is the first example of the abstract structures that Piaget postulates in order to explain the organizational pattern he perceives in the infant's behaviour.

The theoretical move from reflex to scheme is central to the theory and to Piaget's attempt to link biology and psychology; behaviour is established by biological principles but these only serve as the necessary foundation for the further construction of the mind on psychological principles.

As the infant acts, some actions will have consequences on the world. Swiping a hand, for example, may cause a mobile to move, or to make a noise. Actions that are repeated because of the consequences they have on the world define the third substage of sensorimotor development. These actions are called secondary circular reactions. Secondary circular reactions further reflect the drift away from innate behaviours in that they are learnt adaptations to environmental events and they are reinforced by external consequences (as opposed to internal consequences at substage II). Thus, there is now a contingent relation between the infant's behaviour and environmental events. This represents a journey during the first year of life from an organism whose behavioural repertoire consists almost entirely of reflex responses to one that is responsive to the information that can be gained from acting on the environment and observing the consequences of those actions. The infant is still severely constrained in his or her interpretation of the structure of the environment and its relation to behaviour; concepts of causality, space, object permanence and many more still require considerable development during the remainder of the sensorimotor period. Nevertheless, the basic interactive relation between organism and environment is established by substage III. Consequently, substage IV does not consist of the development of new behaviours but of the co-ordination of behaviours already in place.

During substage IV previously acquired schemes are generalized to new situations, and behaviours that have developed independently as secondary circular reactions are co-ordinated to yield more powerful and more adaptive schemes. Where previously each scheme existed in isolation, different schemes can now be combined together in a sequence. One example offered by Piaget (1936a/1952) is the ability to move one object aside (one scheme) in order to grasp an object (another scheme) that it is obstructing. Piaget described the situation as follows:

> I present a box of matches above my hand, but behind it, so that he cannot reach it without setting the obstacle aside. But Laurent after trying to take no notice of it, suddenly tries to hit my hand as though to remove or lower it; I let him do it to me and he grasps the box. I recommence to bar his passage, but using as a screen a sufficiently supple cushion to keep the impress of the child's gestures. Laurent tries to reach the box, and bothered

by the obstacle, he at once strikes it, definitely lowering it until the way is clear. (Piaget, 1936a/1952: p. 217)

The behaviour described by Piaget is an example of the infant's increasing sophistication in reasoning about the external world and in co-ordinating schemes to solve problems that arise when a goal cannot be attained directly.

This increasing facility for problem-solving provides the key for subst-age V, which Piaget describes as the substage of tertiary circular reactions. Primary circular reactions were behaviours repeated for their own intrinsic reinforcement value; secondary circular reactions were behaviours repeated for the environmental effects they produced; tertiary circular reactions are behaviours repeated, *with modifications*, in order to achieve a given goal. They thus constitute a systematic exploration of the relations between means and ends. Piaget describes, as an example, a phenomenon well known to every parent, when the infant discovers the variety of ways in which things can be dropped from a crib, and proceeds to conduct the relevant experiments.

Tertiary circular reactions are the culmination of an intelligence based on schemes. The final substage of the sensorimotor period is the development of a new way of interacting with the environment by mentally representing it. Piaget infers the presence of a mental representation when there is a gap in time between the infant observing something and later repeating what was observed.

Piaget's reasoning is that if a behaviour is observed at some particular time and imitated at some later time, there must be storage of the observed event in the interim and such storage requires a symbolic encoding of events. This ability to represent events by internal symbols brings the sensorimotor period to an end. Once events can be stored symbolically the child has embarked on the long road of learning to process and manipulate stored information. Cognitive development proper has now begun.

Imitation and Representation

Piaget's Account of the Origins of Representations

Piaget (1945/1951) attempts to trace the emergence of symbolic behaviour from its origins in sensorimotor development. His general method is essentially the same as in his other works on sensorimotor development: he presents detailed observational reports on behaviours that might be considered symbolic or proto-symbolic in origin and offers interpretations of these behaviours and their symbolic status. Before discussing Piaget's account in more detail it will be useful to consider the criterion he uses to infer the presence of mental symbols.

Piaget infers the presence of mental symbols that represent the external world on the basis of one criterion: 'the deferred character of the reaction' (p.98). That is to say, there must be a temporal interval between the behaviour that serves as evidence for a mental symbol and the event in the world to which the behaviour relates. Thus, imitation has a representational basis when it occurs sometime after the event imitated and language has a representational basis when words describe events that occurred some time previously. The criterion of temporal delay is used to infer a symbolic system that mediates between the original stimulus and its later reproduction by the child.

It is easy enough to see that this criterion of temporal delay allows Piaget to infer a representational system with some certainty. However, it is not self-evident that the criterion is necessary. Piaget's criteria, in general, tend to err on the conservative side in the attribution of cognitive structures; the criterion for representational thought is no exception. While the representation may be inferred from 'the deferred character of the reaction', a representation is not defined by a delay between stimulus input and response output. In order to understand the origins of mental representations it is necessary to define, within a theoretical framework, what are to count as representations, and then to propose ways of detecting the presence of representations. It is not adequate, as a methodological practice, to work backwards from a convenient, probably overcautious, measure to the theoretical construct. An objection to this criticism might be that Piaget intends the term 'representation' to stand for that which makes deferred responses possible. Unfortunately, this simply creates a circular relation between the construct and its operational measure. In any case, this is patently not what the term 'representation' is intended to capture. There is a reasonably clear theoretical view of what a mental representation is: it is a symbolic encoding of some aspect of the external environment. Mental representations can be legitimately attributed to the child once evidence exists for the use of symbolic encoding in the organization of behaviour. The major methodological task that this creates is to show how symbolic encodings can be detected in an unambiguous fashion. We shall return to this issue later.   Given Piaget's criterion for inferring cognitive representations, imitation is an obvious behaviour on which to test the account. In order to imitate it is necessary at minimum (1) to observe the behaviour of another, (2) to process and encode that observation, and (3) to use the results of that processing to effect a similar sequence of behaviour in the correct serial order. If there is a time lapse between (1) and (3) then clearly we are observing a behaviour that is controlled by a cognitive representation.

Piaget does not report any examples of imitation during the first of his six substages of sensorimotor development. It will be recalled that this substage consists entirely of reflex behaviours. Since imitation involves reproducing some behaviour of a model, and therefore depends upon experience, it would be odd for it to be observed among the reflexes of substage I. It is not until substage II that some sporadic imitation is observed. Piaget reports instances of both vocal imitation of sounds and visual imitation of head movements. However, there are constraints on what can be imitated; the model that the infant imitates must be assimilated to a circular schema that the infant has already acquired. Thus, imitation will only occur if the model presents behaviours that the infant has already performed spontaneously.

During the third substage of sensorimotor development imitation of sounds occurs for quite long periods and imitation of movements continues provided, still, that the infant can make these movements spontaneously. However, Piaget claims that the infant is not able to imitate new sounds that he or she has not previously produced spontaneously. Imitation of movements will only occur if the infant can observe the movement while he or she is making it. Thus, an infant could imitate hand gestures made in front of the face because these can be observed while they are being made but could not imitate scratching the back of the head because the infant cannot observe his or her own movements in doing this. However, Piaget was too inquisitive an observer and too honest a scientist not to report some success at eliciting imitation of tongue protrusion from his daughter Jacqueline. For example, he reported some observations that did not neatly fit his framework. He accommodates these observations to his theory by categorising them as 'pseudo-imitations' on the grounds that the behaviour is not maintained unless its training is prolonged and constantly kept up.

> Obs. 17. At 0;5 (2) J put out her tongue several times in succession. I put mine out in front of her, keeping time with her gesture, and she seemed to repeat the action all the better. But it was only a temporary association. A quarter of an hour later, no suggestion on my part could induce her to begin again. There was the same negative reaction the next few days.

Substage IV, it will be recalled, consists of the co-ordination of schemes. Once this co-ordination is achieved the infant begins to imitate movements of the body not directly visible while being carried out. Piaget argues that this development is a result of the infant assimilating the movements of others to those of his or her own body. At this point let us pick up the story of tongue protrusion.

Obs. 20. At 0;8 (9) I put out my tongue in front of J, thus resuming the experiment interrupted at 0;8 (3) which up till then had given only negative results (Obs. 17). At first J watched me without reacting, but at about the eighth attempt she began to bite her lips as before, and at the ninth and tenth she grew bolder, and thereafter reacted each time in the same way. The same evening her reaction was immediate: as soon as I put out my tongue she bit her lips.

Here, the infant responds predictably and consistently to the adult's behaviour but she does not imitate that behaviour; when Piaget puts out his tongue, Jacqueline bites her lip. This continued for nearly a month until biting the lips and tongue protrusion began to co-occur. About a week later tongue protrusion has become the dominant response. Piaget reports:

At 0;9(11) she finally succeeded in definitely distinguishing between the two schemas. I put out my tongue at her when she had not been doing it just before. Her first reaction was to bite her lips at once, and then after a moment, to put out her tongue several times. I interrupted the experiment, and then again put out my tongue. She watched me attentively, biting her lips, but she put her tongue out more quickly and more distinctly. After a second pause, I put out my tongue, and she then put hers out very definitely without biting her lips, after having watched me very carefully. This must obviously have been conscious imitation.

During substage IV direct imitation of actions that the infant cannot see becomes fully developed. What then of imitation of sounds during this substage? Piaget remarks that when the infant becomes capable of imitating movements he or she has already made but cannot see, attempts are then made to imitate sounds and gestures that are new. It is interesting to note the strong priority given to motor movements in this account. Given that the imitation of movements that cannot be seen and sounds that are new both occur within the same substage, there is no logical reason to see one development as the result of the other.

Substage V is the period of exploring means–end relations. The infant, during this substage, engages in systematic exploration of the various elements that constitute an imitatory scheme.

Obs. 39. At 1;0 (20) J watched me removing and replacing the top of my tobacco jar. It was within her reach and she could have tried to achieve the same result. She merely raised and lowered her hand, however, thus imitating the movement of my hand but not its external effect.

In this example, the infant is obviously capable of isolating the behavioural component of the adult's act from its effect on the environment; the means and the end are clearly differentiated from each other.

According to Piaget, three new elements can be evidenced in imitation during substage VI: immediate imitation of complex new models, deferred imitation, and imitation of material objects resulting in representation. Of these, the latter two are of most theoretical importance. The following two examples are reported by Piaget. The first is of deferred imitation and the second is of imitation of material objects.

Obs. 52. At 1;4(3) J had a visit from a little boy of 1;6, whom she used to see from time to time, and who, in the course of the afternoon got into a terrible temper. He screamed as he tried to get out of a play-pen and pushed it backwards, stamping his feet. J stood watching him in amazement, never having witnessed such a scene before. The next day, she herself screamed in her play-pen and tried to move it, stamping her foot lightly several times in succession. The imitation of the whole scene was most striking. Had it been immediate, it would naturally not have involved representation, but coming as it did after an interval of more than twelve hours, it must have involved some representative or pre-representative element.

Obs. 57. At 1;4 (0) L tried to get a watch chain out of a match-box when the box was not more than an eighth of an inch open. She gazed at the box with great attention, then opened and closed her mouth several times in succession, at first only slightly and then wider and wider. It was clear that the child, in her effort to picture to herself the means of enlarging the opening, was using as 'signifier' her own mouth, with the movements of which she was familiar tactually and kinesthetically as well as by analogy with the visual image of the mouths of others. It is possible that there may also have been an element of 'causality through imitation', L perhaps still trying, in spite of her age, to act on the box through her miming. But the essential thing for her, as the context of the behaviour clearly showed, was to grasp the situation, and to picture it to herself actively in order to do so.

With the development of deferred imitation Piaget is willing to attribute a representational capacity to the child. He remarks: 'representation begins when sensorimotor data are assimilated not to elements that are actually perceptible but to those that are merely evoked' (1945/1951; p. 277). Thus, as a result of the emergence of representation at substage VI, behaviour in which a symbolic system plays an essential role becomes possible for the first time.

Piaget's account of the development of mental representations is best exemplified in his account of the development of imitation. His account contains an astonishing wealth of detailed observation and a consistent attempt to do justice to those observations by interpreting them within a theoretical framework of stage-like development.

Replication Studies

Let us turn now to subsequent studies of imitation and compare their findings with those of Piaget. The studies that will be discussed fall into two broad types. First, there are replication studies that attempt to repeat the observations of Piaget. Second, there are a number of experimental studies of neonatal imitation, some of which challenge Piaget's conclusions.

Uzgiris and Hunt's (1975) studies are the most detailed attempt to replicate Piaget's observations. They were concerned, in general, with attempting to devise a detailed scale of the major content areas of sensori-motor development – namely space, object permanence, circular reactions, imitation and causality – and to address issues such as whether homogeneous substages existed during which behaviour in the various content areas were all at the same level of development. They found little evidence of substage homogeneity across the different behaviours studied. Infants were quite likely to show a spread of development with one type of behaviour being more advanced than average and another type less advanced. In other words, substages do not exist in the sense that there are superordinate organizing constructs determining the developmental level of all behaviours at a given time. However, Uzgiris and Hunt did support the *sequence* of behaviours observed by Piaget in the different content areas. Similar findings for the two content areas of object permanence and space have also been reported by Corman and Escalona (1969).

As far as imitation is concerned Uzgiris and Hunt (1975) report the results of several cross-sectional studies, while Uzgiris (1972) reports a longitudinal study of 12 infants between the ages of 1 month and 2 years. Overall, their findings lend broad support to Piaget's observations. At first infants only reproduce actions that are in their repertoire, such as cooing sounds. This is similar to the observations reported by Piaget at substage II. A more complex form of imitation is reported by Uzgiris and Hunt when infant and experimenter alternate in turntaking in imitation. Contemporaneous with this observation is the observation that infants will now attempt to imitate complex actions (although they may not successfully imitate the whole act). These observations correspond to Piaget's substage III. The next step reported by Uzgiris and Hunt is the successful imitation of actions that cannot be seen by the infant, which corresponds to the observations reported by Piaget for substage IV. Finally, Uzgiris and Hunt report the imitation of unfamiliar sounds and actions, which corresponds to Piaget's substage V.

The studies reported by Uzgiris (1972) and Uzgiris and Hunt (1975) serve to confirm the sequence of imitation reported by Piaget. However, they do not critically test that sequence as do other studies discussed below nor do they address the underlying theory that postulates that representations are absent during the entire period of sensorimotor development.

Neonatal Imitations

A number of investigators have claimed that the imitation of facial gestures, which, according to Piaget, first occurs during substage IV of sensorimotor development, can actually be observed during the early weeks of life. Gardner and Gardner (1970) reported a single case study of facial imitations at 6 weeks. The first systematic experimental evidence was provided by Meltzoff and Moore (1977). Because this study is controversial and because it helps to illustrate the methodological issues that surround research with infants, we shall discuss it in some detail.

In their first experiment Meltzoff and Moore modelled four different gestures to six infants between 12 and 21 days old and videotaped the infants' responses. The gestures were tongue protrusion, lip protrusion, mouth openings, and sequential finger movements. (The last of these will be ignored in the rest of the discussion.) The gestures were modelled for each infant in a different order. Each gesture was modelled four times in a 15-second modelling period followed by a 20-second response period in which the experimenter faced the infant with a neutral unresponsive face. The infants' responses were recorded on video during this period. The videotape recordings were then scored by judges who did not know which gesture had preceded the response being coded. For purposes of analysis, facial and manual gestures were coded separately. The six judges who coded facial responses were informed that the infant had been shown one of four gestures: lip protrusion, mouth opening, tongue protrusion, and passive face. They were instructed to order these four gestures by rank from the one they thought it most likely the infant was imitating to the one they thought was least likely. The two highest and the two lowest ranks were then collapsed yielding a 'yes'/'no' judgement as to whether or not the infant imitated the gesture presented. This means that if, for example, lip protrusion had been modelled and a judge scored the likelihood of the gesture being imitated in the order mouth opening, lip protrusion, tongue protrusion and passive face, the infant would be credited with imitating lip protrusion. This is a somewhat unconventional method of scoring observer judgements. A further caveat that could be entered about the method is that it presumes that the infant is imitating; there is no category equivalent to 'did not imitate'.

Meltzoff and Moore reported that in all four cases the judged behaviour of the infant varied significantly as a function of the gestures shown. Meltzoff and Moore concluded that babies can imitate during the second week of life.

In a second experiment Meltzoff and Moore reported data for 12 2-week-old infants. In this case the rates of mouth-opening and of tongue protrusion were compared during three 150-second time periods. The first was a baseline period during which the experimenter stared at the infant with an impassive face. One of the two gestures was then demonstrated repeatedly for a 15-second period and a further 150-second observation period ensued during which the experimenter resumed his impassive face. The other gesture was then demonstrated and the final 150-second observation period followed. The infants' faces were videotaped during all three observation periods. An independent coder viewed the recordings and scored the number of tongue protrusions and mouth openings for each infant during each period. It was found that significantly more tongue protrusions occurred following tongue protrusion by the experimenter and significantly more mouth openings following mouth opening. Again, the conclusion is that infants are capable of selective imitation. However, as Kaye (1982: p. 163) has pointed out the data seem less than impressive on close inspection:

> The 12 infants opened their mouths a total of eight times (on the average, once every 225 seconds) after the experimenter did so; but they only opened their mouths a total of two times (once every 15 minutes) in each of the other two conditions. Tongue protrusions were a little more frequent, and they too were significantly more frequent after they had been modeled: The 12 tongues were protruded 39 times during the segments following the tongue-protrusion demonstration, 15 times after each of the other conditions. A problem with this study was that Meltzoff and Moore, by reporting the total numbers of occurrences instead of the actual rates or the numbers of babies producing any responses at all, accentuated the (statistically significant) differences between experimental conditions and played down the fact that the rates of responding were extremely low. Very few of the 12 babies produced any imitative responses at all; but a few of them did so, at a sufficient rate to make the total numbers significantly different under each of the conditions.

Since Meltzoff and Moore's original study there have been several attempted replications. Some attempts have failed (Hayes and Watson 1981; Koepke, Hamm and Legerstee, 1983; McKenzie and Over, 1983), while others have succeeded (Field, Woodson, Greenberg and Cohen, 1982; Meltzoff and Moore, 1983). This suggests that the phenomenon is far from robust. Some babies appear to imitate some of the time.

What implications do such findings have for the origins of mental representations? Consider the fact that the infant receives perceptual input and uses motor output to reproduce the form of the input. This might seem to imply that infants are capable of creating some perceptual representation of an adult's behaviour, possibly as an image, and then of using this representation to create a motor output. In order to do this, infants would have to be able to link, in some way, elements of the image with components of the motor behaviour. This would seem to demand rather a lot from an infant's information processing system during the first few weeks of life. Meltzoff and Moore overcame this problem by arguing, following Bower (1974), that the translation from a perceptual representation to a motor output is not necessary because information is initially represented in a form common to all the senses. They state (1977: p. 178):

> The hypothesis we favor is that this imitation is based on the neonate's capacity to represent visually and proprioceptively perceived information in a form common to both modalities. The infant could thus compare the sensory information from his own unseen motor behaviour to a 'supramodal' representation of the visually perceived gesture and construct the match required. In brief, we hypothesize that the imitative responses observed are . . . accomplished through an active matching process and mediated by an abstract representational system . . . The ability to act on the basis of an abstract representation of a perceptually absent stimulus becomes the starting point for psychological development in infancy and not its culmination.

This is a radically different interpretation of the cognitive abilities of infants from that offered by Piaget. It encapsulates something that will recur frequently throughout this book: the extreme contrast between how the cognitive system is viewed by theorists disposed towards interpretations in terms of innate representational abilities and those not so disposed.

A study by Jacobson (1979) is of particular interest in relation to infant imitation. She observed infants at 6, 10, and 14 weeks in a longitudinal study. Two of the gestures modelled by Meltzoff and Moore were studied, namely tongue protrusion and hand movements. In addition three other stimuli were presented, namely a ball, a pen being moved towards the infant's mouth, and a ring being raised and lowered. Jacobson found that tongue protrusion *and* the movement of a ball or pen towards the infants mouth all produced tongue protrusions. Jacobson suggests that the infants' behaviour may not have been genuine imitation but more like the fixed action patterns described by Tinbergen (1951), which are automatically released by certain stimuli. However, by 14 weeks tongue protrusion was primarily elicited by adult tongue protrusion. Thus, even if the behaviour of the infants is initially akin to a fixed action pattern, it is certainly much less stereotyped than the fixed action patterns described by Tinbergen. Meltzoff and Moore (1977) argue against such an interpretation on the grounds that it is unwieldy in view of the fact that infants imitate a variety of different behaviours. The logic of this point is sound but its empirical basis is not. In Meltzoff and Moore's (1977) first experiment the rate of imitative responses was not directly measured. In their second experiment there was a moderate number of tongue protrusions but a very low number of mouth openings. Thus the only behaviour for which there is at present a reasonably clear case to be made for neonatal imitation is tongue protrusion. This conclusion is bolstered by the results of two further studies. Kaitz, Meschulach-Sarfaty, Auerbach and Eidelman (1988) compared the ability of infants to imitate tongue protrusion and facial expressions (for which positive results had been reported by Field et al., (1982)). Kaitz et al. replicated the positive findings for tongue protrusion but failed to replicate the imitation of facial expressions. Abravanel and Sigafoos (1984) modelled five actions three times in succession for infants between the ages of 4 and 21 weeks. The actions were tongue protrusion, mouth opening, and chest tapping. They found no evidence of imitation for any of the actions. However, in a second study they increased the amount of modelling to an unlimited number for the duration of the infants' attention during a 3-minute period. They also decreased the number of actions to three: tongue protrusion, hand opening, and chin tapping. With this procedure there was evidence of imitation of tongue protrusions only for infants in the 4 to 6 week age range. No other comparison was statistically significant at any of the ages sampled. In fact, there was a significant *decline* in the amount of imitation with increase in age.

The issue of infant imitation is currently a hotly-debated topic. It is difficult at this stage to draw definite conclusions because there are too many conflicting results for a clear pattern of empirical data to emerge that call for interpretation. At present, both data and interpretation are at issue. The best that can be done is to consider the current alternatives.

Meltzoff and Moore (1977; 1985) have urged the strongest interpretation. They argue that infants are capable of creating abstract mental representations of the behaviour of others and of using this abstract representation to create a matching response of their own. In order to create a mapping from the visual input to the proprioceptive output they postulate (following Bower, 1974) that infants represent the adult act not as an image or other perceptual representation (which would leave the problem of 'translating' this image to a motor output) but as a 'supramodal' or non-modality-specific representation. Unfortunately, there is no further specification of the nature of this supramodal representation. It was argued in chapter 2 that there is little empirical support for Bower's position.

The major alternative interpretation is that the infant's imitations derive from innate reflexive behaviours that are elicited by various stimuli in the environment. The strongest version of this argument would have it that tongue protrusions are elicited by a range of different stimuli and that there is little evidence for other types of imitation. It is at this point that the debate about the status of the empirical data is critical but is, unfortunately, unresolved. Kaitz et al. (1988) point out that tongue protrusion in infants is a behaviour with a high base-line relative to other behaviours and thus has a high probability of being involuntarily triggered by a variety of stimuli. Kaitz et al. doubt that the reproduction of tongue protrusions in response to a similar facial gesture of the model is true imitation. True imitation, in their view, requires the voluntary co-ordination of motor output to produce the same behaviour as the adult. They argue also that if the intermodal skills postulated by Meltzoff and Moore (1977) were generally available to the infant, imitation would not have been limited to one of four expressions, as found in their own study. Vinter (1986) draws attention to the role of movement in eliciting neonatal imitation and suggests that the behaviour may be controlled by subcortical rather than cortical mechanisms. This suggestion is consistent with the decline in imitation reported by Abravanel and Sigafoos (1984) and is reminiscent of the findings reported on the development of visual orientation to the source of an auditory stimulus reported in chapter 2. Many investigators of neurological development have stressed the continuity from prenatal to postnatal neurological control of movement and a subsequent change in the developmental course of neurological and behavioural variables around the end of the second month (Prechtl, 1984). It may be a general rule of development that as control of motor behaviour moves from subcortical to cortical mechanisms, there is a general decline in early reflexive actions (McGraw, 1943; Touwen, 1976). If this is true, then neonatal imitation is a behaviour of a fundamentally different type from later imitation.

Summary of Imitation and Representation

The discussion of imitation began by considering Piaget's account. His account stressed the gradual emergence of more complex forms of imitation throughout the first two years of life. The general pattern he observed has been confirmed by others, notably by Uzgiris (1972). The greatest challenge to Piaget's account has come from the experiments on neonatal imitation. If the interpretation urged by Meltzoff and Moore (1977, 1985) is accepted then the Piagetian *theory* of imitation is completely erroneous. However, the type of interpretation of neonatal imitation urged by others such as Abravanel and Sigafoos (1984), Kaitz et al. (1988) and Vinter (1986) is much closer to Piaget's general view that early imitations are not indicative of mental representations. While the debate about neonatal imitation has been a lively issue it has had one unfortunate consequence: the fact is that, however one interprets the neonatal evidence, imitation itself undergoes developmental change by mechanisms that are still little understood. The debate on neonatal imitation as an encapsulated phenomenon has taken the emphasis off the need to create a theory of the origins of mental representations that accommodates within its framework the changes in the infant's abilities to imitate.

Imitation provided Piaget with the most direct type of evidence for his claim that mental representations are absent until the end of the sensorimotor period. However, his claim was a general one about the child's thought during the first year and a half or so of life. Accordingly, we can ask to what extent evidence from other areas of sensorimotor development supports Piaget's claims. The area for which the greatest amount of evidence is available is that of object permanence. We shall now consider its development.

The Object Concept

Perhaps the most intriguing aspect of Piaget's research on sensorimotor development is that concerned with the concept of object permanence. A series of ingenious explorations of his children's reactions to the disappearance of objects led Piaget to conclude that until the end of sensorimotor development children do not fully understand that an object that is occluded continues to exist. This may seem like a startling conclusion but the reaction of an infant is equally startling in failing to search for an object over which a cloth has been draped in full view of the infant in such a way that the object's outline is clearly visible underneath the cloth. Piaget claims that the infant has to construct a concept that the world consists of permanent enduring objects and not merely of perceptions and sensations. It is worth bearing in mind that at the time Piaget wrote, very little was known about the actual perceptual capacities of infants.

Piaget's investigation of the infant's object concept employs one particular methodology: an object is occluded in full view of the infant and the infant's attempts to retrieve the object are observed. During the early stages of sensorimotor development, infants simply lose interest when an object is hidden – it seems as if out of sight is out of mind. Piaget concludes that the infant believes that an object is re-created each time it appears. Only perceptual appearances exist for the infant; there is no independent world of objects that gives rise to these perceptual appearances as there is for the adult.

By 6–8 months, during substage III of sensorimotor development, the infant has discovered by active exploration that his or her own actions can produce perceptual contact with objects. An infant will now recover a partially occluded object but fail to recover one that is completely occluded. The reason Piaget advances for this failure is central to his theory of sensorimotor development. The sensorimotor period is one in which the external world is known by the actions performed on it. Thus, an object is known by the action schema that the infant performed in interacting with it. An object grasped is known only through the act of grasping. If an object has been grasped previously then it may elicit the same response when encountered again. However, an occluded object cannot elicit this behaviour in virtue of the object being hidden. The fact that the outline shape of the object may be visible under the cloth that occludes it is irrelevant. Infants cannot reason that the shape is related to the object that was visible previously because that object was known only as a graspable phenomenon.

By substage IV infants will recover a completely occluded object. They have now begun, in some sense, to be able to relate the occluded object to the object that disappeared. This appears to be a significant step forward as far as the mental representation of objects is concerned. However, the infant is still, according to Piaget, constrained by the action schemas used to recover objects. Infants will not recover an object occluded in any place; they will only recover an object if it is occluded in a location where it was previously found. This can be illustrated by the following experiment. Two cloths are placed side by side and an object is hidden under one cloth. The infant retrieves the object. This is allowed to occur several times and then the object is hidden under the other cloth. The infant will usually search under the cloth where the object was previously found and not under the cloth where the object has been hidden. The infant frequently looks very puzzled on failing to find the object and may turn the cloth over and over but still fail to search under the other cloth, through which the outline of the object may be clearly visible. This suggests that the improvement that has occurred over substage III is simply one of a more sophisticated action schema: an object can be retrieved if it has successfully been retrieved from that location previously. However, the story is not this simple. The first retrieval at any given location cannot be explained in this way. More importantly, the infant's behaviour, when faced with occluded or hidden objects at substage IV is more complex than the outline account suggests. We shall return to this below.

By substage V the error of searching where an object was previously found has been eliminated but the infant may still be fooled by more devious hiding. If an object is hidden in the experimenter's hand and the hand then placed under a cloth and withdrawn again, leaving the object behind, the infant will search for the object in the hand, where he or she has seen it hidden, but will fail to search under the cloth. By substage VI the full object concept is acquired and infants will search in all probable places where the object may have been hidden.

Piaget used his findings on the object concept to illustrate his argument that the infant only knows the world through the action schemas used to act on the world. But Piaget also saw the infant as having a more profound difficulty due to egocentrism. Because the infant only knows the world through his or her action schemas, the infant believes that the schemas themselves cause events in the world; the world is not seen as having an existence independently of the action schemas. Thus, the act of searching for an object at a location caused the object to be at that location because search has previously located objects there. From this perspective, searching where an object was previously found rather than where it has just been observed to be hidden is not odd at all; it is a perfectly natural consequence of the infant's egocentrism.

Such is the outline of Piaget's account of the development of object permanence. His observations have given rise to a very large number of experimental studies of this concept. In the main, studies that employ Piaget's criterion of search for a hidden object support the general outline of Piaget's account. As is usual when modern developmental psychologists consider Piaget however, the interpretation of the findings are in dispute. Various interpretations of the infant's failures in object search have been offered, and we shall discuss some of these. However, the more radical challenge comes from a different type of research. Search is not the only behaviour that can be used in investigating how infants respond to the disappearance of objects. Due to refinements in experimental procedures in the last quarter-century, it is now possible to conduct sophisticated experiments on the infant's visual and surprise responses to the disappearances and reappearances of objects. These experiments have the advantage that they can be conducted with young infants who are not capable of searching. Thus, we shall begin with these studies.

Measures of Disappearance and Reappearance

The pioneering experiment in this area was carried out by Bower (1967). He investigated the reactions of 2-month-old (substage I-II) infants to various different types of disappearance. Infants were trained to suck for an auditory reward and a sphere was visible throughout the training period. The sphere was then made to disappear in one of four ways: (1) gradual occlusion by a screen; (2) gradual fading; (3) instantaneous occlusion by a screen; and (4) instantaneous implosion. Bower compared the effect of these four conditions on sucking. He found that sucking was least disrupted by the first condition, which, according to Michotte's (1955) theory, specifies the continued existence of an invisible object, unlike the other three conditions. Bower concluded that the infants believed that the sphere continued to exist behind the screen.

In a series of follow-up studies Bower examined the effect of disappearance and reappearance under the various conditions, this time using spontaneous sucking as the dependent measure. He found that gradual occlusion led to the most suppression but that sucking recovered when the object reappeared so long as the interval between disappearance and reappearance was not longer than five seconds. Bower interpreted these results as showing that the infants suppress sucking while they wait for the occluded object to reappear. Bower interprets this as evidence that the infants possess object permanence. However, it should be noted that the sucking response is different in the two experiments. In one it is maintained, in the other it is suppressed, in response to the same condition. This creates an interpretive problem: it cannot reasonably be maintained that both responses indicate a belief in object permanence. While it certainly seems that gradual occlusion is seen as different from other types of disappearance by young infants, it is not clear that this indicates that young infants possess object permanence. As Brainerd (1978a) has pointed out, it is not possible to separate what may be responses to visual displays from what may be responses to objects in these experiments.   Bower and his associates have also conducted a series of experiments with substage III infants. These experiments used the infants' tracking of objects as they moved across the visual field as a dependent measure. In one experiment (Bower, Broughton and Moore, 1971a) a train was made to move along a track containing a tunnel across the infant's line of sight. The issue of interest is what the infant does when the train enters the tunnel. If the infant immediately loses interest then it can be concluded that the infant was simply responding to the perceptual phenomenon and that, once the phenomenon has disappeared from sight it has, effectively, ceased to exist for the infant. Out of sight is out of mind. However, the infants did not immediately lose interest. Bower et al. found that, by about 3 months of age, the infants immediately looked to the opposite end of the tunnel as if anticipating the re-emergence of the train. They concluded that this indicated that object permanence had developed by this age. However, further research by Bower and others has suggested that there may be alternative explanations of the infant's behaviour. Bower and Patterson (1973) used a train and tunnel but stopped the train just before it entered the tunnel. Even though the train was in full view the infants continued to track along the trajectory the train would have taken for some distance and then stopped. This result was also obtained when the tunnel was removed altogether and the train simply stopped at some point. This would seem to suggest that what Bower et al. (1971a) had interpreted as anticipation of the train's reappearance was simply the result of perseverative tracking. This interpretation is bolstered by the findings of Nelson (1971) who tested children's tracking of a train around an oval track, with a tunnel on one side. The infants tracked the train when it was visible but when it disappeared and then reappeared there was a delay of one to two seconds before the train was spotted. Clearly, if the infants had anticipated the re-emergence of the train there would have been no such delay. More recently Meicler and Gratch (1980) have replicated this result.

It would seem that there is no clear evidence from these tracking experiments that infants possess object permanence during the early months of life. The experiments do not, of course, show that infants do not possess object permanence. The real problem is that it is extremely difficult to relate how an infant tracks in any simple way to a belief in object permanence. Perseverative tracking, does not, for example, indicate an absence of object permanence because Chromiak and Weisberg (1981) have shown that adults track moving objects that stop suddenly in exactly the same way as infants: their eyes continue along the expected path of movement. This is an extremely important result that tells us a good deal about the relation between infant and adult behaviour. It also suggests that tracking is not a behaviour that has direct or automatic dependency on a belief in object permanence.

A number of studies have used tracking in a different way to investigate object permanence. In these studies an object moves along a track, disappears behind a screen and a different object re-emerges at the other side of the screen along the same track. Will infants exhibit any surprise at such a change? The reasoning here is that if infants of this age possess the concept of object permanence they should clearly expect the same object that disappeared to reappear. If, on the other hand, tracking is a behaviour that occurs independently of a concept of object permanence, infants should not be particularly surprised at the disappearance of one object and the reappearance of another.

Goldberg (1976) found no difference in surprise (as measured by heart rate) or in visual fixation in infants of 5 months between the reappearance of a novel and a familiar object. Two later studies have replicated this result. Muller and Aslin (1978) tested 2-, 4-, and 6-month old infants and altered either the shape or colour of the object to no effect on tracking. Meicler and Gratch (1980) reported similar results with 5- and 9-month olds. However, Moore, Borton and Darby (1978) reported more looking back towards the place of re-emergence when identity was altered than when it was not.

On balance, studies that have replaced one object by another during the disappearance of a tracked object behind a screen have not provided positive evidence that infants possess a concept of object permanence. Again, these findings do not prove that infants do not have a concept of object permanence. The negative results may be due to reasons other than an absence of a belief in object permanence. The infant may, for example, regard the disappearance of one object and the reappearance of another as an interesting game. However, there is no need to indulge in this type of speculation to make the essential methodological point: failure to observe surprise in the infants simply fails to support the hypothesis that infants do possess object permanence without telling us that they do not.

Recently, an experiment by Baillargeon (1986) has tipped the balance of interpretation positively in the infant's favour in a more complex tracking experiment. Infants of 6 and 8 months were first shown a car travelling along a track, disappearing behind a screen, and then reappearing at the other side. After several such presentations the screen was removed so that the complete track was visible and a box was placed either on the track or beside it. The screen was then replaced and the infants saw the car move along the track, disappear behind the screen, and reemerge at the other side. The infants looked longer at the car that emerged when the box had been placed on the track than when it had been placed beside it. This could be taken to suggest that the infants were puzzled as to how the car had managed to move through the box placed on the track, which in turn suggests that the infants were aware that the box continues to exist when it has been occluded by the screen.

There are two points to which it is worth drawing attention in the design of Baillargeon's experiment: The first is that the experiment is designed in such a way that the infant's surprise can be attributed to the presence of the box on the track, which is out of sight at the time that the measurement is made. This contrasts with the design in which one object disappears and a novel object reappears. In these experiments, the object intended to elicit a surprise reaction is present at the time of measurement, which would make the interpretation of positive results somewhat problematic. The second point is that the experiment includes a control condition in which all the elements of the first condition are present, but arranged in such a way that the infant should not be surprised to see the car emerge. This condition reduces the likelihood that any positive results might be due to an artifact of the experiment.

The results of Baillargeon (1986) suggest that 6-month-old infants possess a concept of object permanence. Nevertheless infants of 12 months and older make a variety of errors in searching for hidden objects, which led Piaget to conclude that object permanence had not developed at this age.

Search

If we now turn to search itself, then the general sequence of development reported by Piaget has been verified in a number of replication studies (Corman and Escalona, 1969; Kramer, Hill and Cohen, 1975; Uzgiris and Hunt, 1975). These studies show that the sequence reported by Piaget constitutes an accurate description but they do not address the interpretation of that sequence.

Studies of the emergence of manual search during substage III show that the infant's failure to search under a cloth is not due to a lack of manual skill. Bower and Wishart (1972) and Gratch (1972) compared a transparent with an opaque cloth and found that infants were more likely to retrieve the object when it was under the transparent cloth. Presumably the same degree of manual skill is required in both situations. However, an object covered by a transparent cloth can itself be seen, and thus may elicit an action to effect its recovery whereas an object under an opaque cloth cannot be seen and must be represented as being hidden before it can be searched for.

The infant's substage IV error in continuing to search where an object has been previously found rather than where it has been hidden has been widely researched. Although the research has added considerable detail to the original picture, it has not quite succeeded in clarifying the cause of the infant's error. To begin with, the error does not always occur; in fact it seems to occur on approximately 50 per cent of trials (Butterworth, 1975; 1977). This is essentially a pattern of random responding rather than a pattern of perseverating where the object has been previously found. A further factor is that the error disappears altogether if the infant is allowed to search immediately (Gratch, Appel, Evans, Le Compte and Wright, 1974; Harris, 1973). Putting these findings together suggests that the difficulties infants have at substage IV is due to limitations on their information processing capacity rather than to their egocentrism as Piaget had suggested. When search is immediate and the ability of the information-processing system is, presumably, less strained than when there is delay, the error does not occur. However, when search is delayed by more than a few seconds a pattern of random responding to the cloths occurs. This suggests that the infants no longer have access to the stored information about the object. In this context a longitudinal study by Diamond (1985) of infants between 7 and 12 months is of particular significance. Like previous studies, she found that when an object was hidden at a new location, having been previously hidden repeatedly at another location, the delay between the hiding of the object at the new location and the commencement of search was a crucial determinant of the infants' behaviour. The delay needed to elicit a perseverative error at the old hiding place was three seconds at 8 months but increased continuously over time to 10 seconds at 12 months. Diamond suggests that these data can be interpreted as a product of competing response tendencies generated by information in short-term memory and a conditioned tendency to repeat a previously successful response. Information about the new hiding place is stored in short-term memory. If acted upon more or less immediately, this information will form the basis of the infant's search. However, if not acted upon there is a competing response tendency to repeat previously successful searches.

A number of experimental results suggest that the likelihood of a perseverative error (i.e. a true perseverative error as opposed to searching under the cloths in a random fashion) is reduced if objects are hidden under, in, or behind salient landmarks. Bremner (1978b) and Butterworth, Jarrett and Hicks (1982) showed that when two hiding places were distinct from one another infants tended to search correctly. In these experiments the infants appear to have used the salient landmark cues provided to guide their search. An earlier study by Acredolo (1978) lends further weight to the importance of landmark cues in object search. In this study the presence or absence of useful landmarks was systematically varied and children of different ages were tested. Children of 6 months tended to perseverate irrespective of the presence or absence of a landmark. The 11-month-old infants were more accurate if a landmark was present, whereas the 16-month-old infants were accurate whether or not a landmark was present.

In summary, the perseveration error of substage IV seems to depend crucially on there being a delay before search is allowed and an absence of distinctive landmarks. This suggests that the final answers to the infant's errors are to be found in a detailed understanding of the constraints of the infant's information-processing system and how this system uses environmental information.

By comparison with substage IV, substages V and VI of the development of object permanence have not been heavily researched. Several studies have replicated Piaget's finding that visible displacements are easier than invisible displacements (Kramer, Hill and Cohen, 1975; Uzgiris and Hunt, 1975). However, more recent studies have found that if the object is hidden under one of two distinctive containers, and the containers are then rotated, search is fairly accurate (Bremner, 1978a; Cornell, 1979; Goldfield and Dickerson, 1981). This suggests that landmark cues again play a large role in helping the infant discover the location of an object.

By substage VI Piaget claims that the infant is able for the first time to represent mentally the absent object. An experiment by Ramsay and Campos (1978) attempted to assess Piaget's claim. They used the technique of hiding one toy but surreptitiously substituting another in its place before the infant had searched. Infants who had reached substage VI were more likely to smile if they found the toy they had seen hidden but to persist in searching if they found a different toy. Ramsay and Campos argue that it is only at substage VI that the infants can recall the identity of the object to be found so that its recovery elicits a smile and its absence elicits further search. However, there are several factors confounded in this interpretation. Failure to search for a toy is not definitive proof that its identity cannot be recalled. The child may recall the identity but given the absence of any clue as to where the object might be, simply has no idea of where to search. A further factor to be considered as a general issue in relation to such experiments is whether such odd conditions of environmental manipulation are really the most appropriate way to unlock the cognitive system that the infant uses in dealing with the natural environment.

The Origins of Representations

The ability to represent mentally events in the world is the foundation of human cognitive development. In this chapter we have considered two views that are at opposite extremes as far as development is concerned.

One view postulates an innate ability to represent the world. The evidence in favour of this view is, at present, somewhat weak. The other view denies that the infant is capable of any representations at all until well into the second year of life. The evidence against this view is accumulating. Where then does the truth lie?

A characteristic of much recent debate on the origins of representations is a lack of critical reflection of what constitutes a representation. As the introduction to this chapter pointed out, it is possible to have multiple representations of any event, with each one serving to highlight and encode a different aspect of the event. Unfortunately, this point has often been pushed to the background in the welter of methodological and empirical controversy over whether or not an example of representation has been demonstrated. This point applies equally to innatist and Piagetian research. The point is probably obvious enough in relation to recent innatist claims to have demonstrated mental representations in the first few weeks of life, not to need further labouring. It may be less obvious in relation to Piagetian research. Piaget, however, relied exclusively on one type of evidence for representation: temporal delay between the environmental stimulus and the infant's response, during which a 'mental copy' of the event was preserved. Kaye (1982) has argued that this is an unnecessarily restrictive view of representations. He comments:

> When schemas accommodate in some lasting way to some class of stimulating events, we can say that a schema *represents* that class of equivalent events in terms of a class of appropriate intentional actions. The 3-month-old has a representation of bottles in the form of the ability to recognize them visually and orient to them correctly with hand and mouth. That is the dawn of representation. (p. 167)

This is not to say that representation begins at 3 months rather than 18 months but to argue that once mental computation of some sort is involved – such as categorizing events into a class whose members will be treated as functionally equivalent – then it is meaningful to make claims about the infant's mental representation of events. The major emphasis of a theory of the development of representation (which we do not yet possess) should be on what types of more complex representations emerge during the course of development and the mechanisms by which they develop from earlier representations. Kaye, for example, goes on to emphasize that the kind of representations possessed by a 3-month-old are not the kind that use one thing to stand for another, which is what Piaget wished to reserve the term 'representation' for. That is an unacceptable reservation, if only because of the apparent discontinuity it needlessly introduces.

If we consider the object concept, then it would seem that infants do not so much lack a concept of object as lack a representation system that links objects with the spatial cues in the environment. Why this should be, does, of course, require explanation and, to date, no entirely satisfactory explanation has been proposed. However, to explain the infant's behaviour in these terms does represent a shift in emphasis from Piaget's perspective on the problem.

If representations do not begin in the middle of the second year, they do not end there either. The major issue to which Piaget drew attention in relation to representation was the way in which objects and events could be represented by symbols in the forms of images and words. Some recent research by De Loache (1987) has brought a renewed interest in the development of symbolic representation. In De Loache's experiment children 2.5 and 3 years of age watched an attractive toy hidden within a scale model of a room. The children were then required to find an analogous toy in the real room. In one example, a miniature dog was hidden behind a small couch in the model. The child was then asked to find a larger stuffed dog hidden behind a full-sized couch in a regular-sized room. In order to perform the task correctly the child has to use the model as a representation of the full-size room.

De Loache found that 2.5-year-old children were very poor at finding the toy hidden in the regular-sized room, whereas the 3-year-olds were very good at this task. The 2.5-year-olds made fewer than 20 per cent errorless retrievals in the regular-sized room whereas the 3-year-olds made almost 80 per cent errorless retrievals. The difficulty of the younger group cannot have been due to a failure to remember where the object had been hidden in the model because they were subsequently able to retrieve the object originally hidden at a similar level to the 3-year-olds – approximately 80 per cent errorless retrievals for both groups.

De Loache postulates that the younger children were unable to treat the model of the room as both a model and an object in its own right. Quite why this should be so is, at present, an open question. The data serve to highlight, however, the fact that the development of mental representations is not a phenomenon that occurs at a given point in time, but extends throughout the whole period of development. The issue is not whether representation (in the singular) is absent or present but what types of representations (in the plural) are available to a child at any given point of development and, of course, how these representations come to be available and to change.

4

Concepts and Words

Categorization, Concepts, and Names

In this chapter we shall explore the process of categorization, the concepts that result from this process and the words that are used to name these concepts. Categorization is the process by which entities are grouped together because they are similar to each other in certain respects. All objects are unique but categorization allows us to treat some objects as similar or identical while differentiating them from others. Categorization allows dogs to be dogs, dogs to be different from cats, and dogs and cats to be animals. Categorization is an example *par excellence* of how cognition has a representational organization. Although each object is unique, it is generally identified and named as an instance of a class of objects. In order for this to occur there must be a cognitive representation that is more abstract than its instances. This representation is generally called a *concept*.

Concepts are the products of categorization. The term 'concept' refers to a mental representation that determines how entities are related. There are two important types of conceptual relation that will be of concern: the relations among entities that form a conceptual category and the relations that determine hierarchical organization among concepts. The first issue concerns what it is that makes a dog a dog and a table a table. What principles determine how the human cognitive system forms concepts in the way that it does? The second issue concerns the fact that a dog is not just a dog or a table a table. A dog is also an animal, and may be a pet, a collie, and this particular dog Fido. A table is an item of furniture and may be a dining table, and a precious heirloom. There is a rich variety of concepts available to categorize an object in a variety of different ways. There is also a rich variety of names available to communicate about concept. Following Jackendoff (1983), the relation between words and concepts will be treated as a transparent one – that is, it will be assumed that words directly label concepts. Thus if a child forms a concept DOG* and attaches the label *dog* to this concept, then *dog* labels the child's concept DOG. However, we must investigate the process by which the child attaches labels to concepts. Suppose a child hears *dog* uttered by someone else in the presence of a dog. Let us assume, for convenience, that the child instantaneously acquires the label *dog* by mapping it to a concept. To which concept should the word be mapped? The issue here is that there are endless possibilities. If the child assumes the word *dog* labels a whole object then does it label DOG, ANIMAL, PET, COLLIE, or some other? It is also possible that the word labels a part of the object or one of its properties: size, shape, colour or various others. Thus, for each word learnt, the child is faced with a large range of potential mappings. The child is faced with making an inductive inference about the best possible mapping. Given that children readily acquire the correct labels for concepts, there must be considerable constraints imposed by the cognitive architecture on the inductions made about the mapping between words and concepts.

The background to the recent research on how children acquire concepts lies outside the field of cognitive development itself. In recent years there has been considerable research on the way in which concepts are mentally represented by adults. This research has largely overturned a view of conceptual organization that had prevailed since the time of the Greeks. Much of the terminology and results of this research have been used in the study of concept acquisition by children. Accordingly, we shall briefly review this background before discussing the developmental issues. (For a thorough review of the issues see Smith and Medin, 1981.)

The Structure of Concepts

The Classical Theory of Concepts

The classical theory of concepts can be traced back to the ancient Greeks. It received its first detailed exposition in Aristotle's (384–22 BC) *Poetics*.

---

* The following conventions are used to distinguish reference to objects, words, and concepts. When it is the object to which reference is made, ordinary orthography is used; a dog is an object in the world. When it is a label or a name (the terms are used interchangeably) to which reference is made, italics are used; *dog* is a label for a dog. When it is the concept to which reference is made, small capitals are used; DOG is the concept that is labelled *dog* and that categorizes dogs.

The classical theory was, until recently, the dominant theory of concepts (Smith and Medin, 1981). The classical theory held that all instances of a concept shared one or more common properties; that the common properties defined the concept; and that the common properties are necessary and sufficient for an entity to be categorized as an instance of the concept. Smith and Medin (1981: p. 2) illustrate the classical theory as applied to the concept of a square:

> Suppose that people in general represented this concept in terms of four properties: (1) closed figure, (2) four sides, (3) sides equal (in length), and (4) angles equal. Since these four properties, or criteria, would be applied to any object whose squareness is at issue, we have a unitary description of the concept 'square'. Moreover, the four properties that make up this concept are precisely those that any square must have. Roughly, then, to have a classical view concept is to have a unitary description of all class-members, where this description specifies the properties that every member must have.

It does not seem to be necessary that a person actually be consciously aware what the common properties of the members of a concept are. This was demonstrated in an early study of concept acquisition by Hull (1920) using the symbols shown in figure 4.1.

Hull attempted to discover how people learn new concepts. He asked subjects to learn a separate nonsense name for each of 12 Chinese characters. When the subjects had learned the name of one such set, they had to repeat the process with a new set. However, the same names were used. In all, each subject saw six sets of characters but only one set of names. On each occasion, a particular name was paired with a perceptual pattern contained within the overall character. Hull reported that the percentage of correct responses on the first trial with each new pack improved over the course of the experiment. At the end of the experiment a subject was often able to name characters without being able to say what the common element was. Hull drew two conclusions: that concepts are defined by some common element and that recognition of this element may be an unconscious process. These conclusions were generalized to concepts at large. Hull's method of investigation and his conclusions were to influence several generations of studies of concepts. His emphasis on easily manipulable perceptual features as an experimental technique was powerfully attractive. Essentially the same technique formed the basis of Bruner, Goodnow and Austin's (1956) work on concepts. For a brief review of this tradition of research see Johnson-Laird and Wason (1977).

The classical view is that concepts are monothetic (Beckner, 1959; Sokal, 1974); that is, the members of a class share at least one common

Figure 4.1 *Examples of Chinese letters used by Hull (1920) to study the development of concepts. Six variants are shown for each letter. Each row was given the name shown in the first column. The critical feature for membership of the concept is shown in the second column.*
Source: Hull, 1920.

property. The heart of the classical theory of concepts is that every concept has a set of necessary and sufficient features that defines the concept (Smith and Medin, 1981). Every member of the concept possesses these necessary and sufficient features and no non-member possesses them. A statement of the necessary and sufficient features for any given concept would serve to define that concept. The necessary and sufficient features of any concept can form a criterial test of whether or not a given instance belongs to that concept. If the instance possesses the relevant features then it belongs to the concept; if it does not possess them it does not belong. The classical theory offers a very clear view of concepts and a very clear-cut principle for determining what does and does not belong to a concept. This clarity is undoubtedly responsible for the popularity of the theory. However, the clarity is illusory; the principle is clear but natural concepts do not appear to obey the principle. Although laboratory studies of concepts such as those cited have manipulated artificial concepts that obeyed the principles of the classical theory, natural concepts do not appear to categorize entities according to a set of necessary and sufficient conditions.

Family Resemblance

Probably the best-known assault on the classical theory of concepts was conducted by Wittgenstein (1953 §66).

> Consider for example the proceedings that we call 'games'. I mean board-games, card-games, Olympic games, and so on. What is common to them all? – Don't say: 'There *must* be something common, or they would not be called 'games'' – but *look and see* whether there is anything common to all. – For if you look at them you will not see something that is common to *all*, but similarities, relationships, and a whole series of them at that. To repeat: don't think, but look! – Look for example at board-games, with their multifarious relationships. Now pass to card-games; here you find many correspondences with the first group, but many common features drop out, and others appear. When we pass next to ball-games, much that is common is retained, but much is lost. – Are they all 'amusing'? Compare chess with noughts and crosses. Or is there always winning and losing, or competition between players? Think of patience. In ball games there is winning and losing; but when a child throws his ball at the wall and catches it again, this feature has disappeared. Look at the parts played by skill and luck; and at the difference between skill in chess and skill in tennis. Think now of games like ring-a-ring-a-roses; here is the element of amusement, but how many other characteristic features have disappeared! And we can go through the many other groups of games in the same way; can see how similarities crop up and disappear.
>
> And the result of this examination is: we see a complicated network of similarities overlapping and criss-crossing: sometimes overall similarities, sometimes similarities of detail.

Wittgenstein called the network of overlapping and criss-crossing similarities a 'family resemblance' among instances of a concept. In recent years considerable empirical support has accumulated for this position, both for natural concepts (Rosch and Mervis, 1975) and for concepts employed scientifically in biological taxonomies (Sokal, 1974).

Rosch and Mervis (1975) measured family resemblance among instances of a concept by asking subjects to list the features of 20 instances of concepts such as furniture, fruit, and vehicles. They then determined which features were shared by the various instances. Although some features listed were shared by all members of the concept, these features did not serve to define the concept in that these features did not serve to distinguish between instances and non-instances of the concept – that is to say, many non-instances also possessed these features. An example is the feature 'you eat it' listed for fruits, which clearly applies also to many non-fruits. When more specific features were considered – the type of features that might be suitable candidates for a necessary and sufficient criterion of membership – it was found that these features were not shared by all instances of the concept. Rosch and Mervis (1975: p. 580) comment:

> The salient attribute structure of these categories tended to reside, not in criterial features common to all members of the category which distinguished those members from all others, but in a large number of attributes true of some, but not all, category members.

The notion of family resemblance breaks with the classical theory of concepts in that it denies that concepts have necessary and sufficient features that define the instances of the concept. But there is another important aspect of family resemblance also. The features that create the family resemblance structure are highly correlated. Given one feature, it is possible to predict the very likely occurrence of other features. Thus, for example, wings and feathers are features of birds and they are highly correlated; the presence of one is a very reliable guide to the presence of the other. On the other hand, the combination of wings and fur is very unlikely. Rosch (1978) has argued that the objects in the world possess, in general, high correlational structure (see also Garner, 1974). The human information processing system is, as we shall see, highly sensitive to the presence of correlated features. There is considerable gain to be made from this. The presence of one attribute can be used to predict the presence of other correlated attributes if, for some reason, information about these other attributes is not directly available, as might happen when the input that an organism receives is 'noisy' for some reason. This type of inferential process could greatly speed decision-making by an organism about the implications of stimulus information.

Prototypicality

Rosch and Mervis also obtained another measure for the instances of a concept by asking their subjects to rate how typical or representative of the concept any instance was. Subjects were quite willing to assign such ratings to the instances. A typical example is that a subject would rate an orange as a more typical fruit than a melon. Rosch and Mervis found that there was a high correlation between the ratings of typicality and the family resemblance scores. They called this the *prototypicality effect*. The high correlation between measures of family resemblance and measures of prototypicality suggests that an instance of a concept is judged to be more typical of the concept to the extent that it shares features with other instances and vice versa. There are other effects of typicality also. Both Rips, Shoben and Smith (1973) and Rosch (1973) have shown that typical instances of a concept can be identified as instances more quickly than less typical instances. This finding has been replicated many times for a wide variety of concepts. The usual experimental procedure is to present subjects with the name of a target concept, such as BIRD and then to present a variety of words, some of which are bird names and some not. The subject simply has to judge as quickly as possible whether the named entity is an instance of the target concept or not. The reaction times of the subject's responses are measured. For instances of the concept, reaction time in making a decision is a function of the typicality of the instance – the more typical the instance is, the more quickly is the judgement that it belongs to the concept.

The prototypicality effect is another piece of evidence that weakens the model of concepts contained in the classical theory. According to the classical theory there are necessary and sufficient conditions that *define* whether or not an instance is a member of a concept. Since all instances supposedly possess these features there is no reason to propose that any one instance is a better exemplar of the concept than any other instance. The finding that there are better and worse exemplars of a concept is an embarrassment for the classical theory. Although the effects of prototypicality and family resemblance do not disprove that concepts have necessary and sufficient features (it would be possible, for example, for concepts to be defined by necessary and sufficient features and for prototypicality to be determined by other non-criterial features), such effects render necessary and sufficient features as less than centrally relevant to a psychological theory of concepts.

The prototype theory of concepts has come to replace the classical theory as the dominant theory of the mental representation of concepts. The prototype theory emphasizes that instances of a concept will vary in the extent to which they are 'good instances' as a function of family resemblance. This view leads to an interesting testable prediction. Suppose a subject were to be taught a concept by being exposed to instances of the concept that varied in their typicality except that the subject is never exposed to the most typical instance. Once the concept has been learnt the subject is then shown the most typical instance. Will it be recognized as an instance of the concept? The prototype theory clearly predicts that it would, by virtue of the fact that the most typical instance will have a high degree of family resemblance to the instances already encountered.

In a series of studies Posner and Keele (1968, 1970) examined this issue. They first generated a set of four random nine-dot patterns, examples of which are shown in figure 4.2. Each pattern was given a name. These patterns were termed the prototypes. For each pattern, four distortions of the original prototype were created. These had the same name as the prototype. Subjects were then presented with the 16 distorted patterns and had to learn to categorize them into four piles reflecting the concept names. After the subjects could do this perfectly they were presented with a further set of patterns to sort. This set included the old distortions, some new distortions, and it also included the original prototypes. The subjects made some errors, even with the old patterns (random dot patterns are not the easiest thing in the world to categorize). Of most importance, they made significantly fewer errors with the prototypes than with the new distortions. Clearly, the subjects had learned about the prototypes even though they had not studied them explicitly.

Further research by Homa and his associates (Homa and Chambliss,

Prototype A Prototype B

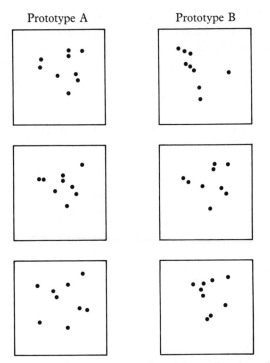

Figure 4.2 *Two random-dot prototypes together with two distortions of each prototype similar to the stimuli used by Posner and Keele (1968). (After Posner, 1969.)*

1975; Homa, Cross, Cornell, Goldman and Schwartz, 1973) has extended
the findings of Posner and Keele (1968, 1970). Homa et al. (1973) found
that increasing the number of instances presented during the learning
phase led to an improvement in performance for the prototype and new
patterns and a deterioration in performance for the old patterns. This
suggests that as the number of instances encountered in learning increases,
the representation of the detail of particular instances becomes less discri-
minable, but the representation of the general structure of the concept
becomes more robust. Homa and Chambliss (1975) found that learning
several related categories led to better performance for the prototype and
new patterns than learning a category in isolation. This suggests that
contrast between related concepts plays an important role in concept
acquisition by highlighting what is distinctive between one concept and
another. Homa and Chambliss suggest that the prototype of a concept is
a list of the most common features that are also distinguishing features.

Basic Level of Categorization

The vast majority of everyday concepts can be organized into hierarchical
classification schemes. Figure 4.3 shows a portion of a typical hierarchical
classification scheme. As the hierarchy is ascended there is a gain in
inclusiveness but a loss in distinctiveness; COLLIE for example is a more
distinctive but less inclusive concept than DOG, which in turn is more
distinctive but less inclusive than MAMMAL or ANIMAL. However, the
changes are not uniform across levels of the hierarchy. Rosch, Mervis,
Gray, Johnson and Boyes-Braem (1976) have suggested that within a
taxonomy there is one level of categorization at which there is a large

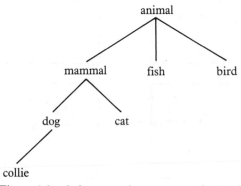

Figure 4.3 *A fragment of a taxonomy of animals.*

gain in distinctiveness relative to the category above but only a small loss relative to the category below. Rosch et al. have called the level at which there is a maximum increase in distinctiveness over the level above the *basic level of categorization*. The levels above and below are called the *superordinate* and *subordinate* level respectively. The basic level is the highest level at which objects share such things as common form, common actions, and common utility for humans.

Rosch et al. (1976) presented subjects with words that designated entities at different levels of categorization and asked them to list all the attributes they could think of for the entity designated. In one example *furniture* was the superordinate term, *chair* the basic level term, and *kitchen chair* the subordinate term. Rosch et al. found that very few attributes were listed in response to the superordinate term, a significantly greater number were listed in response to the basic level term, and only a few more were listed in response to the subordinate level term.

The notions of basic level concepts, family resemblance among instances of a concept and prototypical exemplars of a concept present a very different view of mental representation than the classical theory. In the following section we shall discuss the recent work that has utilized these notions in studying the origins of concepts.

The Origins of Concepts

From where do concepts originate? Several times in this book, it has been stressed that categorization must be a fundamental innate ability of all organisms that learn, simply on the grounds that for learning to be possible an organism must be able to treat different stimuli as equivalent. This ability requires that an organism categorize the stimuli. However, the implications of this must be considered carefully. Postulating an innate ability to categorize does not mean that an organism is born with preformed concepts; it means that an organism is born with the ability to form concepts – that is the ability to detect similarity among instances along certain dimensions and also to detect dissimilarities between these and other groups of instances. In order for such a system to be functional at birth the human infant must be equipped with a set of preferences that determine which stimulus dimensions are to form the representational basis of concepts. These preferences act as constraints on concept formation. Jackendoff (1983: p. 17) puts the point thus:

One could not learn color distinction if the mind did not provide a conceptual dimension in terms of which color distinctions could be mentally represented. It is the existence of such conceptual fields, not the precise distinctions within them that must be innately specified.

One example of the operation of a constraint is the categorical perception of speech sounds, which was discussed in chapter 2. In this case the constraint is some, as yet ill-understood, process that determines that a certain continuous dimension is perceived as two or more discrete categories. More generally, a constraint is an innate predisposition to impose some particular structure on the data of experience. Part of the task of a developmental theory of concepts is to discover what constraints determine the child's initial concepts. Constraints may sometimes dictate that particular dimensions are to be treated in particular ways – as seems to be the case for categorical perception – but more generally constraints will apply a set of principles that will be used in discovering the dimensions of a category through experience. For example, the cognitive system seems predisposed to notice correlations among features in the environment and to treat these correlations as a basis for constructing concepts. In this case, nothing about the particular dimensions is specified by the constraint but the structure to which the dimensions will conform is specified.

In attempting to study the origins of conceptual organization it is necessary to find a methodological technique suited to the abilities of infants. Infants cannot be asked to make judgements of conceptual equivalence, as is common in the study of adults. However, the same group of methodological techniques that were discussed in Chapter 2 in relation to perceptual development in infancy have also been used to good effect recently in studying the origins of concepts in infancy. In particular, the phenomena of habituation and stimulus preference can be used to determine which stimuli are treated as equivalent by infants. If stimuli are treated as equivalent by infants then the inference can be drawn that the infant has formed an abstract concept of these stimuli.

Bomba and Siqueland (1983) used the technique invented by Posner and Keele (1968) of distorting a prototype to investigate whether 3- and 4-month-old infants could form concepts from sets of dot patterns, and if so whether the concept had a prototypic structure. They first selected a prototype instance of three concepts: square, triangle, and diamond, made up of dots and then generated distortions of these exemplars. Figure 4.4 shows the prototypes and three of the distortions. Bomba and Siqueland familiarized the infants with one concept by presenting several of the distortions and then presented the previously unseen prototype of that concept together with the unseen prototype of one of the other novel

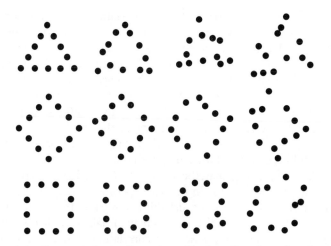

Figure 4.4 *Prototypical stimuli together with three distortions of each, used by Bomba and Siqueland (1983) to study concept acquisition.*

concepts. The issue of interest here is which of the two stimuli the infants will look at. If the prototype of the concept with which the infants have been familiarized is recognized as an instance of the concept then the infants should look longer at the instance of the novel concept. If, on the other hand, the infants have failed to form a concept during the familiarization period they should look equally often at the instances of the 'familiar' and the novel concepts. Bomba and Siqueland found that infants preferred to look at the novel instance, thus indicating that they had formed a concept from the instances and recognized the prototype as an exemplar of the concept.

The prototype theory of concepts emphasizes that there is a high degree of correlation among the attributes of the world (Rosch, 1978); wings tend to co-occur with feathers and beaks, for example. The human cognitive system is highly developed for detecting correlations and using this information in constructing representations of the world. Younger and Cohen (1983) have investigated the sensitivity of infants to the correlational structure of the world. They presented 10-month-old infants with schematic drawings of animals composed of five attributes – body, tail, feet, ears, and legs. Each attribute could have one of three values – for example webbed, club, and hoofed feet. Younger and Cohen constructed two sets of four animals and manipulated the correlation among attributes within a set. For example, in one set, body, tail, and feet were perfectly correlated in that a particular value for one of the attributes always co-occurred with particular values for the other two attributes. Infants were habituated to these stimuli and were then presented with either (1) a novel animal preserving the correlation among the attributes; (2) an animal containing familiar features but failing to preserve the correlation; and (3) a completely novel animal. Let us consider what might happen in these three conditions. If the infants had habituated to the correlated structure with which they had been presented, they should dishabituate to both the novel and the uncorrelated stimuli. If, on the other hand, the infants were responding only to the attributes presented, but not to the correlational structure among the attributes, they should dishabituate only to the novel stimuli. Younger and Cohen found that 10-month-old infants dishabituated to both the novel and the uncorrelated stimuli, thus suggesting that the infants had encoded the correlational structure among the stimuli. In further experiments they showed that 4- and 7-month-old infants do not dishabituate reliably to familiar uncorrelated stimuli. This suggests that infants may initially encode the attributes of a stimulus but not the relations of correlation among the attributes. However, by the latter part of the first year the ability to encode correlated relations has developed and is used as one of the bases of conceptual structure.

What is the significance of a sensitivity to correlated information? Naturally occurring categories tend to have correlated attributes and there is evidence from experiments of adults learning artificial categories that correlated attributes are a common means of forming categories (Medin, 1983). Correlational information may be of critical significance because it provides a basis for using one feature to infer others. This, in turn, provides a basis for primitive explanations of category structure (Murphy and Medin, 1985).

Children's ability to differentiate among everyday concepts during the second year has been demonstrated by Ross (1980). Children aged between 12 and 24 months were first familiarized with multiple examples of food in one experimental condition and of furniture in another. When children were presented with a novel instance of the category with which they had been familiarized and an instance of the unfamiliar category they looked more and reached out more at the instance of the novel category. Other techniques of measurement, especially sequential touching of similar objects among a larger group of mixed objects (Nelson, 1973; Ricciuti, 1965; Starkey, 1981; Sugarman, 1981), have also been used to infer the presence of concepts during the second year. In this procedure young children are given objects to play with and their spontaneous manipulation of the objects is observed. Ricciuti (1965), for example, presented a collection of dolls and cubes to 18-month-olds and asked the infants to 'fix them all up'. The infants touched the dolls in turn, passing over the cubes. Using the same technique Nelson (1973),

Starkey (1981), and Sugarman (1981) showed that infants from 9 months onwards sequentially touched objects in one category after another.

Research with slightly older children has shown that the distinction between superordinate, basic, and subordinate concepts is also applicable to the child's conceptual organization. Mervis and Crisafi (1982) taught 2-, 4-, and 5-year-old children superordinate, basic, and subordinate categories of abstract figures that were defined by their shape. The superordinate categories were angular and curved figures. The basic level categories had similar overall shapes. The subordinate categories differed only in where a detail was placed within the overall shapes. Mervis and Crisafi hypothesized that the degree of differentiation between categories would determine the ease of acquisition. A category is highly differentiated when the members of that category are very similar to each other but not similar to members of other categories at the same level. Mervis and Crisafi found that basic level categories were easiest to learn. The superordinate categories were easier to learn than the subordinate ones, in line with the hypothesis that degree of differentiation determines ease of acquisition. However, a certain caution is called for in generalizing this result to natural categories; this study directly manipulated the concepts, so that the superordinate categories were more differentiated than the subordinate ones; it is not evident that this applies to natural hierarchies.

The evidence from recent research on infants suggests that the way in which infants form concepts is essentially similar to the way in which adults do. It is unlikely that the principles of categorization are learnt; more likely that as Quinn and Eimas (1986) suggest, categorization is part of the innate architecture of cognition. This view is yet another of the revisions that have taken place in recent years in our assessment of children's abilities. Earlier influential studies of cognitive development in children, notably Vygotsky (1934/1962) and Bruner et al. (1966) had stressed that children's concepts are different in kind from those of adults. However, this view was very much the product of the *type of research* on concepts that earlier studies conducted. The earlier research was influenced by the classical theory of concepts (Smith and Medin, 1981). The predominant paradigm of research was one in which the child had to discover the necessary and sufficient features that defined an arbitrary concept specified by the experimenter (in the manner of Hull's (1920) study). In a typical experiment a child might be given blocks that varied on dimensions such as colour, height, width, depth, and shape. The child would then be given a block of particular dimensions – for example, a tall red cylindrical block – and asked to find other blocks that belonged to the same category. Adults typically focus on one dimension and, in the example cited, most adults would form a category of cylindrical blocks. Children do not, however, do this. Having used one dimension to match the first block they choose, they may change the dimension used in the choice of later blocks. Vygotsky (1934/1962) called the categories formed *chain complexes*. He drew the conclusion that children's conceptual structures differ from those of adults.

While it is true that children and adults differ in the way they solve the types of task described by Vygotsky (1934/1962) and also those described by Bruner et al. (1966), it does not follow that children have different principles of conceptual organization from those of adults because the tasks used do not tap the natural process of conceptual organization. As has been discussed previously, everyday concepts are not characterized by necessary and sufficient conditions that define membership of the concept, nor are they characterized by arbitrary variation among the features of a concept. When the experimental stimuli conform to the natural structure of the world, then children have no difficulty in processing information in the same way as adults because evolution has fitted them with the cognitive constraints to do this.

Although there appears to be considerable similarity between the structure of infants' concepts and those of adults, there are differences in the amount and type of information represented in a typical adult and infant concept. In fact, it could be argued that the structural similarity provides the necessary basis of development from the child's more primitive concept to an adult's more elaborated version. As an example of what is involved here, consider the concept of a triangle. Children can recognize triangles readily; they clearly have a usable concept of a triangle. However, an adult may know a great deal about the trigonometric properties of triangles and the use of these properties in a wide variety of scientific applications that no child is likely to know about. The structural similarity of the child's and adult's concept means that the concepts of each will pick out the same set of entities in the world as instances of the concept. This provides an important basis for communication. Not only do humans categorize the world, they also communicate about this categorization through language. The process of communication will be aided to a very considerable extent if the entities to which a parent makes reference are instances of the same concept for parent and child. As the child hears and learns words, the common conceptual structures of parent and child will facilitate the child's attempts to determine the meaning of the words that are heard.

Words and Concepts

Reference, Denotation, and Sense

There are two general issues about which it is necessary to be clear in discussing words and concepts: the relation between words and concepts and the relation between words and the world.

Lyons (1977a) has drawn a useful distinction between the terms 'reference', 'denotation', and 'sense' that will help to keep clear the relation between words, concepts, and the world. Reference is the relation between an expression and the entity in the world that the expression is intended to identify. Reference is a way of describing what a speaker is doing when using words in a certain way (i.e. to refer). Thus, to take a simple example, the utterance *that's a dog* makes reference to some entity in the world and will, on different occasions, make reference to different entities.

The word used to refer to one entity of a class can also be used to refer to any entity of the class. Thus, there is a class of entities to which a word can refer. This class constitutes the word's denotation. Denotation is thus a relation between a word and the world and it is independent of particular utterances. Lyons (1977a) uses the term 'denotation' to express the relation between a word and the class of objects in the world to which it can legitimately refer. This use bypasses the role of concepts in creating representations of classes of objects. The use of the term 'denotation' in the present context will assume that classes of objects are known through the concepts we possess and, thus, the denotation of a word is the concept onto which the word is mapped. The major issue of interest as far as a word's denotation is concerned, is how the word is mapped onto the appropriate concept. This will be referred to as the process of establishing the denotation of a word. As an example let us assume that a child uses the utterance *that's a dog* (or, perhaps, just *dog*) on some occasion to refer to a cat. The child may be quite successful in the attempt to refer but has made a denotational error about the word *dog* – that is, *dog* has been mapped on to an inappropriate concept.

If we continue the example of the child who misuses *dog*, we could also enquire what concept the child had mapped the word *dog* on to. Has the child perhaps mapped the word dog on to the concept ANIMAL? If so, then the child has not failed to understand the distinction between dogs and cats but has created the wrong mapping between word and concept.

Words are related to each other in a rich variety of ways. Lyons

(1977a), for example, discusses relations of synonymy, contrast, opposition, hyponymy (the relation between a word and a superordinate word; e.g. *dog* is a hyponym of *animal*), superordination (*animal* is a superordinate of *dog*) among others. Lyons calls these various relations, relations of sense. An analysis of a word's sense is an analysis in terms of its relations with other words.

The relations of reference, denotation, and sense will help us to analyze the process by which children acquire words. The term 'word' is usually used to refer to the meaningful basic elements of a language. Words can be spoken or written. When they are written the boundaries of a word are clear because words are separated from each other by spaces. When words are spoken the boundaries are less clearly marked – we must draw on our knowledge of the language to segment the speech we hear into meaningful units. That this is not a trivial task is evident if a comparison is made between the tasks of counting the number of words written in a language we do not understand and counting the number of words spoken in the same language. The former task is extremely easy and the latter extremely difficult. This consideration of words is important to the language acquisition process. Children must segment the speech they hear into the appropriate-sized units in order to learn a language. If we were to say that a child learning language has heard words when what has been heard was a continuous stream of speech that was not understood, then, clearly, we would not have provided a good description of the stimulus input that the child has received. Accordingly, we need a term for a continuous period of speech that does not carry with it presumptions about the decomposition of the speech. The term 'utterance' is usually employed in this context.

How do Children Know What Adults are Talking About?

How do children extract words from utterances? There seem to be complementary processes at work in the input that the child receives and the way the input is processed that act jointly to simplify the child's task of extracting words from utterances. First, input to children is simplified by comparison with speech among adults. Adults talk to children more slowly, in shorter utterances, with repetition of key words, and in a higher pitch than they talk to other adults (Garnica, 1977). This makes it easier for children to identify the units (i.e. the words) that make up the utterance. Second, in conjunction with this environmental help, children selectively attend to stressed elements of the adult utterance and, to a large extent, ignore the rest (Gleitman and Wanner, 1982). Since the referential words of an utterance are typically the ones that are stressed (and repeated) in adult speech to children, this means that children will extract the major content words initially from a sentence. It is because of this selective filtering of the input that children's own initial utterances are comprised largely of content words and lack the functor words (such as articles and prepositions) that are unstressed in adult speech. It is this that gives children's speech its characteristic 'telegraphic' character in the early stages of word combination (see Chapter 7).

Even if children initially extract referential words from the input they receive, they must still be able to map the word extracted to an appropriate utterance. The communicative interaction between mother and child is regulated in a variety of ways so that the expressions used by the mother to refer to entities in the world are understood by the child as references to just those entities and not some others. Imagine a child of about 1 year in interaction with his or her mother. The mother wishes to name some object for the child. If she simply names the object, the child may not register the particular word-referent relation either because of inattention or not knowing which referent is being named. From the mother's point of view the situation is problematic because her utterance may never succeed in its intention unless she adopts some special measures to ensure that it does. The most basic requirement for a child to map a word to an appropriate referent is that the attention of both mother and child be focused on the same entity when the mother names it. The most basic form of joint attention is when two people look at the same object (visual orientation). Studies of the development of joint attention between mothers and infants have revealed that the achievement of visual co-orientation is initially due largely to the efforts of the mother. Collis and Schaffer (1975) and Collis (1977) have shown that with infants of 10 months, mothers allowed their attention to be directed by the infants' behaviour and continually monitored the infants' focus of visual attention. Scaife and Bruner (1975) have shown that, provided eye-contact is initially established, infants will follow another person's line of gaze. Murphy and Messer (1977) have shown that mothers use pointing to direct an infant's attention from the time the infant is 9 months of age. These studies demonstrate the presence of behavioural acts of reference in mother-infant interaction by the end of the infant's first year. There is a close link between behavioural reference and linguistic reference in the sense that the interactive pattern of behavioural reference serves to support linguistic reference in its early stages.

Murphy and Messer (1977), in their laboratory study of joint attention, reported that 423 out of 428 points were accompanied by maternal vocalizations, and 40 per cent of these vocalizations consisted of naming the object pointed to. Naturalistic studies have also shown the close relation between joint attention and naming. Ninio and Bruner (1978) reported data from spontaneous sequences of picture-book reading. Several findings are of interest in their study. Naming by the mother usually occurred while looking at books with the child. Within this regular ritual of interaction other regularities were apparent. The mother usually ensured that the child was attending by uttering a vocative such as *look*; then a query, *what's that?*; then a name, such as *it's a dog*; and finally feedback if the infant participated. This pattern of interaction was observed even when the infant was as young as 8 months, even though no linguistic behaviour could have been expected. However, the mother continued to provide this supporting framework of social interaction for several months. As the infant's participation grew, so did the demands on participation.

In a situation such as that outlined by Ninio and Bruner, it is probable that the referential use of language will develop through participation in the ritual naming game of the mother. The child does not need, at the initial stages, to know that there is a symbolic relation between word and object. He or she need simply learn the words as participating responses associated with particular stimuli. Such learning will serve to create the beginnings of a semantic network of words. At first the mapping between these words and the concepts with which they are associated may be limited to expressing a single functional relation. Thus, referential words may be used initially exclusively to request the object to which they refer (McShane, 1980). However, this constraint does not last. Toward the latter part of the second year, naming is well-established as a context-free behaviour and a symbolic relation between words and objects has been achieved. This development will be discussed below.

The accounts discussed place considerable emphasis on the environmental support that help the child establish a referential relation between word and object. The basic form of environmental support to which they appeal is the look-and-name routine – more formally known as ostensive definition. Objections have been raised to ostensive definition as a means of learning names (Quine, 1960). The usual objection is that even if an ostensive definition is provided, we can not be sure that the child assumes that the word refers to the object and not to its colour, or one of its parts or some more global event.

There are two ways round the problem raised by Quine. One is to accept that ostensive definition could not possibly work as a means of teaching names because of the indefinite number of potential interpretations. If that is the case then some alternative means of mapping words on to concepts must be proposed. To date no convincing alternative has been proposed. The second way round the objection, and the one that has gained increasing theoretical popularity in recent years, is to demonstrate that although there are many potential interpretations of what the referent of a word is, the child, in fact, does not get into a muddle about this because the cognitive system is constrained in the interpretations it makes. Specifically, it is constrained to treat ostensive definitions as names for whole objects. Children do not have to eliminate the various logical possibilities raised by Quine because they never consider them in the first place. This claim is essentially a further claim about the architecture of cognition.

If the child's default assumption is that an ostensive definition makes reference to an object, then it would seem that the adult input is maximally sensitive to this assumption. Ninio (1980), in a study of 40 mother–infant dyads, found that ostensive definitions were used almost exclusively to name objects: 95 per cent of ostensive definitions referred to the whole object depicted rather than to its parts or attributes. Further, when mothers named parts of objects, they avoided misunderstanding of the level of reference either by naming the part immediately after naming the whole or by including a reference to the whole in the definition of the part.

One-Word Speech and the Development of Reference

Two primary methods are used to study children's words. In the early stages of development observational research has been widely employed because the data of interest – words – are spontaneously generated with a relatively high frequency. The observations have varied from naturalistic – typically diary studies reported by parents who were linguists or psychologists with a special interest in language – to task-based in which mother and child are asked to perform some task and their spontaneous behaviour in doing so was recorded. The primary purpose of these studies has been to chart the nature and use of the child's earliest words. The observational method has yielded a rich harvest of data in the area of language development. However, it has some limitations. It is not always possible to tell, using this method, whether or not a child's use of a word is the same as an adult's. In order to determine whether the boundaries of reference, denotation and sense for a particular word are the same between children and adults, it is necessary to obtain more systematic and more controlled data from children. For this reason, observational evidence needs to be complemented by experimental evidence in order to obtain a soundly based account of the process of lexical development.

Children begin to use single-word utterances during their second year. During the early months of word learning the child's vocabulary may be limited to a small number of words. However, sometime from the middle of the second year onwards there is a noticeable increase in vocabulary size, shortly followed by the beginnings of combinatorial speech (Halliday, 1975; McShane and Whittaker, 1983; Nelson, 1973). Figure 4.5 shows the average rate of vocabulary increase up to 50 words for 18 children studied by Nelson (1973). It is evident from these data that vocabulary growth is not a simple cumulative affair with more words being added at a steady rate. At a certain point there is a rapid increase in vocabulary. Other studies have reported similar findings (McShane and Whittaker, 1983). This sudden increase requires explanation over and above the natural accumulation of more words.

In order to discover in more detail what is happening during the one-word stage it is necessary to determine how children *use* words and what particular representational system is likely to support such usage. An examination of use is important because children do not necessarily use a word initially in the same way that adults do. For example, in the early stages of language development, words such as *here* and *there* are common but are used exclusively as accompaniments to an exchange of objects and rarely, if ever, to indicate location (McShane, 1980). At this stage of development, *here* and *there* are terms used in the process of particular social interactions. There is a small variety of words of this type. They are most commonly used as part and parcel of the process of social interaction. Other typical examples are *hi*, *bye-bye*, and *no*. These words

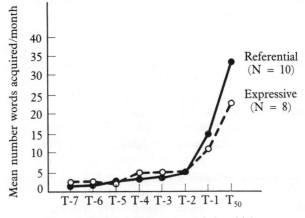

Figure 4.5   *Rate of acquisition of first 50 words for referential and expressive speaking styles reported by Nelson (1973).*

do not represent the world in the sense that they do not map on to conceptual categories. Rather they serve an expressive and personal interactive purpose. Nelson (1973) has reported that children in the early stages of language development can be divided into two groups on the basis of the relative balance of expressive and referential words in their vocabularies. The group she called 'expressive speakers' had a 50/50 balance of expressive and referential words in their early vocabulary. In the group she called 'referential speakers', about 80 per cent of the children's words referred to entities and only about 20 per cent had an expressive function. As development proceeds, the number of referential words increases dramatically, while the number of expressive words increases only very slowly. A small number of words is, apparently, sufficient for the basics of social interaction whereas an increasingly large vocabulary develops to encode the child's conceptual representation of the world.

Referential words primarily encode a relation between word and object. That relation has been expressed in various ways; words have been said to symbolize, signify, or stand for the object to which they refer (see Lyons, 1977a, ch. 4 for a discussion). Whichever term is adopted, the basic idea is that a word can be used in communication to refer to an object or to represent a concept of an object or class of objects. Here, we shall say that words are symbols for objects; that there is a symbolic relation between a referential word and its referent.

The developmental issue that now arises is how this symbolic relation is established. One answer to this is to argue that it does not need to be established; that it is innately given. Although it is difficult to prove that this is *not* the case, there are reasons for suspecting that symbolization is not innate (although in some sense, the capacity for symbolization must derive from innate abilities). One of the major reasons for arguing that the symbolic relation between word and object has an important developmental component is that the earliest uses of referential words appear quite different from later uses. Many observers of children's language have been reluctant to treat early reference (i.e. in the early part of the child's second year) as being on the same representational plane as later reference. The major source of this reluctance is that the child does not appear freely to control his or her use of words to refer or to communicate. At best, the use of referential words occurs sporadically and idiosyncratically. When asked to name things, the child will rarely respond at this stage. This can be contrasted with a child towards the end of the second year who will readily name objects on request and will use an object's name spontaneously to refer to that object.

At present there is no satisfactory answer to the nature of the earliest representational relation between words and objects. There does not seem to be a behavioural test or experiment that might settle the issue. Based on my own observations (McShane, 1980), I have also been reluctant to regard very early reference as qualitatively similar to later reference. I have proposed that words may be initially associated with an object and elicited as associative responses to that object in particular contexts, without the child conceptualizing the relation between word and object as one of symbolization – that is to say, the child does not regard the word as a word that can be used independently of a particular object to refer to that object. If that is the case then somehow or other the child must make the transition from association to symbolization. That transition point seems to occur when the rapid vocabulary increase depicted in Figure 4.5 occurs.

A rapid increase in vocabulary is characterized by a rapid acquisition of one particular type of word: names for objects. From a behavioural point of view, the child's behaviour at the time of vocabulary increase seems unequivocally to be naming whereas the same utterance in the same context some months earlier would not have produced this unequivocal impression. Furthermore, vocabulary continues to increase rapidly from this point on but after the initial burst of names there now begin to appear words for attributes and for actions and also the earliest word combinations. This pattern of development suggests that a major representational change occurs that initially leads to the development of naming and subsequently to the beginnings of two-word utterances. I have proposed that that change can be characterized as an insight that words are not simply associated with objects but also symbolize objects. The details of the argument can be found elsewhere (McShane, 1979; 1980). Suffice it to say here that by the end of the second year language is definitely established as a means of symbolizing entities and the beginnings have been made of a grammatical system that will symbolize the rich variety of relations among entities.

Denotation

Reference is a way of using words; denotation is the concept on to which the word is mapped. When a child hears a word how does he or she establish its denotation? Brown (1958: p. 14) addressed this issue as follows:

> The most deliberate part of first-language teaching is the business of telling a child what each thing is called. We ordinarily speak of *the* name of a thing as if there were just one, but in fact, of course, every referent has

many names. The dime in my pocket is not only a *dime*. It is also *money*, a *metal object*, and *thing*, and, moving to subordinates, it is a *1952 dime*, in fact a *particular 1952 dime* with a unique pattern of scratches, discolorations, and smooth places. When such a object is named for a very young child how is it called? It may be named *money* or *dime* but probably not *metal object*, *thing*, *1952 dime*, or *particular 1952 dime*. The dog out on the lawn is not only a *dog* but is also a *boxer*, a *quadruped*, an *animate being*; it is the *landlord's dog*, named *Prince*. How will it be identified for a child? Sometimes it will be called a *dog*, sometimes *Prince*, less often a *boxer*, and almost never a *quadruped*, or *animate being*.

Brown argued that, when seeking to tell a child what something is named, parents provide names that are most functionally appropriate for children. Thus, all coins may initially be called *money* because, to a child, differences in value are not yet salient. Brown argued that for most objects there is a referential term that has greater behavioural significance than other terms. Thus, for most practical purposes the set of dogs represents a set of entities to all of whom the same behaviours would be appropriate, while the set of animals does not generally do so. Thus *dog* is a more functionally appropriate term for a child than *animal*.

Implicit in Brown's thesis is the claim that the child is most likely to infer that the denotation of a word is a category at a level of functional appropriateness. This view accords well with the more recent work on basic level categorization by Rosch et al. (1976), which suggests that there is a 'natural' level of categorization that contains a balance of increased similarity over that obtained with a superordinate category and increased contrast over that obtained with subordinate categories. It might therefore be expected that these features would aid categorization by children and that therefore they would find it easiest and most natural to map words and concepts at this level. There is a variety of evidence to support this view. Rosch et al. (1976) have shown that on a categorization task, children had little difficulty sorting basic-level categories into a conventional taxonomy but failed to sort superordinate categories in this way and, instead, formed categories akin to Vygotsky's (1934/1962) 'chain complexes'. Rosch et al. (1976) also conducted an analysis of one child's initial vocabulary and showed that the great majority of early words were basic-level terms. Horton and Markman (1980) examined how children aged 4–6 would learn artificial animal categories. They presented children with both exemplars and definitions of basic level and superordinate categories. The categories in question were animals from a strange planet – i.e. ordinary animals to which the experimenters had applied the creative licence common in science fiction. Children were familiarized with instances of two categories in which they either saw exemplars or both saw exemplars and heard verbal descriptions of the category. In each case, half of the categories were basic level and half were superordinate. The children were then presented with a range of further animals, some of which belonged in the category and some of which did not. They were asked to sort these. Horton and Markman found that for the basic level, the addition of linguistic information led to no improvement in performance over the presentation of exemplars alone. However, for superordinate categories, the 5- and 6-year-olds benefited considerably from the provision of linguistic information. Horton and Markman suggest that superordinate categories may sometimes be learned in this explicit way.

An assumption, by the child, that names denote concepts at the basic level of categorization is a powerful means of ensuring that basic-level names, which is mostly what the child hears, are mapped to the appropriate concepts. However, there is also a potential cost to such a constraint. Basic-level concepts are part of a taxonomic hierarchy. The rigid application of such a constraint would mean that children would never learn the names for concepts above and below the basic level.

It is obvious that children do not apply such a constraint rigidly to word learning, since they do, in fact, learn names for superordinate and subordinate categories. Yet they do not do so easily. Young children learn very few words that denote superordinate concepts (Markman, 1989) and will frequently interpret superordinate terms as basic level terms. There is also evidence from class-inclusion studies (Inhelder and Piaget, 1959/1964) that children find it difficult to understand the principles of taxonomic categorization until middle childhood.

 How then do children manage to learn names for superordinate concepts given their difficulties with such concepts and given also the constraint of assuming that names refer to basic-level concepts? In outline, the answer would seem to be that children develop a rich network of relations among their concepts, and this network paves the way for taxonomic categorization, which is a relatively late acquisition. Thus the assumption that names refer to basic-level concepts is under continual stress during the process of language acquisition.

The best example of this process in relation to taxonomic categorization was provided in an experiment by Callanan and Markman (1982). They drew a distinction between collections and classes. For example an oak is a tree, but it may also be part of a forest. The former is a class relation; the latter is a collection relation. The distinction can be brought to bear even more closely on class relations. A ball is a toy, but it may also be part of a collection of toys. The former is a class relation (and it is also an abstract conceptual relation), the latter is a collection relation (and it is a concrete physical relation). Callanan and Markman showed that 2- to 4-year-old children frequently interpreted class-inclusion questions as questions about collections. Thus, for example, a child would accept that a group of toys could be called *toys* but would not necessarily accept that each individual toy could be called a *toy* rather than its more specific name, such as *doll*.

Interpreting class-inclusion questions as collection questions does not, of course, help a child to learn about class inclusion. But it may serve another function that, ultimately, will aid the construction of a taxonomy of concepts and of the appropriate sense relations among the words that denote concepts at different levels of the hierarchy. That function is that having terms for collections breaches the constraint that names refer to basic level concepts without challenging it directly in the way that acquiring a name for a superordinate term would. Thus, by the time children succeed in constructing a taxonomic hierarchy of concepts the constraint that operates in favour of basic-level mapping between words and concepts may have all but vanished.

Markman (1985; 1989) has suggested that mass nouns may aid children in learning class-inclusion relations. Many superordinate terms of English (and of other languages also; see Markman, 1985) are mass nouns: for example *furniture*, *money*, and *jewellery*. The linguistic implication of this is that the superordinate term does not directly replace the basic level term in reference. Although we can substitute *toy* for *ball*, and say *a ball is a toy*, we cannot substitute *furniture* for *chair* and say *a chair is a furniture* but must instead say something like *a chair is a piece of furniture*. Markman (1985, 1989) suggests that by using mass nouns to refer to superordinate categories, languages may help speakers learn hierarchical relations between the superordinate and basic level categories. Markman (1985) used a puppet to teach 3- to 4-year-old children novel 'puppet' words, such as *veb*, for both mass and count nouns. In the mass noun condition the children were shown items such as bathroom supplies and told 'here are some pieces of veb'. In the count noun condition the children were told 'here are some vebs'. After hearing the word used several times, always consistently as either a mass or a count noun, the children were tested on their ability to distinguish category exemplars from distracters. The children were then re-trained and re-tested. Markman found that the children who heard mass nouns were better able to discriminate category exemplars from distracters, especially after the second training session.

One possible way in which children may be helped to construct both superordinate categories and lexical terms for these categories is through verbal definitions. The role of definitions in lexical acquisition has not been studied intensively. However, it may be recalled that Horton and Markman (1980) found that the acquisition of superordinate categories by 4- to 6-year-old children was facilitated by explicit verbal information about the criteria for category membership. Such information had no beneficial effect on the acquisition of basic-level categories. Thus, the developmental processes by which basic- and superordinate-level concepts, and their labels, are acquired may be somewhat different. Superordinate concepts and labels seem to arise out of prior conceptual and lexical achievements. Basic level concepts and labels seem to arise out of the organization of the basic cognitive architecture and the child's initial tendency to create basic level concepts and to match names to these concepts.

There is one apparent problem with this line of interpretation. It has often been claimed that when children initially learn words, the extensions of these words are much wider for the child than for the adult. Thus, a child might learn the word *dog* as a name not just for dogs but for all four-legged animals. In this case the child has apparently mapped the word *dog* to a concept that is certainly not a basic level concept; it seems in fact that the concept approximates to the superordinate concept ANIMAL. If this is the case then it would pose severe problems for the type of developmental relation between words and concepts proposed above. We shall now turn to an examination of this issue and the theories of lexical development to which the issue has given rise.

Overextensions have played a prominent role in theories of the development of word meaning. Clark (1973) was among the first to highlight the role of overextensions in the development of word meaning. Her Semantic Feature Theory can be seen as the reference point for modern theories of the development of word meaning. Clark argued, based largely on the fact that children overextend words, that the meaning of a word was learnt component by component. Thus, a child on hearing the word *dog* might initially represent the meaning of the word as a small number of component features such as [+ animate] and [+ four-legged]. Such a representation would capture more than dogs; it would capture all four-legged animals. Clark argued that such word acquisition strategies were consistent with the data on overextensions.

According to Semantic Feature Theory, the child gradually learns the meaning of a word by learning the set of features that characterizes a word's meaning. Lexical development is regarded as a process of adding more features of meaning to the lexical entry for the word until the child's combination of features corresponds to the adult's combination of features.   Semantic Feature Theory was influential in the study of lexical development because it gave a precise account of how the acquisition of meaning might develop across the complete range of a child's vocabulary. The theory could be applied to almost any area of the lexicon. Moreover, it yielded readily testable predictions and thus generated a wide range of experimental evidence. These experiments substantially increased the understanding of the process of lexical development but they also, ultimately, served to undermine the theory that had spawned them (Richards, 1979).

Semantic Feature Theory included the following three assumptions: (1) word meaning can be represented as a set of semantic features that are learnt one by one with the most general features being acquired first; (2) for contrasting words (such as *big – small* or *deep – shallow*) one word of the pair can be used neutrally to refer to the dimension and this word is acquired first; and (3) words are initially overextended because their limited semantic representation defines a wider range of referents than is the case for adult speakers.

In his extensive review of the literature on Semantic Feature Theory, Richards (1979) concluded that the basic assumptions of the theory were not supported. In particular, there is extensive evidence that indicates that the child's initial names for objects are learnt at what Rosch et al. (1976) have called the basic level of categorization. In a model of development that relates the development of word meaning to the development of concepts, this is exactly what would be predicted, as earlier sections of this chapter have emphasized. However, it is not too surprising that a closer theoretical integration between words and concepts was not provided because our understanding of conceptual structure was less advanced when Clark first proposed Semantic Feature Theory than it is now.

As has been pointed out, a major empirical basis of Semantic Feature Theory was the evidence on overextensions of words during the early stages of language development. Can the data on overextensions be reconciled with the view that words map on to concepts that are essentially similar in structure and extension to adult concepts? In fact, there is much less discrepancy to be explained here than might at first seem to be the case. Overextensions are not especially prevalent in children's speech, although they do occur. In discussing and evaluating the evidence on overextensions it is important to be clear about the nature of the data base and the line of inference from this data base to the child's representation of word meaning. As McShane and Dockrell (1983) have pointed out, many reports of overextensions fail to distinguish between persistent overextensions and occasional or even single occurrences. Occasional occurrences of overextensions tell us very little, if anything, about the semantic representation of a word. They are most probably due to the inaccessibility of the correct word at the time of speaking and the consequent adoption of an associated word to meet the needs of communication. In order to establish that a word used in an overextended way is the result of an overextended representation there should be evidence that a word overextended in production is also overextended in comprehension. In comprehension there is no communicative demand, simply a demand to select the correct referents for a word. If a word is overextended in comprehension, then this is solid evidence for an overextended conceptual representation. A number of studies have examined this issue.

Thomson and Chapman (1977) studied the comprehension of words that children spontaneously overextended in production. They found that not all words overextended in production were also overextended in comprehension, although some were. Kay and Anglin (1982) carried out a somewhat different study. They assessed 2-year-olds' production and comprehension of five words and then trained each child to produce one word that had been previously comprehended but not produced. The training was done by pairing the word with a prototypical referent. Subsequently the child's comprehension and production were assessed for eight referents and eight non-referents of this word. Half of the referents had been judged (by adults) to be central (i.e. prototypical) referents and half to be peripheral. Half of the non-referents were perceptually similar to the prototype and half were dissimilar. Kay and Anglin found that children often *underextended* the words to legitimate referents – that is, they did not always use the words to label these referents. There was a greater tendency to do this for peripheral than for central category members, which may, of course, have reflected the children's current conceptual organization of the category. Kay and Anglin also found overextensions to the non-referents, especially to those that were perceptually similar. The pattern of underextension–overextension occurred for both comprehension and production but there was a twist: overextensions occurred more frequently and underextensions occurred less frequently in comprehension than in production. In other words, the mapping from word to concept was wider when assessed by comprehension for both legitimate but peripheral category members and illegitimate but perceptually similar (along some dimensions) non-category members.

There are many interpretations that could be placed on the Kay and Anglin results but it is difficult to be definite in the conclusions one draws without further evidence. Too few studies have studied both comprehension and production with respect to overextensions and underextensions. However, with that caution in mind, the following pointers seem to be contained in the results. First, the more prototypical the referent, the more likely it is that a word, not previously used for that referent but used for the conceptual prototype, will be extended to include the referent. This no doubt reflects the fact that children map words on to concepts and not on to single instances. Second, the fact that words are not always extended to include the peripheral instances of a concept suggests that the concept itself may not be fully developed but may instead be concentrated around prototypical exemplars. It must be remembered that children are simultaneously learning words and elaborating their conceptual representation of the world. Peripheral instances of a concept are less likely to be included in the initial representation of a concept – this almost by definition. Third, children are, if anything, more conservative in the entities that they are willing to call by a particular label, than in the entities that they are willing to accept a label refers to. This is a non-obvious result, which suggests that conceptual representations may be actively changed while words are being learnt (see Bowerman, 1987; Karmiloff-Smith, 1986). The conservatism of production reflects existing conceptual representations; when a concept is used to generate a label, as in production, only existing instances of the concept can be appropriately labelled. By contrast the greater radicalism of comprehension may reflect the reverse process; when a label is used to access a concept, the prototypical representations can be used to predict new instances that should possibly be included, along one of the relevant dimensions of the concept. This would lead to fewer underextensions but also to a greater number of overextensions in comprehension. False extensions will presumably be weeded out by various processes, such as the later provision of alternative more suitable words that suggest another concept for the instance in question or by the setting of boundaries on the concept by other means that lead to the exclusion of the instance from that concept.

The setting of boundaries on the extension of a concept, and thereby on the extension of a word mapped on to that concept is an issue that must be addressed by theories of concept development and of word meaning. Barrett (1978) was one of the first to raise the issue in the context of lexical development. Barrett's discussion focuses almost exclusively on words without reference to the concepts on to which they are mapped. This has been a common feature of discussions of lexical development. However, implicitly, the claims made can be extended to the concepts on to which words are mapped. Barrett argued that the key features in establishing a word's denotation are those that serve to contrast a word from related words. Thus, the denotation of a word such as *dog* is not acquired by determining the prototypical features of dogs but by learning the relevant contrasts between dogs and other animals such as cats and bears. Barrett's initial hypothesis was that children represent the meaning of referential words as a set of contrasts between one word and other related words. An example he offers is that horses have hooves while dogs have none.

As presented in its original form, the theory emphasizes the importance of contrasts to the exclusion of all else. However, a more plausible version of the theory was offered by Barrett (1982) in which a word is initially mapped on to a prototypical representation; the more salient prototypical features are then used to group the word with other words that share similar features; then contrastive features are used to differentiate between words. This is one version of the Contrastive Hypothesis of word meaning. The hypothesis has been extended as a general principle covering all of lexical development by Clark (1983, 1987). Just as her Semantic Feature Hypothesis heavily influenced research on lexical development in the 1970s, so the Contrastive Hypothesis is exerting a strong influence on this research in the 1980s.

Gathercole (1987) has pointed out that there are two versions of the Contrastive Hypothesis. The first, which I shall call the Restricted Contrastive Hypothesis, is essentially the version outlined above and is designed to account for how the boundaries of a word are determined such that incorrect referents are excluded from the extension of a word. In this version of the hypothesis the words in question all occur at the same level of representation – typically at the basic level. The second version of the hypothesis, which I shall call the Extended Contrastive Hypothesis, applies the principle of contrast beyond object words and across levels of representation. Thus, for example, Clark (1983: p. 802) states:

> The word *dog* contrasts with the word for other animal categories at the same level of abstraction, for example *cow, horse*, and *sheep*. It also contrasts with both superordinate and subordinate terms, like *animal, canine, terrier*, or *Pekingese*. To go further, the term *dog* for adults, at some level or another, contrasts with every other term known to them.

The Extended Contrastive Hypothesis takes on board all the relations of sense discussed by Lyons (1977a). It will be recalled that Lyons defines sense as the meaning relations that a word contracts with other words. In Lyons's theory contrast is only one of these relations; in Clark's Extended Contrastive Hypothesis contrast is *the* relation.

One implication of the Contrastive Hypothesis is that when children learn a new word, it will be pre-empted from overlapping with existing words and will have to find its place in some gap; it will have to map on to a concept that does not already have a word mapped on to it. However,

Gathercole (1987) has observed that the data on lexical acquisition do not support this position. Overlapping extensions in children's use of object words are not uncommon initially (Merriman, 1986a, 1986b) but become less so later in development. If there is a principle of non-overlapping labels, then this principle would seem to be derived from experience with the lexicon rather than being a primitive mechanism used to guide acquisition. The results of Merriman (1986b) suggest that pre-emption comes into play once a basic lexicon exists; it is not the process by which the initial lexicon is acquired. He taught 2.5-, 4-, and 6-year-olds a nonsense name such as *pilson* for nonsense object – i.e., artefacts that exhibited a particular set of characteristics. The child was then shown a set of probe objects each of which shared some characteristic with the original trained object. The child was asked to pick out the pilsons and the extension of the term was noted. Subsequently a second nonsense name was taught for one of the objects to which the original name had been extended. After this the child was tested on the extensions of both nonsense names by being asked to pick out the referents for each from the set of probe objects. The Contrastive Hypothesis would predict that once children had learnt the second nonsense name they should no longer apply the first to that object. However, Merriman found that younger children were less likely to treat the two trained words as mutually exclusive than older children.

There seem to be two general conclusions suggested by these results. The first is that the use of contrast as an organizational principle for lexical acquisition emerges during the course of language development rather than being the primary driving force behind the system. The second is that contrast cannot therefore be the sole basis that determines the extension of a word; from the beginning of referential speech children use the majority of words appropriately and would seem to establish, without noticeable difficulty, the correct denotational representation for the words they hear. The mechanism for this is less likely to be the application of a principle of contrast than the mapping of words on to concepts that, as has been argued earlier, are mostly unambiguous in the entities they categorize.

Although younger children do not adhere very strongly to a principle of pre-emption, older children seem to do so (Au and Markman, 1987; Carey and Bartlett, 1978; Dockrell and Campbell, 1986; Markman and Wachtel, 1988). Markman and Wachtel (1988) examined what occurs when children are presented with a novel label for a concept for which they already have a label. When presented with a choice between a familiar object (for which the child had a label) and a novel object, as possible referents of the novel label, children interpreted the novel label as a term for the novel rather than the familiar object. In further studies Markman and Wachtel removed the novel object so that children were now faced with a potential label for an object for which they already had a label. Under these conditions children tended to interpret the term as either a term for a part of the object or as a term for the substance from which the object was made. Thus, existing terms in the lexicon tend to pre-empt new terms from being mapped to the same concept. The operation of a principle of pre-emption would help explain further why children initially have difficulty learning superordinate terms for objects. The cognitive system must remain flexible enough to accommodate the overlaps that do occur among words, in spite of a principle of pre-emption. The system must also work with several different types of information. For example, grammatical information will set its own constraints on whether or not a word labels an entity or a relation, or an action, or labels nothing at all such as the so-called functor words. It is worth noting, in this context, that all the experiments cited thus far have tested for constraints on mapping words to concepts within the constraints imposed by the grammatical structure of the language. That is to say, phrases such as *this is a* . . . imply on grammatical grounds that an entity is being labelled.

The words that children hear are embedded in utterances and, in various ways, these utterances themselves provide clues as to the type of concept on to which a word should be mapped. Brown (1957) and Dockrell and McShane (1990) have shown that 3- to 5-year-old children draw on their knowledge of grammatical information in order to map a word to a concept. Dockrell and McShane showed that the feature of plural inflection on a novel word led a child to select a picture that contained several novel referents rather than a picture that contained a single novel referent. However, when the same inflection, -*s*, was used on the same words but the words had the grammatical function of verbs, children interpreted the words as referring to actions. The use of syntactic information to constrain meaning can be detected even earlier than 3 years. Both Gelman and Taylor (1984) and Katz, Baker and Macnamara (1974) found that 2-year-olds interpret unfamiliar names for objects differently depending upon whether they are labelled with proper or common nouns.

Induction and Conceptual Change

A child who learns a concept, such as DOG and a word for that concept such as *dog* learns the same concept as an adult, in the sense that the concept will have the same extension for both child and adult. However, the adult's and the child's concepts will undoubtedly be different in spite of this. The adult's concept will include much more information about the characteristics of dogs, their relations to other species and so forth. The way in which the knowledge structure of a concept changes over time, and the role of language in these changes is a topic of considerable developmental importance that is only beginning to receive appropriate attention. Carey (1985) emphasizes the importance of the child's developing theories about the world and the role of induction in the process of conceptual change. The role of theories, Carey argues, is to constrain the inferences that are made about a concept. The role of induction is to allow generalization of new information beyond the instances about which the information was acquired. As one example, Carey found that children initially organize biological knowledge around humans as a prototype. Inferences about biological properties of other species are based both on what children believe about humans and how similar the other species is to humans. The main emphasis of Carey's (1985) analysis is how children make inductions about the properties of concepts such as PERSON, PLANT, ANIMAL, and so forth. If a child finds, for example, that a property previously unknown to him or her – perhaps a property relating to internal organs in the case of animals – applies to one instance of a concept, what, if any, inductions will the child make about this property in relation to other instances of the concept?

A basic problem that must be addressed in considering induction is how the human cognitive system chooses the properties of the environment over which to make inductions. In chapter 1 the example of inducing the general rule that 'all swans are white' from observing several white swans was considered. There, it was pointed out that the rule induced is, in fact, false; there are also black swans. Nevertheless, the induction is one that a cognitive system might easily make. It raises the issue of why one property is chosen as the basis of induction. Because there is a multitude of properties in the world over which inductions might be made, the cognitive system must be selective in what it chooses to subject to the inductive process, otherwise it will be overwhelmed by a mass of useless analyses (Holland et al., 1986).

Gelman and Markman (1986) addressed the issue of how children make inductions about natural kind concepts (concepts such as BIRD, FISH, and so forth). Natural kind concepts have a rich structure of properties, some of which may be known only to experts. In spite of this we all readily form natural kind concepts and we continue to extend our knowledge of these concepts throughout our life. Gelman and Markman examined how children decide between conflicting information on how to categorize a novel living entity. In particular they wished to contrast perceptual similarity and lexical information as potential sources of induction about the category to which an entity belonged. In order to do this they presented triads of pictures such as that shown in figure 4.6, in which the owl bears a greater perceptual similarity to the bat than the flamingo, but the owl and the flamingo are both birds, while the bat is a mammal.

In their experimental work with 4-year-old children, Gelman and Markman presented triads similar to that in figure 4.6 and gave the children information about two of the pictures in each set and then asked a question about the third picture. In one example children were shown a tropical fish, a dolphin, and a shark. The shark was perceptually similar to the dolphin but was given the same label, *fish*, as the tropical fish. (The dolphin was labelled *dolphin*.) The experimenter then told the children that the tropical fish breathes underwater but the dolphin comes above the water to breathe. The children were required to predict what the shark would do. In almost 70 per cent of the cases children based their answers on the category information. This suggests that words themselves, by the fourth year, come to be important determinants of concepts. When a novel entity is labelled with a familiar word, the label alone is sufficient in many cases, to suggest assimilation of the entity to the concept.

Figure 4.6   *Examples of stimuli used by Gelman and Markman (1986).*

Further evidence that children rely on their growing knowledge structure rather than on perceptual appearance comes from Carey (1985). In one study she showed several groups of children aged between 4 and 10 a mechanical monkey that looked much like a real monkey. The children were asked whether the mechanical monkey could breathe, eat, and have babies, like a real monkey can. The vast majority of children denied that mechanical monkeys possess these properties. In this instance, children appear to be using their knowledge of the distinction between animate and inanimate entities to control the generalization of properties from one group (real monkeys) to a perceptually similar group (toy monkeys).

The results of these experiments are at odds with the widely held view that children's thinking is dominated by perceptual appearances. Children may, perhaps, rely on perceptual appearance when there is little else to go on, but it is not the case that they rely on perceptual appearances exclusively. Rather, as Carey (1985) has emphasized, their inductions are largely governed by their developing theories of the world.

Summary

Cognition depends upon categorization. We cannot understand learning, language, memory, or perception without understanding how categorization works. Categorization is the process by which the human information processing system determines which stimuli and entities can be treated as equivalent.

The classical theory of concepts argued that instances belonged to a concept because each possessed some small set of necessary and sufficient features that defined the concept. The evidence against this view of conceptual structure is by now overwhelming. Few concepts possess defining features. Instances of a concept typically share many features in common with other instances but no one set of features is common to all instances. Concepts also have an internal structure in terms of which some instances are more prototypical of a concept than others.

The world can be categorized at different levels. Concepts of objects can usually be arranged in a taxonomic hierarchy. As one ascends such a hierarchy, the similarity among instances within a concept decreases while the contrast among different concepts increases. There is one level of the hierarchy at which there is a maximal balance between within-category similarity and between-category contrast. This is called the basic level.

Although it has often been assumed otherwise, recent evidence indicates that children's concepts are structured in a way similar to adult concepts, although the children's concepts do not contain the same richness of knowledge as adult concepts. The structural similarity ensures that communication is possible between adult and child without serious danger of misunderstanding. Adults help to avoid misunderstandings where language acquisition is concerned, by providing the child with names that are typically at the basic level of categorization. This fits neatly with the child's own tendency to assume that a name should be mapped to a basic level concept. However, there is a tension between this constraint and the fact that an object can be named in many different ways. The constraint on mapping words to basic level concepts serves to get the lexical system off the ground in a maximally useful way but it is continually weakened thereafter by the relations that exist between concepts and between words. An early example of this is the fact that objects can be instances of a basic level concept and also of a higher level collection. Verbal definitions may play an important role in the acquisition of a taxonomic hierarchy of concepts.

Concepts undergo change throughout childhood, and probably throughout all of life. The extension of a concept may not be subject to radical change (although children appear initially to underextend many concepts) but the knowledge structure of the concept is continually enriched and refined. The way in which conceptual change occurs appears to be determined by the child's own beliefs about the structure of the world – that is, the process of conceptual change is determined by the knowledge structure of other concepts.

5

Memory Development

Memory and Information Processing

The cognitive system has evolved to process and store information. If we consider an information processing system in the abstract then it must have two major features: component processes to manipulate sensory input and a way of storing the representations that result from information processing. The human infant at birth must have a basic memory capacity in order to learn from his or her encounters with the world. We have already seen that human infants are capable of learning from birth, which implies the presence of a basic memory system and that the basic structure of the memory system is part of the innate architecture of cognition. However, the content of what is stored will be a function of the child's ability to represent input in different ways. Accordingly, although the structure of memory is unlikely to change much during childhood, the information stored is likely to change greatly. Before considering development, we shall consider how research on memory fits into the overall framework of an information processing approach.

Historically, memory has been a topic of central interest to psychology, since the pioneering research of Ebbinghaus (1885/1913). The way in which memory has been conceptualized and studied has changed, as paradigms of psychology have changed. Ebbinghaus himself was interested in what factors affected how learned material was recalled. In order to minimize the effects of previous knowledge, Ebbinghaus studied memory for lists of nonsense syllables. The idea that the most important facts about memory could be ascertained by studying the recall of lists continued unhindered until comparatively recently. Lists have now lost some of their popularity as the key stimuli for the investigation of memory, although they have by no means vanished. The data of list-based studies have formed some of the core data around which theories of memory have been constructed. Miller's (1956) famous paper 'The Magical Number Seven, Plus or Minus Two' was the first attempt to offer an information-processing account of list recall. Atkinson and Shiffrin (1968, 1971) provided the first detailed model of memory within the information processing paradigm. Their model (see figure 5.1) consists of three memory stores – a sensory register, a short-term store, and a long-term store – and control processes that operate on the short-term and long-term stores.

Since Atkinson and Shiffrin's first presentation of their model there have been many suggested revisions and alternatives. Among the more important is the suggestion by Baddeley and Hitch (1974) that we should replace the idea of separate short- and long-term stores with a single permanent store, part of which is activated and becomes 'working mem-

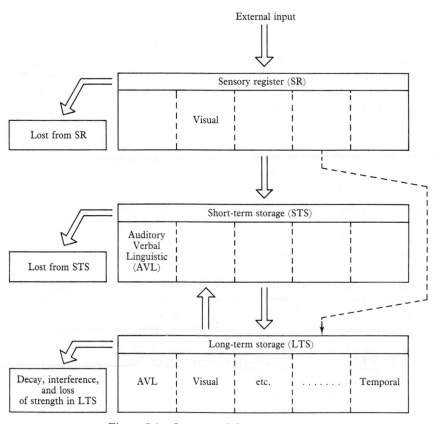

Figure 5.1 *Structure of the memory system.*
Source: Atkinson and Shiffrin, 1968.

ory' when information is being processed. Working memory in this conceptualization fulfils the same function as short-term memory in the Atkinson and Shiffrin model.

A major critic of the Ebbinghaus approach to memory was Bartlett (1932). Bartlett's chief objection was to the use of nonsense syllables. He argued that the exclusion of meaning from the stimuli resulted in experimental findings that had little to do with memory in everyday life. Bartlett argued that 'effort after meaning' was central to human learning and that subjects actively tried to impose meaning on a situation. His own experimental approach was to demonstrate this 'effort after meaning' by having subjects recall such things as American Indian ghost stories. He found that subjects typically distorted the unusual stories to bring them into line with their own experiences. Bartlett interpreted this as showing that our knowledge of the world is interpreted through schemata based on past experience. Subsequently, several theoretical proposals about the role of past experience in interpreting and remembering events have been made that are very much in the spirit of Bartlett's original proposal. Rumelhart's (1975) 'schemas', Minsky's (1975) 'frames' and Schank and Abelson's (1977a) 'scripts' can be mentioned in this context. These proposals have influenced some developmental work on memory directly. Additionally, there is increasing awareness among developmental psychologists that the child's 'knowledge base' is a crucial factor in explanations of memory development. A knowledge base, of course, can only be gained from experience and therefore its effect must be studied in relation to meaningful material.

There is one further distinction that should be mentioned at this point. Tulving (1972) distinguished, within the long-term store, between episodic and semantic memory. Episodic memory is memory for personal experiences and their temporal relations – such as what happened yesterday, where I went on holiday last year, or even what words were present in a list I learned yesterday. Semantic memory is memory for facts that transcend individual experience, such as the meanings of words and concepts. An example of the latter would be remembering a mathematical formula. The distinction between episodic and semantic memory can be a useful convenience, but it is probably no more than that. It is doubtful that there are different types of long-term stores (Baddeley, 1976) and it is also doubtful that either category identifies a homogeneous set of phenomena.

There are several techniques of studying memory in adults and children. By far the most popular is the study of recall, in which an event that occurred at time t_1 is recalled at some later time t_2. There are various issues of interest here, such as the effect that the length of the interval between t_1 and t_2 has on recall, and also the effect of any intervening activity. An intervening activity can have positive or negative effects; one of the most heavily researched developmental issues is the effect of rehearsal sometime between t_1 and t_2 on recall at t_2. A further issue of interest is how events at t_2, the time of recall, can facilitate the recall. Even if some episode is difficult to recall, the recall may be facilitated if some cue associated with the original event can be used.

Sometimes events recur in the environment, either completely or partially. We may see a person at t_2 and recognize him or her as the person we saw previously at t_1. In order to do so we must have stored some information about the episode at t_1, which is activated by the information processed at t_2 when we see the person again. Recognition would seem to be the most basic form of memory, in that there is rich stimulus input at the point of performance and it does not require the construction of output of some sort, as recall does. We might therefore expect recognition memory to be more advanced at an early age than other types of memory. In fact, we could go further and argue that recognition memory must almost certainly be innate because, in order for any learning to occur, the child must be capable of recognising some stimulus situation as being the same as an earlier stimulus situation. Since we know that learning can occur in infants only a few hours old (see chapter 2) we can assume the ability to recognize stimuli is a hard-wired information processing facility. Indeed, the phenomenon of habituation, which is widely used in the study of young infants, crucially depends upon recognition.

Recognition Memory in Childhood

Recognition memory involves the ability to determine if a stimulus is novel or familiar. If the stimulus is familiar recognition may trigger recall. However, here we are concerned simply with issues of recognition. The typical laboratory experiment on recognition involves showing slides to subjects for relatively brief amounts of time. After an interval some or all of the slides are mixed with novel slides and the subject is required to identify the ones that he has seen before. Adult recognition abilities are impressive. Shepard (1967) showed adults 612 pictures and tested recognition immediately, after two hours, three days, one week, and four months. The immediate and two-hour delay conditions yielded practically 100 per cent recognition. After one week the average recognition score was 87 per cent. By four months it was just above chance level at 58 per cent. However, recognition is considerably more durable than this if the subject has had repeated exposure to the stimulus. Bahrick, Bahrick and

Wittlinger (1975) found that 35 years after graduation from high school, adults recognized photographs of their class mates with 90 per cent accuracy.

What are the origins of recognition memory? If we consider the minimum cognitive requirements for even the simplest of conditioned learning to occur, then it will be apparent that learning requires recognition memory in order for a stimulus to be identified as having previously occurred. The ability to recognize some form of similarity must, therefore, be innate or learning could not occur. We should expect therefore to find primitive recognition abilities in infants. However, there is an obvious difficulty in the way here: it is difficult to conduct experiments with young children. Conventional experimental techniques require an adult or child to verbalize his responses, and thus these techniques cannot be used with infants. However, as we have discovered in chapter 2, there is a variety of specialized techniques that can be used to study the abilities of young children. In general, these same techniques will serve us well here.

The habituation paradigm was discussed in chapter 2 as a common technique used to study visual discrimination. The technique exploits the fact that after repeated exposure to a stimulus an infant's response to the stimulus diminishes. This is not usually due to fatigue because presentation of a new stimulus invariably leads to an increase in the rate of response. The conventional interpretation of habituation is that the infant ceases to attend to the stimulus because he or she recognizes it as familiar. Thus, the technique requires recognition memory for its success and can, therefore, be used as a test of recognition memory.

The studies that most clearly demonstrate the newborn's abilities of memory are those conducted by Friedman and his associates (Friedman, 1972a; 1972b; Friedman, Bruno and Vietze, 1974). Friedman (1972a) showed infants 1 to 4 days old black and white checkerboards for 60 seconds and recorded how long the infant looked at the board. After several presentations interest declined significantly. This was not a fatigue effect; when a more complex checkerboard was presented, the rate of looking increased again. The most plausible explanation of these results therefore is that the infants recognized the original checkerboard, became less interested in it, and looked less.

Although Friedman's results demonstrate a basic ability to recognize similarity in the newborn, we know relatively little about the dimensions of similarity that are encoded. The newborn knows relatively little about the world, so we must be wary about making generalizations about which stimuli will be regarded as similar and which not, or about how long recognition will last. The latter question is one which the habituation

paradigm will not answer; it is a technique best suited to the demonstration of basic abilities. In order to examine the longer-term abilities
of infants we shall have to use alternative techniques.

A technique that can be used over the longer term is to compare how
long infants attend to stimuli when first presented and then when presented again a day or two later. Using this procedure Martin (1975) tested
infants aged 2, 3.5, and 5 months old over a two-day period. On the first
day a geometric figure was shown six times for a period of 30 seconds.
The procedure was repeated on the second day. The infants looked at
the figure less on the second day than they did originally. The decline
in looking also increased slightly with age, suggesting that the 5-month
old infants may have been more sure of the familiarity of the stimulus.

How do infants recognize a stimulus that they have seen before? An
experiment by Strauss and Cohen (1980) showed that some features of
the stimulus are better remembered than others. They showed infants
aged 5 months either an arrow or a 'Y' for 60 seconds. In the test of
recognition memory the original stimulus was paired with another arrow
or 'Y' that differed in some way from the original. Strauss and Cohen
varied the comparison stimuli along one of four dimensions: orientation,
size, colour, and form. For example, if the original stimulus was an
upright arrow it might be paired with a rotated arrow. Tests of recognition
memory were carried out immediately and after delays of either 15
minutes or 24 hours. The measure of recognition was the relative amount
of attention paid to the two stimuli. Since infants are known to prefer
novel to familiar stimuli (see chapter 2), greater attention to the stimulus
not seen before can be taken to imply recognition of the other stimulus
as familiar. Strauss and Cohen found that immediately after presentation
infants always recognized the original stimulus; 15 minutes later they
recognized only the form or colour; 24 hours later only the form of
the stimulus was recognized. This study shows that different types of
information may be lost from infant memory at different rates.

If we now consider children of preschool age, recognition memory is
remarkably effective under laboratory conditions. Brown and Scott (1971)
investigated 4-year-olds' recognition of distinctive colour pictures of familiar objects over varying intervals. Immediate recognition (with 'filler'
pictures being shown in the interval between test and re-test) was almost
perfect. Over the longer term recognition was a function of both the
interval and how frequently the pictures had been seen. Pictures that
were seen twice initially were recognized with 94 per cent accuracy after
one day and 75 per cent after a month. Pictures that were seen only once
were recognized with 84 per cent accuracy after one day but only 56 per
cent after a month.

One limitation of the Brown and Scott study is that the pictures were very distinctive from each other. Would children perform as well with less distinctive pictures? The answer appears to be 'yes'. Brown and Campione (1972) showed 4-year-olds 80 pictures and then later showed them 120 pairs of pictures. The same character was depicted in each picture of a pair but in different poses. One pose had been presented previously for 60 of the pairs; for the remaining 60 neither picture had been presented previously. After two hours, if a character was recognized, the correct pose was chosen 95 per cent of the time. After one week, the accuracy was 85 per cent.

The results of these studies reveal impressive recognition abilities. It might seem that little remains to develop as far as recognition memory is concerned. However, although the basic ability to recognize is well-developed, there are factors important to recognition that are not revealed in the studies discussed thus far. All of the studies have involved children's abilities to recognize single objects. It is probable that the information gained by a child from looking at a picture of an object differs very little from the information gained by an adult. But what of more complex situations, where the information may have to be sought and organized before it is stored? A study by Newcombe, Rogoff and Kagan (1977) is instructive here. They compared children's recognition of objects and scenes. The scenes consisted of objects clustered together in a meaningful way. Six objects and six scenes were presented and recognition was tested either immediately or after five days. Children aged 6 and 9 years were tested as well as a group of adults. As might be expected from previous results, recognition of the objects was excellent. However, recognition of the scenes was quite different. The 6-year-olds performed only slightly above chance level. The 9-year-olds were more accurate; they recognized an average of about 80 per cent of the scenes in contrast to over 90 per cent of the objects. The performance of the adults was essentially similar for the scenes and the objects.

What is the difference between objects and scenes? The difference lies less in the stimuli themselves than in the information processing strategies that they require. Scenes require scanning and the extraction of information. Young children are not especially good at such tasks (Mackworth and Bruner, 1970). Once extracted, the information contained in a scene can be stored as a set of separate features or it can be organized into more meaningful chunks. As we have seen already, young children are not adept at organizing information. When recognition requires strategic behaviour (either at encoding or recall or both) then young children are shown to be at a disadvantage. When the stimuli are simple objects and it may be presumed that information processing is a more or less automatic perceptual process, then the performance of children is comparable to that of adults.

Recall

Research on recall can be traced back at least to Jacobs (1887) who reported age differences in digit span. Work continued in this tradition during the first half of the twentieth century. Throughout this period the main focus of the research was to measure memory differences and to relate these differences to global IQ measures. Measures such as digit span are a component of many IQ tests. This research was concerned with documenting individual differences but there was very little attempt to construct a theory of memory development or to focus on the way in which memory processes (as opposed to products such as digit span) might change during the course of development. It is only comparatively recently that attempts have been made to construct theoretical accounts of why memory span improves with age (Belmont and Butterfield, 1969; Case, Kurland and Goldberg, 1982; Chi, 1976, 1977; Huttenlocher and Burke, 1976).

The developmental study of memory processes began in earnest in the 1960s. This occurred in the context of a cognitive *zeitgeist* fostered by a renewed interest in Piaget's work and the research of Bruner et al. (1966), to mention but two major influences. The line of research that was to prove most influential from this period was that initiated by Flavell and his associates (Flavell, Beach and Chinsky, 1966). Interestingly, the direct issue that prompted their studies had nothing to do with memory *per se* but was an issue that arose out of learning theory. Research on discrimination learning (e.g., Kendler, 1961; Reese, 1962) had suggested that in early childhood children do not use verbal symbols as mediators between a stimulus and a response, whereas older children do so. This was called (Reese, 1962) *the mediational-deficiency hypothesis*. Flavell et al. (1966) pointed out that the child's difficulty could be of two sorts: the child might produce verbal mediators but these failed to work as mediators as they did for the older child; Flavell et al. restricted the phrase *mediation deficiency* to this situation. Alternatively, the child might fail to produce any mediators at all at an appropriate point in performing a task. They called this a *production deficiency*. An obvious way to disentangle mediation from production deficiencies is to study children's verbal rehearsal on short-term memory tasks. Do young children rehearse (i.e. use verbal mediators) on such tasks? If not, can they be induced to do so, and what effect would this have on their performance? These questions formed the background to early research on children's use of memory strategies. The memory task was not itself the object of interest initially; it was simply a convenient way to investigate the production-mediation deficiency issue. However, things soon changed and the memory phenomena themselves became of primary interest. Flavell et al. (1966) showed children aged 5, 7, and 10 years seven pictures of common objects. The experimenter pointed to a subset of these pictures and asked the children to remember this set in serial order, either immediately or after a delay of 15 seconds. The latter condition is the one of interest. The experimenters reasoned that if children rehearsed the list, they would do so overtly rather than silently. Accordingly, a trained lip-reader was employed to observe the children during the 15-second interval. In order to prevent the children continuing to observe the pictures during this interval and also to allow the lip-reader to observe the children closely, each child wore a toy space helmet with a translucent visor, which was pulled down during the delay interval.

With 20 children in each of the three age-groups only two of the 5-year-olds rehearsed, whereas 12 of the 7-year-olds and 17 of the 10-year-olds did so. Thus, a clear increase was observed in spontaneous verbal rehearsal.

Having discovered that young children do not rehearse, Flavell and his associates proceeded to explore why this is so. Are young children incapable of rehearsing or are they simply unfamiliar with the strategy of rehearsal in particular and in general with the notion that memory tasks may require strategic behaviour to be initiated and used by the child? In order to determine whether young children would benefit from rehearsal Keeney, Cannizzo and Flavell (1967) trained 6- and 7-year-old children who did not rehearse spontaneously to do so and observed the effects on performance. A control group of spontaneous rehearsers were also tested, and of this group half were given the same training as the non-rehearsers. The results are shown in figure 5.2. It can be seen that before training the non-rehearsers were significantly worse than the rehearsers at recall but that this difference was much smaller after training. It is apparent from these results that the reason why young children fail to rehearse is not because they are incapable of doing so.

However, even though Keeney et al. succeeded in inducing children to rehearse, they discovered that the children did not maintain the strategy after the training trials had been completed. After the tenth recall trial following training, the experimenter explained to the children that they could continue to say the names if they wished to but that they were no longer required to do so. During three subsequent recall trials almost 60 per cent of the children trained to rehearse abandoned the strategy. Thus,

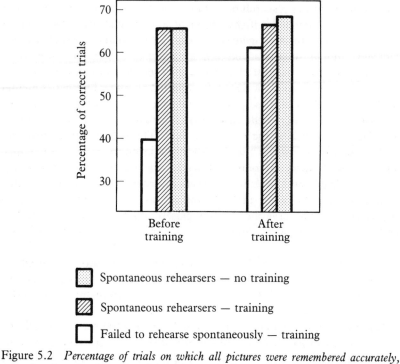

Figure 5.2 *Percentage of trials on which all pictures were remembered accurately, as a function of rehearsal training, for 6- and 7-year-old children who rehearsed spontaneously and those who did not rehearse spontaneously.*
Source: Kail (1990).

although rehearsal could be induced, it was not spontaneously maintained as a memory strategy by the children.

It was evident on the basis of this research that young children do not rehearse spontaneously and that this is not because of the intrinsic difficulty of the rehearsal process itself. Clearly, young children *could* rehearse but they did not usually do so. In the original terms of Flavell et al. (1966), the children had a production deficiency. The nature of this production deficiency now began to emerge as an important research issue. As a result of the findings that young children are apparently not willing strategy users, researchers began to probe in more detail the behaviour of young children in memory tasks. The basic tenor of the researcher's reasoning was something like the following: we know that young children do not rehearse in memory tasks; is there any evidence that they engage in strategic behaviour of some sort, even if it is ineffective? In other words: do children understand that some memory requires effort?

One popular method adopted in research on strategy use was to compare children performing a task who had been instructed to remember ('the memory group') and children performing the same task without such instructions ('the control group'). The research rationale is that if the memory group behave differently from the control group then this can be attributed to their efforts to do something that will facilitate recall.

One of the earliest studies to address the relation between the instruction to remember and the child's activity was that of Appel, Cooper, McCarrell, Sims-Knight, Yussen and Flavell (1972). They showed pictures to 4-, 7-, and 11-year-old children under two conditions. In one condition the children were instructed to remember the pictures for later recall, while in the other they were simply told to look at the pictures. Both groups of children were, in fact, asked to recall. The question at issue is: what observable differences are there between the children instructed to remember and those not so instructed? It was found that only the 11-year-olds showed conspicuous differences in the two conditions; the group instructed to remember engaged in more mnemonic-like activities than the group instructed to look. On testing for recall the memory group had superior recall. There was little difference between the two groups of 4-year-olds. Both of these results are in conformity with previous findings. The 7-year-olds behaved differently in the two conditions; the memory group did engage in more mnemonic activities. However, this failed to lead to improved recall. This led the researchers to conclude that the 7-year-olds had identified a memory task as one requiring special mnemonic activities of encoding but the children were not yet effective users of such mnemonics. However, even if children are not effective users of rehearsal, subsequent research showed that they recognized that an instruction to remember required some special effort. Yussen (1974) studied attention rather than rehearsal in 4-year-olds. Using the same technique as Appel et al. (1972) he instructed children either to remember the items that a model pointed to or simply told the children that later they would play a game with the model. Both attention and recall were greater in the first condition. Thus, even 3-year-olds appear to understand that remembering requires an effort. A similar result was reported by Wellman, Ritter and Flavell (1975). They told children a story about a dog using four identical inverted cups as props in the story. Midway through the story the dog was placed 'in the doghouse', which was in fact under one of the cups. The experimenter then left the room on the pretext of obtaining some more props and asked the child to remember where the dog was. The child's behaviour was observed through a one-way mirror during the next 40 seconds. The children engaged in such activities as looking at and touching the cup where the dog was hidden.

Together these studies suggest that from a very early age children recognize that memory requires encoding effort. However, the studies that have detected strategy use by younger children require only simple strategies of encoding such as looking and touching. They do not require rehearsal, which involves symbolic representation of an object by its name and the use of repetition in order to preserve a list of symbols in working memory. The results of Keeney et al. (1967) suggest that rehearsal itself is not intrinsically difficult, and the results of Appel et al. (1972) and Wellman et al. (1975) suggest that the child has no great difficulty in understanding that a memory task requires mnemonic activity. It seems that the child's problem lies in identifying the rehearsal strategy as a relevant mnemonic strategy.

Evidence to support this suggestion came from Kennedy and Miller (1976). This experiment was, in essence, a replication of Keeney et al. (1967). Recall that Keeney et al. trained children to rehearse and observed improved performance but also observed that children did not maintain use of the strategy when instruction to use it ceased. In the Kennedy and Miller experiment two different types of training were conducted with non-rehearsers. One group was trained to use the strategy as children had been in the Keeney et al. study. The other group were given feedback concerning the effectiveness of the rehearsal on their recall by being told 'You did much better when you whispered those names over and over. I guess whispering helped you remember the pictures better.' Later, when rehearsal was optional, as it had been in the Keeney et al. experiment, only the children given feedback continued to use the strategy. Thus, Kennedy and Miller secured maintenance of the strategy where Keeney et al. had failed to. For now, let us draw out two implications; a practical one for training and a theoretical one for memory development. The practical implication is that training is more likely to lead to maintenance of the strategy trained if the child is informed of the strategy's function and its effect. The theoretical implication is that being capable of rehearsal does not ensure that the strategy will be accessed at the appropriate times. Even though rehearsal may improve recall, it may not be obvious that it has done so to the young child. Without this awareness there may be little reason, from the child's point of view, to engage in the effort of rehearsal.

The Development of Mnemonic Strategies

Even when the child does begin to engage in rehearsal there is not a simple shift from no rehearsal to rehearsal. In a series of studies Ornstein, Naus and Liberty (1975) and Ornstein, Naus and Stone (1977) asked subjects ranging from 7-year-olds to adults to remember up to 20 words and instructed their subjects to 'think about' the words aloud. They found that the *overall amount* of rehearsal was similar in all age groups but there were age differences in the number of different words that were rehearsed. The younger children often rehearsed a single word over and over whereas older children and adults rehearsed several words simultaneously. Thus, there are developmental differences in the rehearsal strategy itself.   What elaboration of rehearsal occurs, once the basic strategy itself has been mastered? One key fact about material to be rehearsed is that it often makes more sense, from the learner's point of view, to rearrange the input into a more familiar form. This is the case where, for example, the child is required to learn a list of words drawn from a limited set of superordinate categories but presented in random order. For example the list *dog, shoe, cabbage, hat, cat, shirt, carrot, cow, leek* consists of words for animals, clothes, and vegetables in random order. To recall such a list it is easier to group the words together in categories. Most adults would do this in a recall task. Do children do so?

A number of experiments have reported that children do not cluster words until sometime between the ages of 10 and 12 years. However, other studies have reported clustering in much younger children. Part of the problem here is what is to count as clustering. If *cat* and *dog* are part of a list and they are recalled together, is this evidence of clustering? Some researchers would argue that it is (so long, of course, as the juxtaposition is statistically respectable in the data). Others would be less happy. Lange (1978) has argued that evidence of early clustering can be re-interpreted as the effect of inter-item associations. Even so, inter- item associations may be the developmental basis of clustering. If we assume that inter-item associations are a more or less automatic output of semantic memory and that clustering is the deliberate organization of output into superordinate categories, then a possible mechanism for the emergence of clustering as a rehearsal sub-strategy can be suggested. Early clustering, let us assume, occurs as a result of strong inter-item associations. If the child detects such associations in recall then they may serve as a spur for actively seeking further associations and, in time, this could lead to the strategic deployment of superordinate categories as aids to encoding and retrieval. In short, an involuntary product of semantic memory is monitored and turned into a strategy that can be deployed to add further power to encoding and retrieval. It is worth remarking, parenthetically, that there are two ways in which clustering aids recall. Firstly, it takes advantage of inter-item associations which may be useful both for encoding and retrieval. Secondly, if it is known that n, or approximately n, items belonged to a particular category, then, at retrieval, the category label can be used to turn a recall task into something resembling a recognition task. The category label can be used to generate subordinate items (e.g. by saying all the animal words you know) and each item can be checked for recognition as it is generated. Thus, having a category label can serve to identify a manageable search space in semantic memory, thereby changing a recall task to a recognition task.

In order to investigate clustering in children, Ornstein, et al. (1975) asked children aged 8, 10, and 12 years to 'think aloud' while rehearsing a 20-item list of four words in each of five categories. They found that 8- and 10-year-olds did not cluster the items but that 12-year-olds did. Similar results were reported by Moely, Olson, Halwes and Flavell (1969). Children aged 5 to 11 years were shown pictures of animals, furniture, vehicles, and clothes and instructed to study them for later recall. The pictures were arranged in a circle with no two pictures from the same category adjacent. The children were told they could move the pictures about if they wished. Only children aged 10 to 11 showed any significant degree of clustering as a mnemonic strategy.

These experiments show that deliberate clustering at input is absent in young children. Why do young children fail to cluster? It could be that they do not recognize the words presented as being related or it could be that if they do, they do not see the taxonomic relation as a useful strategy to be deployed in a memory task. In fact, as the evidence reviewed in Chapter 4 suggests, young children may have difficulty constructing a superordinate category at all.

Earlier, it was suggested that deliberate clustering may develop as a result of monitoring involuntary inter-item associations. If it is the case that initial clustering is 'forced' on the child by strong inter-item associations then we might predict that for young children high-associate items will cluster in recall, while low-associate items will fail to do so, even though the child may be aware of the taxonomic relation. Several experiments indicate that this indeed is the case. Corsale and Ornstein (1980) asked children aged 4 to 5 years and 8 to 9 years to group items for recall. Half of the subjects received high-associate examples of the categories whereas the other half received low-associate examples. The older group were much more likely to form taxonomic categories as a preparation for recall with both high and low-associate items (although they exhibited more variability with the latter items). Although independent evidence showed that the young children could sort the high-associate items taxonomically, very few did so as a preparation for recall. When asked to recall, however, there was a high level of clustering for the high associate items among the younger children, and this was true even for children who did not sort items on the independent sorting test. Frankel and Rollins (1985) constructed two recall lists that had either high or low categorical relatedness among the items and two lists that had either high or low associativity. Each list consisted of four sets of six items. Children older than 9 years performed well on recall when either associative strength or categorical relatedness was high. However, children aged 5 only performed well with the list high in associative strength. Bjorklund and Jacobs (1985) reported a similar result. Subjects from 5 years to adult were asked to recall lists that contained both high and low associates within the same list. Subjects of all ages from 5 years to adult used associative relations to begin category clusters but only subjects over the age of 10 years used non-associative categorical relations to begin clusters. Thus, the origins of clustering do not lie in deliberately imposed organizational strategies but in the automatic associations of semantic memory. What young children lack is the realization that these associations can be deployed as a mnemonic strategy through the use of superordinate taxonomic categories.

What Causes Strategy Changes?

Two key issues that have emerged from the preceding discussion are the importance of having a strategy and of knowing when to use it. Much of the early research on memory development seemed to indicate that children's awareness of a strategy's use might play a crucial role in its spontaneous deployment. This suggests that an understanding of memory development requires an understanding of the processes that control the use of strategies. In particular it would be useful to know how control strategies develop and whether or not they are consciously deployed. Essentially, we are concerned with how the cognitive system manages its own memory resources. Since the issue is one of management the processes are given executive status.

Executive Processes in Memory Development

Executive processes seem to be a necessity for theories of cognition. Such processes are in accord both with introspection and with experimental evidence. However, there is no satisfactory general theory of the executive control of cognition. Any attempt to construct such a theory faces considerable epistemological difficulties about the attribution of reflective awareness of the processes of thought. In the absence of theoretical guidance, there is something of a rag-bag of executive processes to choose from in the literature on cognition. However, there seem to be two typical requirements placed on an executive system: that it can monitor the performance of the rest of the system and modify strategies in the light of monitoring.

It may help to begin by stepping outside developmental models of memory for a moment to examine briefly the general model that has influenced most information processing theories. In their influential model of the memory system Atkinson and Shiffrin (1968, 1971) distinguished between memory stores and control processes that govern the flow of information to and from the stores. As examples of control processes Atkinson and Shiffrin (1971) cited rehearsal, coding, decision rules about the deployment of strategies and retrieval strategies. The first two of these processes operate on incoming information, the third is an executive decision process and the fourth operates on long-term memory. This is something of a mixed bag of processes. In particular it should be noted that the model contains strategies that apply to the content of cognition and executive processes that do not themselves affect content directly. Information processing theories of memory have been strongly influenced by the Atkinson and Shiffrin model. As a result, the control structure of the memory system has been conceptualized as a set of higher-level executive processes. The basic requirements of such executive processes are that they control the deployment of strategies according to the task; monitor performance; and change the strategies being used if necessary.

Much of the research on executive control has addressed the issue of the selective deployment of attention and effort to particular elements of a task. For instance, if a child had achieved partial mastery of a piece of text that needs to be memorized then it obviously makes sense for the child to concentrate further rehearsal on the new unlearned parts rather than on the parts that are familiar. To do so requires that the child monitor his own learning and then use the results of this monitoring as input to strategy deployment.

Masur, McIntyre and Flavell (1973) examined the extent to which children can monitor their own performance and use the results to control further rehearsal. Children aged 6, 8, and college students were asked to remember a set of pictures that was 1.5 times greater than their memory span. The subjects were initially allowed a 45-second study period followed by a recall test. After recall the subjects were allowed to select half the pictures for a further 45 seconds of study. This alternation of study and recall continued for several trials. The 8-year-olds and the college students almost always selected pictures for study that had not been recalled on the previous trial but the 6-year-olds picked approximately equal numbers of recalled and unrecalled pictures.

The results of Masur et al. concern the learning of lists of isolated items. It might be objected that the reason why young children are so strategically poor with such items is that they are alien to the child. However, research on study with more 'natural' material supports the view that young children are poor spontaneous users of memory strategies. Brown and Smiley (1977) asked adults to rate on a four-point scale the importance of units of text to a theme. They then asked students aged 6 to 18 years to perform the same task and compared the results with those of the adults. The performance of the 17- to 18-year-olds was similar to the adults. Children aged 11 to 12 could reliably distinguish the least and the most important units but could not differentiate the intermediate units from each other. The 9- to 10-year-olds could distinguish the most important units from the others but beyond that they could make no further differentiation. Children aged 7 to 8 could not make any distinctions at all. Commenting on this result, Brown, Bransford, Ferrara and Campione (1983: p. 91) remark:

> These initial findings have important implications for studying. To go beyond retention of just a few main points, that is to achieve a more complete fleshed-out memory of the text, one must engage in active strategies to ensure increased attention to important material that will not be retained automatically. If young children have difficulty distinguishing what is important, they will also have difficulty studying. Quite simply, one cannot selectively attend to important material in the absence of a fine sensitivity to what *is* important.

In a follow-up study, Brown and Smiley (1978) investigated the use of study strategies in students from 10 to 18 years of age. When given extra time to study a text children aged 10 to 12 engaged mainly in passive re-reading of the text. As age increased a greater proportion of students took notes or underlined. Those who did so concentrated on the important elements of the text. When recall was tested it was found that active strategy users had superior recall to those students who simply re-read the text. However, of more importance is the finding that students with an efficient study strategy showed an adult pattern of recall; some 12-year-olds were as good as 18-year-olds. This result suggests that developmental improvement in recall is not simply a function of age but is determined by the strategy available, regardless of the student's age. We shall encounter this phenomenon again when we discuss the effect of the child's knowledge-base on performance.

The results of these, and similar studies (Brown and Day, 1983; Brown, Smiley and Lawton, 1978) have important educational implications. First, they suggest that study strategies are of central importance to the learning process. Second, they suggest that children can develop efficient and sophisticated strategies relatively early in the developmental process, but they will not necessarily do so. This latter fact might itself suggest that study strategies should be taught more formally than they are at present – in conjunction, of course, with relevant content. However, we need also to understand why it is that some children may fail to use efficient strategies. There are probably several reasons for this. One is that the child may possibly be ignorant that a strategy is called for. A second possibility is an ignorance of what the strategy should be, even if called for. A third possibility is a failure to monitor that a strategy is actually effective. A fourth is that an existing, less efficient strategy, may be relatively entrenched and serviceable. In relation to the last of the issues mentioned, Brown et al. (1983) suggest that children are often impeded in replacing primitive strategies with more sophisticated ones because the primitive strategies work reasonably well. As an example, Brown and Day (1983) contrasted how students from 9 to 18 years of age summarize a text. Highly proficient subjects used five summary rules: (1) deletion of trivia; (2) deletion of redundancy; (3) substitution of one superordinate for several superordinate units (such as words, or events); (4) selection of topic sentence (if one has been provided); (5) invention of a topic sentence (if one has not been provided).

Brown and Day found that even the youngest children could use the deletion rules with over 90 per cent accuracy, but rarely used the more complex rules. Brown et al. (1983) suggest that because the deletion strategy is effective, it may hinder the development of the more complex strategies, which require a greater degree of cognitive manipulation. Students, of course, do overcome this hindrance but the fact that many junior college students performed like 12-year-olds on the summarization task suggests that progress can be very slow.

Awareness and Memory Development

Flavell (1971) argued that the development of knowledge about memory might be an important factor in age-related improvements in memory performance. He used the term *metamemory* to denote knowledge of memory. However, knowledge of memory is a rather vague concept. It has been used to cover things as various as a sensitivity to the need to use strategies, through an explicit knowledge of these strategies, to general knowledge of the capacity and limitations of the memory system. Studies of metamemory soon began to proliferate. Several lines of investigation were pursued. One was to ask children direct questions about their knowledge of memory (e.g. Kreutzer, Leonard and Flavell, 1975); another was to ask children the relative difficulty of different tasks (e.g. Moynahan, 1973); another was to ask children to predict their own performance on memory tasks (e.g. Flavell, Friedrichs and Hoyt, 1970); another was to study how children monitored their own memory attempts (e.g. Brown, 1978).

In their review of metamemory Cavanaugh and Perlmutter (1982) argue that the lack of distinction between executive processes and memory knowledge has been counterproductive and has led to conceptual confusion. They advocate that the term 'metamemory' be reserved for knowledge about the contents of memory. We shall use the term 'metamemory' in this sense and distinguish it from executive processes. Although we can regard metamemory as the result of deliberate and conscious reflection upon cognitive activity it is quite important to resist the implication that executive processes are invariably conscious processes (Klatzky, 1984). In skilled performances, in particular, executive processes appear to operate in an automatic fashion not susceptible to conscious control (Hasher and Zacks, 1984; Schneider and Shiffrin, 1977; Shiffrin and Schneider, 1977). However, the less skilled performer may bring a great deal of conscious executive control to a task. Given that developmental psychology invariably studies the inception of a skill to a greater degree than its consolidation into expertise, the conscious executive control of cognition is likely to be a particularly pertinent issue.

It may be useful to consider first how executive processes and awareness of memory are related. To some extent both constructs address the same data, but with a different emphasis. Executive processes are the control processes of the memory system, whether or not these processes are accessible for introspection. A person may be aware of some of the control processes of memory but his or her awareness will also extend to other aspects of memory. Thus, the constructs of executive processes and awareness partially overlap. This is not necessarily a problem in itself, but confusion can occur when a term such as 'metamemory' is used for both constructs, thereby implying a theoretical unity that does not exist.

Klatzky (1984) distinguishes three general types of awareness of memory: conscious awareness of the mental processes in which one is engaged; awareness of the contents that are stored in memory; and awareness about memory as a human capacity.

Research on metamemory has demonstrated that the older the child, the more detailed and more accurate is knowledge about memory (Flavell and Wellman, 1977). However, any attempt to summarize this research to produce a coherent developmental picture is beset with the problem that a wide variety of measures of metamemory have been used on a wide variety of tasks without there being any obvious or theorized relation among either measures or tasks or between measures and tasks (Whittaker, 1983). Although the concept of metamemory may have given impetus to these various lines of investigation it was to prove incapable of holding them together. Metamemory was not a well-defined construct to begin with and, perhaps because of this, it came to serve as a label for all manner of phenomena whose connection with each other was, at best, unclear. Under the circumstances it seems better to consider the difficulties that vitiate previous studies and that future studies must overcome.

The first difficulty is the extent to which people can report on their own mental processes. One of the most commonly used interview techniques in studies of metamemory is to present children with hypothetical memory situations and then ask the child what he or she would do (e.g. Kreutzer, Leonard and Flavell, 1975). Can children's introspections be trusted on such issues? There is, after all, a long-standing distrust within psychology of introspective reports. However, recently, Ericsson and Simon (1980, 1984) have advocated that verbal reports on mental processes provide acceptable data under certain conditions. Unfortunately, hypothetical situations are one of the conditions they regard as likely to provide highly untrustworthy reports.

A second difficulty is that studies of metamemory are highly reliant on verbal ability in addition to accessibility to mental processes. Young children have limited skills in this domain. This is a fact that hinders rather than prevents research but it is a considerable difficulty nevertheless.

A third difficulty, at least with the majority of the research up to now, is that the research designs used do not allow the issue of the developmental relation between metamemory and memory to be addressed. Many studies have employed a correlational design in which both strategy use and knowledge about a strategy has been measured at the same point in time. Such studies cannot, by their nature, reveal whether memory development depends on metamemory or whether metamemory follows memory development. The results of such studies have, in addition, been frustratingly disappointing; they have yielded only moderate correlations at best (Cavanaugh and Borkowski, 1979; 1980; Kelly, Scholnick, Travers and Johnson, 1976; Salatas and Flavell, 1976; Yussen, Levin, Berman and Palm, 1979).

A fourth difficulty is the unique nature of many of the research designs that have been employed. Cavanaugh and Perlmutter (1982: p. 16) comment: 'By and large, unique interviews, materials, or tasks are used in separate experiments. an equally serious problem is the general lack of reliability measures.' Thus, it is difficult to compare or summarize the results of different studies.

In the face of these difficulties it is not surprising to record that studies of metamemory have failed to deliver much in the way of tangible reliable findings. Despite this, many remain convinced of the potential of metamemory as a useful construct and of the possibility of better methodological studies. Cavanaugh and Perlmutter (1982: p. 22) conclude that 'in its present form, metamemory has little value' but add 'there is no compelling reason why its future must be considered bleak, however'. However, that future depends critically, in their view on improvements in assessment techniques and more extensive theoretical considerations of the relation between metamemory and memory.

Knowledge of Results and Memory Development

There is one area in which there seems to be a definite positive relation between 'awareness' and memory. This occurs when the child becomes aware that use of a strategy produces a desired result, as, for example, in the Kennedy and Miller (1976) study already discussed. It is difficult, if not impossible, to measure awareness of this type directly. The studies we shall discuss are all training studies in which children who are made aware of strategy's effectiveness are contrasted with children who are not given this knowledge. Although these studies have sometimes been cited as examples of a metamemory–memory relation, it is probably best to distinguish between measuring awareness in the traditional ways and manipulating awareness in a training study. Another reason for maintaining the distinction is that the awareness in question concerns neither introspection about one's own mental processes or a general knowledge about memory as a human capacity. It is, instead, the knowledge that there is a rationale for a strategy's use.

We have already drawn the contrast between the efforts of Keeney et al. (1967) and Kennedy and Miller (1976) to produce maintenance of rehearsal. Kennedy and Miller achieved maintenance by providing feedback to the children about the effectiveness of the rehearsal strategy. Borkowski, Levers and Gruenenfelder (1976) investigated how effectively children learnt prepositional relations between paired-associate objects under four different training conditions: passive observation, active manipulation, active manipulation together with viewing a film that portrayed the strategy's effectiveness, and a control condition. After training, the subjects were given additional similar tasks designed to measure the extent of transfer. The factors that determined extent of transfer were active participation for all groups and, of most importance in the present context, watching the film that portrayed the usefulness of the strategy. Thus, the children benefitted considerably if they were informed about the effectiveness of the strategy they were shown.

The results of these studies could be interpreted as suggesting that a major reason for children's failure to use a strategy is a lack of awareness that strategy use will make any difference. In order to have such awareness children must either be told that strategies are effective, as in the studies described, or they must monitor their own performance. A direct test of these issues was provided by Ringel and Springer (1980). They tested children aged 7, 9, and 11 years on a semantic sorting strategy as a preparation for retrieval. The children were first matched on five recall scores and then assigned to one of three treatment groups or a control group. The treatment groups were given instructions in sorting pictures according to semantic similarities and two of the groups received feedback about the improvement in performance that resulted from this strategy. Although results for the 7-year-olds were equivocal, the provision of feedback had a definite effect on the amount of transfer that occurred on subsequent trials for the 9-year-olds. The 11-year-olds in the treatment group improved their performance (over the controls) whether or not feedback about a strategy's effectiveness was provided. This implies that the 11-year-olds were capable of monitoring the strategy's effectiveness, and feedback therefore conferred no additional advantage. This was confirmed in a metamemory interview that was conducted as part of the study. In all of the 11-year-old treatment groups the children said they would 'group' items to facilitate recall. Among the 9-year-olds, children were much more likely to say this if they had been in one of the groups given feedback.

The implication of these studies is that a major barrier to strategy use is the ability to monitor the effectiveness of a strategy. The studies do not reveal how such monitoring develops but they do show that it can be induced successfully. This has important implications for training and instruction. A key piece of input to training or instruction should obviously be some sort of feedback about the effectiveness of a strategy's use. Training without such feedback may not be maintained or transferred beyond the initial learning situation.

A theoretical conundrum remains. If monitoring a strategy's effectiveness is the key to maintenance, how does the strategy develop in the first place? Monitoring cannot cause a strategy to become effective - it is parasitic on some independently motivated use of the strategy. For the strategy of semantic clustering we have, as previously discussed, the possibility that some clustering, especially that observed in young children, is a by-product of the associative mechanisms of semantic memory. This by-product may be a sufficient basis for a monitoring mechanism to elaborate it into a deliberate strategy. However, it is not known at present whether or not a similar mechanism could explain the development of other strategies. If it could then it will be necessary to rethink many of our assumptions about the causes of development.

The Knowledge Base and Memory

In the recall of events, it is an obvious fact that what a person knows will influence what he recalls. This has been demonstrated by Bartlett's (1932) famous research on remembering and by countless other experiments since. However, that line of research essentially concentrates on the way in which pre-existing knowledge distorts the recall of some, often unusual, event. More recently, there has been a different interest in the effect of knowledge on memory: the way in which changes in the knowledge base are related to changes in recall. This differs from the Bartlett tradition in that the distorting effect of knowledge is not the issue and it differs from the classic experimental paradigm in that the effect of experience is under direct investigation rather than prior experience being regarded as a variable that creates 'noise' in the data and that must therefore be controlled.

The importance of the knowledge base is most vividly demonstrated in an experiment conducted by Chi (1978). Chi tested a group of children (of average age 10 years) and a group of adults and asked them to recall a list of 10 digits in one condition and the pattern on a chess board in the second. As might be expected the adults had superior recall on the digits but the children were considerably better at recalling the chess positions. There is no mystery about this; the children were skilled chess players and the adults were novices. The experiment was designed in such a way as to maximize the children's expertise. The arrangement of the pieces was taken from real chess games. This would allow the skilled chess player to recognise the organization of the pieces whereas to the unskilled player the arrangement of the pieces would appear rather random. Chi's experiment demonstrates that the availability of a knowledge base can have a considerable effect on recall. The expert can recall more because the expert can encode more; specifically, configurations of stimuli form meaningful chunks to the expert whereas to the novice they may be just a lot of stimuli that have to be encoded and recalled independently.

The precise nature of the difference in the knowledge base as a function of increasing expertise has been demonstrated in a study by Chi and Koeske (1983). This study did not compare one group with relatively little expertise with another group of greater expertise, which might seem the obvious way to explore this issue. In fact, Chi and Koeske studied just one 4.5-year-old boy who happened to be something of an expert on dinosaurs. The child had knowledge of some 46 dinosaurs. Two groups of dinosaurs were selected – a better known and a lesser known group – based on the frequency with which the child mentioned a dinosaur and the frequency with which the dinosaurs were mentioned in the books that had been read to the child. Chi and Koeske explored, over a number of sessions, the extent of the child's knowledge of various properties of the dinosaurs and their lifestyle. They then used this information to construct a network representation of the relation between dinosaurs and properties. When the better known group was compared with the lesser known group it was found that the former had more properties associated with its members and there were more interrelations among the properties than was the case for the lesser known group.

Chi and Koeske's study is one of the few to quantify what an increasing knowledge base means. They did not neglect to demonstrate the effect this can have on recall. The child was asked to recall two lists of ten items – one chosen from the better known group of dinosaurs and the other from the lesser known group. Recall of the better known group was almost perfect over three recall trials whereas only half of the lesser known group were recalled.

Up to this point we have used the phrase 'knowledge base' without being at all specific about its meaning. Although the phrase is now used widely in discussions of cognitive development, it is rarely given any extended discussion as a construct. In cases like chess and dinosaurs it is relatively easy to see what the knowledge base might be – i.e. lots of detailed and organized knowledge about a particular topic. However, if we are to use the knowledge base as a construct in the explanation of development we must explore its utility beyond the prototypical cases of specific and well-circumscribed content domains. In particular we need to know about the relation between everyday knowledge of events and recall.

Memory for Everyday Events

Children's memory for everyday events has not been studied nearly as intensively as memory for laboratory events. Both types of event are temporally-dated personal experiences and so would be termed episodic memory in Tulving's (1972) terms. However, the two types of event may be radically different. Laboratory events usually require that deliberate strategies be employed if the event is to be remembered. Everyday events, by contrast, are remembered usually without any deliberate attempt at remembering. This suggests that the processes that serve to determine encoding and retrieval may be different. In this section we shall discuss the research on script-like representations and the role that they may play in memory development.

A script is a temporally organized representation of how events are related in some stylized everyday activity. Because the activity is stylized the sub-sequence of events is highly predictable, even stereotyped. These stylized activities constitute a script that may be accessed and used in comprehension and in recall. A script is, thus, a mental representation of a stylized or stereotyped everyday activity. Scripts organize input in terms of previously stored knowledge. Because they do so, communications about a stereotyped activity can be relatively brief, with many causal links left unspecified; the script provides the missing links as default values. Consider Schank and Abelson's (1977b) restaurant script:

John went into a restaurant.
He ordered a hamburger and coke.
He asked the waitress for the check and left.

As Schank and Abelson point out: 'We do not need to say that a waitress took the customer's order or that he ate the hamburger. These ideas are firmly part of the story because the restaurant script requires them. In understanding a story that calls up a script, the script becomes part of the story even when it is not spelled out.' (p. 425)

Although the concept of a script provides a useful starting point in the exploration of the representation of events, there are some obvious weaknesses that make scripts a treacherous theoretical concept. First, there is the danger of scripts being invoked post hoc to accommodate all manner of phenomena. Second, usage of the concept has been inconsistent from one researcher to another. Third, the relation of scripts to other forms of knowledge is far from clear. Schank and Abelson (1977a) distinguished between plans and scripts, but the distinction is not always easy to draw. In short, scripts fulfilled a theoretical need but they addressed one issue within a yawning gap of theory and came to be a panacea for the absence of that theory rather than a stimulus to improve the theory. Many of these issues have been addressed by Schank (1983), who has abandoned the construct of scripts. Nevertheless, flawed though the concept is, it has a certain utility and will serve to organize our discussion of the origins of event memory. The aim is to illustrate broad principles of representation in a field that is currently in considerable theoretical ferment. We shall begin with some empirical research on how adults represent events.

Bower, Black and Turner (1979) conducted a number of experiments on how adults represent routine activities such as eating in a restaurant or going to the doctor. Bower et al. found that when subjects were presented with stories describing such activities, they tended to recall both actions that were mentioned and actions that belong to the script but were not actually stated. Subjects also showed a strong tendency to recall scrambled stories in their canonical script order. Deviations from a script were also recalled well, especially if these were relevant to the overall goal. Similar results were reported by Graesser, Woll, Kowalski and Smith (1980). Clearly, the concept of a script, whatever its short-comings, captures the essence of an important fact about the represen-tation of everyday events. Such representations provide the organizational framework for the comprehension of input. Because the representation is relatively permanent, the recall of everyday events is greatly facilitated. The developmental question that obviously arises is: do children have a script-like representation of everyday events?

The major developmental research on scripts has been conducted by Nelson and her associates (Nelson 1978a; 1978b; 1985; Nelson, Fivush, Hudson and Lucariello, 1983; Nelson and Gruendel, 1981). Nelson (1978a) elicited descriptions from 4- to 5-year olds about the events that occur when eating at home, in their daycare centre, or at McDonald's restaurant. Her results are similar to the results for adults reported by Bower et al. (1979). There was a common skeletal structure representing the mealtime event. The children generally appealed to the same type of event at the same level of generality. Thus, the McDonalds script con-sisted of the elements:

- Transportation
- Arrival
- Enter
- Order
- Receive
- Pay

- Sit
- Eat
- Garbage
- Leave
- Transportation

The elements were usually in the correct sequence, with the exception of paying (which was frequently assumed to happen at the point of leaving). Even 4-year-olds, it would seem, have accurate scripts, for at least some events. In a second study Nelson (1978a) investigated the effect of experience on a child's script by comparing children's scripts for eating at the daycare centre shortly after they began school for the first time and three months later. At the first interview the children did have a basic script and within three months a more elaborated version. The fact that children had a basic script initially, gives an important clue to the development of script representations and to the nature of event memories in general. It is perfectly possible that the organization represented in scripts is built up over time by the gradual accretion of isolated bits of a repeatedly experienced event type. Nelson's result suggests that this is not the case. What repeated experience appears to bring is greater detail; organization seems to be the basis on which event memory works. Confirmation of this is provided in a study by Ratner, Smith and Dion (1986) who studied how single events are recalled by 5-year-old children and by adults. They found that the major goals of the events were best remembered at both ages and that children reported these as often as college students. The adults were superior to the children in the amount of minor detail recalled. Thus, as with Nelson's result, experience brings more detail but not a change in basic organization. The findings of Ratner et al. also suggest that one important dimension of memory organization is the goal-based structure of the event. This suggests that so long as a child can comprehend or attribute a goal, he or she will encode and recall an organized representation of the event.

Why is it that we can recall a great deal about our past life but typically can remember nothing about the first few years (so-called infantile amnesia)? In this context we might speculate that the phenomenon of infantile amnesia is to be accounted for by either the absence or the relative weakness of everyday scripts in the early years of life. There are two possible ways in which an absence of scripts could account for infantile amnesia. The first is that because of this absence relatively little information is encoded and stored. The second is that, early information is stored but either its organization is disrupted by the later development of everyday script representations, or it is no longer easily accessible because it is not organized in the form of scripts, which have become the major means of access to stored information. However, these are speculations, and, as Spear (1984: p. 327) has noted 'infantile amnesia is a problem for which plausible theories far outnumber substantial facts'. Kail (1990) presents a useful short review of the available theories and evidence.

The research on the development of children's event representations is still in its infancy. Nelson has shown that young children know about and rely on the sequential structure of everyday events. Ratner et al. have demonstrated the importance of goals. Further, children seem to have little problem about what constitutes basic units of events. Thus, from an early age script-like representations of events are being built. These representations undoubtedly play an important role in many aspects of comprehension and recall. However, much remains to be done in this area. To date we have had 'existential demonstrations' of scripts but as yet no clear theoretical statement of the role of scripts in cognitive development. It may also be that although scripts capture an essential truth about event representation, scripts are not actually the appropriate theoretical construct with which to pursue issues of event representation. Schank and Abelson's (1977a) original theory was that scripts are stored chunks of knowledge. Schank (1983) has more recently proposed that scripts are not stored chunks of knowledge but are dynamically constructed from smaller chunks as needed.

A special case of real-life events are stories. Stories are narrated events and, from an experimental point of view, they have many attractions. In particular, it is easy to manipulate experimental variables in a story but more difficult to do so in real life events. Stories and events have much in common, including sequencing of episodes and causal and temporal connections between episodes. However, it would be unwise to regard studying memory for stories as a shortcut to studying memory for events. Sequences and temporal connections can be and are manipulated in stories; in events the sequence is fixed. Stories can and do juxtapose events that are separate in real life. The temporal duration of an episode is very different in a story and an event. The medium of presentation for stories is oral; for events it is visual. All of these factors are likely to affect recall. Indeed there is evidence that memory performance for the same event differs as a function of the medium of presentation (Baggett, 1979; Mandler and Murphy, 1983). Accordingly, it is best to regard stories as events of a special type, to be studied in their own right. Given that much of our information comes through the oral and written medium, the study of the development of story comprehension and recall is an important task.

Much of the interest in the recall of stories is due to the availability of story grammars as a means of analysing text into meaningful units. Story grammars derive primarily from two sources: the work of Kintsch and Van Dijk (1978) and Rumelhart (1975). The basic idea of story grammars is that stories have a structure that consists of a setting in which the characters and background information are introduced, followed by episodes of activity that form the plot. Each episode can be further analysed into more detailed components. Of particular interest, in view of our previous discussion, is the importance of goals in the structure of episodes. It is assumed in story grammars that the main character acts within an episode to achieve a goal. The goal is not always explicit in the surface structure of the story but is assumed to be present in its underlying structure. In traditional stories, the temporal and causal connections among the constituents of an episode occur in the correct sequence. With the availability of story grammars developmental questions can be asked about the extent to which children of different ages are sensitive to various 'units' of a story; the extent of differential attention to important and less important units; how cohesive the recall is, and so forth.

One of the more robust findings of memory research on stories is that stories that correspond closely to the natural order of temporal and causal connections are more readily comprehended and recalled than stories that do not (Mandler, Scribner, Cole and De Forest, 1980; Nelson and Gruendel, 1981; Stein and Glenn, 1979; Yussen, Matthews, Buss and Kane, 1980). In fact, children and adults will usually rearrange a story so that it is recalled in the natural order of the events. Nelson and Gruendel (1981) presented children either with a correctly arranged script-like story or with one that had an event out of its correct sequential position. When recalling the misarranged stories, the children tended either to omit the misordered event altogether or put it back in its canonical position.

Mandler (1978) presented subjects from 7 years to adulthood with stories in which two episodes were interleaved. During recall the episodes were separated by most subjects. Mandler and De Forest (1979) found that even when instructed to maintain the presented order, subjects had great difficulty in doing so. This difficulty was greater for the children than the adults, suggesting that children are very reliant on being able to arrange events in conventional sequence.

It may be recalled that, when discussing memory for events, it was found that the pattern of recall does not vary very much between children and adults (Ratner et al., 1986), although the amount of detail does. The same is true for story recall (Mandler, 1983). However, age differences are readily apparent at a finer level of analysis. The ability to distinguish major and minor elements of a story varies as a function of age. Using relatively simple stories Yussen et al. (1980) found a considerable improvement between the ages of 8 and 10 years in the ability to distinguish major from minor episodes. Brown and Smiley (1977) reported a similar result for older children and more complex stories. In addition, children have poor awareness of story structure. Markman (1979) found that children were poor at monitoring inconsistencies.

Story schemas seem to be a close analogue of event scripts. Both emphasize the importance of a structural framework that is readily available to interpret particular content. Of the two concepts, schemas are the more general, being receptive to a variety of content, while scripts are specific to a particular type of content. Both constructs emphasize the importance of incoming information. Although neither construct is very watertight theoretically, they do serve to draw attention to the organizational patterns that characterize memory for events. Human information processing seems to be innately disposed to temporal and causal organization of information and automatically exploits this organization when it can. In this there is a parallel with the automatic associative mechanisms discovered in the study of list learning. Although researchers have only begun to scratch the surface of memory structures and processes, some issues seem to emerge with reasonable clarity. Certain structural properties such as association, and the apprehension of temporal and causal links may be innate organizational properties of the memory system. On these are built more complex organizational structures such as hierarchical categories and, possibly, scripts and schemas. The basic organizational framework is sufficient to ensure a functional memory for everyday purposes. However, much of the information we encounter does not conform to the canonical organization. Encoding and recall of such material requires special effort and strategies. These strategies are the most obvious source of major developmental changes in memory during childhood.

Children as Witnesses

Memory is a topic of considerable practical as well as theoretical interest. One obvious area of application is study techniques, which have already been touched upon. Another area of application is to the testimony of children in courts of law. Given that children may sometimes be crucial witnesses to a crime, it makes sense to ask to what extent we should trust their testimony.

The first thing to say about the issue of the child as witness is that much of the academic research on memory development does not translate directly into an answer about the reliability of children's testimony. One major reason for this is that the conditions under which a laboratory experiment is conducted may vary greatly from the conditions under which a crime was observed. If these conditions themselves are a variable that affects memory then it is important to know what degree of confidence we can have in a generalization from a laboratory study. Let us consider, for example, the difference between a laboratory study of face recognition, and seeing a face during a crime. In the laboratory study the child knows the nature of the task whereas in the real life situation the child may be frightened and pay little attention to the assailant's features. In the real life situation identification or recall may take place months, or perhaps even years after the event has occurred, unlike the laboratory situation. The child's trauma on giving testimony may be aggravated further by hostile defence questions. It is evident that there is much more to the reliability of eye-witness testimony than what laboratory studies tell us about a child's memory. However, memory research should tell us at least part of the story.

Face Recognition

The obvious question to ask about face recognition in this context is how children's recognition compares with adults'. However, this is a very general question because there are many variables that may affect face recognition and not all may have the same developmental effect. Therefore, the question must be decomposed into a set of more specific questions.

The first issue we shall examine is the age effects on recognition memory. A variety of studies support the conclusion of Carey and Diamond (1977) that level of accuracy improves with age (Blaney and Winograd, 1978; Carey, Diamond and Woods, 1980; Chance, Turner and Goldstein, 1982; Flin, 1980). In a review of the relevant literature Chance and Goldstein (1984) concluded that beyond 12 years of age, children are equal to adults in their performance on face recognition tasks. However, this is not necessarily the key piece of information from a legal point of view. Although young children may be poorer at recognition, what trust should we put in a positive identification, if one is made. To answer this we need to know the rate at which false positive identifications are made. Several studies have reported that the proportion of false positive identifications decreases with increasing age (Chance et al., 1982; Cross, Cross and Daly, 1971; Flin, 1980). A further factor that affects recognition is whether or not the faces to be recognized are drawn from the subjects own ethnic group. It is an extremely robust finding that subjects have more difficulty in recognizing faces of groups other than their own (Chance and Goldstein, 1984; Yarmey, 1979). Curiously, young children of 6 to 7 years are no worse at recognizing faces from other ethnic groups than their own but from 10 years on a difference emerges in favour of recognition of one's own ethnic group.

It would be useful to know to what extent these findings would be affected by the situational differences that obtain between the laboratory and real life. Perhaps the closest we can come to answering this question is by conducting studies that simulate some of the conditions of real eyewitness tasks. Regrettably there are very few such studies with children. In one of the few, Marin, Holmes, Guth and Kovac (1979) studied how well children remembered an intruder who burst into a room where the subject and experimenter were supposedly about to begin testing. The intruder harangued the experimenter for 15 seconds before departing. Children aged 5 to 6 years later selected the correct intruder 54 per cent of the time; 9- to 10-years-olds 46 per cent and 13- to 14-year-olds 75 per cent. However, college students were no better than the youngest children! Although this study simulates some aspects of a real eye eyewitness task, the nature of the intrusion ensured that the intruder would be looked at. This condition may not always pertain. Further, the intruder wore no disguise and was clearly visible, conditions that also may not invariably pertain. As Chance and Goldstein (1984: pp. 74–75) have argued: 'We cannot ask about the adequacy of face recognition in relation to subject variables such as age, unless we also define important situational variables. We must devise and describe those situational variables along useful dimensions relevant to events in an eyewitness-culprit interaction rather than limiting our comparison to one between the laboratory and real life.'

One important situational variable that bears on eyewitness testimony is the variation that may occur between the face witnessed and the face to be identified. Perpetrators of a crime often effect deliberate disguises or may, wittingly or unwittingly, change various facial characteristics before being apprehended and paraded for identity. How well can children cope with such changes? Diamond and Carey (1977) tested immediate recognition of previously unfamiliar faces as a function of changes in facial expression and changes in 'paraphernalia' such as hats, glasses, wigs and so forth. They found a steady improvement from 6 years up to 10 years but little change from 10 to 16 years. These experiments suggest that children under 10 years may have particular difficulty at identifying a culprit who has changed either some aspect of his or her appearance or the paraphernalia of his facial presentation. This issue should not be confused with the issue of deliberate disguise on the occasion of a crime. Research with adults (Patterson and Baddeley, 1977) suggests that recognition of faces previously seen in disguise is untrustworthy at any age.

One very prominent feature of eyewitness testimony is that the testimony often takes place some considerable time after the event. There is little relevant research with children on the effect of retention interval on recognition. A study with adults by Egan, Pittner and Goldstein (1977) showed that correct identifications remained above 90 per cent up to 56 days later but false positive identifications grew to an alarming 93 per cent.

An important issue for courtroom testimony is the stress that it may cause the child. There is evidence that confrontation with a culprit (whether or not the culprit was actually an assailant of the child) is both stressful and an impediment to accurate recognition. Dent and Stephenson (1979) tested children's recognition of a workman who had visited the classroom for two minutes one week previously. The children were asked to identify the workman either from a live parade or from colour slides of the parade members. Accuracy was significantly higher in the slide condition with 29 per cent correct identification versus 12 per cent in the live parade. Dent and Stephenson comment (1979: p. 199) 'The majority of [children] who went in front of the live parade were nervous, embarrassed and even frightened'. Dent and Stephenson attribute the poor recognition performance to the children's anxiety rather than to a superiority of photographs over people. In a further study they compared identification from a live parade, a parade viewed from behind a one-way screen, and colour slides of a parade. Identification was best in the one-way screen condition with 40 per cent correct identifications compared with 30 per cent for the slides and 18 per cent for the live parade. (The performance in the latter two conditions is similar to that of the children in the previous experiment.) It would seem that the one-way screen method of identification may be preferable both from the point of view of accuracy and of stress reduction.

Overall, although the evidence is scanty, it would seem to indicate that young children are less reliable than adults at identification along several dimensions. Although further research is unlikely to change this conclusion, there is clearly a need for more detailed and more accurate information about the extent to which different dimensions affect recognition. In particular the issue of false positive identification is an important one. From a legal point of view, a failure to make an identification may be of less concern than an incorrect identification of an innocent person. The conditions under which an identification is made are also obviously of crucial significance both for the accuracy of testimony and the welfare of the child. More evidence and a legal system more sensitive to the needs of children are highly desirable.

Verbal testimony

How accurate is children's recall of events they have witnessed? Laboratory studies indicate that children are less efficient than adults in recalling events they have witnessed (Loftus and Davies, 1984). This might not be such a problem if we were sure that we could rely on the child's recall being accurate as far as it goes; incomplete but accurate. However, there is considerable concern that children's recall may be inaccurate. Saywitz (1987) asked children aged 8, 11, and 14 years to read a story about a crime and then to recall the story. The recall of the 8-year-olds was less complete and more embellished than that of the other groups. Wells, Turtle and Luus (1989) showed a film of a staged abduction to children aged 8 and 12 years, as well as to adult subjects. One day later all subjects were asked a series of 10 direct questions about what they had seen and were also asked a further seven questions typical of a cross-examination. The 8-year-olds were somewhat less accurate than the other groups in their recall of what had happened under direct questioning but the difference was not significant. However, under cross-examination type questioning the 8-year-olds performed significantly less well than the other groups. This finding addresses an issue that is of considerable significance for courtroom testimony. Even if children's recall is reliable under conditions without stress, can it be trusted under conditions of stress? There are two sides to this issue: to what extent are children suggestible such that their recall in court is inaccurate and to what extent can accurate recall withstand the stress of cross-examination in court? (See Davies (1989) for a recent review.)

Historically, there has been a strong belief in children's suggestibility (Goodman, 1984a). However, in order to understand children's suggestibility one has to appreciate that under a variety of conditions adults have been shown to have far from reliable recall (Loftus, 1979). Thus, research on the suggestibility of children requires adult controls for proper evaluation.

In the Marin et al. (1979) study in which an intruder burst into the room, the subjects were asked to provide an account of what had happened immediately the intruder had left. A number of questions were also asked by the experimenter, one of which implied the presence of either a non-existent object or an event. Two weeks later a follow-up study of recall was conducted. Memory for the actual event was quite accurate at all ages from 5 years to adulthood and there was no apparent age difference in susceptibility to the inaccurate suggestions made two weeks earlier – about half the subjects proved susceptible. This may seem like good news for the reliability of children's testimony but it must be borne in mind that the study does not probe a range of suggestions nor a range of methods of suggestion. Other studies have reported different results. Ceci, Ross and Toglia (1987) exposed children between 3 and 12 years to misleading information after they had been presented with a story to be recalled later. Their general finding was that the younger the child, the more susceptible he or she was to misleading information. A similar finding has been reported by King and Yuille (1987), but Zaragoza (1987) failed to find any effect of age on suggestibility.

A detailed study of suggestive questioning has been conducted by Cohen and Harnick (1980). They showed a film depicting two petty crimes to children aged 9 and 12 years and to college students. Immediately after the film they asked 22 questions, half of which were straightforward, (e.g., *'What was the young woman carrying when she entered the bus?'*) and half of which were leading questions (e.g., *'The young woman was carrying a newspaper when she entered the bus, wasn't she?'*). A week later the subjects were administered a multiple choice test of 22 items (one for each question asked). Cohen and Harnick found a large increase in accuracy with age and also an increase in the resistance to suggestibility.

However, a contrary picture about suggestibility emerges from a study by Duncan, Whitney and Kunen (1982). They showed subjects ranging from 6 years to adulthood a slide sequence and asked a series of questions. Some questions were straightforward; some were leading questions suggesting events consistent with the slide but which had not been shown; some were leading questions but suggesting events inconsistent with the slides. Accuracy of recall improved with age, as in Cohen and Harnick's study. However, children and adults were equally influenced by the leading questions.

It is evident that there is no clear answer to the question of children's suggestibility. Perhaps the problem is that we expect an absolute answer to whether or not children are suggestible rather than an answer that tells us under what conditions children are likely to prove suggestible. If we were to adopt the latter approach then we could begin to map out the areas where testimony is more and less likely to be reliable. There is, for example, a finding reported by Allport and Postman (1947) that children are less likely than adults to misidentify the race of an aggressor in a violent incident. In addition to needing to know the dimensions of testimony that are likely to be reliable we need to know a great deal more about appropriate techniques of questioning. Although some studies have set out to investigate the effects of leading questions, very few of these have compared different methods of questioning with a view to ascertaining how it can best be done.

The need for an improvement in the techniques used in interviewing children seems a critical issue. Asking questions, whether leading or not, is surrounded by a host of difficulties. There is some evidence that narrative reports are more accurate than reports obtained through questioning (Dent and Stephenson, 1979). However, even if narrative reports were to prove the ideal method for eliciting information about a crime, there remains the crucial issue of how courtroom testimony will be heard, if the child is a crucial witness.

Children are not likely invariably to produce well structured narratives when required. However, there are techniques that can be used to aid recall. In particular, props may be useful. There is a growing trend towards the use of anatomically correct dolls in obtaining testimony about sexual abuse from children (Berliner and Barbieri, 1984). The use of props may have more widespread potential. Goodman (1984b: p. 162–3) cites a study by Price (1983) that investigated the use of props. In this study, children aged 2.5, 4 and 5 years repeatedly participated in a sequence of seven events involving 21 details in a novel play setting. Both 4- and 5-year-olds remembered an average of 19 to 21 details if they were provided with a small model of the playroom they had visited, along with miniatures of relevant items. While the 5-year-olds' performance remained at about 18 details when the props were unavailable and only oral prompts were provided, the 4-year-olds' performance dropped to only two and a half items. The performance of the 2.5-year-olds did not rise above an item and a half in either condition; however their performance rose to 63 per cent of that of the 4-year-olds when they were placed back in the original room. Moreover, despite the use of toy props, not a single child's account or reenactment contained elements of fantasy.

There seems to be sufficient evidence here to warrant further investigation of the use of props in recall. In particular, it needs to be determined whether props retain their usefulness following single exposure to an event, as is common in many eyewitness situations.

We can summarize the main outstanding issues in relation to children's recall of an event they have witnessed:

1 There is a need for more detailed information about children's long-term memory for realistic events similar to those about which a child might have to testify.

2 The conditions under which recall is more or less likely to be reliable needs to be determined. This approach may be more useful than simply regarding accuracy as a function of age.

3 Inaccuracy and confabulation may be more critical factors than accuracy from a legal point of view. We need to know under what conditions children are especially likely to be unreliable or to lie.

4 Too little attention has been paid to the methods used to elicit information from children who have witnessed a crime. There are several dimensions to this issue; the role of questioning; the use of props to aid recall and to supplement verbal descriptions; whether or not specialist interviewers should be trained to interview child witnesses.

5 Last, but not least, the present system of investigation and courtroom confrontation may have long-term emotional consequences for children who are witnesses. This factor alone should impel a search for a more satisfactory way of treating child witnesses.

Summary

Memory is a central construct to information processing theories. Theories of memory are theories of how information is stored by the cognitive system. This information will be used, in various ways, by the cognitive system on later occasions. Thus, any information in the original stimulus that is not processed and stored is lost forever and can play no part in future cognitive activity.

At birth the human infant's innate cognitive architecture processes and stores basic elements of stimulus input. This means that a recognition memory is functional from birth, which allows the human infant to learn from his or her encounters with the world. For some types of input, infants have remarkably good recognition memories. However, complex aspects of a stimulus, such as the arrangement of objects in a scene, require more sophisticated processing strategies than the innate architecture provides. For these types of stimuli there is an evident developmental trend.

Recall is a more complex phenomenon than recognition because it requires the organization of output from a stored representation. Recall is greatly enhanced by the use of strategies for encoding and retrieving information. Much recent research has focused on the strategies used by children when required to engage in some act of deliberate recall. The most obvious gross account of memory development is that older children use more strategies, and use them more effectively, than younger children do. The more detailed issues of memory development concern how strategies develop. Initially, some strategies may be by-products of other aspects of the cognitive architecture. For example, the strategy of clustering semantically similar items seems to derive from associative links among items that could be clustered. The strategy of rehearsal simply involves repetition of the names of objects to be remembered but the deployment of this strategy seems to depend crucially on the development of an awareness that repetition of names is of benefit to recall. More generally, the development of effective monitoring of one's own behaviour and efforts is central to the successful deployment of memory strategies.   The understanding of memory development also has important practical implications. Children are often the victims of crime. Their testimony can be of crucial significance in legal proceedings. However, children are generally regarded as unreliable witnesses, prone to error, exaggeration, and confabulation. This is too sweeping a judgement of the young child's reliability, but it is all too common. Recent research has begun to clarify our understanding of the extent to which children make reliable witnesses. There is a long way to go, both in terms of obtaining a clear answer as to the reliability of children's testimony and in terms of adjusting the established adversarial style of courtroom practice so that it is more suitable to the child as a witness. Nevertheless, significant gains in understanding have already been achieved.

6

Reasoning about Quantity and Number

Number and Quantitative Reasoning

Psychological interest in the learning and teaching of calculation dates back at least to Thorndike's (1922) work, *The Psychology of Arithmetic*. Thorndike's book placed a strong emphasis on the importance of knowing basic arithmetic 'facts', such as $4 + 2 = 6$. The memorization and recall of facts was seen as the key to successful arithmetic computation. Much of the research in the Thorndike tradition aimed to establish the relative difficulty of acquiring various facts and of solving various types of problems. While it is undoubtedly important to know arithmetic facts, it is not the whole or even the major part of calculation with numbers. The reasoning that goes on in performing calculations is of prime importance. The case for studying mathematical reasoning is fairly evident if one considers even a moderately difficult piece of subtraction such as $1304 - 979$. Very few, if any, will know the result of this as a stored 'fact'. Therefore an understanding of general arithmetic procedures is necessary to solve the problem. The obvious developmental issue is to explain how children acquire such procedures.

Unfortunately, the study of how children learn to reason about quantities became largely divorced from the practical issues of learning about number. The tone of later research on quantitative reasoning was heavily influenced by Piaget. Piaget gave great prominence in his theory to one aspect of quantitative reasoning: conservation. For him, conservation lay at the heart of a system of logical and rational thought. According to Piaget, other quantitative reasoning, such as arithmetical reasoning, was dependent in a very fundamental way on the ability to conserve. Piaget's analysis exerted a large influence on psychologists and educationists concerned with issues of number development. The reason is partly due to the persuasive analysis offered by Piaget (1941/1952) and partly to the fact that the tasks he introduced to study conservation provided a very adaptable experimental technique, even beyond the issues to which they were initially addressed.

Piaget emphasized reasoning about conservation at the expense of other aspects of number such as the basic mastery of the counting sequence. In recent years, new theoretical perspectives on numerical reasoning have been developed within the information processing framework that place considerably more emphasis on counting and on reasoning about numbers than Piaget did. The first part of this chapter discusses experimental research on conservation that has tried to unravel what the conservation experiment actually measures. Not everybody has been convinced that the typical conservation experiment is as clear a measure of quantitative reasoning as Piaget assumed it was. Although there is not a simple conclusion to be drawn from these experiments, the methodological lessons to be learnt are instructive.

As imaginative adaptations of the conservation test were made so that they could be administered to children as young as 2 years, counting began to assume a more central role in the development of quantitative reasoning. The latter part of this chapter considers the development of counting skills and the role that counting plays in the development of arithmetical reasoning.

The Centrality of Conservation to Piaget's Theory

Conservation is one of the most thoroughly researched topics in cognitive development. It occupies a central role in Piaget's theory of cognitive development. For him, conservation lay at the heart of rational thought.

> Every notion, whether it be scientific or merely a matter of common sense, presupposes a set of principles of conservation, either explicit or implicit. It is a matter of common knowledge that in the field of empirical sciences the introduction of the principle of inertia (conservation of rectilinear and uniform motion) made possible the development of modern physics, and that the principle of conservation of matter made modern chemistry possible. It is unnecessary to stress the importance in every-day life of the principle of identity; any attempt by thought to build up a system of notions requires a certain permanence in their definitions. In the field of perception, the schema of the permanent object presupposes the elaboration of what is no doubt the most primitive of all these principles of conservation. Obviously conservation, which is a necessary condition of all experience and all reasoning, by no means exhausts the representation of reality or the dynamism of the intellectual processes, but that is another matter. Our contention is merely that conservation is a necessary condition for all

rational activity, and we are not concerned with whether it is sufficient to account for this activity or to explain the nature of reality. (Piaget, 1941/1952: p. 3)

Having thus located conservation at the centre of human thought processes, Piaget continues:

> This being so, arithmetical thought is no exception to the rule. A set or collection is only conceivable if it remains unchanged irrespective of the changes occurring in the relationship between the elements. For instance, the permutations of the elements in a given set do not change its value. A number is only intelligible if it remains identical with itself, whatever the distribution of the units of which it is composed. A continuous quantity such as length or a volume can only be used in reasoning if it is a permanent whole, irrespective of the possible arrangements of its parts. In a word, whether it be a matter of continuous or discontinuous qualities, of quantitative relations perceived in the sensible universe, or of sets and numbers conceived by thought, whether it be a matter of the child's earliest contacts with number or of the most refined axiomatizations of any intuitive system, in each and every case the conservation of something is postulated as a necessary condition for any mathematical understanding.

Piaget's own investigation of number gives a central role to studies of number conservation. In the course of these studies he came to the conclusion that counting plays little role in the development of number reasoning. He concluded that 'there is no connection between the ability to count and the actual operations of which the child is capable' (p. 61). The general technique for investigating number conservation is as follows. Two collections of objects, typically counters, are set out as shown in figure 6.1. The child is asked whether each row contains the same number

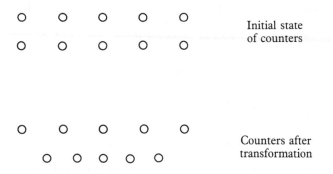

Figure 6.1 *Typical arrangement of counters in a conservation of number experiment.*

of counters. Usually, the answer is 'yes' because the basic process of one-to-one matching between the rows allows the child to form an immediate judgement; there is no need to count the rows. One of the rows is then lengthened or shortened and the question is repeated. Children who can conserve will say that the rows contain the same amount and when asked why will offer a justification something like 'because they were the same before, you just moved them about'. However, below the age of about 6 years, after rearrangement, children usually maintain that the longer row now has more. This constitutes a failure to conserve. The difference between the two groups is explained, in Piaget's theory, by the presence of *concrete operations* of reversibility and compensation. The presence of these operations is detected by asking the child to justify a correct response. A justification that the rows could be returned to their original state is evidence of reversibility; a justification that one row is shorter because it has been squashed up without affecting the amount it contains is evidence of compensation. It is the development of these operations that moves the child from being a non-conserver to being a conserver.

Conservation of number is but one of several conservation phenomena that can be observed in mid childhood. Other well-researched conservation issues are those of length, mass, weight, and liquid. In a conservation of mass experiment two equal balls of plasticine or some similar substance are made. Once the child has agreed that the balls are equal one is rolled into a sausage shape and the child is asked whether the two still contain the same amount. Children who can conserve maintain that the amounts are the same; those who fail change their judgements, often in favour of the longer shape containing more. Conservation of weight involves the same materials but equality of weight is established using a balance scale before one shape is altered. Conservation of liquid involves pouring equal amounts of liquid into two similar glasses and then transferring the liquid in one into a different-shaped glass, typically a taller thinner glass. The non-conserver usually maintains that the tall thin glass contains more liquid. The phenomenon of conservation is one of the most reliable developmental phenomena there is. Countless experiments have replicated Piaget's basic findings and the difference between conservers and non-conservers is very noticeable to anyone carrying out a conservation experiment. In spite of this the conservation experiment has aroused considerable methodological controversy.

Assessment of Conservation

The Piagetian method for detecting conservation requires the child not only to give a correct answer but also to provide a justification for the answer given, and often, to meet further stringent criteria of resisting countersuggestion. The rationale for seeking justifications is fairly evident: if a child can verbalize the principle on which a judgement is based then clearly the child is in possession of those principles. However, if a child gives a correct answer but fails to give an adequate justification, can it be concluded that the child does not possess a principled basis for his or her conservation response? To argue that the child does not possess such a basis runs the risk of an overconservative criterion that fails to attribute conservation when it is actually present. To argue that the child does possess a principled basis of conservation on the basis of a judgement alone runs the risk of an overlenient criterion that fails to detect possible sources of bias that may yield the correct judgement for the wrong reason. There is no simple answer to this dilemma but there are reasons for resisting both extremes.

The case against the Piagetian criterion has been forcefully put by Brainerd (1973). Brainerd's objection is not just that Piaget's criterion is overconservative but that the criterion of justification is fundamentally at odds with basic tenets of Piagetian theory. The reason for this lies in the relation between cognitive structures and language within Piagetian theory. According to Piaget cognition precedes language: the concepts expressed by language are a result of prior developments in cognition. This ensures that justifications are a *sufficient* criterion for inferring the presence of cognitive structures but it also ensures that, logically, they are not a *necessary* criterion. Brainerd concludes that requiring explanations is overstringent and argues that judgements alone are a more satisfactory criterion.

This issue of how to assess whether or not a cognitive structure is present is an important general issue. To date most researchers have sought a single criterion, probably in the belief that there is a single structure that is or is not present. The judgement versus explanation controversy is an example of this belief at work. An alternative to the single criterion would be to have a scale of criteria that reflected various levels of accomplishment of a particular cognitive skill. On this scale explanations would rate higher than judgements because clearly there is some developmental difference between a child who can articulate a principled basis for a judgement and one who cannot. The scale would not simply be a binary scale of judgements and explanations. Where the conservation of number is concerned one could add ability to conserve small versus large numbers for instance, on which there are age differences. The import of this proposal is that a cognitive skill may emerge slowly and only be accessible under certain conditions. If these conditions form a reliable developmental scale (in the sense that the same sequence is reliably observed among children) then it would be more informative to discuss a child's position on this scale than to seek for one absolute, and possibly mythical, measure of conservation (or of any other cognitive structure).

Can 2-year-olds Conserve?

Several investigators have claimed to detect conservation in children very much younger than those who normally succeed on the Piagetian task. The common factor of all these experiments is that the method is deliberately varied in order to overcome postulated 'biases' in the Piagetian procedure. These biases, it is claimed, cause the child to fail who can, in reality, conserve. The point needs to be stressed that there comes a time when 'biases' do not affect a child's ability to conserve and thus, even if there are biases in the Piagetian procedure, these are not artifacts to be eliminated from good research practice but are themselves factors to be explained as part of the developmental account. However, that said, the main thrust of the experiments to be discussed is that conservation is an ability possessed by children younger than the standard Piagetian account allows and thus its development may require a theory different from the standard Piagetian theory. We shall discuss a selective number of such experiments for their methodological and theoretical implications.

Mehler and Bever (1967) claimed to detect conservation in children aged 2 years. In their experiment children were shown two rows of four items of equal length. Then, one row was shortened and two further items were added to it. Each child was given two trials in this experiment. The first trial was conducted with clay balls and the child was asked which row had more.

The second trial was conducted with pieces of candy and the child was asked to choose the row he or she wanted to eat. Figure 6.2 shows the results for the two conditions. In the latter condition there was a uniformly high rate of correct responding among all age-groups. However, in the former condition there was a U-shaped pattern of results. The 2 -year-olds responded correctly but there was then a fall-off in the number of correct responses by 3-year-olds, while 4-year-olds performed at the same level as 2-year-olds.

What is most surprising about these results is that children aged 2 years can, apparently, conserve. However, the Mehler and Bever experiment confounds the effect of shortening the row and, at the same time, adding items to it, so it is not a true test of conservation. Nevertheless, the experiment reveals a previously unsuspected capacity in very young children.

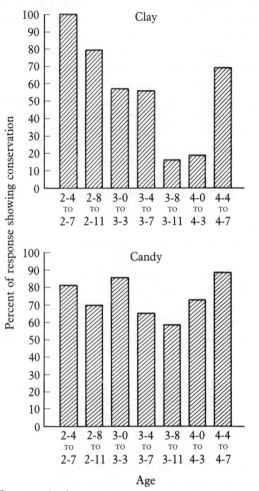

Figure 6.2   *The proportion by age of conservation responses to rows made up of clay balls and candy, reported by Mehler and Bever, 1967.*

Mehler and Bever argue that the cognitive structures on which conservation depends do not develop in mid-childhood but are present in the young child and are, presumably, innate. The question naturally arises of why these structures are so difficult to detect in young children and why, especially, do children below about 5 years consistently fail conservation tasks. Mehler and Bever argue that this failure is a result of interference between perceptual strategies and cognitive structures. As the child learns to reason on the basis of perceptual appearances he or she comes, for a time, to rely more on these appearances than on innate cognitive structures. Thus, the strategies overlay the structures. The child has to learn to overcome the competing pull of perceptual strategies in order to achieve the conservation abilities typical of mid-childhood.

Mehler and Bever's data and their interpretation have not gone unquestioned. A number of studies have questioned the reliability of the finding. Beilin (1968), Piaget (1968), and Willoughby and Trachy (1971) failed to replicate the result. Hunt (1975) showed that the results are very susceptible to experimenter bias. Telling an experimenter that 2-year-olds will do well at the task makes the experimenter more likely to replicate the original finding. However, Bever, Mehler and Epstein (1968), and Calhoun (1971) have reported replications.

Can young children conserve? The different results are sufficient to suggest that judgement be withheld. But, even if the results were unanimous in showing that children achieve a high level of performance on the task used by Mehler and Bever, it would still be difficult to conclude definitely that an ability to conserve has been demonstrated. Mehler and Bever assume that the performance of the 2-year-olds and the performance of the 4-year-olds, which is at the same level, reflect the same underlying cognitive structures. This is not necessarily the case. It is possible that the responses of the 2-year-olds and the responses of the 4-year-olds have a different cognitive basis. Although there is no direct evidence that this is what occurred in these experiments, there is evidence from other experiments that U-shaped patterns of results cannot reliably be taken as an indication of common cognitive structures shared by children performing at the different peaks of the curve.

In a study reminiscent of Mehler and Bever (1967), Walkerdine and Sinha (1978) reported that 3-year-old children could compensate for different widths of container in judging liquid equality but that when the children were re-tested at age 4 they failed to compensate. The task required the child to pour equal amounts to drink for two toy animals into two glass containers, one taller and narrower than the other – glasses A and B as shown in figure 6.3. To provide a correct solution the child must compensate for differences in the width of the containers by judging that the liquid column will have to be higher in the narrower container. The typical response of most non-conserving children to this task is to pour equal height columns of liquid into the two containers. However, as Walkerdine and Sinha showed, this is not what 3-year-olds do. If this result were to prove reliable it would provide support for the general thesis advanced by Mehler and Bever that skills of logical reasoning can be detected in young children.

McShane and Morrison (1983) replicated the Walkerdine and Sinha

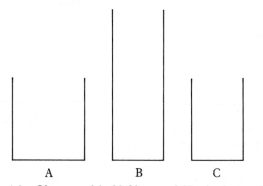

Figure 6.3   *Glasses used in McShane and Morrison's experiments.*

result. In this experiment 3-year-old children had a success rate of 80 per cent, which dropped to a success rate of only 3 per cent at about 5 years. McShane and Morrison went on to conduct a further experiment which was designed to test whether the success of the younger children was due to a genuine understanding of the principles of compensation or to some other factors. They suspected that rather than making a logical compensation response the children were ensuring that each glass had the same approximate relative fullness. This strategy is indistinguishable from a compensation response when two glasses are used, so, in their experiment McShane and Morrison added a third glass (glass C in figure 6.3) that was the same height as the original wide glass (glass A) and the same width as the original tall glass (glass B). The children's response to glass C when asked to judge when the same amount of liquid has been poured is now crucial. If the 3-year-olds are making genuine compensation responses the same height column of liquid should be poured into glasses B and C. If, on the other hand, their response strategy is one of judging relative fullness, then the same height column of liquid should be poured into glasses A and C. The latter was, in fact, what occurred. Apart from showing that young children do not judge the equality of liquid quantities on the same basis as older successful children, this experiment also highlights some issues about judgement- only criteria in tasks of quantitative reasoning. The children involved were unable to give justifications for their responses, so it would have been unreasonable to have used a criterion of adequate justification for inferring the child's cognitive structures. However, the alternative of simply accepting a correct response as an index of a logical competence is also unreasonable. Possibly the best solution to this recurring dilemma is not to opt for one extreme or the other but to seek corroborating evidence for an inferred strategy or structure wherever it may be found – in justifications if these are forth-coming or in predictions about performance on further tasks as in the McShane and Morrison experiment.

Is the Conservation Test Biased?

The argument that children are biased against making conservation responses during early childhood has been advanced by several studies. The most influential of these was a large series of experiments on percep-tual effects and cognitive strategies conducted by Bruner and his associates (Bruner, Olver and Greenfield, 1966). More recently, the child's under-standing of the instructions given in a conservation task has come into question. Rose and Blank (1974) pointed out that in conservation tasks the child is asked to make two judgements, one before and one after transformation. They argue that the repetition of the question may suggest to the child that the original judgement was in error. In order to test this hypothesis they asked children about 6-years-old to perform different versions of a conservation of number task. Group A performed the standard conservation of number task in which the child was asked whether two equally-spaced rows contained the same number of counters, one row was then shortened by having the counters squashed closer together, then the child was again asked whether the rows contained equal numbers of counters. Group B were asked only one question – after the row had been transformed. Group C did not see the row being transformed at all but only the final product. They were also asked one question. Rose and Blank found that Group B made fewer errors than either of the other groups. The fact that Group C made a similar number of errors to Group A suggests that perceptual factors may be less of a hindrance to conservation than other studies have emphasized. Rose and Blank interpret their findings as support for the view that when a child has just declared the rows equal he interprets the request for a second judgement as a signal to change his response.

McGarrigle and Donaldson (1975) approached the child's comprehen-sion of the task demands in a different manner. Like Rose and Blank they were concerned about the child's possible interpretation of the second question in a conservation task. In a typical conservation task the experimenter first asks a question about the equality of the rows and then deliberately transforms one row before asking a second question. They argued that the experimenter's behaviour between the first and second questions – i.e., that of transforming one row of counters – might lead the child to misunderstand the second question as being one about the length of the rows. Consequently, they sought to remove the deliberateness from the transformation of the row. To do this they used a 'naughty teddy'. At the beginning of the experiment the experimenter explained that teddy was very naughty and liable to mess up the counters from time to time. After the two rows had been made equal and the child asked the first conservation question one of two procedures followed. In the first, the intentional transformation (IT) condition, the experiment proceeded without any interference from teddy. This was thus a normal conservation experiment. In the second procedure, the accidental transformation (AT) condition, the experimenter warned with surprise that teddy was about to spoil the game and teddy was then used to disarrange the counters. When teddy had been calmed the experimenter rearranged the counters, ensuring that the necessary transformation was effected. McGarrigle and Donaldson found that over all four situations tested (conservation of equal number, unequal number, equal length and unequal length), nearly three quarters of the responses were correct in the AT condition, whereas only one third were correct in the IT condition. They interpreted these results as support for the view that children often fail the standard conservation task because they assume the experimenter's second question is a question about the irrelevant quantitative change that has been made (i.e., the lengthening or shortening of a row of counters in a conservation of number task). Donaldson (1978) argues that the achievement of Piagetian-type conservation depends upon learning to give primacy to the language over the context in the child's interpretation of the question.

In a recent series of experiments by Neilson, Dockrell and McKechnie (1983a, 1983b) the issues raised by Rose and Blank (1974) and by McGarrigle and Donaldson (1975) have been re-examined. Neilson et al. (1983a) examined the applicability of Rose and Blank's (1974) one-judgement task to the conservation of length, liquid, and weight, in addition to number. If there is such an effect of repeating the same question, it should be general across conservation tasks. Neilson et al. found that the facilitatory effect of the one-judgement condition was specific to number conservation. They suggest that the reason for their results is that the one-judgement condition leads the 6-year-old children to count, a strategy that is only applicable to number conservation. The children thus base their judgements on the result of counting rather than on reasoning from the pre-transformed array. This contention is supported by the fact that a similar level of responding was found in the one-judgement case whether the arrays were transformed or the final state simply presented without any transformation being witnessed. Neilson et al. (1983a) also tested a group of 4.5-year-old children. With this group, the one-judgement condition had no effect on performance, even for number conservation. Why is it that the one-judgement task elicits counting from 6-year-olds but not from 4.5-year-olds? The answer may lie in the different appreciation of the relevance of counting possessed by 4- and 6-year-old children. Michie (1984a, 1984b) examined children's counting and its role in reasoning about the relative numerosity of two arrays. In one experiment (Michie, 1984b), she compared the relative use of different strategies for judging relative numerosity by 3- and 4-year-olds. She found that children rarely counted spontaneously when judging which of two rows had more although they could easily be induced to do so, and accuracy of judgement improved significantly when the children did count. In a second experiment Michie (1984b) examined the effect of various types of training on children's tendency to count when asked to judge relative numerosity. The only type of training that had any effect was that which included feedback on the reliability of counting. Michie concludes that young children do not deploy counting because they are not aware of its value as a strategy in number reasoning. In particular, when confronted with alternative bases for making a judgement, such as the length of a row of counters, children will use these cues because they mistakenly believe that these are reliable indicators of numerosity.

In their re-examination of the results of McGarrigle and Donaldson (1975), Neilson et al. (1983b) examined the justifications offered by the children. Because of the problematic relation between verbal justifications and the cognitive structures to which they relate, most research in recent years has dispensed with justifications and simply measured the level of correct responding. The danger of this is, of course, that it is impossible to detect when the correct response has been arrived at for the wrong reasons. The relation between justifications and responses is raised again by the Neilson et al. report. It was found that, taking responses alone, the results of McGarrigle and Donaldson's experiment were replicated. However, only 22 per cent of the children who gave correct judgements in the AT condition were capable of providing adequate justifications. Neilson et al. argue that the nature of some of the justifications offered in the AT condition suggest that the children may be basing their judgements solely on the pre-transformed arrays and ignoring the transformed array as a 'mess' created by teddy. The results of Neilson et al. (1983a, 1983b) emphasize that the relation between performance and cognitive structures needs to be examined with care. It is necessary to determine, when children give conservation responses, why they have given them. Piaget used justifications as his yardstick here. It may be that justifications are not the most appropriate method of determining which cognitive structure has generated a response, as Brainerd (1973) has argued. However, this should not mean that the attempt to obtain some measure of the cognitive structure, other than a simple correct or incorrect response should be abandoned. Apart from the inherent methodological danger of relying solely on correct/incorrect responses, measures of how the child actually solves the problem will be necessary to address other issues such as whether the different types of conservation have a developmental origin in a common cognitive structure, or whether, in fact, they derive from quite different information processing strategies.

What Strategies are Used to Solve Conservation Problems?

There are good grounds for believing that at least the conservation of number relies on different principles than the other conservations. The major bases for judging equivalence in a conservation of number test are one-to-one matching and counting. Neither of these strategies can be applied to the conservation of length, mass, or liquid. In fact, as Siegler (1981) has shown adults were not always correct when asked to judge the equivalence of post-transformation displays of liquid and mass, although they were always correct for number. Presumably the difference is due to the verification procedures available: rows can be recounted if necessary; there is no such readily available procedure for checking whether or not the transformed display is the same as the nontransformed display with liquid and mass.

Siegler (1981) tested children from 3 to 9 years on number, mass, and liquid conservation problems in order to determine the order in which the ability to conserve emerged. He found that number conservation developed earlier than the other conservations. The childen's performance on the conservation of liquid and mass was very similar suggesting that these tasks may share a common underlying structure. In fact, the difference between children's performance on the conservation of discrete and continuous quantities has been noted by Genevan researchers:

> Some subjects had great difficulty in applying a reasoning which had proved adequate for problems dealing with discrete elements to other situations where quasi-continuous materials were used. This would suggest that the developmental link between the conservation of discrete and continuous quantities is neither simple nor direct. (Inhelder, Sinclair and Bovet, 1974: p. 80).

If the development of number conservation can be explained by the deployment of such procedures as counting and one-to-one matching, what procedures could account for the conservation of continuous quantities such as liquid, mass, and weight? Piaget's own view was that conservation depended on the prior development of two rules of reasoning: compensation and reversibility (Piaget, 1941, 1952, 1968). Compensation involves reasoning that, for example, when liquid rises higher in a tall thin glass than a similar volume of liquid in a short fat glass, the rise in height is compensated for by the decrease in width. Compensation involves an appreciation that the height of a column of liquid is a function of the width of the container. Reversibility involves reasoning that if liquid is poured from a short wide glass into a tall thin glass and, in the process, rises higher, then the operation can be reversed and the same height column as originally will be obtained in the short wide glass. According to Piaget these reasoning processes underlie the ability to make judgements of conservation; it is their development that moves the child from nonconserver to conserver.

Others have disputed Piaget's claims and argued that an identity rule may be sufficient for conservation. Bruner (1966; Bruner et al., 1966) stressed the importance of qualitative identity – 'is it the same water as before?', while Elkind (1967; Elkind and Schoenfeld, 1972) stressed the importance of quantitative identity – 'is there the same amount of water as before?'. It should be possible to test the various rules proposed as a necessary basis of conservation independently of conservation itself and thus determine what relations hold between the proposed rules and conservation. A number of studies have attempted to do this.

It has been claimed at one time or another that all four of the rules implicated in conservation – qualitative and quantitative identity, compensation, and reversibility – precede the ability to conserve. Bruner (1966) and Hamel (1971) both demonstrated that children understood that the liquid after transfer is 'the same liquid' as prior to transfer much earlier than they understood conservation. Research findings showing that quantitative identity precedes conservation have been summarized by Brainerd and Hooper (1975). The lag between quantitative identity and conservation is much shorter than the lag between qualitative identity and conservation. Some studies have reported no consistent relation between compensation and conservation (Larsen and Flavell, 1970; Gelman and Weinberg, 1972). However, others (Curcio, Kattef, Levine and Robbins, 1977; Brainerd, 1977) have reported that children grasp the principle of compensation before they can conserve. Finally, Brainerd (1977), and Murray and Johnson (1969) found that children understand the principle of reversibility well in advance of being able to conserve. Brainerd's (1977) study showed that children understood reversibility first, compensation and qualitative identity next, and finally quantitative identity. However, this is a trend, not a universal order.

What can we conclude from these studies? Overall they are consistent with the view that each of the four rules plays a part in the development of conservation. However, none of the studies shows that any particular rule is a necessary and sufficient condition for conservation. But to phrase the issue in this way is to assume that there is one unitary cognitive ability that can be described as conservation. It is probably more profitable to see conservation as a way of reasoning that can exist at various levels. It is possible that some children may appreciate quantitative identity but not compensation, while the reverse may hold for other children. It would surely be more profitable to treat both groups as having particular conservation abilities rather than arguing about whether either can truly conserve.

A study by Acredolo and Acredolo (1979) illustrates the way in which patterns of development can vary in relation to conservation. They tested children on a sequence of anticipation-of-liquid conservation, anticipation-of-water-levels, and standard liquid conservation tasks. The background to their study is a familiar debate that we have previously examined in relation to number conservation: that children are misled by the actual transformation itself, which brings their logical reasoning into conflict with more overriding perceptual strategies. Bruner (1966) showed that there was a high incidence of anticipation of liquid conservation among otherwise nonconserving children. He argued that this demonstrated that failure to conserve in the standard task was not due to a lack of logic but to the child being seduced by perceptual appearances. Piaget, for his part, retorted that the anticipation task is not a case of genuine conservation but of pseudoconservation based upon the child failing to appreciate that the water heights will be different following transfer of water to a different-sized container (Piaget, 1967b, 1968). It is possible to test these alternative views by presenting children with an anticipation-of-conservation task, then an anticipation-of-levels task, and finally a standard conservation task. This is essentially what Acredolo and Acredolo (1979) did.

Piagetian theory would predict that 'pseudoconservers' would pass the anticipation of conservation task but fail the other two tasks. By contrast a theory that emphasizes the importance of identity relations in conservation would predict that although some children might show the above pattern, there would also be children who would pass both anticipation tasks but fail the standard conservation task – i.e. they would anticipate a change in liquid height but when confronted with it would change the basis of their conservation judgement from one of reasoning by identity to reasoning by liquid height. In addition, identity theory would also predict a group of children who would fail to anticipate a change in level but would both anticipate conservation and pass the standard conservation task – i.e. although the children do not anticipate a change in liquid height, when it happens in the standard conservation task it is effectively ignored by them and they continue to reason on the basis of amount rather than liquid height. Acredolo and Acredolo tested children aged 5 and 6 years and found an 18 per cent incidence of pseudoconservation but also an overall 37 per cent incidence of the two patterns not predicted by Piagetian theory. Of particular interest was the fact that 29 per cent of the children anticipated conservation and a change in liquid level but failed to conserve when confronted with the change – a result that suggests that there can be a conflict between perceptual appearances and judgements of amount and that stability between these conflicting judgements must be achieved before conservation judgements become robust. However, the lack of robustness is no reason to deny any appreciation of quantitative reasoning to a child who fails the standard conservation test. The results of Acredolo and Acredolo would seem to suggest that children often rely on an evaluation by identity in judging amount but that the younger child's confidence in this judgement can easily be jolted or overridden by other considerations. The developmental path would appear to be not one in which a logical appreciation suddenly transforms the basis of quantitative reasoning but one in which different modes of reasoning can develop simultaneously and to some extent independently. One or other of these modes may be differentially accessed by different stimulus conditions in the early stages of a skill's development. If the modes give different results (as judgement by amount and by liquid column height in a conservation of liquid experiment will do) then the child's responses may appear contradictory – a fact of which the child may for a time remain blissfully unaware. Instead of regarding contradictory judgements as the absence of a 'true skill' - as has so often been the case in research on cognitive development – it would seem better to seek an understanding of the modes of reasoning that are in contradiction and the conditions under which a particular mode is accessed.

The importance of conditions under which children are asked to make a judgement and the extent to which the young child's reasoning is stimulus-dominated is illustrated in an experiment by McShane and Morrison (1985). They asked children to judge which of two amounts of liquid was greater under two conditions. In the first condition the amounts were first shown in two standard bottles and both amounts were then poured into glasses. The larger amount was poured into a short wide glass and the smaller amount into a tall thin glass. The glasses and the amounts were so arranged that the liquid levels were equal after this transfer. In the second condition, only the final state of the liquid in the glasses was presented without any transfer being observed. McShane and Morrison predicted on the basis of their previous research (McShane and Morrison, 1983) that when only the final state of the liquids was presented, younger children (3- to 4-year-olds) should be as good as when the transfer was actually observed. The rationale for this is that young children will judge only the relative fullness of the final state of the glasses. By contrast older children (4- to 5-year-olds) should perform at a random level on the no-transfer task but above random on the transfer task. This pattern of results was indeed observed. It would be tempting to conclude that younger children judge amounts only depending on the final state of the liquid and ignore prior information. They might thus be judged to be in a pre-identity phase of development. However, this conclusion would not be justified as a second experiment showed. In this experiment the tall thin glass used in the previous experiment was modified. It was still thin but it was no longer tall – in fact it was the same height as the fat glass. The problem that faces the younger children in this condition is that there is now no relative fullness cue because the liquid levels are equal and the glass heights are equal. (A potential cue exists in the width of the glasses but Anderson and Cuneo (1978) have shown that this dimension is not accessed by children below about 6 years.)

It was found in this experiment that in the no-transfer condition the younger children's performance fell to chance-level, as would be expected from the absence of the relative fullness cues. However, in the transfer condition they maintained their previous high level of performance showing that they are capable of using pre-transfer information as a basis for their judgements. It may be that they also used this mode of reasoning in the transfer task, even when relative fullness information was available. However, even if they did do so, the fact that they succeeded in the no-transfer condition and failed a standard conservation task shows that they do not always use this mode of reasoning. McShane and Morrison proposed that, with younger children, judgements will be highly influenced by the most salient stimulus dimensions. This proposal helps explain the inconsistency exhibited by children who succeed on anticipation of conservation and anticipation of levels tasks but fail a standard conservation task; the basis of judgement changes from one task to the other. In the conservation task the salient liquid height dimension becomes the basis of judgement.

Conservation in developmental theory

The development of conservation has been a central issue for theory and research in cognitive development. It has been central both because it plays such a prominent role in Piaget's theory and also because it is a rich source of experimental hypotheses. Studying conservation has helped researchers to understand a great deal about how children select and process information in early childhood and about how the conduct of an experiment, both verbally and non-verbally, can be factors that affect the child's reasoning. As a methodological technique the conservation experiment has been invaluable.

However, the great mass of research on conservation has also served to weaken its central role in a theory of cognitive development. There are many reasons for this. For one thing, conservation itself is a complex judgement that depends on the presence of various information processing strategies and the recognition that a particular strategy should be deployed. For another, the use of a strategy crucially depends on *other* developments that determine the child's interpretation of the task that is being posed. In view of this complexity, conservation has become a skill to be explained by other processes rather than a basis on which to build theories of cognitive development.

There have been numerous research attempts to link the development of other cognitive skills to conservation. In general, these attempts have been unsuccessful. The ability to conserve has not been implicated as a crucial determinant of other cognitive skills, nor has failure to conserve been reliably implicated as a central cause of any cognitive delays. These results are further reasons why conservation does not today assume the theoretical centrality that Piaget assigned to it.

Number Development

Researchers have explained children's ability to conserve number in terms of the application of one-to-one matching and counting. However, none of the research that has yet been reviewed has explained how these procedures develop. The procedures are of considerable interest in their own right because, irrespective of the role they play in number conservation, they are fundamental skills on which numerical reasoning is based.

Numerical reasoning is of central theoretical importance because it is a domain in which all the major issues relevant to the development of information processing are in clear focus. First, there is the issue of how representations of a precisely specified set of words and concepts develop.

Second, there is the procedural skill of manipulating numbers for computational purposes. Third, there is a gradient of complexity from counting, through simple numerical operations of addition and subtraction, to complex abstract reasoning about number. Fourth, although number reasoning begins early, number is essentially an abstract concept; there is no physical 'number 2'. This means that the information processing system must, in some sense, be innately sensitive to the property of number. Thus, number is a key area in which there is an opportunity to explore some properties of the human cognitive architecture and also, because there is much that must be learnt about numbers, how this architecture interacts with learning from experience. Numbers have many applications. At the most basic level numbers are used to count. Although this may seem a simple skill it has its developmental complexities. Historically, the evolution of a counting system took a considerable time. The counting system that we use is of comparatively recent origin. The last section of this chapter contains a brief outline of the evolution of our counting system.

Counting involves establishing a one-to-one relation between number words and objects that are being counted. Number words have two important properties: they are ordered and the last count word is a measure of the number of objects that have been counted. These properties are known as *ordinality* and *cardinality* respectively. Numbers may also be manipulated by processes of addition, subtraction, division, and multiplication. These processes are usually referred to as *mathematical reasoning*.

The Development of Counting

Counting is probably the most basic use to which numbers can be put and developmentally it is the first use of numbers to appear. Contemporary work on number development views counting both as an important developmental process in its own right and as playing a central role in number reasoning (Fuson, 1988; Gelman and Gallistel, 1978).

Counting involves establishing a one-to-one correspondence between objects being counted and some representation of those objects. The representation that we employ is the system of number or count words *one, two, three,* etc. Counting requires several cognitive skills. The number words must be mapped in a one-to-one fashion onto the entities being counted and then, when the last entity has been counted, the cardinality of that entity – i.e., the number word used to count it – must be taken as the total of the number of entities. These are two basic counting principles. In addition to these principles there is a requirement for consistency in the order in which the count words are used. A child who counts *one, two, three, four, five,* on one occasion but *one, four, six, seven* on another, would hardly be credited with an ability to count. Although it was once believed that children initially count in this sort of erratic fashion, recent evidence has challenged this view.

It is possible to contrast two approaches to early development of counting. The first is represented by Gelman and Gallistel (1978) and has been further elaborated by Greeno, Riley and Gelman (1984). According to this approach counting results from the application of cognitive principles by the child. These principles are presumed to be part of the cognitive architecture with which the child is innately endowed. This does not mean that the child has nothing to learn. The principles do not replace learning but rather serve to channel the learning and the inferences that the child makes. The second approach to the development of counting is represented by Fuson (1988). Fuson does not find consistent evidence for the principles proposed by Gelman and Gallistel (1978). She offers an alternative set of principles that imply a considerably less powerful innate cognitive architecture than that proposed by Gelman and Gallistel (1978) and Greeno et al. (1984).

According to Gelman and Gallistel (1978) counting involves the application of five principles: the one-to-one principle; the stable-order principle; the cardinal principle; the abstraction principle; and the order-irrelevance principle. The first three principles are *how to count* principles. The fourth, the abstraction principle states that counting can be carried out on any collection of entities and the fifth, the order-irrelevance principles states that the order in which items are counted is irrelevant.

Gelman and Gallistel argue that some children as young as 2 years obey the three 'how to count' principles. Although children as young as this do not usually know the standard count words, Gelman and Gallistel maintain that the child's own idiosyncratic list (for example *one, two, five, four,* etc.) is used systematically and in conformity with the one-to-one principle, the stable-order principle, and the cardinal principle.

Gelman and Gallistel cite two sources of evidence in favour of their claim that children obey 'how to count' principles. The first source is an experiment conducted by Gelman (1972a, 1972b). This experiment was designed to investigate children's reasoning about number and this aspect of the experiment will be discussed later. In this experiment children were presented with rows of 2 vs 3, or 3 vs 5 toy mice, and were required to make certain judgements about which row was 'the winner'. The children had previously been provided with feedback that the row containing more was the winner. Everything the children said in the experiment was tape recorded. It transpired that there was much talk about number and much spontaneous counting. The tape recordings thus provided a data-base for retrospective analysis of the children's counting by Gelman and Gallistel (1978). They found that for two- and three-item arrays, 14 out of 16 children as young as 2 years obeyed the one-to-one principle and 9 of these obeyed the stable order principle. For three- and five-item arrays, 20 out of 24 children obeyed the one-to-one principle and 17 of these obeyed the stable-order principle. Gelman and Gallistel also reported that the majority of children had some knowledge of the cardinal principle.

The second source of evidence comes from a direct study in which children aged 3 to 5 years were asked how many items were in a particular set. Sets were presented in pairs of 2 and 3, 4 and 5, 7 and 9, and 11 and 19. One set was 'for the child' and the other 'for a puppet' that the experimenter had brought along. The child was required to indicate how many items each had. The children's application of the one-to-one principle varied as a function of set size. For set sizes up to 5 the performance of all three groups was impressive, if not perfect. Thereafter the performance of the 3-year-olds declined rapidly and the performance of the 4- and 5-year-olds less rapidly. Further, the majority of children of all ages used the same list on all their trials, thus applying the stable-order principle also. Although the study was not designed specifically to test the cardinal principle, Gelman and Gallistel report that there was evidence that children used the cardinal principle, although support for this was not as marked as support for the one-to-one and the stable-order principles.

Fuson (1988) agrees with Gelman and Gallistel that children must possess one-to-one and stable-order principles in order to be able to count at all. However, although these principles may guide the child's behaviour, Fuson's analysis reveals that the skilled mastery of the principles takes some considerable time to develop.

One-to-one matching   The principle of one-to-one matching is basic to counting. Its application requires that each object be counted once and that it only be counted once. This requires two important subskills: matching count-words and objects and separating counted from to-be-counted objects. In the early stages of counting children make frequent errors, especially as set size increases (Fuson, 1988; Gelman and Gallistel, 1978). In particular, children have difficulty in separating counted from to-be-counted objects, even when the objects are arranged in a row. Typical errors involve skipping an object altogether and multiple counts of the same object. By age 4, the error-rate drops considerably (Fuson, 1988). This may be due to developmental changes in the way in which children use pointing within the task of counting. Saxe and Kaplan (1981) have proposed that children initially use pointing as a referential gesture when counting and that, at this time, it plays little if any role in coordinating the sequence of number words with the objects being counted. Thus, the child may simultaneously be doing two things – uttering number words and pointing at objects. However, the activities may be unco-ordinated and, as a result, the common errors observed in children's counting will occur. Between the ages of 2 and 4 years Saxe and Kaplan argue that children come to be able to use pointing in a regulatory way to match number words to objects.

The analysis of errors made by children in carrying out some task is an important method by which information processing theories study the underlying skill required on a task. In the case of counting there are two important types of error that can be made in coordinating pointing and counting: errors in which the pointing is accurately done but the counting is not and errors in which the counting is accurately coordinated with the pointing but the pointing itself is inaccurate, with a consequent loss in the overall accuracy of the count. Fuson (1988) calls these two types of errors *word-point errors* and *point-object errors* respectively. Of the two types of errors point-object are more common initially (Fuson, 1988). This finding is consistent with the argument of Saxe and Kaplan (1981) that children have some initial difficulties in using pointing to regulate the objects being counted.

Figure 6.4 shows the error data from a study reported by Fuson (1988) in which children were asked to count blocks either in rows or in disorganized arrays. The children were initially presented with a row of four or five blocks and then blocks were added, one or two at a time, until the child either counted 33 or 34 blocks, refused to go on, or ceased to pay attention. The differences among the various conditions were more marked for the younger than the older children. The youngest children – those aged between 3 and 3.5 years only succeeded in preserving a low error rate for word-point errors when the blocks were in rows. When the array was disorganized word-point errors increased significantly for this group but to a much lesser extent for the other groups. All groups made more point-object errors, whether counting a row or a disorganized array. The fact that there is not a large effect of rows versus disorganized arrays on the rate of point-object errors suggests that the major contributing factor to this error is a cognitive one of coordinating the two behaviours. Fuson (1988) found that children aged between 4.5 and 6 years eliminated such errors entirely when they were asked to 'try really hard' whereas those aged between 3.5 and 4 years only reduced their error rate slightly.

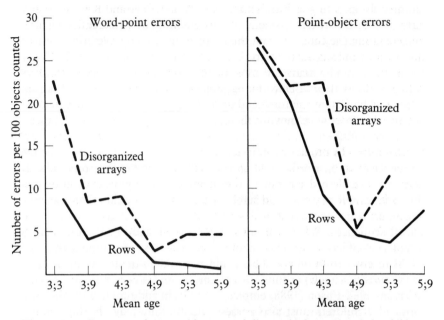

Figure 6.4   *Frequency of errors with rows and disorganized arrays made by children counting. (Derived from table 4.2 in Fuson, 1988.)*

Thus, younger children have a fundamental difficulty in integrating pointing with counting effectively.

The most common type of word-point error is pointing without a count-word. The most obvious explanation of pointing without a count-word would seem to be that children have to search for the number word, having pointed and, by the time the word is retrieved, the pointing finger has moved on. However, if this were the case, it would be expected that the rate of this error would increase as the number of objects to be counted increases and, accordingly, the number words known to the child decrease. Yet Fuson (1988) has found that in 3-year-old children point-no word errors are distributed equally over objects in the first and second half of rows ranging from seven to 14 objects. It seems therefore that the most significant cause of these errors is simply the lack of co-ordination between the two behaviours.

In addition to its function in relating number words to objects, pointing serves another important function: it is one means by which children can separate counted from to-be-counted objects (Beckwith and Restle, 1966). Pointing serves this function best when the objects to be counted are in an orderly fashion – a line is the ideal example. When objects are not arranged in an orderly fashion, pointing is not such an effective means of separating the counted from the to-be-counted. An alternative method is to move objects as they are counted. Fuson (1988) found that only between 5.5 and 6 years did most of the children move a pile of blocks while counting them. Below this age approximately 50 per cent of children separated blocks into counted and uncounted piles; the remainder pointed at the blocks without moving them.

Stable-order   In order to count accurately it is necessary to use a stable sequence of count words. Gelman and Gallistel (1978) have proposed that keeping a stable order is one of the innate counting principles possessed by children. However, a rigid stable-order principle would militate against changing from unconventional sequences of number words to conventional sequences. What is needed is the preservation of stability unless there is conflicting evidence about the sequence from inputs that the child receives from others. This could be through deliberate instruction (as occurs in schools) or intermittent correction (as occurs in interactions with parents). Fuson (1988) emphasizes that, in addition to a stable-order principle, children must also possess specific knowledge of the number word sequence in order to be able to count. According to Fuson, children regard counting as an activity that is carried out by using a special list of counting words. Children also understand that the list is composed of number words only. (Gelman and Gallistel place little emphasis on this, requiring only that the child use a stable list of some sort, whether count words or some other sequence such as letters of the alphabet.) Fuson's emphasis is that the child is concerned with learning the list of count words and, in doing so, learns about other features of number.

Fuson, Richards and Briars (1982) have examined the extent to which 3- to 5-year-old children obey a stable-order principle when counting. They asked children to count as high as they could. They found that children's count sequences could be sub-divided into three portions: an accurate number-word sequence, a stable incorrect sequence, and a non-stable incorrect sequence. The accurate number-word sequence consisted of the smaller number words; the stable incorrect sequence (which began anywhere from five onwards) mostly had the number words in the correct sequence but contained omissions; the non-stable sequence consisted of the final number words produced by the child and were, by definition, irregular over trials. Even for the two stable sequences, the children were not consistent on every trial. Apart from the fact that this lack of consistency is to be expected from children learning the number words, the inconsistency reflects a *necessary feature of learning*: if children were bound rigidly by a stable-order principle, they would be locked forever into an initially acquired incorrect sequence.

As we have seen, children master the sequence of count words gradually. Initially, a child will learn a portion of the list accurately, but then become increasingly inaccurate with later portions of the list. How do unconventional sequences of count words come to be corrected? The fact that the number words can be learnt by rote is undoubtedly of considerable significance here. The sequence itself can be detached from the act of counting and learnt simply as a list. The focus of the child's attention, and that of the child's tutor, can be placed on the structure of the list itself, without the additional cognitive loads imposed by counting. As the list becomes more stable, so counting will become more accurate. Thus, an accurate list of count words can be acquired independently of counting but then applied to the task of counting.

Cardinality   Gelman and Gallistel (1978) argue that children possess a principle of cardinality that involves the knowledge that the number of objects in a set corresponds to the last numeral used. This claim is based on the fact that when children are asked how many objects are in a set, they respond with the last number counted. Fuson (1988; Fuson and Hall, 1983) however, regards the same data as only showing that children give a 'last-word response' when asked how many objects are in a set – that is, the children simply repeat the last count word used in response to a 'how-many' question. The basis of Fuson's argument is that in many experiments on the cardinality principle, no evidence was obtained as to whether the child understood that the last counted word referred to the cardinality of the set. In attempting to obtain independent measures of a principle of cardinality, Fuson found that many children who answered a question such as '*How many stars are there?*' by saying n failed to answer correctly the further question '*Show me the n stars.*' Faced with such questions 2-year-olds gave correct demonstrations 20 per cent of the time and 3-year-olds, 53 per cent of the time. These data do not support a universal cardinality principle that is part of the innate organization of counting.

Abstraction and order-irrelevance   There were two further counting principles proposed by Gelman and Gallistel (1978): the abstraction principle, which stipulates that any objects can be counted, and the order-irrelevance principle, which stipulates that the order in which items are counted is irrelevant. In general, there seems to be consistent evidence that children conform to these principles, although to do so does not require any particular knowledge about count words. In this, they differ from the other principles.

Summary   There is still considerable debate about the extent to which counting is done in accordance with innately specified principles. Some principles must exist to make the ability possible at all. However, there is, at present, dispute over whether principles such as cardinality are innate or constructed from experience. There also seems room to doubt whether a stable-order principle is really an innate regulator of counting in view of the fact that children produce some very unstable count lists, beyond the initial segment (Fuson, 1988). It may be that the stability of the early part of the list is of an entirely associative character. As the list lengthens the associative connections will weaken and instability will result. The stable portion of list will gradually become longer as associative strengths increase through more frequent exposure to and use of longer lists. However, final stability of the list in the tens and hundreds portions will only be achieved when the child induces a generative rule for decade and century structure.

Learning Arithmetic

Arithmetic skills cover a wide range from a basic understanding of the principles of addition and subtraction to accurate calculation with many large numbers. The teaching of arithmetic is a major task of primary education and a basic competence is a prerequisite for life in our society. The psychological principles of arithmetical reasoning and calculation can therefore be regarded as of major importance to an understanding of cognitive development.

Arithmetical skills are of fundamental theoretical significance because, more than in any other area of cognition, it is possible to articulate the rules and procedures for arithmetical computation. Thus it should be possible to examine clearly the relation between the developmental representations and strategies used to solve arithmetical problems and the formal representations and procedures that define arithmetic. In other areas of cognition, such as language development, this relation is much more difficult to examine because there is no generally agreed formal representation of the language system.

Arithmetic is also of particular interest because it possesses both a syntax and a semantics that can, to some extent, be treated independently. It is possible, for example to learn to perform written arithmetic by learning a set of syntactic principles that specify how the numbers are to be manipulated. For example, it is possible to learn how to manipulate the numbers in problems such as 92 − 67, in which we are required initially to subtract seven from two. We can proceed by decrementing the next leftmost digit to 2 by one unit and add this value to 2 making the initial subtraction 12 − 7. This can be represented as follows:

$$\begin{array}{r} ^{8}9^{1}2 \\ -\ 6\ 7 \\ \hline \end{array}$$

A child may learn to carry out this, and many other operations, without understanding the meaning, or semantics, of the procedure. The fact that there is both a syntax and a semantics to numerical computation, and that they are frequently dissociated, makes it possible to study the extent to which the acquisition of procedures depends on understanding what the procedure does. Answering this question is fairly fundamental to educational issues about arithmetic. Educational practice has tended to move from an emphasis on the purely formal syntactic structure of arithmetical problems to an emphasis on comprehending the problem structure (Resnick and Ford, 1981). This seems to be a desirable move but the fundamental evidence about how children best learn arithmetical skills is still unclear. Therefore, addressing the issue of the syntactic-semantic relation in the domain of arithmetic is of fundamental importance.

The acquisition of arithmetic procedures is a topic that is too large and and detailed to review thoroughly in a book such as this. Therefore, the focus will be on illustrative examples of how these procedures can be studied and on the relation between the earliest aspect of number development, counting, and the later acquisition of arithmetic procedures.

Counting is basic to the acquisition of arithmetic procedures. This is true, both in general terms – arithmetic procedures are simply counting shortcuts – and also in developmental terms: children deploy counting as a way of solving problems that do not specifically request that the child count. One of the most interesting demonstrations of this is an experiment conducted by Groen and Parkman (1972). The experiment is interesting both for what it reveals about children's arithmetic and for the methodology employed.

One of the most difficult aspects of studying cognition is finding a methodology that can be used to test the cognitive processes that are hypothesized to underlie behavioural responses. Consider the task presented by Groen and Parkman. They gave children all possible combinations of addition problems that sum to 9 or less. Children saw the problems on a screen and had to indicate the correct answer as quickly as possible by pressing a numbered key. In abstract terms, children saw all problems of the type

$$m + n = ?$$

What Groen and Parkman wished to discover was how the children arrived at their answers. They had a number of hypotheses about how this might be done. These were:

- *Counting-all model.* The child counts up to the first number m and continues for n more numbers. For $2 + 4$ the child would count 1, 2, 3, 4, 5, 6.
- *Counting-on model.* The child starts from m and counts on for n more numbers. For $2 + 4$ the child would count 3, 4, 5, 6.
- *Min model.* The child starts from the larger of m or n and counts on by the other. For $2 + 4$ the child would count 5, 6.

In order to test these models, Groen and Parkman used a technique developed by Sternberg (1969). Sternberg showed that the reaction time taken to perform a task is a linear function of the number of computational operations carried out. Applying this reasoning, Groen and Parkman assumed that the reaction time required to count on from the lesser of the two numbers would be greater than the reaction time required to count on from the greater of the two. Similarly, if children counted on from the first of the two numbers, the reaction time would have a different pattern than if they counted on from the second of the two. Given that each model implied a different pattern of reaction times, the actual reaction times could be tested against the five models to determine which model best fitted the data.

Groen and Parkman found that one model fitted their data quite precisely: reaction time was a linear function of the smaller of the two numbers to be added. This has become known as the min model because reaction time is a linear function of the minimum of the two addends. The psychological process implied by the model is one in which the larger of the addends is taken as a starting point and the child then counts on from this point by the value of the second addend. It made no difference in Groen and Parkman's study whether the larger or smaller number was presented first. This further suggests the operation of a principle of commutativity (or order irrelevance) whereby it is recognised that the ordering of numbers in calculation is irrelevant to the result. Groen and Parkman's initial results were replicated and refined by a variety of other studies (Groen and Poll, 1973; Svenson, 1975; Svenson, Hedenborg and Lingman, 1976; Woods, Resnick and Groen, 1975).

The *min* model is a genuine surprise because the algorithm it implies is not usually taught directly to children as a calculation procedure. Where then does it come from? The obvious inference is that it is invented on the back of the counting model. In order to test directly whether the algorithm is indeed invented Groen and Resnick (1977) taught a number of children, who did not yet know how to add, an addition algorithm significantly different from the min algorithm, and then observed any changes in the algorithm being applied over an extended period of time. To add $m + n$, five children aged 4 years were taught to count out the number of blocks that represented m, then the number that represented n, then to combine the sets and count the combination. This model is called the sum model, because its application would lead to reaction times that are a linear function of the sum of $m + n$.

Having taught the children the sum algorithm, Groen and Resnick presented children with a variety of addition problems. The results for two of the subjects were consistently best fitted by the sum model over a range of trials while the results for a further two were consistently best fitted by the min model. The remaining subject changed from a sum to a min model over the tests.

How did the children change the algorithm used? Groen and Resnick point out that although the sum algorithm is easy to demonstrate and teach to young children, it is inefficient as a performance routine both because of its limitation to objects that can be counted there and then and because of time taken. Once the algorithm was well established the children moved from block counting to finger counting (sometimes on the experimenter's suggestion) and from there to the immediate display of the correct number of fingers for each quantity without counting them out one by one. Eventually finger counting was dropped by the children. The min algorithm is completed by representing (overtly or covertly) the larger of the two addends and then counting on by the smaller.

If we consider the process in a little more detail then it becomes clear that in order to move from a sum algorithm to a min algorithm the child must recognize a cardinal-to-count connection (Fuson, 1982) for the larger addend, which obviates the need to count out the larger addend. Fuson (1982) argues that the control of different meanings for number words is a vital part of learning to count-on. In particular, she argues that establishing a cardinal-to-count connection should be distinguished from a count-to-cardinal connection. The latter is the cardinality rule and states that the last ordinal number in a count sequence is the cardinal value of that sequence. The rule summarizes an action that has been completed. The cardinal-to-count connection by contrast predicts an action that may be carried out; that is given '6 + 3' for example as an arithmetic problem the child knows by applying a cardinal-to-count rule that the production of the final count word 'six' and counting on the remaining quantity from this will give the correct answer. In a study with children aged 6 to 8 in which relatively large numbers were used (12 through 18 for the first addend and 6 through 9 for the second addend) Secada, Fuson and Hall (1983) found that 5 out of 27 subjects used a sum algorithm in conditions where collections of squares were visible for the addends despite the relative effort of counting such large numbers for the first addend. When squares were not present the children counted on. Thus, the acquisition of counting-on is not an all-or-none phenomenon and may co-exist with other, less efficient procedures. This is a characteristic of cognitive functioning: efficient procedures are not necessarily universally deployed by a person; under various conditions less efficient procedures may be elicited or chosen.

Counting models have been applied to other simple arithmetic tasks, such as subtraction (Woods et al., 1975; Svenson and Hedenborg, 1979) and addition with the sum known but one of the addends unknown (Groen and Poll, 1973). Further, overt counting has been observed in a variety of problem-solving situations including work with children as young as 2 years (Gelman, 1972a, 1972b). Thus, counting, which appears to be a natural human activity, spontaneously engaged in, provides also the initial means of arithmetical calculation.

The use of counting in subtraction displays the versatility in using procedures of which children are capable. Both Woods et al. (1975) and Svenson and Hedenborg (1979) have shown that from about the age of 7 years children will often work out the answer to a subtraction sum by either counting down from the minuend (the number from which the subtraction is to be made) by the value of the subtrahend (the number to be subtracted) or by counting up from the subtrahend to the minuend. Thus, 8 − 2 is solved by counting *eight . . . seven, six* and obtaining the answer directly and 8 − 6 is solved by counting *six . . . seven, eight* and keeping track of the number of digits required to reach the minuend. It is worth stressing again that the majority of children observed using these procedures had not been taught to use them; they spontaneously invented them. To do so, they not only needed to be competent at counting, they also needed to be able to reason about counting. Resnick (1983, 1986) has suggested that for children to solve such problems they must understand that a number can be decomposed into parts. In the case of 8 − 2 this means that 8 can be decomposed into two numbers, one of which is given as 2. The task is to find the other one. To do so it is possible either to count up from 2 to 8 or to count down from 8 by 2. If we also assume that children's knowledge of number allows them to reason that 2 is the smaller part of the decomposition of 8 then the obvious strategy is to count down from 8. By a similar process of reasoning, the obvious strategy for 8 − 6 is to count up from 6, although here there is the additional task of counting the number of count words used. The analysis of these simple tasks shows the amount of combination of basic number skills that is necessary to solve even simple tasks. The fact that it is done spontaneously shows the extent to which the cognitive system actively engages in problem solving.

Counting may provide the initial entry-point to arithmetical calculation. However, the counting involved quickly becomes cumbersome when larger numbers are involved. These numbers require the application of procedures to a small stock of number facts (which are perhaps initially established or consolidated by counting algorithms). It is to the study of these procedures that we now turn.

Arithmetical Errors

Children make a variety of errors in arithmetical calculation. Some of these errors are simply errors of number facts but many involve misconceptions about arithmetic operations. It is with this latter group of errors that we shall be concerned. It is a common assumption that the erratic application of principles is the primary cause of arithmetical errors. However, misconceptions are not usually a random affair but involve the application of incorrect principles to arithmetic calculation. It is an important task to diagnose these principles in order to aid the student in mastering the correct principles. Systematic but incorrect principles also have an important theoretical status. Obviously such principles are not taught, so they must represent constructions or inventions by the learner. They thus reveal the natural inferences that the child makes in learning mathematics.

Recent research on children's mathematical skills has focused on errors as 'faulty algorithms' rather than as faulty application of a correct algorithm (Brown and Burton, 1978; Brown and Van Lehn, 1980; Young and O'Shea, 1981). As an illustration, let us consider the following examples of one student's addition from Brown and Burton (1978):

41	328	989	66	216
9	917	52	887	13
50	1345	1141	1053	229

The errors may appear random but they could also be the result of a faulty algorithm. In order to understand what this might be it is necessary to consider the process of addition in a little more detail. The issue that requires particular attention is what happens when the sum of two digits $m + n$ is greater than 9. For digits, the correct procedure is to 'carry' units of ten to the next leftmost column. If the calculations above are examined it will be found that this is always done; the sum for the units and tens columns is correct in all cases. Errors only occur in the hundreds columns, and they also only occur when a carry has occurred from the units to the tens column. This suggests that the student *accumulates* the amount carried across columns. Thus, in the second sum a value of one is carried from the unit to the ten column and correctly added to this column. The same value continues to be carried to the hundreds column and is incorrectly added to it. This is a case where the student has learnt a faulty algorithm of syntactic principles and obviously fails to understand that the 'one' being carried from the units to the tens column is one unit of ten. In order to diagnose faulty algorithms such as the above a model must be created of the correct and incorrect procedures used. In practice this requires breaking down a complex procedure into a set of more elementary procedures. This elementary set will include various incorrect procedures, whose application is responsible for incorrect output. As an example of 'breaking down' a procedure, consider multi-digit subtraction. This requires the separate procedures of single digit subtraction, borrowing, and, as a special case, borrowing across zero. This is only a rough and ready breakdown; finer details will be necessary. But it conveys the flavour of the analysis that is necessary.

Once such a set of correct and incorrect procedures has been created, it can then be used in attempts to simulate particular patterns of errors made by students. Brown and Burton (1978) attempted to do this for subtraction by creating a computer program BUGGY, that contained a large set of possibly faulty algorithms (or 'bugs') and then used the program to examine an extensive data-base of 19,500 problems performed by Nicaraguan grade-school children. BUGGY was used to determine how well a given student's responses could be explained by a simple bug. This is an important attempt to use the power of a computer to aid in the diagnosis of faulty algorithms, so we shall examine the method closely.

Brown and Burton first compared how well a student's responses could be explained by any simple bug. This simply shows the extent to which particular errors can be generated by BUGGY. It does *not* show that the student and BUGGY arrive at the answer in the same way. Following this first run, Brown and Burton then returned to analysis by hand of responses not captured by existing bugs. This led to an increase in the number of bugs from an initial 18 to 60. At this point BUGGY could identify examples of a single faulty algorithm (so long as it contained the relevant bug) but not yet examples of combined bugs. BUGGY was then programmed to try all pairs of bugs in its attempt to match an incorrect answer. This led to some non-obvious interactions, which we shall not pursue, but which illustrate the power and use of a computer in testing all possible combinations of bugs – a daunting if not impossible task by hand.

Further analysis by hand now followed in order to identify students making algorithmic as opposed to careless or random errors. From this followed a set of criteria for diagnosing whether or not a student's performance was consistent with a bug or pair of bugs. These criteria were computerized. BUGGY was now in a position to *diagnose* a student's problem. It was found that nearly 40 per cent of the students made consistent algorithmic errors. Although this is by no means a perfect diagnostic tool, it is a major advance in analysis because it indicates, in some cases, precisely why a student is going wrong. This indication suggests where remediation should be directed.

Although BUGGY included a large number of bugs, a small number occurred with a relatively high frequency. The most common bugs cited by Brown and Burton are shown in table 6.1.

The theoretical model proposed by Brown and Burton to account for their findings is based on the premise that students often consistently follow algorithmic procedures. They call their model of these algorithms a procedural network. A procedural network is, essentially, a list of interconnected instructions of how to do arithmetic.

When algorithmic errors are made it is assumed that a 'buggy' procedure has replaced a correct procedure in the network. Thus a particular child's algorithmic errors can be modelled by a procedural network containing appropriately faulty subprocedures in place of the correct procedure. An alternative model of subtraction errors has been offered by Young and O'Shea (1981). The major difference between the two models is that whereas Brown and Burton claim that errors are made because children have faulty versions of certain algorithms, Young and O'Shea claim that children's algorithms are incomplete in that certain subcomponents are not functional. Empirically, there is little to choose between the two theories (Young and O'Shea, 1981) and thus the main differences are in the conceptualization and modelling of cognitive processes. The procedural networks advocated by Brown and Burton contain a series of subprocedures some of which may be faulty. The production system approach (Newell and Simon, 1972) advocated by Young and O'Shea consist of a series of rules each representing some local knowledge

Table 6.1   *The 14 most frequently occurring bugs found by Brown and Burton (1978), in a group of 1325 students.*

Frequency	Description
57	*students used: BORROW/FROM/ZERO (103−45=158)* When borrowing from a column whose top digit is 0, the student writes 9, but does not continue borrowing from the column to the left of the 0.
54	*students used: SMALLER/FROM/LARGER (253−118=145)* The student subtracts the smaller digit in a column from the larger digit regardless of which one is on top.
50	*students used: BORROW/FROM/ZERO and LEFT/TEN/OK (803−508=395)* The student changes 0 to 9 without further borrowing unless the 0 is part of a 10 in the left part of the top number.
34	*students used: DIFF/0−N=N and MOVE/OVER/ZERO/BORROW* Whenever the top digit in a column is 0, the student writes the bottom digit in the answer; i.e., $0-N=N$. When the student needs to borrow from a column whose top digit is 0, he skips that column and borrows from the next one.
14	*students used: DIFF/0–N=N and STOPS/BORROW/AT/ZERO* Whenever the top digit in a column is 0, the student writes the bottom digit in the answer; i.e., $0-N=N$. The student borrows from zero incorrectly. He does not subtract 1 from the 0 although he adds 10 correctly to the top digit of the current column.
13	*students used: SMALLER/FROM/LARGER and 0–N=N (203−98=205)* The student subtracts the smaller digit in each column from the larger digit regardless of which one is on top. The exception is that when the top digit is 0, a 0 is written as the answer for that column; i.e., $0-N=0$.

12   *students used: DIFF/0–N=0 and*
MOVE/OVER/ZERO/BORROW
Whenever the top digit in a column is 0, the student writes
0 in the answer; i.e., 0–N=0. When the student needs to
borrow from a column whose top digit is 0, he skips that
column and borrows from the next one.

11   *students used: BORROW/FROM/ZERO and DIFF/N–0=0*
When borrowing from a column whose top digit is 0, the
student writes 9, but does not continue borrowing from the
column to the left of the 0. Whenever the bottom digit in a
column is 0, the student writes 0 in the answer, i.e., N–0=0.

10   *students used: DIFF/0–N=0 and N–0=0 (302–192=290)*
The student writes 0 in the answer when either the top or
the bottom digit is 0.

10   *students used: BORROW/FROM/ZERO and DIFF/0–N=N*
When borrowing from a column whose top digit is 0, the
student writes 9, but does not continue borrowing from the
column to the left of the 0. Whenever the top digit in a
column is 0, the student writes the bottom digit in the answer;
i.e., 0–N=N.

10   *students used: MOVE/OVER/ZERO/BORROW (304–75=139)*
When the student needs to borrow from a column whose top
digit is 0, he skips that column and borrows from the next
one.

10   *students used: DIFF/N–0=0 (403–208=105)*
Whenever the bottom digit in a column is 0, the student
writes in the answer; i.e., N–0=0.

10   *students used: DIFF/0–N=N (140–12=121)*
Whenever the top digit in a column is 0, the student writes
the bottom digit in the answer; i.e., 0–N=N.

9   *students used: DIFF/0–N=N and LEFT/TEN/OK*
(908–395=693)
When there is a 0 on top, the student writes the bottom
digit in the answer. The exception is when the 0 is part of 10
in the left columns of the top number.

about subtraction. The rules proposed by Young and O'Shea are more molecular than the procedures proposed by Brown and Burton, in that several rules may have to be combined to form what would be an effective procedure. It may be that, despite differences in the nomenclature of the systems, the approaches are complements to each other and serve to demonstrate that a skill can be decomposed to varying degrees of granularity. The grain of the decomposition that is necessary will depend on the task at hand and on the utility of model that the decomposition results in.

The analyses offered by Brown and Burton and by Young and O'Shea are static in the sense that they attempt to model procedures at a particular point in time. Neither addresses in a principled way the question of how faulty algorithms arise or of how they are eventually resolved in favour of the correct algorithm. Young and O'Shea do make some informal observations that the origin of *always borrowing* in subtraction may be due to the fact that as soon as students are introduced to the concept of borrowing they are presented with a series of problems, all of which require borrowing. This may lead to the induction of an erroneous rule.

An attempt has been made by Brown and Van Lehn (1980) to provide a principled account of the origin of bugs. The theory assumes that a student attempts to follow existing procedures in calculation. If the student arrives at a point at which the existing procedure dictates a step that cannot be carried out, an impasse has been reached. For example, if a student has a decrement rule but has only so far encountered decrementing numbers greater than zero, then an attempt to decrement zero, as in 204–17, will lead to an impasse. At such points human problem-solvers are unlikely just to quit, but will seek ways to resolve the impasse. This assumption leads Brown and Van Lehn to propose that students invent 'repairs' or 'patches' for their existing procedures at points of impasse. Such repairs will often be erroneous, causing bugs in the model, and faulty algorithms in the student's set of calculation procedures. Brown and Van Lehn call their theory Repair Theory. They point out that the theory has two parts; the first is a series of operations that leads to an impasse and the second is a series of operations that repair the procedure so that it can proceed. We shall concentrate on the generation of repairs.

Repairs are implemented by a set of repair heuristics and a set of 'critics' to filter out some possible but unreasonable repairs. As an example, suppose a student does not have a 'borrow' rule and is presented with the problem of

$$\begin{array}{r} 15 \\ -\ 7 \\ \hline \end{array}$$

If, as we shall assume, the student has a rule that says that larger numbers cannot be subtracted from smaller then he or she has reached an impasse in the right-most column. The student can now either quit or implement a repair. Implementing a repair such as subtracting the smaller from the larger number regardless of position will create a bug. Brown and Van Lehn argue that students use general purpose problem-solving heuristics to guide their repairs. This is an interesting proposal in that it allows control of a skill at an impasse to pass outside domain-specific procedures – the procedures that have just caused the impasse – and thus allow the student to continue his or her efforts at a solution. However, Brown and Van Lehn do not stipulate in detail which general problem-solving heuristics give rise to which repairs. Repairs, such as subtracting smaller from larger regardless of position seems to be a rather domain specific repair with minimal input from more general heuristics. To some extent, much depends on the definition of such terms as 'domain' and 'general strategy'. For example, repairing by analogy with an addition heuristic, involves the general strategy of seeking an analogy outside the domain of subtraction but within the larger domain of number operations. This, of course, is the sensible place to look for an analogy at an impasse, but it points up the necessity of being clear about what constitutes a domain in appealing to domain independence, and what constitutes a 'general problem-solving strategy'.

There is one other important component to Repair Theory: critics. Critics play the role of blocking possible but improbable repairs. If a repair is possible, but is never observed to occur, this must be because there is a principle at work to prevent this. Critics are the theoretical nomenclature for these principles in Repair Theory. Brown and Van Lehn discuss a variety of critics including such principles as 'don't leave blanks in the middle of an answer' (which prevents just passing over an impasse) and 'don't change a column after its answer is written'. The presence of critics explains why certain procedures are avoided in generating repairs.

Summary

Reasoning about quantity and number are fundamental skills. In this chapter we have explored how children's ability to conserve develops. The conservation task itself is a complex cognitive phenomenon. To succeed the child must bring to the task the fundamental principles of reasoning required by the task and must realize that these principles are appropriate to the task. A variety of experiments have shown that children who fail the standard Piagetian conservation task, will succeed on alternative versions of the task. The fundamental commonality of the alternative versions is that they serve to elicit the reasoning strategy that the standard conservation task would diagnose as being absent. This suggests that the task itself is not a reliable indicator of the presence or absence of these strategies of reasoning although it may indicate the more sophisticated skill of knowing that a strategy in one's repertoire is relevant to this task on this occasion.

The fact that conservation judgements can be induced by manipulating the experimental context has led some researchers to conclude that even 2-year-old children are capable of conservation. On the present evidence, these claims are not well-founded. Although it is possible to perform experimental manipulations that lead to conservation judgements by very young children, there is no evidence that these children understand the principle of conservation. The judgements elicited are due, it would seem, to the constraints introduced by the experimental manipulation rather than to the uncovering of a previously unsuspected cognitive skill. There is an important methodological lesson to be drawn from all of this.

Demonstrations that very young children can make apparently sophisticated judgements need to be treated with caution, especially if there is no independent evidence for the information processing strategy that the child is presumed to use. When researchers have attempted to create models of the strategy use that underlies judgements, the developmental picture has become more complex and more interesting. In the case of number conservation, in particular, counting has emerged as a strategy of central importance.

Counting has a complex developmental history in its own right. Children have to learn an appropriate set of count words, and how to match these count words to objects to be counted. In addition they must learn a principle of cardinality so that the result of counting an array can be represented by a single number. This number can, in its turn, be stored, if necessary, for comparison with other numbers in judgements of numerosity.

The development of counting is only the starting point for arithmetical reasoning. Having learnt to use numbers, children must come to treat numbers as objects in their own right, capable of being manipulated by rules and algorithms. The cognitive system seems to be readily disposed to this task, able and prepared to invent algorithms if none are available from pedagogy. The min strategy for addition is a good example of this. However, the downside is that faulty algorithms are often invented.

Understanding the generation of these, the way in which they can be detected, and, ultimately, the way in which they can be corrected is one of the more important tasks for an information processing approach to cognitive development.

A Historical Note on the Development of Counting

Counting is probably the most basic use to which numbers can be put and developmentally it is the first use of numbers to appear. Our counting system uses a base 10 system but there are many other systems in existence. The most basic system is a 2 system and there are a number of tribes who still use such a system (Flegg, 1983). In theory a 2 system can do anything that a 10 system can but a 2 system quickly imposes considerable demands on short-term memory. It is probably for this reason that most known 2 systems are only used for numbers up to about eight, thereafter the equivalent of 'many' is used for all further numbers.

A 5 system is common, particularly among people who use a system of finger-counting. In many systems the base 5 is only preserved for numbers up to 10 or 20 and then abandoned in favour of a 10 or 20 system. Flegg (1983) remarks that there is no known example where a 5 system is extended to large numbers. There are also some systems that use a base 20, usually with some base 10 intermixed.

The existence of a counting system does not necessarily imply any abstract awareness of number. It is impossible to say when such an awareness occurred historically but there is no evidence that numbers as abstractions were an important part of mathematical thinking before the Pythagoreans. The system of counting that we use today, the 10 system, is presumed to have been a part of Indo-European, a language from which most of the languages spoken from India to Western Europe are derived. However, it is not necessarily the case that Indo-European contained the full decimal system that we use today. Flegg (1983) remarks that the largest number word was probably that for 1,000.

Thus far we have considered, albeit briefly, some of the varieties of spoken number systems. Probably the earliest permanent record of numbers was made by tallying, which consists of marking a stick or bone in some way. The simplest form of marking is with notches although tallying can be considerably more sophisticated than this. Tallying was in use until quite recent times, especially for recording taxation payments it seems. Flegg (1983: p. 45) recounts:

During repairs to Westminster Abbey in 1909 a number of surviving British Exchequer tallies were unearthed. These are of the split kind, and have notches of different sizes carved on them representing different denominations of currency. Officially their use was forbidden by statute in 1783, but they were not entirely replaced by handwritten records and the use of paper money until about the end of the first quarter of the nineteenth century.

The simplest system of recording numbers is to mark each unit in some way. Very often this way was a short horizontal line so that || represented 2, ||||| represented 5 and so on. The obvious limitation of such a system is that it quickly becomes difficult to read at first sight. Without counting it is not obvious what |||||||||||||||||||| represents. Improvements can be introduced by grouping; ||||| ||||| is better than |||||||||| . Such groupings appear to be present in all ancient numeral systems that used the repetitive principle. A further improvement was the introduction of distinct symbols for fixed numbers of units. It seems that even in palaeolithic times some such distinct symbols were used. The Roman system, which is still visible on old clock faces and on film copyright dates is an example of a system with distinct symbols for units, fives, and tens (and larger multiples of ten). While such systems do not have major disadvantages for tallying purposes they are inherently inimical to the symbolic manipulation of numbers for purposes of computation, which is possibly why the Romans were not noted for their contribution to mathematics.

Computation is greatly facilitated by a place-value system in which the value of a numeral is determined by its place in a sequence, as for example in our present system in which the value of '1' in 1, 10, and 100 signifies one unit, ten units, and a hundred units respectively.

The Babylonian numeral system is the oldest surviving example of the principle of place-value. The base of the Babylonian system was 60. Up to 59 the Babylonians used symbols for units and tens without place-value; the symbol for 60 was the same as the symbol for a single unit with further numbers represented by numerals written to the right of this unit. Such a system has advantages of economy in the use of symbols but it also has a built-in ambiguity about the value of a particular symbol. This may not have been important in everyday commerce, where the approximate price of something would be known, thus making it unlikely for confusion to arise as to whether it cost one shekel or sixty shekels. However, the ambiguity was there in principle. The way to resolve it is to have a symbol denoting that a place to the right of a given symbol is empty. The place-value principle inevitably throws up a requirement for a symbol to represent zero.

The Babylonians did invent such a zero symbol but they used it only to denote internal empty places; it was not used to denote that a final place to the right of a number was empty.

A different line of development was the use of the alphabet, which is of North Semitic origin and dates from the second millennium before Christ, to denote numbers. There is evidence that the Hebrews and the Greeks used the alphabet to represent numbers. Early alphabetic number systems simply assigned numbers to letters up to the end of the alphabet and then combined letters in various ways for larger numbers. The obvious improvement, probably taken by the Greeks, was to allocate the first nine letters to the numbers one to nine, the next nine letters to the multiples of 10 between 10 and 90, and a further nine letters for multiples of 100 up to 900. It is worth remarking that this system does not have a symbol for zero in it: what we would represent as 10, was represented by a new letter, not the repetition of the letter for 1 combined with a 0. Zero, in fact, proved one of the more difficult notions about number to accept; European mathematicians debated its acceptability for some time after the introduction of the present Hindu-Arabic system of numerals. This has a developmental parallel; zero poses considerable problems when computing with numbers.

The system of written numbers that we use today was invented in India and transmitted via the Arabs to Europe. The system incorporates two important principles: it consists of unique individual symbols for the numbers 1 to 9 together with a zero symbol and it is a place-value system. The Greek system contained the decimal principle but it was not a place value system. The Roman system was a place value system but it was cumbersome to operate with, particularly when numbers grew large. Several different ways of writing numbers evolved in India of which the most important was the Brahmi numerals, which are shown in figure 6.5. The Brahmi numeral system was a decimal system but it did not yet contain a zero nor was it, for that reason, a place-value system. It is not entirely clear how the transition came about but it seems that there was a need by Indian astronomers for a numeral system in which very large numbers could be easily represented and that these astronomers were familiar with the Babylonian sexagesimal astronomical system, which, as we have seen, incorporated the notions of place value and the marking of empty places internally. It may be, however, that the Indians invented a zero symbol independently. By whatever means the transition came about, the Brahmi decimal system became a place-value system with a zero symbol.

The expansion of the Mohammedan empire as far as India in the seventh and eighth centuries resulted in many scholarly works being

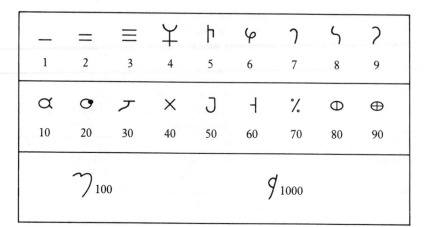

Figure 6.5 *Brahmi numerals, from which our present numerals are descended.*
Source: Flegg, 1983.

brought back to such centres as Baghdad to be translated and studied. Among these works was an Indian astronomical textbook, the *Siddhanta of Brahmagupta*, making use of the decimal place-value system. The dissemination of the Hindu System came about largely as a result of a booklet written in AD825 by the great Arab mathematician al-Khwarizmi, which described the numerals and their use in translation. This book was eventually translated into Latin, in the first instance by an Englishman, Robert of Chester, who had become acquainted with the system while visiting Spain to study mathematics. However, acceptance of the new system was slow. In particular, the symbol for zero was a source of difficulty largely because it violated the additive principle on which the Roman system was built; many could not accept that a zero placed to the right of a numeral increased the value of that numeral ten-fold.

One of the most prominent supporters of the new system was the thirteenth-century Italian mathematician, Fibonacci. His book, the *Liber Abci*, played a large part in the eventual triumph of the Hindu-Arabic system. Although Roman numerals did not disappear completely, the increasing need of mathematicians for elaborate calculation, and the obvious superiority of the Hindu-Arabic system in this respect, ensured its eventual adoption.

7

The Development of Grammar

Language and Learning

Although children are communicative during their first year of life, there is little that can be recognized as language until the second year. At about the age of one year children begin to acquire their first words. The initial acquisition of words is a slow process, but by about 18 months many children will have acquired a vocabulary of 50 words (see figure 4.5, which shows the rate of acquisition of the first 50 words reported by Nelson, 1973)). After a prolonged period of slow steady acquisition, there is a rapid increase in vocabulary size at about 18 months. Shortly after this rapid increase, two-word utterances begin to appear (McShane and Whittaker, 1983). Two-word utterances mark the beginning of word combinations and are the first primitive signs of children's attempts to construct a syntax for their language.

For a period of some months after the first two-word combinations, children continue to expand the range of two-word utterances, without any further significant increase in the length of the utterance. Most two-word utterances combine a content word with a word for an attribute or an action, as in the utterances *more duck* and *dog run**. Beyond two-word

---

*In this chapter it will be necessary to distinguish among reference to words, utterances by children, illustrative sentences, and utterances by adults. I have used the following convention: Italics are used to indicate either a child's utterance, a word, or a constituent of a word (such as *-ing*); illustrative sentences and adult utterances are indicated by single quotation marks. Italics and quotation marks are also used for emphasis and quotation respectively, as they have been in other chapters. It is also necessary to distinguish conceptual categories from formal grammatical categories. Small capitals are used for conceptual categories, as in other chapters, and initial large capitals for formal grammatical categories.

utterances, the child begins both to modify words by adding inflections (such as the plural -s or the progressive -ing) and to include the articles, conjunctions, and prepositions that are so conspicuously absent from two-word utterances. By the age of 4 years most children will be fluent speakers of their native language. This is not to say that acquisition is complete at this stage, but certainly a great deal of the work will have been done. It is a remarkable achievement in a relatively short time. How do children do it?

In order to appreciate better the child's accomplishment, one has to look at the structure of language itself. Languages have a complex structure at different levels of representation, which include the phonological, syntactic, semantic, and pragmatic levels. Phonology is concerned with the sound structure of language; syntax with the rules of word combination; semantics with the meaning of utterances; and pragmatics with how language supports interpersonal communication. The child thus acquires a system that has different levels of representation with a variety of interactions among the levels. Theories of language development have been largely concerned with how children acquire the grammar of their language. This puts the emphasis firmly upon the syntactic level. For reasons that will become evident, the interaction between syntax and semantics is of great importance in theories of language development. It is with these two levels of the child's linguistic development that this chapter will be concerned. Analysis of the phonological and pragmatic levels of language will not feature prominently.

Languages have complex grammatical structures. Native speakers of a language can readily agree on what are acceptable sentences of a language (that is, the sentences that can be considered grammatical) and what are unacceptable. Even though this can be done with ease, the vast majority of people are unaware of much of the grammatical structure of their language. The grammatical structure of language involves dependent relations between words. Sometimes the words that have a dependent relation with each other are conjoined as in 'the big dog', where the adjective *big* modifies the noun *dog*. Sometimes they are separated by intervening material as in 'the dog that chased the cat jumped over the moon', where *dog* is the subject of *jumped* but the subject and predicate are separated by the intervening relative clause 'that jumped over the moon'. In this example two things have been deliberately mixed: the words of the sentence and a description of the grammatical categories (noun, verb), grammatical functions (subject, predicate) and grammatical phrases (relative clause). The words that make up the sentence are called the *surface structure* of the sentence. However, the rules for constructing sentences are not rules for combining specific words but rules for combining abstract grammatical categories and phrases. In some sense adults 'know' these rules because they adhere to them when they talk. By about the age of 4 years children appear to speak a simple but close approximation to the adult language. This means that the child has acquired a set of grammatical rules for combining form-class categories such as NOUN, VERB, and ADJECTIVE in various ways. Neither the rules, nor the categories over which they operate are readily detectable in the input the child hears. The input consists simply of words, or, more precisely, it consists of a continuous linear stream of acoustic energy that must be segmented into words. For the sake of simplicity it will be assumed that segmenting the input into words is unproblematic. The problem that this chapter addresses is how each child manages to construct a grammar for the particular language to which he or she is exposed.

In order to construct a grammar children must bring learning mechanisms to operate on the linguistic input to which they are exposed. Traditionally, the child has been attributed with only a few basic general-purpose learning mechanisms. Almost every theory of learning presumes an ability to make associations. However, associations are not remotely powerful enough to account for language acquisition. The basic argument against an associationist account of language has been laid out by Chomsky (1957, 1959), and never answered. Chomsky argued that the production of an utterance is not simply a matter of stringing together a chain of associations. Utterances obey grammatical rules, often of a fairly complex sort. Chomsky argued that the rule-system of language could not be learnt by children. The reason for this is not that the rules are complex (although they are) but that it is not possible to work out the rules from the input that the child receives by any conventional learning procedure. This argument has come to be known as the *poverty of the stimulus argument*. Since children do, obviously, acquire their native language, the poverty of the stimulus argument has been a major justification for proposing that language acquisition is guided by innate constraints. Chomsky (1965) argued that children are born equipped with an innate Language Acquisition Device (LAD) that guides the learning process. Chomsky did not specify what the LAD was. His proposal was more a logical than an empirical claim: conventional learning mechanisms are not sufficiently powerful to learn the abstract structure of language from the input available to a child; therefore the child's learning must be guided by innate processes.

From the above considerations it is possible to identify two key issues that a theory of language development must address. The first is that it is necessary to describe the abstract structure of the language that the child is presumed to acquire. The second is that it is necessary to examine in detail under what constraints the learning mechanisms available to the child could derive the abstract structure from the input that the child receives. These issues are the *what* and *how* questions for language development.

The Structure of Language

Since Chomsky (1957), linguistics has attempted to provide a generative model of language structure. A generative model is one that contains a finite set of rules, which are capable of generating an infinite variety of sentences. The need for such a system is fairly obvious: Speakers of a language are capable of producing and understanding sentences they have never heard before. There is an infinite variety of these sentences because some of the properties of language, such as co-ordination as in 'John and Mary and . . .' or relativization as in 'this is the dog that chased the cat that . . .' can be expanded indefinitely.

To date there is no unanimous agreement on what constitutes the finite set of rules of a generative grammar. A number of different proposals have been advanced and, as weaknesses have been discovered in each set of proposals, new models have been proposed. This might seem to create something of a problem for a theory of language development. Since the goal of a theory of language development is to explain how children acquire the rules that are used to generate utterances, it might be presumed that it is necessary first to work out the rules and then to work out a theory for their acquisition. In an ideal world this might be the case. In the world of real scientific practice it is common to advance on different interrelated fronts at once. For such advances to be mutually profitable it is helpful to understand how advances on one front can be used to inform theories and models on the other. This issue will be examined in due course. Before doing so it will be helpful to have some grasp of the type of models of language structure that are common in linguistics. The classic model is that proposed by Chomsky (1965).

Chomsky assumes that a spoken utterance signal can be regarded as a string of discrete words (morphemes actually – this will be clarified shortly). If we consider the simple sentence 'The dogs chased the cats' then it is intuitively obvious that the words *the* and *dogs* belong together. This intuitive notion is captured by the formal notion of a Noun Phrase (NP). It is also intuitively obvious that the remaining three words can be grouped together as a phrase representing what the dogs did (and to whom they did it). This phrase is called a Verb Phrase (VP). It is now possible to form a simple rule for any straightforward declarative sentence (S):

$$S \rightarrow NP\ VP$$

Rules such as this are called phrase-structure rules. A phrase-structure rule simply takes a grammatical unit, such as S, and decomposes it into sub-units, such as NP and VP. We could continue with this process and decompose NP and VP in turn, and their sub units in turn, until we reach the basic building blocks of the sentence. In order to illustrate this process it is easiest to begin with an example. Consider again the simple sentence 'The dogs chased the cats'. If phrase-structure rules are applied to this sentence it will be decomposed into basic grammatical units, each of which represents a class of morphemes. A morpheme is a 'unit of meaning'. The word *dogs*, for example, consists of two morphemes, the Noun Stem *dog* and the Plural operator, which, in this case, adds *s* to the noun stem to produce a single word *dogs*. The complete phrase-structure rules needed to deal with the sentence 'The dogs chased the cats', can be expressed as follows:

$$
\begin{array}{rcl}
S & \rightarrow & NP\ VP \\
VP & \rightarrow & V\ NP \\
NP & \rightarrow & Det\ N \\
N & \rightarrow & NS\ Plur \\
V & \rightarrow & VS\ Past \\
Det & \rightarrow & the \\
NS & \rightarrow & dog \\
NS & \rightarrow & cat \\
VS & \rightarrow & chase
\end{array}
$$

Each rule is an instruction that rewrites the symbol on the left as the symbol or symbols on the right. The sentence is first rewritten as two constituent parts, NP and VP. VP consists of a Verb and an NP. NP is rewritten as a Determiner and a Noun; Noun itself is rewritten as the Noun Stem and the Plural operator. Verb is rewritten as the Verb Stem and the Past Tense operator. These are the basic categories and operators of which the sentence is constructed. The remaining rewrite rules show the words that instantiate these categories. The process is one in which the symbols on the left are gradually refined into smaller and smaller syntactic divisions until the basic syntactic categories such as noun and verb are reached. The words that make up the sentences are instances of these categories. Figure 7.1 is a tree diagram that reveals this process more clearly. The bottom of the tree in figure 7.1 consists of what are called *terminal nodes*. Terminal nodes have the property that they only

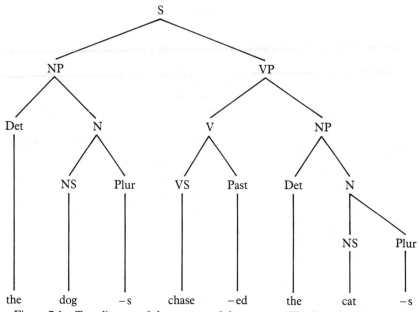

Figure 7.1   *Tree diagram of the structure of the sentence: 'The dogs chased the cats'.*

appear on the right-hand side of phrase-structure rules. They represent the basic building-blocks on which the rules operate.

Phrase-structure rules provide a method of converting a sentence into a linear sequence of morphemes. In modern versions of grammatical theory the rules would probably be stated in a somewhat different form, known as $\bar{X}$ ('X bar') syntax (Jackendoff, 1977). However, this is not of major relevance to the exposition so the older, simpler notation will be preserved.

The phrase-structure rules given above will provide only a limited number of English sentences. Strictly, they will only generate the sentences, 'The dogs chased the cats', 'The cats chased the dogs', 'The dogs chased the dogs', and 'The cats chased the cats'. However, the range covered can easily be extended by providing more words as instantiations of each category and by making the Plural operator and the Past operator optional. Further rules to allow adjectives, adverbs and so forth can also be added. A larger set of rules of this sort could generate a large number of declarative sentences. However, they would still only generate declarative sentences. There would be no way of accounting for the obvious similarity of meaning between 'The dogs chased the cats' and

'The cats were chased by the dogs'. These similarities were handled in Chomsky's theory by transformation rules, hence the name Transformational Grammar.

Chomsky proposed that non-declarative linguistic structures, such as the passive, the imperative, and so forth could be derived from the declarative base structure (i.e. the terminal nodes of the tree) by applying a systematic set of transformation rules to the phrase-markers (i.e. the NPs, VPs and so forth) of that base structure. The details of these rules are not of central concern here (see Huddleston (1976) for a clear exposition). The major point of importance is that Chomsky provided a principled set of explicit procedures which, when applied to an explicitly specified set of terminal strings, generated sentences of a language (English in this case). The aim of Chomsky's grammar was to provide a set of rules with the capability to generate all possible sentences of English and no non-sentences. A grammar that could meet these requirements was claimed by Chomsky to represent an ideal speaker's linguistic *competence*. A real speaker will, of course, generate occasional ungrammatical utterances. These are regarded by Chomsky as due to *performance* limitations, such as lack of attention, memory limitations and so forth.

Following Chomsky's proposals there was considerable discussion among psychologists about the extent to which Transformational Grammar should be considered as a 'psychologically real' model of how a speaker produces and comprehends utterances. Should a psychology of language seriously entertain the notion that when someone spoke an utterance, that utterance was the product of transformations carried out on a base structure representation by transformational processes? To some psychologists such a prospect was anathema; to most others it was strange, at best. The type of cognitive computations that seemed to be required by the theory of Transformational Grammar were quite different from what most psychologists were used to. Today, the whole prospect is less strange. The potential complexity of subconscious cognitive processing is now widely recognized. In principle, Transformational Grammar could be accommodated as a model of the mental representation of the structure of language. However, Chomsky's own theory has changed considerably since his original proposal of a transformational grammar and there are now several major additional theories of grammar. This raises the issue of what the relation is, or should be, between formal models of grammar and psychological models of language learning.

Grammar and Learnability

The relation between formal models of grammar and models of language learning has been, and continues to be, a problematic one. There is, first of all, the issue of whether the grammars proposed by linguistic theories should or should not be interpreted as proposals about the mental representation of language. If they should, then such grammars are proposals about the types of mental representation that characterizes the endpoint of the developmental process. If they should not, then the issue must be addressed about what, if anything, formal grammars have to say about the mental representation of language. Discussions of the 'psychological reality' of formal models of grammar by linguists abound with equivocations (see e.g., Black and Chiat, 1981; Lightfoot, 1982), although some linguists have faced the problem and demanded that:

> we take responsibility not only for characterizing the abstract structure of the linguistic knowledge domain, but also for explaining how the formal properties of our proposed linguistic representations are related to the nature of the cognitive processes that derive and interpret them in actual language use and acquisition. (Bresnan and Kaplan, 1982: xxii.)

Many psychologists have simply assumed that formal linguistic theories are theories of mental representations and have attempted to explore the implications of this for language comprehension (see Fodor, Bever and Garrett, 1974) and for language learning. The latter issue will be considered here. The attempt to create a model of the psychological processes that could learn a particular model of grammar can be an instructive exercise, even if the model grammar should ultimately be superseded. The exercise is instructive, not simply as an intellectual challenge, but also, and primarily, as a means of discovering the demands that particular formal models place on learning and the adequacy of theories of learning in meeting these demands. Understanding and resolving these demands, either by adjusting the model of grammar that needs to be learned or by adjusting the model of learning that the child is presumed to use, seems the most likely way to arrive at a satisfactory theory of language development. Thus, it might be expected that something like the following relation should exist between linguistic and psychological theories.

Linguistic theories can postulate candidate grammars for a language. Psychological theories can examine what would be required in order for such a grammar to be learnable. This can benefit both disciplines. The psychological theories can examine the extent to which the rules of the grammar could be learnt by the mechanisms of learning that are presumed to operate given the data available to these mechanisms. If the learning mechanisms are not sufficiently powerful to produce the rules specified by the linguistic theory then there is an impasse that must be resolved. The impasse can be resolved by changing either the theory of learning or the grammatical theory, or both. Thus, the attempt to square models of grammars with models of learning by testing the learnability of a particular model of grammar can be of advantage to both linguistics and psychology. A model of grammar whose rules can only be learnt by implausible learning mechanisms should suggest a rethink about the grammatical model. Equally, the demonstration that particular models of learning are too weak to account for key facts about language should suggest a revision of the learning theory.

There are two major points about the foregoing discussion that are worth emphasis. The first is that it can be extremely instructive to discover the learnability of particular models of grammar, even if the grammar is known not to be entirely adequate. Ultimately a theory of grammar and a theory of learning must meet to show how language is learnt. By discovering the limitations of current models it should be possible to create better theories in the future. The second major point is that the learnability criterion has implications both for theories of grammar and theories of learning. From a psychological standpoint, one ought to be critical of models of grammar that can only be learnt by implausible assumptions about learning mechanisms and the learning process. It is important to preserve this critical scepticism because it is much easier to make demands for adjustment on a model of learning than on a model of grammar. If a grammar seems to make implausible demands of learning it is no easy matter to amend the grammar so that it is learnable in a more plausible way. In such a case, the chances are that it is some fundamental proposal about the structure of the grammar that creates the learnability problem. Therefore, only a radical revision of the grammar (in effect, an alternative model of grammatical structure) is likely to lead to a more plausible learning process. On the other hand, it is relatively easy, when some aspect of a grammar creates a learnability problem to resolve the problem by postulating an appropriate innate representation of language structure that is triggered, but not learnt, as a result of environmental experience. Ultimately, it is possible to trivialize the learnability of any model of grammar by proposing so much in the way of innate representations of language that almost no learning is required. One safeguard against such trivialization is to require that the necessity for any innate representation be demonstrated across a variety of languages. In this way, eventually, bad proposals will be found out.

Most theories of language development assume that children learn language by a process of induction. Induction is a powerful learning mechanism for any theory concerned with a rule-based representation of knowledge because induction derives general rules from specific examples. Since theories of grammatical structure are almost exclusively rule-based theories, induction is the obvious learning mechanism to call upon. Consequently, both innatist and non-innatist accounts assume that induction plays a key role in language acquisition. Innatist accounts, however, place considerable constraints on the inductive process. The reasons for this will be examined later.

Grammar and Meaning

The meaning of an utterance is not determined simply by discovering the grammatical structure of the utterance. Meaning is a mapping between the utterance and some real or potential state of affairs in the world. This mapping is conventionally called semantics. The ways in which language has meaning are multiple. Some idea of the extent and complexity of the issues involved in the semantics of language can be gained from Lyons's extensive but accessible two-volume account (Lyons, 1977a; 1977b). However, complexity need not detain us here. In studying the early phases of language development we shall be concerned with the everyday meaning of straightforward utterances such as *kick ball* and *allgone juice*. The major issues do not essentially concern what these utterances mean but how meaning and structure are related – i.e., how semantics and syntax are related.

There are two ways in which issues of meaning are important to language development. The first is how children determine the meaning of the utterances they hear before they know anything about grammar. Among the first to tackle this issue was Macnamara (1972). Macnamara proposed that children take individual words they hear to be names for objects to which their attention is drawn. Repeated experience of this sort will provide the child with a lexicon of words that can be comprehended. Macnamara then proposed that children can work out the meaning of an utterance by using their knowledge of the meaning of the individual words and the context of their occurrence to work out the meaning intended by the speaker. Thus, a child who knows the content words *dog*, *cat*, and *chase*, saw a dog chase a cat; and was told 'the dog chased the cat', could work out the meaning of the utterance from a knowledge of the meaning of the individual words and the event to which they refer. If the child also notices that the words heard are arranged in a particular order of the actor, the act, and the acted upon, then the child will have received input about grammatical order in English. Thus, the ability to work out the meaning of an utterance is a vital clue to the structure of one's native language according to Macnamara. In considering this thesis it is important to remember that the utterances that an infant hears relate mostly to the here-and-now; in particular, statements made by adults to young children usually describe events that are happening (or have just happened) in the world. Macnamara proposed that a combination of knowing the referents of the individual content words and being able to determine how these referents are related to each other in the world, will enable the child to work out the meaning of an utterance without recourse to syntax. More importantly, once that meaning is available, it can be used to guide inductive inferences about the syntactic structure of the language to which the child is exposed.

Macnamara's proposal lacked detail as to how particular syntactic devices are learnt. (It should be pointed out also that he did not claim that all syntax was learnt in this way.) However, the general flavour of the proposal is important: that the combination of a knowledge of the meaning of individual words together with a knowledge of the event in which their referents are involved (derived from observing the event while hearing the words) may be an adequate basis for working out the meaning of simple utterances.

The second way in which meaning is important is how the child's own utterances have meaning. Even if children obey syntactic rules they are trying to make semantic sense. Thus, in proposing rule structures for children's language attention must be paid to how these structures are capable of realizing the child's intended meaning.

In the sections that follow emphasis will be placed upon the research that has addressed the initial acquisition of grammatical structure. The period covered will be from the child's initial two-word combinations to the point at which the child's grammar can reasonably be claimed to be based upon the categories of NOUN, VERB, and ADJECTIVE. The induction of these categories could reasonably be said to represent the point at which the child's grammar begins to approximate closely to the adult grammar.

It is, of course, possible that children do not learn grammatical categories of NOUN, VERB, and ADJECTIVE, but that these are innate primitives that guide the child in acquiring grammar. These arguments are best understood in the context of a more general discussion of the innatist approach to language development. This will be considered following the discussion of non-innatist theories.

Two-Word Utterances

When two-word utterances make their appearance in a child's language, it is possible to begin to study the emergence of a grammatical system. During the early 1960s a small number of researchers began to study the grammatical structure of children's language. Brown and Fraser (1963) and Brown and Bellugi (1964) characterized children's early word combinations as 'telegraphic'. This description captured the fact that children's utterances contain mostly content words and relatively few function words (such as articles, prepositions, and so forth), the type of words that used to be left out of telegrams when these were a common means of communication. Some typical examples of early word combinations reported by Braine (1963) are *more cereal, more cookie, more read, more sing, all broke, all dressed, all dry, all buttoned, no bed, no down, no fix, no home, other bib, other bread, other milk, other pants, boot off, light off, pants off, shirt off, see baby, see pretty, see train, byebye car, byebye papa.* Although grammatically impoverished, such speech is readily intelligible because the content words establish reference between the utterance and the situation being talked about.

The phrase 'telegraphic speech' was an approximate descriptive characterization of children's early word combinations. However, it is not entirely accurate (Brown, 1973a). Early word combinations do not consist entirely of content words; a small number of 'function' words play an important role in these early combinations – words such as *more, another, allgone,* and locative terms such as *in* and *on*. The most important deficiency of the characterization of children's speech as 'telegraphic' is that such a characterization does not lead us at all towards an account of the rules that determine how children begin to combine words together.

The first rule-based model of the child's grammar was Braine's (1963) 'pivot grammar'. Braine carried out a distributional analysis of the earliest word combinations of three children. He found that most of the initial combinations were just two words long. The majority of the two-word utterances were of the type *more duck* and *no ball*. These utterances have the characteristic that only a few words occupied the first position in the utterance but a much larger set of words occupied the second position. Thus a child might say *more car, more cereal, more juice, more read, more up, no bed, no down, no water, no wet*. The utterances consist of a combination of a content word in the second position preceded by a modifying word. Braine observed that children used only a very small number of modifiers but they used a much larger number of content words. He called the two classes of words he had identified *pivot* and *open* respectively. The combination can be represented as P + O. Braine also found a less frequent O + P combination, in which the O words were essentially the same as the O words that occurred in P + O combinations. However, the two P classes did not overlap; a child who produced the O + P combinations *duck there* and *ball there* would not produce any utterances of the type *there X*. Thus, there were two distinct combinations: P_1 + O and O + P_2. In addition O words were found to combine freely in O + O combinations. These three types of combination, i.e., P_1 + O, O + P_2, and O + O, constituted Braine's proposed grammar for children's two-word utterances. It was a grammar that took syntactic structure seriously but assumed that the child constructed the grammar exclusively from a distributional analysis of the speech he heard. Braine's grammar claims that what a child learns in learning to combine words is that some words (the pivots) occupy fixed positions and that other words (the opens) do not occupy fixed positions. Thus, on this account learning language structure is a matter of learning the permissible position of words.

It has been emphasized that the relation between syntax and semantics is a major issue for theories of language development. Braine's proposal did not address this relation at all except to assume that the meaning of the words provided the meaning of the utterance without problem. Unfortunately, there is a problem. It was brought to light by Bloom (1970). Bloom observed that the utterance *Mommy sock* occurred in her corpus of data with two distinct meanings (as inferred from the contexts in which the utterance was spoken). One meaning was akin to 'this is Mommy's sock' and the other to 'Mommy is putting on my sock'. Clearly, the same linguistic processes did not produce the two utterances *Mommy sock*. The question is: what sort of linguistic processes would do justice to the semantics of the child's utterances while still limiting the syntax to two-word combinations? Bloom's own work was an attempt to apply the principles of Transformational Grammar to the study of children's early word combinations. Clearly, one could generate two different meanings for Mommy sock from two different base structures. However, in her more general attempt to apply the theory of Transformational Grammar to the children's utterances, Bloom could not find a single uniform set of principles to account for the types of utterances produced by the six children she studied. This was an important finding because it was presumed that Transformational Grammar described the common abstract representation of language that all children shared. In addition, some of the ways in which the principles of Transformational Grammar had to be changed – for example by adding a 'deletion' rule that reduced to two words some surface structures that would otherwise be generated – were unduly clumsy.

While developmental psychologists were finding it difficult to apply the principles of Transformational Grammar to children's two-word utterances, changes were occurring in linguistic theory that were to have a profound effect on the next ten years or so of research on language development. Fillmore (1968) was among the first to argue that the underlying structure of language explicitly contained functional-semantic categories (rather than the abstract syntactic categories envisaged in Chomsky's (1965) Standard Theory). Fillmore argued that there was a set of universal semantic concepts, 'which identify certain types of judgements human beings are capable of making about the events that are going on around them, judgements about such matters as who did it, who it happened to, and what got changed' (Fillmore 1968: p. 24). Fillmore proposed that the structure of language is built around these semantic concepts. He postulated a set of grammatical *cases* that represented, in formal terms, the semantic concepts. Fillmore called his grammar Case Grammar. The cases he proposed are shown in the following extract (Fillmore, 1968), and they constitute the semantic deep structure of Fillmore's grammar. They are converted into a surface structure output through the operation of mediating rules.

> *Agentive* (A), the case of the typically animate perceived instigator of the action identified by the verb.
> *Instrumental* (I), the case of the inanimate force or object causally involved in the action or state identified by the verb.
> *Dative* (D), the case of the animate being affected by the state or action identified by the verb.
> *Factitive* (F), the case of the object or being resulting from the action or state identified by the verb, or understood as a part of the meaning of the verb.
> *Locative* (L), the case which identifies the location or spatial orientation of the state or action identified by the verb.
> *Objective* (O), the semantically most neutral case, the case of anything representable by a noun whose role in the action or state identified by the verb is identified by the semantic interpretation of the verb itself; conceivably the concept should be limited to things which are affected by the action or state identified by the verb. The term is not to be confused with the notion of direct object, nor with the name of the surface case synonymous with accusative.

Fillmore's proposal that grammar had a semantic basis made it much easier to tie together the syntax and the semantics of the child's utterances.

Moreover, if the further step were taken of deriving the semantic cases from the child's developing cognitive system then one would have a neat *cognition* → *semantics* → *syntax* equation. This type of equation held considerably more appeal for many psychologists than the proposal that syntax was governed by an innate acquisition device. Following Fillmore's proposal, and Bloom's (1970) demonstration that semantics must play a more central role in the child's system than earlier proposals had allowed, a shift of emphasis occurred in accounts of children's early speech, especially in accounts of two-word utterances. Various proposals were advanced, notably by Slobin (1970), Schlesinger (1971), Bowerman, (1973), and Brown (1973a) about the semantic structure of two-word utterances. With the exception of Bowerman, these proposals were in the spirit of Fillmore's proposal that semantics had a central explanatory role in accounts of language structure rather than being specific applications of Fillmore's Case Grammar.

Brown, (1973a, 1973b) proposed that a list of 11 semantic relations would account for 75 per cent of two-word utterances, with a list of 18 being sufficient to account for the vast majority of the data. The semantic relations he proposed, together with his examples, were:

- NOMINATIVE *that ball*
- DEMONSTRATIVE *there ball*
- RECURRENCE *more ball*
- NONEXISTENCE *allgone ball*
- POSSESSIVE *Daddy chair*
- ENTITY and LOCATIVE *book table*
- ACTION and LOCATIVE *go store*
- ATTRIBUTIVE *big house*
- AGENT–ACTION *Daddy hit*
- ACTION–OBJECT *hit ball*
- AGENT–OBJECT *Daddy ball*

Although the proposals that children's initial word combinations are organized semantically was widely accepted, the conceptual foundations of the approach were a little shaky. To begin with there was no agreed account of what the relevant semantic categories were. The categorization systems proposed, although they were semantically inspired, contained an informal mixture of semantic, syntactic, and intuitive categories. Secondly, the claim that children were *conceptually* able to make the distinctions attributed to them was never adequately established. Piaget's theory was frequently appealed to in a loose way. However, subsequent research (see Golinkoff, 1982) tended to support the assumptions implicit in the semantic accounts. Indeed, the assumptions are thoroughly plausible; it is not their lack of plausibility to which attention is being drawn but the lack of rigour with which the links between cognition, semantics, and syntax were made. Thirdly, there is the question of the categories themselves. Even if they are plausible, are they the correct categories? Is the child organizing a language system around precisely the concepts proposed in the semantic accounts of language?

Braine (1976) sought to answer the last of these questions in particular. He re-analysed the structural patterns of 16 corpora of word combinations that had formed the data base of most of the influential studies up to that point. Braine pointed out that in many of the original analyses, the line of inference from the corpus to the grammatical categories had not been spelled out. On re-examination, many of the categories proposed seemed to be over-general for the data. Many of the children seemed to be learning rules of how to combine an individual word with a category. Of the 11 children studied, six did not show convincing evidence of rules in which both grammatical positions were occupied by a category. Braine proposed that frequently children were learning rules about specific *words* rather than about more general semantic concepts.

Let us consider the example of a child who hears the utterance *more ball* and knows the meanings of both *more* and *ball*. If a child hears the utterance in the context of seeing another instance of a ball (assuming one or several exemplars are already present), then the child could work out that *ball* referred to the object and *more* to the plurality of instances. The child has now derived the meaning of the input string *more ball*. This meaning can now be used to work out a grammatical rule. Most accounts prior to Braine had argued that the grammatical rule would be something like RECURRENCE + ENTITY, which is directly equivalent to the abstract semantic content of the utterance. However, there are other possibilities. One is that the child had learnt a more simple rule about combining the word *more* with a category of words that denote entities. According to this type of account the child is learning rules for combining entity words with particular individual words such as *more* that encode a property of the entity, rather than learning to combine entity words with a more abstract semantic construct such as RECURRENCE. The two alternative accounts can be separated in the case of the example given by considering in more detail the implications of a rule such as RECURRENCE + ENTITY. *More* is not the only word that can be used to encode recurrence; *another* (and *again* under certain circumstances) should occur in free variation if these words are in the child's vocabulary. Braine's study of the corpora revealed that free variation did not always occur when a number of semantically synonymous terms were in the child's vocabulary.

For example, in the case of one child studied by Braine the words *more* and *other* were both used to encode recurrence. *More* was combined with both nouns and verbs in utterances such as *more can, more cereal, more read, more sing,* while *other* was combined with nouns only and then largely with nouns that denoted food or items of clothing, within utterances such as *other bread* and *other shirt.* Braine concluded that the child had learnt specific rules of lexical combination for *more* and *other* rather than a general semantic rule of recurrence with *more* and *other* in free variation. Although Braine found evidence for some rules that combined two general semantic categories, he found much evidence also for rules that combined single specific words with a semantic category; often one that is narrower in scope than the type of category proposed in the existing semantic analyses. This suggests a much more piecemeal and specific method of organizing grammar than had been assumed. The difference between Braine's proposal and earlier proposals can be seen if we consider a child who encounters utterances such as 'more ball', 'more juice' and so forth, knowing the meaning of both *more* and the object words, and assume that the child makes an inductive guess about the structure of his or her native language, as proposed by Macnamara (1972). On a semantic analysis *more* would be regarded as an instantiation of a general concept of recurrence and *ball* as an instantiation of a concept of object. The child might induce that RECURRENCE + OBJECT was a legitimate rule of the language. Braine's analysis would not credit the child with such a general rule unless there were evidence that words other than *more* were used to express recurrence and that all such words had the same scope of combination. Without this evidence Braine suggests the child should be credited with the more specific induction that *more* + OBJECT was a legitimate rule of the language.

The main patterns discovered by Braine are shown in table 7.1. Braine arrived at these patterns by first determining whether the children's utterances expressed manifestly different semantic relations and by then using distributional analysis within a category to determine whether there was one general semantic pattern or a variety of more specific lexical patterns. Table 7.1 shows that children use both general and specific categories in producing two-word utterances. The importance of Braine's analysis is that it reveals that there is much more that is specific about the child's inductions than was previously suspected. The picture that begins to emerge from this is that of a child with a limited number of general semantic categories, and these mostly for basic cognitive categories such as ACTOR, ACTION, and OBJECT, who is sensitive to words as represen-

Table 7.1 *Patterns identified by Braine (1976) in early word combinations.*

Content and/or function of utterance	Typical pattern	Example
Draw attention	*see* + X	*see train*
	here/there + X	*here milk*
Identify	*it/that* + X	*that ball*
Comment on property	*big/little* + X	*big ear*
Possession	X + Y	*Daddy book*
Number	*two* + X	*two spoon*
Recurrence	*more* + X	*more juice*
Disappearance	*allgone* + X	*allgone stick*
Negation	*no* + X	*no water*
Actor-action	X + Y	*Mommy read*
Location	X + *here/there*	*lady there*
Request	*want* + X	*want car*

tational entities in their own right and who is beginning to build a grammar based on rules for combining words as well as rules for combining more general categories.

A further feature of Braine's review was his finding that although the same patterns could be observed across the 16 corpora studied, the order of emergence of the patterns was different for different children. This suggests that there are few dependencies among the patterns and that children are learning a series of independent rules to express particular meanings. From the point of view of learning, the lack of dependency simplifies the child's task; rules can be acquired in any order and learning bottlenecks are not created by the absence of a particular rule.

In summary, research on two-word utterances has been largely concerned with the nature of the rule system that the child acquires for word combinations. Most analyses agree on the general principle that the child acquires a variety of combination rules that encode semantic relations. There was an initial tendency to credit the child with rules that combined very general semantic categories. Following Braine's (1976) influential review, there has been a realization that there is greater specificity in the child's rules and also greater variability among children than had previously been supposed.

The proposals that the child initially organizes language on a semantic basis made it relatively easy to see how the child could begin the task of creating an organizational structure for language. However, such an organizational structure is not an end-point in itself; it is simply an intermediate point in the overall process of language development. In many ways it is an uncomfortable intermediate point. Ultimately, the structure of language obeys syntactic not semantic principles. The structural syntax of English, for example, requires concepts of NOUN, VERB, ADJECTIVE, SUBJECT, OBJECT, ACTIVE, PASSIVE, TENSE, and a variety of other grammatical concepts. These concepts do not reduce to semantic definition in any simple sense. Thus, an outstanding issue is the relation between an early language based on semantic rules and a somewhat later system based on grammatical rules. There are two ways in which the relation between the two can be addressed. The first is to seek continuity through the modification of semantic into syntactic categories. On this view the child begins by inducing semantic categories and rules for their combination and proceeds to modify these rules until syntactic categories and an adult grammar are achieved. As will become evident, this route is fraught with difficulty.

A second way to address the relation between the child's early and later grammars is to see them as largely independent systems, organized over a common lexicon. The emphasis on rules for combining words can obscure the fact that words themselves are key representational elements in the language system. The word is the basic building block of language. It is possible that the child brings a variety of organizational strategies to bear on the lexicon. Semantic analysis may be the first of these, not least because the major purpose of organizational strategies is to combine words to express meanings. Initially, the lexicon is limited in the number of words it contains and simple relational meanings given by direct combination of semantic categories may be the best that the child can achieve. As the lexicon expands the possibility of other analyses arises. On this view the semantic relations of early word combinations are not the direct precursors of grammatical categories but are the most easily applicable initial system of organization. Other systems of organization will later be induced and will come to replace rather than succeed the child's early semantic formulae.

The Origins of Form-Class Representations

A theory of language development must be able to show how the child induces the major grammatical form-classes that are the basis of grammar. In passing, it should be noted that although there is not universal agreement on a generative theory of grammar, there is no serious disagreement that such a theory will manipulate, in some way or other, categories such as Noun, Verb, and Adjective. Hence, it is a strong requirement on a developmental theory of language to show how the child acquires these categories.

The original hope behind the proposal that two-word utterances had a semantic structure was that such a structure would provide a solid foundation for grammar. However, this hope was strongly dependent on the adequacy of some case-like semantic grammar. It transpired that semantic grammars have serious deficiencies and they are no longer considered as serious candidates in the search for a grammatical theory (see Newmeyer, 1980). The main problem is that semantics cannot provide a direct basis for syntax. However, it is possible that early semantic categories could form the prototypes for later syntactic categories. A number of theorists have advanced such a proposal. In order to evaluate the proposal, it is best to begin by considering the relation between semantic concepts and form-class categories.

If we consider nouns as an illustration, then the most obvious semantic property of nouns is that they denote objects. However, this property is not universally shared by nouns. Nouns also denote abstractions, with words such as *idea, knowledge,* and *beauty*, and states with words such as *happiness* and *sadness*. These forms must eventually be accommodated as nouns within the child's grammatical system. However, the presence of such terms in the adult language does not preclude the view that the category NOUN is initially formed around the semantic notion of objecthood. Such a view has an obvious attraction because OBJECT is a basic cognitive category if anything is. Furthermore, the vast majority of children's early nouns are object words rather than words for abstractions or states. Thus, there seems to be little difficulty in imagining a semantic criterion forming the basis for an initial NOUN category. Several theorists have proposed that the NOUN category is first formed in this way (Gentner, 1982; Slobin, 1981). The only problem with such a view is that the category must be restructured in some way to include nouns such as *beauty, happiness* and so forth. There is a variety of ways in which this might be accomplished. One possibility (Bates and MacWhinney, 1982) is that object words form the initial prototypical core of a noun category and that words such as *beauty* and *sleep* are assimilated to the category because they behave, linguistically, in similar ways to the prototypical members – for example, they occur in the same grammatical positions in sentences as prototypical nouns do.

It is somewhat more difficult to apply the same analysis to verbs and adjectives. The prototype for a VERB category would obviously be action. However, even casual inspection of children's early utterances reveals that they use a variety of verbs that do not denote actions: *think, want, need, have, see, know,* and *can,* are just some. In fact, verbs are an extremely mixed bag of relational terms that denote actions and states. Furthermore, they do none of these things exclusively; there are semantic overlaps between verbs and other form-classes. In particular, there is considerable overlap between adjectives and verbs. There are stative adjectives, such as *nice* or *generous*, and adjectives that have an actional basis, such as *active*, or *busy*. If the child were to use a semantic criterion to define form-classes then it is likely that some incorrect assignments of words to form-classes would be made. This would result in errors of inflection. Suppose, for example, that a child assimilated *nice* to the verb category on the grounds that nice is a state and states can be represented as verbs. Such a child should make errors such as *he nices and *they are nicing (the * indicates that the sentences should be considered ungrammatical) until he or she discovers that *nice* is not a verb. As we shall see shortly, children do commonly make inflectional errors but they almost never make this kind of error even though there is ample opportunity for it as a result of semantic overlaps among form-classes. The fact that the errors do not occur suggests that children are not inducing form-classes on a semantic basis.

There are additional arguments that can be advanced against the semantic origins of form-class categories. Maratsos and Chalkley (1980), for example, draw attention to the cross-cultural evidence that indicates that children readily learn what appear intuitively to be difficult formal systems that have no basis in semantics. One example is the gender system for nouns in German. Meaning is a poor cue to the gender of a noun in German, which has masculine, feminine, and neuter genders. In German the moon is *der Mond* (masculine), the sun is *die Senne* (feminine), while child, girl, and woman are *das Kind, das Madchen,* and *das Weib,* all neuter. Children rarely make errors in selecting the appropriate determiner (*der, die,* or *das*) for a noun despite absence of semantic cues (MacWhinney, 1978). This is a significant accomplishment because the selection of a determiner is more complex than a choice between *der, die,* and *das.* German has four grammatical cases: nominative, accusative, genitive, and dative. The determiner varies as a function of the case but there is not a unique relation between determiner and case. The full system of determiners by case for the singular is shown in table 7.2.

It can be seen that *der,* for example, precedes both the masculine nominative and the feminine dative and genitive. In spite of this and other duplications children rarely make errors. The reasons suggested by Maratsos and Chalkley (1980) is that the form of the determiner and the case of the noun *together* are a predictive basis to the noun's gender and to the determiners a noun takes in other cases. This combination of determiner and case also predicts (or can be predicted from) the pronomi-

Table 7.2 *The full system of determiners by case for the singular in German.*

	Masculine	Feminine	Neuter
Nominative	der	die	das
Accusative	den	die	das
Dative	dem	der	dem
Genitive	des	der	des

nal form of the noun. The absence of error by children learning the German noun gender system suggests that children are highly sensitive to non-semantic distributional cues about the structure of their native language. Maratsos (1983) cites various other examples that indicate that children's analysis of the structure of language is not heavily dependent on a semantic basis as a prerequisite.

Once a cross-cultural dimension is added to children's achievements in the early stages of language development the following picture begins to emerge. Children have an ability to organize the lexical data-base of their language in a variety of different and independent ways based on semantic, phonological, and distributional properties. Despite the priority of semantic organization in the combinations of early speech, semantics does not seem to have a privileged organizational status. Thus, it may be that, as has been suggested, the semantic organization evident in two-word utterances is not a precursor for the syntactic classes and syntactic rules that characterize the later organization of language. Early semantic organization may be an adaptive communicative response that is replaced by later developing forms of organization. For example, Maratsos (1979; 1982; 1983; Maratsos and Chalkley, 1980) has proposed that form-classes such as NOUN and VERB are induced on the basis of shared grammatical properties among words. In the case of the category NOUN, the relevant grammatical properties might be that the word can occur in certain privileged positions in an utterance (for instance, at the head of a declarative sentence), can be preceded by a determiner, can be modified by words that denote properties and so forth. The way in which a VERB category could be induced will now be examined in more detail.

The Category VERB

When children progress beyond the two-word stage, they begin to add to their utterances the function words and the inflections that were missing from the two-word utterances. During the two-word stage action words will all consist of the root form of the verb – e.g., *jump, walk, roll*. Beyond the two-word stage children will gradually begin to add the past *-ed*, the progressive *-ing*, and the third person present *-s* inflections to these verbs. What learning process accounts for this? It could be that the children induce, from the language that they hear, some general rule about how to encode the past, the progressive, and the third person present. This might seem to be the simplest and most straightforward way to acquire the grammatical morphemes of verbs. However, this does not seem to be how children progress. If the child induced a general rule for the past tense of the form 'add *-ed* to words that denote actions', then he or she would have induced a rule that does not always work because there are many irregular verbs that do not form the past tense by adding *-ed* to the verb stem. Some sample verbs are *hit, run, do*, and *make*. There is nothing to prevent a child inducing a general rule that is incorrect and simply overriding the irregular verbs. In fact, at a slightly later point in development exactly this happens. However, when verb inflections are first learnt, the correct form of both the regular and irregular verbs are learnt. Since the irregular verbs are irregular in a variety of different ways (Bybee and Slobin, 1982), this pattern of learning suggests that the inflected forms of a verb are initially learnt on a word-by-word basis rather than as the application of a generative rule. Thus, a child learns that *jumped* is the past form of *jump, walked* is the past form of *walk, hit* is the past form of *hit, ran* is the past form of *run* and so forth. Each of these pieces of knowledge is learnt simply by observing the appropriate form being used by others to talk about actions that have happened recently but that are now no longer happening. This type of learning illustrates again the fact that a great deal of language learning consists of the child working directly on the lexical data base.

The pattern of word-by-word learning that this implies is perfectly consistent with the type of learning discussed above that leads to the initial combination of words. However, it is evident that the child must go beyond this. Adults, and even somewhat older children have a generative ability to predict the correct grammatical form of a novel word (Berko, 1958, Brown, 1957). In Berko's famous study she tested this ability with 5- to 7-year-olds. In one of the verb examples she showed a picture of a man swinging an object and told the child: 'This is a man who knows how to rick. He is ricking. He did the same thing yesterday. Yesterday he . . . .' The child was required to provide the final word. The majority of children provided the correct form *ricked*. Thus, by the age of 5 years, children have acquired a rule for forming the past tense by adding *-ed* to the verb stem. Berko demonstrated that children commanded a wide variety of such morphological rules. Evidently, by the age of 5 years children possess a conventional grammar built around syntactic categories. How then, have children progressed from the word-by-word acquisition of verb inflections to a rule-based system for mastering inflections?

For each individual verb in the input the child will learn a variety of related forms; for example *walked, walking,* and *walks* for the word *walk.* At the level of lexical representation these words share a common element of meaning: they all refer to walking. At the level of phonological representation they all share a common root: *walk.* If we assume that the child has the ability to segment the affixes *-ing, -ed,* and *-s* from the common stem *walk* then we can imagine a representational structure something like the following being acquired:

> Root: *walk*
> + *ed* pastness
> + *ing* progressive
> + *s* 3rd person present

This is not the full representational structure – there will be other elements also, especially elements to do with combination rules. However, it is a sufficient amount of the word's representation for exposition. It is worth noting how, even to build such a simple representational system, morphological, lexical, and semantic levels of representation are needed.

Maratsos (1979; 1982; Maratsos and Chalkley, 1980) argues that from the word-by-word acquisition of verb inflections children begin to build a network of words that share the fact that they all take the same inflections. A child may, for example, hear a variety of words used with *-ed* to denote pastness. Many of these same words will be used with *-s* to denote generic present and with *-ing* to denote progressive. The type of network that might result is shown in figure 7.2. Although all the words that belong to the network would be called verbs in the adult language, they do not belong to the network because they are verbs; rather they are verbs because they belong to the network. This is the essence of the argument about form-class origins advanced by Maratsos. His position can be contrasted with that of innatist theorists who assume that the category Verb is part of the innate structure brought to bear on language acquisition and with semantic theorists who assume that the syntactic category VERB is derived from a semantic category that has clustered together words denoting actions. Maratsos argues that the distributional pattern of the inflections is criterial in defining the form-class Verb.

Let us at this point, sketch in the broad picture of what is going on.

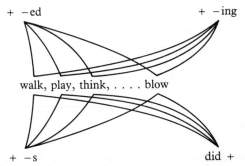

Figure 7.2   *The type of network that Maratsos and Chalkley (1980) suggest for representing the semantic-distribution patterns of the root form of a word with morphemes.*

The child initially learns a variety of words that denote objects, actions, and properties. He or she learns to combine words using a mixture of lexically-specific and more general semantic rules. At this point in development the child is not generally assumed to represent language in terms of grammatical categories such as NOUN and VERB. Development continues apace, with the addition of function words such as determiners and prepositions to the child's linguistic system and also with the addition of morphological modifications to the content words, such as -s to denote plural for object words and, for actions words, -ed to denote pastness, -ing to denote progressive aspect, and -s to denote the third person present indicative (Brown, 1973a). The inflections are initially learnt on a word-by-word basis but morphological segmentation of words into roots and affixes creates a network of words that share a common set of inflections. The inflections and other grammatical properties that they share in common (such as position in declarative sentences) define grammatical categories such as Noun, Verb, and Adjective.

The argument advanced by Maratsos about the derivation of grammatical categories can be put into perspective by contrasting it with the traditional view about grammatical categories. If we consider the category Verb as an example, then the traditional view would have it that Verbs are words that can be inflected by -ed for pastness, -ing for progressive and so forth. Maratsos reverses the direction of the argument and argues that words that can be inflected for pastness by -ed, for progressive by -ing and so forth are verbs. It is the inflections that are criterial for the category rather than the inflections being a consequence that follows from membership of the category.

One reason that we can be certain that children do induce grammatical categories such as VERB is that after the initial correct learning of the past tense of irregular verbs children begin to make errors of regularizing the past tense of irregular verbs. Thus, a child who initially produced *came*, *saw*, *thought*, may now produce *comed*, *seed*, and *thinked*. These errors are among the best-known errors of children learning English and have been widely documented (Brown, 1973a, Cazden, 1968; Ervin, 1964; Kuczaj, 1977); Such errors are strong indications of both the child's own creative role in the language acquisition process and of the fact that initial word-by-word learning has been replaced by a new organizational pattern of a grammatical form-class category.

The pattern of development that appears to fit the data on the move from initial correct usage of irregular past tense forms to overregularized usage is one in which children first learn the correct irregular forms as unanalyzed whole words but later induce a rule that the past tense is formed by adding -*ed* to the root verb. This would produce the characteristic errors observed. However, before accepting this conventional answer to the pattern of development observed, let us address the issues of why they should do so and how exactly the inductive process works.

The question of why children should induce a rule is not often addressed in the language development literature. Yet, it must be remembered that children already have the correct past tense form of the verbs to which they misapply the rule 'add -*ed* to the root to form the past tense' and that they never hear the incorrect past tense forms as speech input. There must therefore be powerful forces at work in the cognitive system that dictate this rule. There seem to be two possible sources of such a powerful force. One is that there is a powerful induction mechanism that is triggered once certain threshold values of a regularity are reached. Initially many of the verbs learnt are irregular, largely because most of the most commonly used verbs have irregular past tenses. However, with time, more and more regular forms are added and eventually a threshold may be reached that triggers an inductive process. This mechanism would then operate to override the previously correct forms.

There are two difficulties that face such an account. The first is that the account presumes that there is a representational category of verbs to which the inductive process can be applied. But, we have seen that the most common explanation of the initial correct usage of irregular past tense forms is that they are learnt on a word-by-word basis. Thus, the account sketched above must be supplemented by an account of how the individual words come together to form the representational category VERB. It is possible, and tacitly present in most accounts that presume a process like the above, that the initial representational category of VERB is formed on semantic grounds. However, such accounts face the difficulty that a semantically-defined category is likely to be over general, which would lead one to expect that the errors following induction would be over general also and apply to some forms that are not legitimate verbs. Yet, such errors are never observed.

The second difficulty that faces the account of induction sketched is that it presumes a mechanism highly sensitive to partial regularities, with the scope to override already established non-regular forms once a partial regularity is encountered. However, there is little evidence that the cognitive system employs such a powerful inductive mechanism. Nor is such a powerful mechanism consistent with the data; children do not unilaterally replace irregular verb forms with overregularized forms; both the regular and overregularized forms co-exist (Kuczaj, 1977).

There is a way round both problems at once. This is that overregularizations are not the direct result of an induction process triggered by the presence of a statistical regularity in an already-formed VERB category but are the indirect result of the formation of a VERB category itself in the way outlined above – that is, formed as a result of a network of correlated privileges of occurrence of various inflections. The formation of this category creates a new level of linguistic representation but at this level of representation the only things that are represented are the correlated occurrences of inflections. Thus, the correlation between -ing, -s, and -ed inflections with a common root are represented. Root words are linked to this new representational structure. The existing lexical representations of the word are preserved however. A word is now represented twice over: as a lexical item in its own right and as a generative product of a form-class category. In the case of regular verbs the two representations will produce the same output. However, in the case of irregular verbs one representation will produce the correct irregular form and the other will produce the incorrect generative form leading to their co-occurrence within the child's output, which is what is observed (Kuczaj, 1977).

Kuczaj (1977) has presented the most complete data on the overregularization of the past tense. He reported cross-sectional data for 14 children together with longitudinal data for one child. The average proportion of overregularizations in the cross-sectional data was 21 per cent, which means that almost 80 per cent of the child's verbs continue to have the correct form. In the longitudinal data the proportion of overregularizations never rose above 46 per cent. These data are entirely consistent with the model of verb learning proposed here. They are not consistent with the view that the child induces a general all-powerful rule 'add -ed to the root to form the past tense'.

The account presented here has several advantages over the conventional account. It does not presume the prior existence of a category of

VERB over which the inductive process operates; it does not predict a monopolistic use of overregularized forms; and it does not require an inductive process of unlikely power operating in the creation of grammatical categories. Instead, the account stresses that overregularization occurs as a side-effect of the induction of the grammatical category VERB. There is, however, another alternative as to how children learn the past tense of verbs proposed by Rumelhart and McClelland (1986), which will be considered in chapter 9.

Innateness and language development

Historically, a contrast has been drawn between innatist and empiricist theories of language development. This characterization is not accurate. There are no modern empiricist theories of language development in the sense in which Skinner's (1957) account was empiricist. The major distinction to be drawn is one between theories that assume that language development is made possible by innate knowledge of the principles of grammar and theories that assume that language development is made possible by innate processes for analyzing language input in order to learn the structures of grammar.

One of the major issues that has faced attempts to construct a theory of language development is the issue of learnability. Part of Chomsky's contribution to thinking about language development is his insistence that the mechanisms of learning must be shown to be capable of generating the structure of any natural language from normal input data. In the preceding sections an attempt has been made to summarize the major lines of empirical research that have addressed the representational structure of the child's developing language system. The emphasis has been placed, deliberately, on theories and research that address the route that leads to the construction of the major grammatical categories. Much has been left on one side, including a more detailed discussion of the semantics of two-word utterances (see Bloom, Lightbown and Hood, 1975; Braine, 1976), the complex semantics of the verb system (see McShane, Whittaker and Dockrell, 1986), the development of complex sentence structure (see Maratsos, 1983), the role of input in language acquisition (see Hoff-Ginsberg and Shatz, 1982), and the way in which cross-cultural studies can be used to test claims about universal mechanisms in language acquisition (see Slobin, 1985). The induction of the major grammatical categories provides the child with a basis for learning the syntactic structure of language. However, the empirical research on language development does not directly address the issue of whether the child's model of grammar eventually converges to an adult model. At best the data reviewed above amount to a partial answer to the learnability question. Ultimately, one must be able to explain how the type of intermediate stages of development described above are converted by precisely specified acquisition mechanisms into a rule system adequate to represent the adult language system.

The Poverty of the Stimulus Argument

Chomsky (1965) proposed that children come equipped to language acquisition with an innate Language Acquisition Device that guides the structural inductions that the child makes. Chomsky saw the necessity for a LAD as arising from the poverty of the stimulus argument.

The basis of the poverty of the stimulus argument is that there is insufficient evidence available to the child in the input received to warrant the kind of rules induced. Lightfoot (1982) lists three ways in which stimulus input may be deficient:

1 The speech the child hears will include some ill-formed sentences. These sentences will not come labelled as defective, and so will create problems when the child tries to generalize to the set of grammatical sentences of the language.

2 A child encounters only a finite range of expressions but comes to be able to deal with an infinite range of novel sentences.

3 Many of the rules of language that people come to 'know' (in the sense that they are adhered to, though not necessarily expressible, by native speakers) could not be learnt from the input to which they are exposed as children.

Of these three arguments, the first and second are of less relevance than the third. Although children undoubtedly hear some ungrammatical sentences when learning a language, it is not certain what significance should be attached to this. If one assumes that the child uses every input sentence as a basis for making new inductions about the structure of language (as much of formal learning theory assumes) then ungrammatical sentences are a problem. However, if one assumes that a sentence-type must occur with some degree of frequency before it is a candidate for induction then ungrammatical sentences are unlikely to be of any relevance to the majority of children learning language.

The second argument advanced by Lightfoot has little force because almost any theory of language learning will postulate that the child induces general rules from particular instances. These general rules will be capable of generating a range of sentences far beyond the examples from which the rules were derived.

The third argument is altogether the most relevant. As an example of this argument Lightfoot (1982) offers the following three sentences, the third of which would be considered ungrammatical.

(a) 'Who did the woman meet in town?'
(b) 'Who did you believe that the woman met in town?'
(c) '*Who did you see the woman that met in town?'

Lightfoot points out that children are not exposed to sentences like (c) and told that they are ungrammatical but nevertheless they come to know that sentences like this are ungrammatical. Lightfoot (1982: p. 18) goes on to draw the following conclusion.

> If the child's linguistic experience does not provide the basis for establishing some particular aspect of linguistic knowledge, some other source for that knowledge must exist. That aspect must be known a priori in the sense that it is available independently of linguistic experience.

In other words, if children acquire rules that are not derivable from the input, they must have some innate knowledge that guided the acquisition of the rule. It should be noted that since the rules a child acquires are the rules of some particular language, such as English, it is not plausible to suggest that the rules themselves are innate. The rules, rather, are seen as the product of innate constraints brought to bear on language acquisition.

In Chomsky's later work the concept of a Language Acquisition Device has been replaced by the concept of a Universal Grammar. Universal Grammar is not a grammar in the sense that Transformational Grammar is; rather it is a theory that attempts to specify the set of primitives, axioms, and rules of inference that would generate a grammar for any natural language to which a child is exposed. The attempt to create a Universal Grammar is an attempt to discover a set of principles and parameters that act as innate constraints on the rules that the child induces.

Induction and Language Learnability

The proposal that there are innate constraints on the inductions that a child makes about the structure of language does not rest entirely on the poverty of the stimulus argument. The issue can also be approached by considering whether or not the mechanism of inductive learning is sufficiently powerful to learn the abstract structure of a natural language. The pioneering work in this area was that of Gold (1967). Before considering this it will be useful to consider induction in more general terms.

In any theoretical account of how children acquire the rules of grammar the problem of constraining the inductions they make is a fundamental one. There are many possible rule systems that could be postulated to account for the limited amount of language that a child hears or produces. The question now arises: could induction serve to generate a grammar of the language to which a child is exposed? This question cannot be resolved by simple experiment. In principle we could answer the question by building an artificial learning system equipped with inductive powers, exposing it to the input that a child receives, and observing the output. However, simulations of learning mechanisms have not yet advanced to the point where this is a feasible proposition on the large scale of learning language as a whole.

Simulation is not, however, the only way to tackle the problem of how language learning might occur. In recent years, an impressive body of formal work has addressed the problem of induction in language learning. This is sometimes called *formal learning theory* or *learnability theory*. Learnability theory consists of a body of formal work that attempts to prove theorems about whether or not language is learnable given certain assumptions about the input, the learning mechanisms the child possesses and the structure of the adult language system. The pioneering effort was that of Gold (1967). Gold attempted to examine the conditions under which blind inductive process might identify the grammar of language. (A blind inductive process is one in which the inductive process has no constraints and therefore has no basis for preference among alternative hypotheses and must choose at random among the alternative hypotheses.) Gold constructed the following scenario: There is some target language to be learned by a learner. The learner receives input one sentence at a time from the language. After each presentation the learner guesses (by induction) what the grammar of the language is. If the existing grammar can generate the sentence, the learner retains the existing grammar; if not a new grammar is guessed that can generate the new sentence together with all the sentences previously heard. The guesses are 'blind', in the sense that the learner systematically works through every possible rule of combination for the grammar. If the learner's grammar stabilizes to the point where it can, over some period of time, successfully generate all new sentences it receives, then it is said to have *identified the language in the limit*.

Gold's work led to an important discovery: So long as an inductive learning process receives only positive examples of the target language, it cannot be guaranteed to discover the grammar in a finite amount of time. Basically, the problem is that unless there is some means of discovering which sentences are *not* in the language, an inductive mechanism will generate too many false but plausible grammars to allow learning of the correct grammar to occur. Since children do not, apparently, receive examples that are not in the language – caretakers do not deliberately produce utterances as examples that are not in the language – it follows from Gold's theorem that induction on its own is not a sufficient mechanism for learning the grammar of a language. Children obviously do learn the grammar of the language to which they are exposed, so it must be concluded that they do not use the type of inductive processes considered by Gold.

Let us dwell on the significance of this result for a moment. Gold's theorem shows that a general-purpose blind inductive process cannot identify the grammar of a language unless it is given examples of sentences that are not in the language. The general-purpose inductive process envisaged by Gold is probably more powerful than human induction in at least one respect: it will guess a new grammar *every time* it cannot generate an input sentence. Even with this powerful ability, blind inductive search among potential grammars will not learn the grammar of language in the limit. It follows from these results that using only blind induction, children could not infer the grammar of their language from the input received. Thus, natural languages are not learnable using only a blind inductive learning process. Therefore, the learning mechanism must be given more power.

The favoured way of making the language learning mechanism more powerful than blind induction has been to assume that the inductive process is not blind but is guided by innate constraints on the structures proposed for the input received. This was the proposal initially advanced by Chomsky (1965). In what follows it is useful to keep two points separate: (a) the proposal that there are constraints is a logical proposal based on the limits of inductive learning mechanisms; and (b) the constraints proposed will depend, to some extent, on what assumptions are made about how the grammar of a language is represented.

What might these constraints be? The answer to this question will depend, to some extent, on one's theory of grammar. There is no generally agreed account of how grammatical knowledge is represented. The early innatist theories of language assumed that grammatical structure is best represented by a transformational grammar and framed their proposals about constraints accordingly. More recent proposals have assumed different theories of grammar resulting in different proposals about constraints.

Thus if one assumes that the structure of language is best represented by Transformational Grammar, the constraints would need to guide hypotheses about transformations. If, on the other hand, it is assumed that surface structures are generated by phrase-structure rules without a transformational component, as in Lexical Functional Grammar (Kaplan and Bresnan, 1982) then the constraints will not need to guide hypotheses about transformations. Whatever grammar is proposed the function of the constraints is to guide the inductive hypotheses that are made by the child about the grammar of the language from the input received.

The issue of learnability and the proposal that there is innate knowledge of the structural principles of language go together in the sense that the learnability issue has been used as a justification for proposing innate structural principles to guide language acquisition. However, logically the learnability issue and any *particular* set of proposals about how language is learnt are separate. The learnability issues must be tackled by any theory of language development. A particular proposal may, as a matter of fact, be right or wrong. Proposals must be tested in the conventional way, by comparing their implications for the learning process with evidence from actual learning.

Innate Processes for Acquisition

Although developmental theories of language acquisition have not paid particular attention of how language is learnt, the issue has been addressed by Slobin (1966; 1973; 1985) in a series of papers. Slobin has argued against a system of structural constraints on language acquisition in favour of a system of innate processing strategies that focus the child's inductions. Slobin (1966: pp. 87–8) stated the basic philosophy of a process-oriented approach to language development:

> It seems to me that the child is born not with a set of linguistic categories but with some sort of process mechanism – a set of procedures and inference rules if you will – that he uses to process linguistic data. These mechanisms are such that, applying them to the input data, the child ends up with something that is a member of the class of human languages. The linguistic universals, then, are the result of an innate cognitive competence rather than the content of such a competence.

Slobin (1973) proposed a set of 'operating principles', which were a summary of the processing strategies that children might use in acquiring their native language. The processing strategies he proposed were supported by evidence from a wide range of languages. Slobin argued that cognitive development was the pacesetter for language development;

the child must first have an independent semantic intention to express something and must then discover the linguistic means of doing so. However, language development was not seen by Slobin as an automatic or trivial product of cognitive development. He pointed to several cross-linguistic examples in which a particular linguistic form is learned very much later in one language than another because of the formal complexity of the linguistic structure. One particular example is the fact that plural markers for the noun are a relatively early acquisition for English-speaking children but for children learning Arabic, the noun plural is not fully mastered until the teens; the reason, Slobin argued, is the extreme complexity of plural marking in Arabic. The processing strategies proposed by Slobin (1973) are:

1 Pay attention to the end of words.
2 The phonological form of words can be systematically modified.
3 Pay attention to the order of words and morphemes.
4 Avoid interruption or rearrangement of linguistic units.
5 Underlying semantic relations should be marked overtly and clearly.
6 Avoid exceptions.
7 The use of grammatical markers should make semantic sense.

Slobin's wide-ranging review and his detailed proposals were influential in turning the attention of students of language to the relation between cognitive and language development. The significance of Slobin's proposals were two-fold: firstly there was the emphasis that what is learned about language structure is learned initially because the structure is of independent semantic significance to the child; secondly there was a detailed set of proposals about universal processing strategies. These latter were an attempt to show *how* the structure of language is learnt. However, there was no attempt to address the question posed by learnability theorists: could these mechanisms be shown to be adequate to learn a grammar of some specified sort? This seems doubtful given that the operating principles proposed by Slobin have little to say about grammatical categories such as NOUN and VERB or grammatical functions such as SUBJECT and OBJECT, or about the complexity of verb relations, or about phrase-structure rules. However, Slobin would not necessarily accept that an attempt to show how some particular model grammar was learnt was the most profitable way to extend our understanding of language acquisition mechanisms. In a later revision of his proposed operating principles Slobin (1985: p. 1158) remarked:

I shall attempt to make use of our cross-linguistic findings to discuss what we currently know about 'LMC' – the LANGUAGE-MAKING CAPACITY of the child. Rather than 'pre-tune' LMC to a particular current theory of abstract syntax, I prefer to work backward from acquisition data to propose systems of knowledge and information processing that seem to be prerequisite for the sorts of data we encounter crosslinguistically.

Slobin's (1985) revision of his operating principles refined the original proposal, added new principles to account for counterexamples to the original set, or to handle phenomena not previously dealt with. The complete set of operating principles is too lengthy to be discussed here but the overall structure is as follows: first there is a set of principles that serve as filters on what enters the cognitive system for further processing from the speech that the child hears. A further set of principles store the filtered speech in different sized 'chunks' of word classes, functor classes, phrases, and clauses. The principles at the heart of the system are those that relate meaning to form. Slobin argues that certain cognitive notions have a privileged status and serve as prototypes for creating semantic-syntactic links. In particular, extracted speech units are mapped, as a first attempt, onto representations of objects and events. Words that cannot be mapped onto entities or events (such as the locative prepositions *in, on,* and *under*) will be assumed to be grammatical units that relate content words together. There is a detailed set of proposals of how semantic-syntactic links are established for such grammatical forms. Further principles deal with other aspects of grammar such as word order, and the placement of affixes. Slobin also proposes a set of 'review strategies' that serve to control the child's system in various ways, such as by strengthening good rules and by reorganizing the system on a piecemeal continuous basis.

Slobin (1985) has presented the most thorough attempt to account for *how* language is learnt without proposing strong innate structural constraints on the child's inductions. However, the attempt cannot be judged entirely successful at this point. Although there is a wealth of operating principles it is not entirely clear how these could be applied in an explanatory way to the sequence of development of a child learning some particular language. The problem with the wealth of principles proposed is that for any observed pattern of development it is likely that some principle can be found that will apply to 'explain' that pattern. At present the principles lack any ordering relations or as Bowerman (1985) has pointed out, they lack a conceptual 'glue' to bring them into a theoretically-driven relationship with each other. There is also the further problem raised by Bowerman of the extent to which the principles are testable. In some cases there are complementary principles such that if one fails, the other applies. Bowerman (1985: p. 1267) cites the twin principles that state 'the use of grammatical markers should make semantic sense', and 'if a speech element is frequent and perceptually salient, but has no obvious semantic or pragmatic function, use it in its salient form and position until you discover its function; otherwise do not use it'. If a child is not following the first of these principles then it may be presumed he or she is following the second. Such complementarity makes it very difficult to test how and when a particular principle applies.

The principles proposed by Slobin have very much a goal-directed, problem-solving approach to language learning. This is evident in the way that the principles are couched with recurring phrases of 'pay attention to', 'determine', 'if you discover'. At best, this is curious phrasing for processes that operate largely at the subconscious level; any attempt to translate from the stylistic conscious phrasing to unconscious information-processing mechanisms will not be an easy task and may impose more strain than the principles can bear. The learnability of grammar has become a major issue for theories of language development. This is all for the good: learnability sets a challenge to theories of language development to demonstrate that some target grammar can be learnt by clearly specified procedures that operate on a specified type of input. Slobin (1973, 1985) has presented the most sustained attempt to specify a set of procedures that operate without strong reliance on innate constraints about the structure of the language. At present, the operating principles proposed by Slobin cannot be judged to have met the challenge of learnability.

Learnability and Developmental Evidence

There are two major contrasts between innatist and developmental approaches to language acquisition. Innatist theories are much concerned with issues of learnability and the constraints that might guide learning but pay very little attention to the empirical details of actual learning. By contrast developmental theories pay considerable attention to detailed empirical findings and attempt to construct models adequate to these data. But, the accounts do not cumulate to deliver a theory of how language is learned by the child.

However, in recent years there have been attempts to bring the two lines of research closer together – to treat both the learnability problem and the empirical data with equal respect. The most serious and sustained attempt in this direction is that of Pinker (1984). Pinker places a number of requirements on learnability. First, the rule system proposed at a particular stage of development must have been constructed by an acquisition mechanism that began with no knowledge of the child's native language. Second, the system must have arrived at its current state on the basis of the input it has received in the interim. Third, each intermediate rule system must be the result of specified acquisition mechanisms operating on the preceding rule system. Fourth, the end result of acquisition must be a grammar adequate to represent adult abilities.

Pinker's approach to these issues is, in common with all learnability work, to commit himself to a model of the adult language and then to enquire how that model might be learned. Although the issue of how the adult language system ought to be described or represented is not settled, Pinker argues that it is important to make a commitment to some model in order to force one's acquisition theory to be explicit and the final theory adequate to the full complexity of the adult language. In making such a commitment one may, of course, choose an adult model that will, in time, turn out to be inadequate. However, theories can only be constructed in the light of the available evidence; it seems entirely reasonable as a theoretical enterprise to explore the learnability of some plausible model of adult language.

The model of adult grammar that Pinker espouses is Lexical Functional Grammar (Kaplan and Bresnan, 1982). Lexical Functional Grammar is a theory of generative grammar with no transformational component, in contrast to Chomsky's (1965) Standard Theory discussed earlier. So, whereas in the Standard Theory two sentences with the same meaning such as 'the dog chased the cat' and 'the cat was chased by the dog' would be generated from some common underlying base structure by the application of different transformations to that base, in Lexical Functional Grammar each sentence would be generated directly by the application of different phrase structure rules for active and passive sentences.

Lexical Functional Grammar is, in many ways, a more apposite model to choose to test learnability than Transformational Grammar. The reason for this is that Lexical Functional Grammar is committed to a close link between the formal properties of the grammatical theory and the cognitive processes that derive and interpret these properties in language use and acquisition. Bresnan and Kaplan (1982; xxiii) make this evident:

> In attributing psychological reality to a grammar, then, we require more than that it provides us with a description of the abstract structure of the linguistic knowledge domain; we require evidence that the grammar corresponds to the speaker's *internal* description of that domain.

Transformational Grammar, by contrast, does not have this commitment. A second major difference between Lexical Functional Grammar and Transformational Grammar is that the lexicon has a much bigger role to play in Lexical Functional Grammar than in Transformational Grammar. In Transformational Grammar the lexicon is simply a repository of the words in the language and their meaning. In Lexical Functional Grammar the lexicon includes information with each word about the grammatical roles it may have and how it may be modified (if it may) for such things as number and tense.   In Lexical Functional Grammar a sentence is given two different types of syntactic description. The first type is a *constituent structure* description, which results from the application of phrase-structure rules to produce a conventional phrase-structure tree. The second type is a *functional structure* description, which is a representation of the grammatical relations in a sentence – relations such as subject, predicate, object, tense and so forth. The functional structure of Lexical Functional Grammar is the syntactic input to the semantic interpretation of a sentence. Although constituent and functional structures are separate they interact in the following way. In constructing a constituent structure, phrase-structure rules are annotated for functional relations by templates associated with the phrase-structure constituents. Thus, a noun phrase that is the subject of a sentence would be annotated as NPsubj. If we consider the phrase-structure rules for 'the cats chased the dogs', these would be identical in Lexical Functional Grammar to the rules for the standard theory of Transformational Grammar presented earlier, except that the constituents would be annotated for grammatical function. In Lexical Functional Grammar, the phrase-structure rules would be:

$$
\begin{array}{lcl}
\text{S} & \to & \text{NPsubj VP} \\
\text{VP} & \to & \text{NPobj} \\
\text{NP} & \to & \text{DET N} \\
\text{N} & \to & \text{NS Plur} \\
\text{N} & \to & \text{VS Past}
\end{array}
$$

The annotated phrase-structure of a sentence is a half-way house between the constituent structure and the functional structure. It contains some functional information but within the overall framework of phrase-structure rules.

The annotated phrase structure rules and the lexical entries for the words in the sentence, together generate the functional structure of the sentence. The functional structure is, in effect, a test of whether the functional relations of the annotated phrase-structure tree are compatible with the grammatical information stored in the word's lexical entry. An important property of Lexical Functional Grammar is that a string of words may have a constituent structure but it may be impossible to generate a functional structure.

Having briefly explicated a portion of the model of the adult grammar to which Pinker commits himself we can now proceed to discuss how Pinker proposes that such a grammar is learned. His method is two-fold: first he proposes that the child is innately equipped with many of the components that enter into the grammar. This, he argues, provides for continuity between the child's rules and the final rules of the adult grammar. Equipping the child with a large range of innate components is, of course, controversial, but it does not mean that the child knows the grammar of the language from the start. What the child must do is assemble the components together in the appropriate way so that the particular phrase-structure of the language is induced. Pinker tackles that induction issue by proposing a set of subtheories, each of which is designed to acquire some particular subset of the rules of Lexical Functional Grammar. We shall examine some of these proposals.

The learnability of Lexical Functional Grammar is, in effect, ensured by the proposal that the components necessary to assemble a Lexical Functional Grammar are part of the child's innate knowledge. Specifically, Pinker proposes that the child is innately equipped with representational categories such as NOUN and VERB for language and that the child is innately disposed to induce phrase-structure rules for the particular language encountered.

Even though the child is equipped with innate grammatical categories such as NOUN and VERB, it is still necessary that he or she learn which particular words in the input are to be treated as members of a particular grammatical category. This is not a trivial problem. As Pinker points out, such entities are not marked in the linguistic input in any way. Pinker (1984, 1987) proposes that the child works out which words are nouns, which verbs, and so forth by expanding Macnamara's (1972) proposal that children use meaning as a way of working out the syntax of their language. He proposes that the child first learns the meaning of many content words, then uses these meanings to construct a semantic interpretation of simple input sentences. The child now has two vital pieces of information: the surface structure of the utterance and its meaning. It is then possible for the child to use the meaning as a guide in making inferences about the structure of the language. This is the *semantic bootstrapping hypothesis* (Pinker, 1984; 1987). If it is assumed that the child has available to the inference process universal categories such as NOUN, and VERB, together with a specification of the key semantic concepts that these grammatical categories encode, then it is possible for the child to infer the grammatical structure of the utterance whose meaning has been worked out independently. Thus, in the utterance 'the ball broke the window' the child can identify the referents for *ball*, *broke* and *window*. The child is also presumed to know, as part of an innate knowledge of language, that grammatical functions such as Subject are the universally preferred method of encoding agents (Keenan, 1976) and that actions are universally expressed by verbs. Putting together the child's independent semantic interpretation of the utterance with the innately specified, *semantic* prototypes of the *syntactic* grammatical categories, the child is in a position to induce a phrase-structure for utterances such as 'the ball broke the window'. In order to do so, the child must, of course, use innate knowledge of how to construct phrase-structure rules.

A mechanism such as that proposed by Pinker has certain powerful advantages. It will, fairly obviously, make the task of learning a language considerably easier than would be the case if the child were credited with a less powerful innate system of representation. However, the advantages are not an unmixed theoretical blessing. The presence of a powerful innate mechanism must be reconciled with the actual pace of language development. If one posits a very powerful learning mechanism, which then only yields products that are also capable of being yielded by less powerful mechanisms, the suspicion must be entertained that the extra power is gratuitous and the simpler mechanism is to be preferred. Applying this line of reasoning to Pinker's proposals in relation to early word combinations as reviewed by Braine (1976), the question arises of why the child, equipped with the learning mechanisms proposed by Pinker, apparently represents the structure of the language as a set of limited-scope formulae as Braine reported. This is a problem that must be faced by an account such as Pinker's. He does so by re-evaluating the evidence and arguing against limited-scope formulae.

Pinker's attack is two-fold. The first prong is to argue in favour of the parsimony of grammatical categories and the fact that they provide representational continuity between the systems of child and adult. However, this does not serve to demonstrate that the child's first word combinations actually are the product of a language representation system built around standard grammatical categories. It simply demonstrates that it would be much easier to construct a developmental theory of language acquisition if the world were arranged in this way. The second prong of Pinker's attack is to attempt to nullify the arguments of Braine (1976) and others against attributing grammatical categories to children producing two-word utterances. This is, of course, a much weaker strategy than producing positive evidence in favour of one's own theory. As an example of the type of argument used consider an argument of Braine's to the effect that if a grammar has a rule $A \rightarrow B + C$ and a further rule $C \rightarrow D,E,F$, then once the child has learnt one of the patterns BD, BE, BF, the other patterns should emerge rapidly and none should have their constituents consistently in the opposite order to those of the first pattern. Braine claims that early word combinations violate this condition and uses this violation to conclude that children do not learn general grammatical relations. Pinker counters by arguing that although a child might know the meaning of words D, E, F in the example above he or she may not know the syntactic categorization of all of them. Thus, if a child knows that $C \rightarrow D,F$ but not that $C \rightarrow E$ he or she will not be able to form a rule for the constituent ordering of B and E.

The preceding account offers only a small flavour of the types of mechanisms postulated by Pinker and the range of data over which he applies his theory. However, it does serve to give a general flavour of his attempt to tackle the learnability issue. How should the attempt be evaluated?

It is, at present, difficult to evaluate the overall plausibility of Pinker's approach. His work has the major advantage that it brings together two major approaches to the study of language development that, up to now, have had far too little to do with each other. By comparison with the approaches considered earlier in the chapter, Pinker equips the child with a very considerable system of innate representation. His major justification for doing this is that it ensures continuity between the child's and the adult's system of representation. However, this should not be regarded as a decisive argument in favour of his assumptions. There is no a priori requirement on a theory of language development that it provide continuity in this way. The requirement of learnability is that the child can be shown to arrive at an adult representation of language on the basis of specified learning mechanisms that operate on the input available from the environment. If a learning mechanism can be specified that leads to the induction of, say, a grammatical category that is a constituent element of the adult grammar then the learnability criterion will have been met without the need for a continuity that is guaranteed by innate representations. Pushed too far, the arguments for continuity begin to sound like preformationism in biology.

Theory and Data in Language Development

Language is probably the most complex representational structure possessed by humans. It is acquired with relative ease by the vast majority of children. Explaining that acquisition will require a bold theoretical approach coupled with methodological rigour in the analysis of data. There have been two major traditions of work on language development; one has displayed a bold theoretical approach without much regard for the compatibility between theory and data, the other has displayed an industrious concern with its own methodology without serious attempt to construct an overall theory of how language is learned. It is surely only by marrying the best parts of these approaches that we will achieve an adequate understanding of how language is acquired by children.

8

Basic Reading Skills

The Origin of Reading

Reading is a vital skill in the world in which we live. Printed text is ubiquitous. Learning to read is arguably the most important thing a child has to learn in the early school years. Failure to learn to read at this stage effectively locks the child out of much of the remainder of the school curriculum. Although reading has long been neglected as a central topic of cognitive development (there is, for example, no chapter on reading development in the four-volume *Handbook of Child Psychology*, Mussen, 1983), there are signs that this is changing. The change has come about partly as a result of increased attention to research and reading difficulties within the community of developmental psychologists and partly as a result of the fact that many cognitive psychologists working within the information processing framework have turned their attention to the analysis of developmental reading difficulties. Much of the research on reading, in fact, focuses on reading difficulties.

Before discussing reading difficulties it may be useful to get some perspective on normal reading development. Reading is not a 'natural development' in the way that language is. Left to his or her own devices a child will not learn to read or write just from casual encounters with the world. Reading is a skill that must be taught. It is worth remembering that reading is the product of cultural rather than biological evolution. Hence, we are unlikely to have brains that are specially adapted to process written material. Reading must therefore take advantage of other cognitive abilities. We each must assemble a cognitive skill out of component parts that are not specialized to perform the particular task of reading. In spite of this the ability to read is among our most significant cognitive and cultural achievements.

Reading presumes writing. If nothing were written there would be nothing to read. Historically, writing began with 'picture writing' (Gelb, 1963). True writing systems emerged when symbols were used to represent words of the language. The earliest systems were based on the one-word-one-symbol principle. Initially these systems, called 'logographic systems', were still strongly pictorial but gradually they became more stylized.

Logographic systems take no advantage of the fact that language itself is built from a small number of phonological units that can be combined and recombined in infinitely many ways. The progression towards a system of writing that represents sounds (rather than words) began with Egyptian hieroglyphics and moved forward in earnest when the Phoenicians borrowed the Egyptian symbols to represent syllables of their language. The conversion from a logographic to a syllabic system of representation was completed around 1500 BC. The final stage was the invention of an alphabet in which individual letters represent different sounds. This transition was made by the Greeks, who borrowed the syllabic system of the Phoenicians, but added to it symbols to denote vowels, which had been absent from the Phoenician system. A full alphabet developed gradually over a period of about 200 years during the first millennium BC in Greece, and spread across the ancient world (Gleitman and Rozin, 1977). Our own alphabet is directly descended from this source.

The relation between the alphabet and speech is complex. The alphabet is a representation of units of sound at approximately the level of the phoneme – i.e. the level at which sound differences convey meaning differences for a given language. Thus, *bar* and *car* differ only in their initial phoneme and this distinction is captured by the alphabetic letters b and c. The notion that there is a letter-phoneme relation between written and spoken English is a convenient first-order approximation but is not entirely accurate. However, it will serve for our purposes. (For more detailed discussion of the relation between the alphabet and the phonological structure of language see Gleitman and Rozin, 1977).

The Reading Process

Reading researchers can be divided into two camps: those who study the way in which written words are decoded and those who study more global issues concerning the comprehension of text. Ideally, the two approaches should complement each other but, at present, the appearance is more one of separate endeavours, with separate issues and separate objectives defining the fields of study. The study of decoding is mostly concerned with the information processing mechanisms involved in the recognition of a single, usually isolated, word. The study of comprehension is concerned, in the main, with the contextual factors that determine how the meaning of a word, a sentence, or a piece of connected text is arrived at. These studies largely concern 'higher cognitive processes' of inference and integration, while the study of decoding concerns the cognitive processes involved in word recognition. Skilled reading consists of a complex set of coordinated processes, from decoding words on the printed page, through determining the reference and meaning of words and phrases, to coordinating this meaning with the general theme of the text. The cognitive processes that support this activity operate on a variety of representations from letters to text. The fluent reader obviously computes many different kinds of information in a relatively short time. How does the cognitive system manage this considerable task? If each level of representation were computed one after the other then the task of reading would take much longer than it does and would not proceed with the smoothness that it does. There is considerable evidence that the different levels of representation are computed in parallel rather than in a serial fashion (Just and Carpenter, 1980; McClelland and Rumelhart, 1981; Rumelhart, 1977) with mutual interaction among the levels of representation. Although the evidence for parallel processing is strong, as yet there is no integrated model of the reading process.

Much of the developmental research on reading concentrates on the initial stage of reading development – the decoding of words. Although decoding a word is only one part of the reading process it is an essential part, and it is, moreover, the part that is often the source of reading difficulties. It is, in some ways, fortunate that the study of decoding has yielded such a rich harvest of data, theory, and application, because decoding is considerably easier to study in an experimentally rigorous way than are the higher level cognitive processes of inference and integration. Nevertheless, it should be remembered that the main purpose of reading is not to recognize words, but to comprehend the concepts described in a text. The ultimate aim must be to develop an integrated theory of all the processes that lead to comprehension of written text.

We read both by ear and by eye. When we read by eye alone we recognize words directly; when we read by ear we transform the visual input into a phonological representation. We do this when we sound out a word that is unfamiliar in order to determine whether its pronunciation is familiar and the word recognizable. This process is extremely important in the development of the ability to decode written text. The most influential model of the decoding process is that developed by Morton (1969) and refined in various papers since (e.g. Morton, 1979; 1982;

Patterson and Morton, 1985). Morton calls his model a *logogen model*, from the Greek *logos* meaning word, and *genus* meaning birth. The logogen model is a model of how input is processed before any meaning is derived from the input.

Recent versions of the logogen model emphasize two routes by which access can be gained to the semantic system. The first of these involves direct recognition of a word by a visual word recognition system as shown in figure 8.1. Direct lexical access by word recognition does not necessarily require one to have any knowledge of the components (i.e. the letters) that make up a word. Many systems for teaching reading, in fact, begin by teaching children to recognize whole words.

However, skilled readers can read by ear as well as by eye. Reading by ear means one has to convert from a written code to a speech-based code. This is the second route by which logogen-inspired models propose that access is gained to the cognitive system. The route is essentially parasitic on the prior establishment of a word recognition and production system for spoken language. Figure 8.2 shows a logogen-type model for the recognition and production of spoken language. The analysis of input

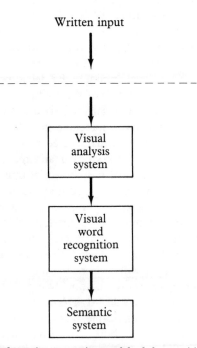

Figure 8.1   *A simple information processing model of the cognitive systems involved in the direct visual recognition of words.*

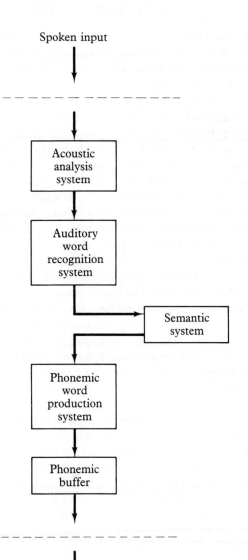

Figure 8.2 *Model of the cognitive systems involved in the recognition and production of spoken language.*

for spoken language parallels that for written language. Figure 8.3 shows the composite model for reading. Reading by ear is achieved by converting the written input to a phonological representation, which is done by the orthography to phonology translator (Patterson and Morton, 1985), and then passing the output of this translation process through the phonemic buffer to the auditory word detectors and thence to the semantic system. (For a more detailed exposition of logogen models see Ellis, 1984). In figures 8.1 to 8.3 the analysis of information processing terminates when the information arrives at the semantic system. Of course, it is at this point that the work of comprehending what has been read begins.

Models such as figure 8.3 represent the adult reading process. In what way can it help us understand the development of reading? One important way in which such models can be helpful is in identifying the processing strategies used by skilled readers and thus guiding the analysis of the development of reading strategies. Thus, for example, the model of figure 8.3 identifies orthography to phonology translation as a key route in skilled reading. Since reading is a cultural rather than a biological skill there is no possibility that we are innately disposed to perform this translation. Accordingly, a key component of a developmental account will need to be the learning of orthography-phonology conversion rules. However, once these rules are learnt the model shows that further analysis takes advantage of the older (in both onto- and phylo-genetic terms) auditory word recognition system. One prediction that can be made from the model in this context is that any weakness in the phonological representation system will impose a heavy penalty on reading development.

Models such as those in figures 8.1 to 8.3 identify what are the key processes involved in reading but they do not reveal in detail how the processing occurs. Therefore, the input–output relations in these figures must be complemented by an account of what the input–output transformations are and how these are achieved. We shall discuss one account of how direct visual recognition of words might occur both to illustrate the level of detail that must be considered in specifying how processes operate and also to illustrate the parallel interaction that occurs between different levels of information processing.

McClelland and Rumelhart (1981) have produced a model of the parallel interaction between features, letters and words in reading by eye. We shall outline the model to illustrate the nature and the importance of parallel processing in reading. The model is a computer simulation of how features, letters, and words could interact in reading. It is consistent with a large range of experimental evidence on the direct visual recognition or words (McClelland and Rumelhart, 1981).

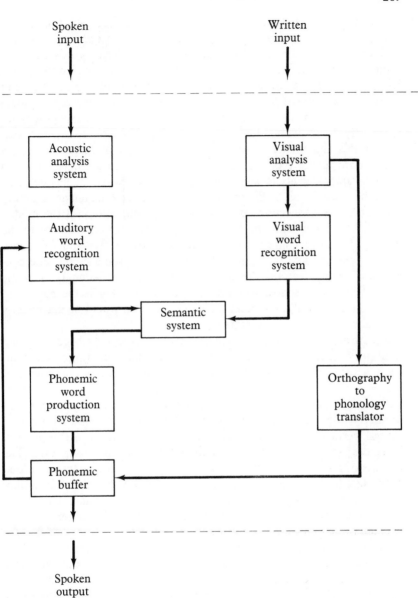

Figure 8.3 *Model of the two routes by which written input can be processed by the cognitive system.*

Because the McClelland and Rumelhart model is a computer simulation, it contains a variety of simplifying features in order to allow the program to run. The model recognizes only four-letter words and only if they are presented in a particular angular typeface, in which the letters are made up of straight lines without any curves. (Recently, McClelland (1986) has attempted to produce a model that is not restricted to four-letter words.) When a word is presented to the model, the computer tries to identify the individual line features of which the letters are composed. To do this the model is equipped with a range of feature detectors appropriate to the typeface. Upon being activated each detector sends out excitatory signals to any letter that has the feature it has detected and inhibitory signals to all other detectors. The combination of excitatory and inhibitory connections is the basic processing feature of the model. This is consistent with the basic principles of neuronal activity in the brain. Excitatory connections are indicated by arrows and inhibitory connections by dots in figure 8.4, which shows some of the interconnections among features, letters and words, for the letter T when the word TRIP is presented to the computer. Figure 8.4 is the pattern of activation for T only; the other letters of the word would be detected by parallel sets of feature detectors.

T activates two detectors, each of which immediately begins to send inhibitory signals to all other detectors at the same level of representation. Each active detector also begins to activate letters at the next level of representation. The leftmost detector in figure 8.1 will activate letters such as E, F, and T, all of which have a horizontal line across the top. Similarly, the second detector will activate I and T because both have a central vertical line. Only T, receives input from the two feature-level detectors, so it will be most strongly activated at the letter level. The process of activation and inhibition at the letter level is identical to that at the feature level. Each letter attempts to inhibit the others. Its ability to do so is a function of the extent to which it itself is activated. Obviously, T will send the strongest inhibitory signals to the other letters.

Once the letter level is activated it immediately begins to activate the word level and also to send further activation to the feature level. Thus, the features that activated T will themselves be more strongly activated by T. This type of mutual activation system is called a cascade model (McClelland, 1979). Although a large number of features and letters may receive some activation, the system very quickly identifies the stimulus correctly through the processes operating in cascade.

If we follow the activation to the word level, T will begin to activate all words that begin with T. Although many irrelevant words will be activated, their activation will be short-lived because the word level will

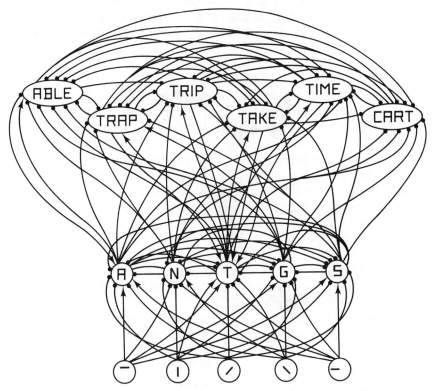

Figure 8.4   *A few of the neighbours of the node for the letter T in the first position in a word, and their interconnections. Arrows indicate excitatory connections and dots indicate inhibitory connections.*
Source: McClelland and Rumelhart, 1981.

receive simultaneous signals from the letters R, I, and P. Only TRIP will be activated by all of these so it will inhibit the other words and TRIP will be read. Figure 8.5 shows some examples of words in which letters are ambiguous but which can all be read easily. The McClelland and Rumelhart model can easily account for the ability to read these words.

We have discussed the McClelland and Rumelhart model in some detail because it is one of the few models that goes beyond specifying what the cognitive system does and illustrates how the system might process information during word recognition. Yet, the model explains only how a single word might be recognized, by one of the possible pathways specified in models of reading. There is no processing model of similar

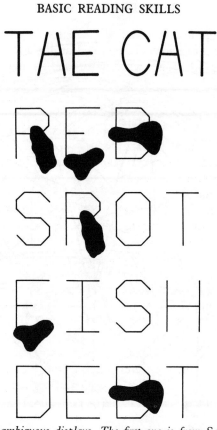

Figure 8.5 *Some ambiguous displays. The first one is from Selfridge, 1955. The second line shows that three ambiguous characters can each constrain the identity of the others. The third, fourth and fifth lines show that these characters are indeed ambiguous in that they assume other identities in other contexts.*
Source: Rumelhart and McClelland 1986.

detail for reading by ear, nor indeed of any of the higher cognitive processes involved in comprehension.

The Development of Reading

There has been much study of reading difficulties but relatively little attention to providing a theory of reading development. Marsh, Friedman, Welch and Desberg (1981) have provided a descriptive account of four stages of reading acquisition that emphasize the strategies used to read unknown words. The emphasis is placed on unknown words because the ways in which children tackle this task gives an indication of their current knowledge and the reading strategies they possess.

The first stage is characterized by rote learning and association between a visual stimulus (which is a whole word) and an oral response (which is a spoken word). (In terms of the model presented in figure 8.3 the child is learning to read words by the direct lexical access route.) The assumption of initial rote learning is supported by evidence from observational studies (Torrey, 1979). A popular pedagogic method at this stage is to use 'flash cards', which present a single word on a card, to which the child is required to give an oral response. In the model of Marsh et al., a rote learning strategy is diagnosed by an inability to respond to novel or unknown words when presented in isolation. This is complemented by a linguistic guessing strategy when the word is encountered in a simple sentence context; the child simply guesses a syntactically and semantically appropriate word at the point at which the unknown word is encountered.

Stage Two is, essentially, an elaboration of Stage One. As the size of the word set that can be recognized increases, the child comes to pay more attention to the alphabetic features of a word. Marsh et al. argue that the child initially only processes individual letters to the extent necessary to discriminate one word from another. This strategy is typical of tasks in which subjects learn novel material by rote. However, it marks the beginning of a phonological awareness of written words.

In contrasting Stage One with Stage Two it is interesting to note the way in which guesses of words in sentences change over time. Initially the child's guesses are contextually appropriate even though the word guessed may bear little resemblance to the word on the page (Biemiller, 1970). Thus, if a Stage One child is presented with 'The cat chased the butterfly', he or she may guess *The cat chased the mouse*. As the child progresses however, the guesses come to be constrained both by context and by the words that the child has already learned to read. Initially only the initial letter may constrain the choice and so the child might guess *The cat chased the bee* to the above. Gradually, the other letters of the target word serve to constrain further the child's choices. This, of course, reflects a growing awareness of the decomposability of words.

Stage Three is characterized by the ability to decode novel words using orthographic-phonological conversions. Gaining access to the phonological representation of a word from its written input is probably the most important part of learning to read. It is also probably the most difficult. The difficulty arises from the fact that the mapping from the alphabet to the phonological system is far from direct. Alphabetic letters do not represent individual phonemes or, to put it the other way round, the sound stream of speech is not divisible into separate elements that correspond to the separate alphabetic letters (see Gleitman and Rozin, 1977;

Liberman, Cooper, Shankweiler and Studdert-Kennedy, 1967). Rozin and Gleitman (1977) have speculated that a syllabic system of writing would be preferable to an alphabetic system because orthographic-syllabic conversions would be relatively easy and straight-forward. However, the majority of children learning to read have to contend with an alphabet.

In the reading literature the term 'grapheme' is often employed to indicate the unit of a written word that is translated into a phoneme in orthographic-phonological conversion. Initially the conversion process was dubbed 'grapheme-phoneme conversion'. However, Patterson and Morton (1985) have proposed replacing this with the more generic phrase 'orthographic-phonological conversion' to take account of the fact that conversion can be in terms of higher-order chunks than grapheme-phoneme pairs. For the child learning to read English, the initial attempts at conversion will usually be at the level of grapheme-phoneme pairs. Grapheme-phoneme conversion initially works on a simple left-to-right principle with the child being relatively insensitive to the effect that surrounding letters may have on the letter being pronounced. The characteristic errors of Stage Three readers are substitution errors with a high graphemic similarity to the correct word and the production of non-word errors (a sure sign that orthographic-phonological conversions are being made).

A wide variety of 'phonics' teaching methods has been designed to facilitate the child's understanding of the relation between written and spoken language. Although there is some evidence that children may naturally progress to this stage without specific phonics teaching (Barr, 1974), instruction must play a large part in further progress in view of the complex relations between orthography and phonology.

The child at Stage Three has relatively simple orthographic- phonological conversion rules. Nevertheless, these rules bring a much greater flexibility in reading than was previously possible. When a word not encountered in print before presents itself, an attempt can be made to decode it phonemically. With any luck the word will be in the child's spoken vocabulary and so its meaning will be accessible.

Stage Four builds on Stage Three. During Stage Four the rules of grapheme-phoneme conversion become context-sensitive. The child can now add another strategy – the use of analogy, in which novel words are pronounced not strictly on dominant phonemic principles but by analogy with particular existing words. As an example, consider pronunciation of the non-word *faugh*. Mostly, it will be pronounced as *faw* in accordance with phonemic principles but occasionally it may be pronounced as *faff* by analogy with *laugh*.

A further characteristic of the skilled reader at Stage Four is that orthographic-phonological relations are now understood in the context of the grammatical and morphological structure of the language. English orthography represents many levels of language structure (Gleitman and Rozin, 1977). One simple example is the use of a regular inflection to form the plural despite variation in its pronunciation. Another example is the presence of homonyms – words that are pronounced the same but spelled differently, as in *chute* and *shoot*.

More recently, Frith (1985) has proposed a modified version of the model of Marsh et al. Frith's model moves the analysis away from stages of reading development to the strategies employed in word recognition and also emphasizes the importance of the relation between reading and writing in the developmental process. Frith suggests a model in which logographic, alphabetic, and orthographic strategies play dominant roles. The logographic strategy is dominant during Marsh et al.'s rote stage, in which familiar words are recognized as whole entities. There is little, if any, role for phonological factors in this stage. The child pronounces a word after he or she has recognized it; if a word is not recognized then the child will not usually respond, but may guess on the basis of contextual information.

The alphabetic strategy is characterized by the use of graphemes and phonemes in word recognition. With this strategy, letter order and phonological factors play a crucial role in word recognition, as they also do in Marsh et al.'s sequential decoding stage. This strategy allows the reader to pronounce novel words.

The orthographic strategy is one in which orthographic units are recognized as wholes without individual grapheme by grapheme analysis. This strategy represents the best of the two preceding strategies: the instant recognition of familiar units, in common with the logographic strategy, but at a finer level of decomposition than the individual word, and the analytic skills of the alphabetic strategy that allows the unfamiliar to be decomposed to units that are familiar. Frith (1985: p. 306) remarks: 'The orthographic is distinguished from the logographic one by being analytic in a systematic way and by being non-visual. It is distinguished from the alphabetic one by operating in bigger units and by being non-phonological.'

Of particular interest is the relation proposed between reading and writing in this model. Frith argues that reading and writing do not develop in synchrony, but rather have a symbiotic relation in which each pulls development in the other at different points. Reading precedes writing developmentally; it is only when logographic strategies are reasonably well-established that writing will begin. However, the alphabetic strategy is first adopted for writing while a logographic strategy may continue to be used for reading. The rationale for this is that the alphabet is tailor-made for writing rather than for reading (Frith and Frith, 1980). However, in the development of orthographic skills, reading is again proposed as the pacemaker, possibly through the development of spelling.

Reading Difficulties

For most children reading becomes a background skill; something to be taken for granted and used in the acquisition of other types of knowledge. Some children, however, experience considerable difficulty in learning to read. Because of the educational handicap that this imposes it is important that a developmental model of reading encompass these difficulties. It also happens that this is a very useful way to advance our understanding of the basic process of reading; developmental difficulties are an important source of evidence about the reading process.

Any account of reading difficulties has to take account of the term 'dyslexia', which is widely but inconsistently used in relation to reading difficulties. An oft-quoted definition of dyslexia is that proposed by members of a congress of the World Federation of Neurology, cited by Critchley (1970: p. 11):

> A disorder manifested by difficulty in learning to read despite conventional instruction, adequate intelligence, and socio-cultural opportunity. It is dependent upon fundamental cognitive disabilities which are frequently of constitutional   origin.

This definition is usually cited, not for the light it casts on dyslexia but as a way of illustrating the difficulties of defining the condition. There are two essential parts to the definition: the diagnosis of the condition and its cause. The diagnosis restricts the term to children who have difficulty in learning to read despite a normal environment. For this group of children dyslexia is a condition they suffer from. Implicitly, children who have difficulty in learning to read and who have the further burden of social or intellectual disadvantage are not dyslexic. This is an unsatisfactory distinction. As the definition states, dyslexia is a cognitive disability. There is no way of telling whether all children who, despite a normal environment, have difficulty learning to read, have a common cognitive disability of dyslexia on the basis of the environmental infor-mation alone. Nor is there any way of telling whether dyslexia is absent in children who have reading difficulties but are further burdened with social and/or intellectual disadvantage on the basis of the environmental information alone. If 'dyslexia' is to be a useful label it must identify the cognitive source of the reading difficulty and it must distinguish dyslexic from non-dyslexic children on the basis of the presence or absence of some particular cognitive difficulty.

The second part of the definition attributes dyslexia to genetic causes. As Seymour (1986) has pointed out, the two halves of the definition fit uneasily together; genetic influences are unlikely selectively to affect only those with a certain background. If the cause of at least some reading difficulties is genetic, as it almost certainly is, then dyslexic problems will occur among the disadvantaged as well as the advantaged.

All this leaves the meaning of the term 'dyslexia' in a parlous state, to say the least. In what follows the term 'dyslexia' will be used as a synonym for 'reading difficulty' without any implication as to genetic or environmental causes. The question at issue is not the meaning of the term 'dyslexia' but the causes of reading difficulties and whether there are distinguishable deficits among children who experience reading difficulties. If it should turn out that there are different deficits then it may be desirable to give them different labels such as 'dyslexia' and so forth, but that will not be of concern to this chapter.

It has already been stated that reading difficulties imply, of necessity, some difficulty in the cognitive processing of written input. What is the source of the difficulty? Is there, indeed, a single source or is there a range of varying and diffuse sources? This is an important question, to which we shall return, but it is not one that is well-addressed in much of the literature on reading difficulties. It has been a tacit assumption of much research that there is a single cause of reading difficulties. Accordingly, the favoured research tactic has been to take a group of children who have difficulty in learning to read and to compare them with a control group of normal readers on some measure hypothesized to be the cause. Usually the slow readers have performed worse on the test, regardless of what the hypothetical cause was, than the control group. This does not, however, mean that a variety of causes for reading difficulties has been discovered. Many experiments that show differences between slow and normal readers are open to the interpretation that the difference is the result of the reading difficulty, not the cause of it. When more tightly-controlled experiments have been conducted, the differences between slow and normal readers have rarely been evident.

The hypotheses tested in the comparison of slow and normal readers span a wide continuum but they are of three general types: hypotheses that reading difficulties are caused by some deficit in processing perceptual input; hypotheses that the deficit has a more central, but nevertheless general, cognitive source – such as in the memory system; and hypotheses that locate the source of the deficit in the processing of linguistic information.

An alternative to comparing groups of normal and slow readers that has recently emerged is to report detailed individual case studies. This strategy derives from the work of cognitive neuropsychologists with adult patients suffering from acquired dyslexia. Acquired dyslexia is a condition suffered by someone who, because of brain damage (due to a stroke or, occasionally, injury) experiences difficulty in reading. These patients were all previously fluent readers. Cognitive neuropsychologists have reported in detail on the syndrome of difficulties experienced by particular patients. As a result of such case studies a number of different types of acquired dyslexia are now recognized. It seems a natural question to ask whether the same types are evident in children with reading difficulty. A number of case studies of children with reading difficulties (often referred to as 'developmental dyslexia' in this context) have been reported that make specific comparisons between the difficulties the child has and the documented difficulties of a particular adult syndrome. However, the comparisons must be treated with caution. Finding a single individual child who has or appears to have a similar pattern of difficulty to some recognized syndrome of acquired dyslexia does not of itself tell us very much about the modal cause of reading difficulties. The basis of comparison is also problematic. There is no standardized procedure for such comparisons, which makes it difficult to decide how close the child and adult syndromes really are. At present, case studies and comparisons with patterns of acquired dyslexia provide an interesting additional perspective on the problem of reading difficulties but it is not yet clear how fruitful the comparisons will be. It should be emphasized in passing that comparisons between developmental and acquired dyslexia are not testing the hypothesis that reading difficulties are the result of brain damage among the developmental dyslexics.

Perceptual Deficit Theories of Reading Difficulties

One widespread belief is that reading difficulties are due to a central cognitive deficit. The most popular of such theories has been that reading difficulties are due to a perceptual deficit of some sort. This idea can be traced back to the end of the last century and was popularized in Britain by the Scottish ophthalmologist, James Hinshelwood, in a book published in 1917 entitled *Congenital Word-Blindness*. Hinshelwood proposed that poor readers have a difficulty in acquiring and storing in the brain the visual memories of words and letters. In America, a neuropsychiatrist,

Samuel Torrey Orton, proposed that a dysfunction in visual perception and visual memory, characterized by a tendency to perceive letters and words in reverse, caused reading difficulties. Orton's book, *Reading, Writing and Speech Problems in Children*, published in 1937, was highly influential. Orton's view encapsulates what is still a common misconception about children with reading difficulties. The proportion of mirror-image reversals (for example, reading 'saw' for 'was') made by children with reading difficulties is small and is no different from the proportion made by normal children (Bryant and Bradley, 1985). These errors are made sometimes by all children learning to read. Errors of this type do not distinguish children with reading difficulties from other children.

Perceptual deficit theories have had something of a magnetic attraction for those interested in reading difficulties. Different theories have entertained different versions of the hypothesis. A detailed review of these theories is provided by Vellutino (1979; see also Vellutino 1987, for a recent synopsis). The balance of the evidence fails to support the view that there is any generalized perceptual deficit associated with reading difficulties. Before we discuss some of the evidence, it will be useful to discuss some methodological issues of research in this area. In order to compare the perceptual abilities of poor readers with those of normal readers we need to form the appropriate groups of normal and poor readers and then test these groups on some perceptual task. There have been criticisms concerning the criteria used to select groups and also concerning the nature of the perceptual tasks in tests of the perceptual deficit hypothesis.

The most common technique that has been used in the selection of groups is to match normal and poor readers for chronological and mental age. This is called the chronological age design. The chronological age design ensures that the general abilities of the two groups are equivalent. However, this may not be the most appropriate technique for ensuring that the normal readers do not have an advantage over the poor readers to start with. If, for example, the task on which the normal and poor readers are to be tested is one on which skill may be acquired through reading, then, despite matching the groups for mental age, the normal readers are likely to be at an advantage precisely because they are normal readers. As an example, let us suppose that we are testing the hypothesis that a poor short-term memory causes reading difficulties. It may be, as Morrison and Manis (1982) have proposed, that practice at reading improves short-term memory (STM) performance. If this is so, then any finding that normal readers perform better on STM tasks than poor readers is more likely to be the result of the differences in reading ability rather than its cause. This is a general difficulty with all positive

differences in favour of normal readers: the difference may be the result
not the cause of the reading difficulty. Given our limited knowledge of
what influences what in cognitive development, we cannot eliminate such
a possibility unless we ensure that the groups of children that we test are
matched for reading ability. One way to achieve this is to compare poor
readers with a group of younger children who have the same level of
reading skill, as measured by a standardized reading test. This is called
the reading-age design.

However, although the reading age design is an improvement on the
chronological age design, it is not perfect because it only yields interpretable results under some circumstances. If the poor readers perform worse
than the controls on a non-reading cognitive task, despite the advantage
that the poor readers have in age, then this would be very strong evidence
for a cognitive deficit. However, if no differences are found then the
interpretation is more equivocal. The finding could mean that there are
no differences or it could mean that the superior age of the poor readers
is masking a real difference. The fact has to be faced that the method of
experimental comparisons only yields unequivocally interpretable results
under two sets of circumstances. When there is no difference between a
normal group and a chronological age-matched group of poor readers on
some task then it can be concluded that the cognitive variable tested is
not implicated in the cause of reading difficulties. When a normal group
perform better than a reading age-matched group of poor readers then it
can be concluded that the cognitive variable tested is implicated in the
cause of reading difficulties. All other patterns of results cannot be readily
interpreted. In particular the finding that a group of poor readers perform
worse than a chronological age-matched group of normal readers does
not indicate that the variable tested is implicated in the cause of reading
difficulties; it could be cause or effect. The methodological issues about
the design and interpretation of experiments that investigate the cause of
reading difficulties are discussed in more detail in Backman, Mamen and
Ferguson (1984) and in Bryant and Goswami (1986). Bryant and Goswami
argue that causal hypotheses are best tested by longitudinal studies combined with intervention.

If we now return to the issue of whether reading difficulties are due
to a perceptual deficit, armed with these methodological caveats, then it
will be found that many experiments that apparently support the perceptual deficit hypothesis are open to the criticism that they have only used
a chronological age-matched group in testing the hypothesis. Many are
also open to another criticism: the 'visual' tasks that they employ use
alphabetic or linguistic stimuli that are likely to be easier to process for
the normal children.

In the light of these considerations, there is little point in reviewing the 'positive' evidence that has been provided by poorly designed studies. Vellutino (1979) has, in any case, done the job admirably. What is worth reporting is that there is a large amount of evidence against the perceptual deficit hypothesis; sufficient to render the hypothesis untenable. For example, Mason and Katz (1976) examined perceptual search rates of poor and normal readers. The task was to find a target shape among a set of other unfamiliar shapes. There was no difference between the groups. Ellis and Miles (1978) compared the speed with which normal and poor readers could judge whether pairs of letters were the same or different. This experiment is of particular interest because it employed alphabetic material but did not require any linguistic processing of the material. Under these conditions there was no difference between the groups. Vellutino and his associates (Vellutino, Pruzek, Steger and Meshoulam, 1973) investigated the ability of poor and normal readers to print words and letters from an unfamiliar writing system: the Hebrew alphabet. Both groups performed equally well on this task.

The view that reading difficulties can be traced to some difficulty in perceptual processing has had a long history but, in spite of that, there is no convincing evidence of such a deficit and much evidence against it. However, this negative finding seems simply to have fuelled alternative deficit theories. Still within the realm of perceptual processing it has been suggested that reading difficulties are due to an 'intermodal' deficit (i.e. a deficit in matching written with spoken words) or to faulty eye-movements. Neither proposal has stood up to empirical test. Stanley (1978), for example, reported differences in eye-movement patterns between normal and poor readers when the task was reading, as might be expected. However, when the task was one that required the children to locate a picture within a scene, there was no difference between the groups. Here again the observed difference on the reading task would seem to be the effect rather than the cause of the reading difficulty.

Memory deficits and phonological encoding

There is considerable evidence that children with reading difficulties perform worse on a variety of memory tasks than age-matched controls (Jorm, 1983). However, the problem of cause and effect is again apparent here. In considering memory let us first of all ask whether or not there is any evidence for a generalized memory deficit among poor readers. If reading difficulties are caused by short-term memory difficulties, then these difficulties should be evident on tasks that do not involve recall of words. Holmes and McKeever (1979) compared a group of 13-year-old poor readers with an age-matched group of normal readers on the recall of faces and of words. They found no differences between the groups in the recall of faces but differences were found in word recall. Liberman, Mann, Shankweiler and Werfelman (1982) reported a similar negative result for the recall of faces between poor and normal readers but the poor readers performed less well than the normal group on verbal recall. These results would seem to indicate that there is no generalized deficit of memory but that there may be a memory deficit specifically for verbal material. In fact, the vast majority of evidence indicates that this is the case. The difficulty lies in interpreting the evidence. First of all there is the cause and effect issue. Do some children read badly because they have a poor memory or do they have a poor memory because they are bad readers? Bradley and Bryant (1983, 1985; see also Bryant and Bradley, 1985) have reported longitudinal data that are relevant to this issue. The study is particularly interesting because it followed a group of 368 children over a period of four years. None of the children could read at the beginning of the study. As they learnt to read, most of the children made good progress but some turned out to have reading difficulties. At the beginning of the study Bradley and Bryant had administered a variety of tests to the children, one of which was a test of verbal recall. If poor verbal memory is the cause of reading difficulties then it should be possible to predict later reading scores on the basis of memory scores. Bradley and Bryant found that memory scores at 4 to 5 years did not predict reading scores a year and a half later. Of further interest, they found that reading scores at 7 years predicted memory scores at 9 years. They concluded that the causal effect is that reading determines memory and not memory reading.

However, this conclusion must be treated with caution. It may be that the strategies used for verbal recall by the children when they were initially tested were different from the strategies that are used later on for recall. If there is a strategy shift (and there is evidence to suggest such a shift) then it is possible that reading difficulties occur among children who have difficulty with the new strategy, which affects both memory and reading performance. The possibility of a strategy shift in encoding verbal information arises because children appear to begin to encode words phonemically at the age of 5 or 6 years. In order to examine the issue further let us stand back from the data for a moment and consider some issues about the cognitive processes that might be involved.

Many experiments comparing the memory of poor and normal readers appear to regard memory as an entity of some sort; if differences are found then some entity called memory is impaired. However, this is not a very fruitful or theoretically sophisticated way to view the memory system. Memory is, primarily, a convenient shorthand label for the system that processes and stores information. The processes are not invariant over time but undergo developmental change (see chapter 4). It is possible that the way in which verbal material is processed and stored changes during the course of learning to read. If this is so, then some children may find themselves at a disadvantage if they are slow or inefficient in developing a new processing strategy. In order to consider these possibilities properly it is necessary to have some theoretically motivated model of the reading process and the course of normal reading development. The opening sections of this chapter have reviewed these issues. It will be recalled that there are two potential routes to accessing the meaning of written words: a direct route via recognition of the whole word and a phonically mediated route via orthographic-phonological conversion. It will also be recalled from the model of strategy development of Marsh et al. (1981) that phonemic mediation is a later and possibly more difficult (Rozin and Gleitman, 1977) strategy than direct visual recognition. Many theorists believe that children with reading difficulties are poor at phonemic encoding and that this retards their reading development. In principle, this is a well-founded view. Reading an alphabetic script demands that the child be aware of the sounds that make up words. Any difficulty in creating representations of sounds is likely to affect reading.

The ability to create a phonological representation of sound seems to be a developmental product rather than a fixed cognitive component. The basic evidence for this (which is slim and ought to be established more solidly) comes from research by Conrad (1971) based on the previously discovered phonetic confusability effect (Conrad, 1964). Conrad (1964) showed that subjects found it more difficult to remember lists of letters when they rhymed with each other (e.g., BCTGP) than when they did not rhyme (e.g. HQSLW). Conrad (1971) found no evidence of phonetic confusability in 4-to 5-year-olds but did find it in 5- to 6-year-olds. This suggest that the 5- to 6-year-olds have begun to use phonemic memory codes. This is of particular interest because there is considerable evidence that poor readers are delayed in their acquisition of phonemic memory codes. Thus, it is possible that a difficulty in creating a phonological representation of a word could be the cause of reading delays because such a delay effectively shuts out access to meaning via the phonological route of the model in figure 8.3. A further reason for suspecting this as a cause of reading difficulties is the fact that children who are delayed in acquiring language often subsequently experience difficulty in learning to read (Fundudis, Kolvin and Garside, 1979).

Evidence for differences in phonological encoding between normal and poor readers has come from a variety of experiments. Much of the evidence is suggestive rather than conclusive because of failure to use reading-age control groups. The crucial question here is whether poor readers cannot encode words phonologically or whether they can do so, but with much more difficulty than normal readers.

Byrne and Shea (1979) presented children with a continuous list of spoken words. As each word was spoken the child had to indicate whether it had been previously presented. Some of the words were phonologically similar to the previously presented words (e.g. ship, grip) while others were semantically similar (e.g. ship, boat). Normal and poor readers performed at the same level on this task but the error pattern of the groups was different. The normal group made more false positive responses to words that were phonologically similar than to words that were semantically similar to a previously presented word. By contrast, the poor readers made more false positives to words that were semantically similar than to words that were phonologically similar to a previously presented word. In a further experiment Byrne and Shea bolstered this finding by presenting pseudo-words (i.e. words that are not meaningful in English but obey its phonological conventions). When the errors were compared for words that were dissimilar to previous words, normal readers made more errors for similar-sounding words but the poor readers showed no difference in the error rate for similar and dissimilar words. Other studies have reported similar results using a recall technique. Mark, Shankweiler, Liberman and Fowler (1977) asked 7-year-olds to read a list of words and subsequently gave the children a recognition test in which the previously presented target words were mixed with distracter items. Half the distracter words were phonologically similar to target words while half were semantically similar. Normal readers made more false positive responses to the phonologically similar than to the semantically similar words. For poor readers there was little difference in the incidence of false positives for the two types of distractors.

Both of these studies suggest that the way in which words are stored in memory differs between normal and poor readers. Other studies (Mann, Liberman and Shankweiler, 1980; Shankweiler, Liberman, Mark, Fowler and Fischer, 1979) have reported that on immediate recall tasks poor readers are less prone to phonetic confusion from rhyming words. However, since all of these studies used a chronological age-match design it cannot be concluded that the memory differences actually caused the reading differences.

A study by Johnston (1982) compared poor readers aged 9, 12, and 14 years with both chronological age and reading age control groups on the recall of rhyming and non-rhyming words. She found that the poor readers' recall was inferior for both rhyming and non-rhyming words to that of the chronological age controls. Bearing in mind the lower level of recall, the proportion of errors on rhyming words was not smaller for the poor readers than for the chronological age controls. This result casts considerable doubt on the view that there is a qualitative difference between the phonological encoding of poor readers and that of normal readers. However, it still remains the case that there are quantitative differences in memory between poor readers and their chronological-age peers. It may be that children who experience reading difficulties are delayed in their acquisition of a phonological code.

Evidence in favour of a delay in phonological encoding of written material comes from Olson, Kliegel, Davidson and Davies (1984). They investigated the performance of poor and normal readers on a test of recognition similar to that used by Mark et al. (1977). Unlike Mark et al., they found that both normal and poor readers made a greater number of errors on rhyming than on non-rhyming distractors. However, the size of the effect differed among the groups as figure 8.6 shows. For 7.5-year-olds there was much greater phonetic confusion among the normal than the poor readers. Among the normal group the phonetic confusion decreased with age but among the poor readers it increased with age. At 16.5 years of age the poor readers were showing approximately the

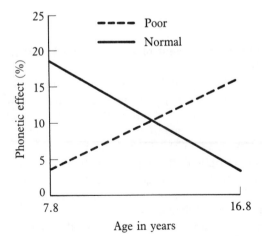

Figure 8.6 *Difference between rhyming and non-rhyming false–positive errors (Phonetic Effect) for poor and normal readers. Best fitting regression lines predicted from age.*
Source: Olson et al., 1986.

same level of phonetic confusion as the normal readers had shown at 7.5 years.

Further evidence that poor readers are best characterized in terms of a developmental lag is provided by Stanovich, Nathan and Zolman (1988). They compared three groups of children aged 9, 11, and 13 years who were matched on reading ability, on a variety of linguistic and cognitive tests. The cognitive profiles of the three groups were strikingly similar despite the age differences. Of particular interest is a comparison of a sub-group of the 11- and 13-year-olds who had been previously tested two years earlier at 9 and 11 years respectively. At that time the 9-year-olds were normal readers and the 11-year-olds were a matched group of poor readers. During the intervening period the younger group of normal readers had made a more rapid improvement in reading ability than the older group of poor readers. This finding is consistent with the view that poor readers are acquiring the same skills as normal readers but at a slower pace.

It is possible, at this point, tentatively to draw the evidence together. There seems to be a link between the use of phonological codes in memory and reading disability. Poor readers seem to have difficulty in establishing a phonological representation for a word, although there is no evidence that they totally fail to establish such representations.

If phonological encoding plays the major role that it seems to in reading difficulties then it would pay to understand its development in more detail.

The Development of Phonological Encoding

The evidence of Conrad (1971), cited earlier, seems to suggest that phonological encoding develops during mid-childhood. Why should it develop at this time? One possibility is that it arises directly as a result of learning to read. The suggestion here is that the process of learning to read draws attention to the phonological structure of a word. The argument might continue in the following way. Prior to learning to read, a child's encounters with language will have been entirely through the medium of spoken language with the attentional focus on words and grammar rather than on phonology.

In this form the argument is overstated. Children are not insensitive to phonology before they learn to read as the pervasive popularity of rhymes shows and also as the mastery of a complex system of inflectional morphology reviewed in the previous chapter shows. There is, however, a close connection between the awareness of sounds and progress in learning to read. Bradley and Bryant (1978) compared the abilities of a group of poor readers and a reading age-matched group of normal readers to detect rhyme and alliteration. In spite of the fact that the poor readers were, on average, 3.5 years older than the normal readers, they performed less well in detecting the word that did not rhyme with the others among a group of four words. Over 18 trials, 92 per cent of poor readers made at least one error and 85 per cent made more than one, in comparison with 53 per cent of the normal readers who made a single error and 27 per cent who made more than one error. In a later study Bradley and Bryant (1983) administered a similar test to 4- and 5-year-olds before they had learnt to read and then followed up progress in reading over the next four years. The average correlation between the rhyming test and reading tests administered three years later was 0.51, which shows that there is a clear, but not determinate, link between rhyming and reading.

A similar result has been reported by Lundberg, Olofsson and Wall (1981). They tested 6- to 7-year-old children in Sweden a few months before they began school. (In Sweden schooling begins at 7 years.) The children were administered a variety of tests of phonological awareness. One year later the groups were given reading and spelling tests. Lundberg et al. found that the results of the tests of awareness of sounds predicted well progress in learning to read. A study of related interest has been reported by Fox and Routh (1983). They compared a group of 10 poor readers with 10 normal readers over a three-year period, between the ages of 6 and 9 years. At age 6 the poor readers performed much less well than the normal readers when tested on their ability to break up syllables into their constituent phonemes. In the follow-up study at 9 years the poor readers had overcome their particular difficulty with syllable segmentation but their reading scores had fallen even further behind the scores of the normal readers. When tested on spelling the poor readers tended to make 'bizarre' errors in that there was often little relation between the spelling and the phonological structure of the words they were trying to spell.

If most reading difficulties can be attributed to difficulties in the acquisition of a phonological code, then it seems reasonable to ask whether intervention techniques that try to increase a child's awareness of the phonological structure of words will help to overcome reading difficulties. There is, in fact, a fair amount of evidence that programmes designed to increase awareness of sounds improves the reading performance of normal children. There is also evidence that the technique is effective, to some extent, as an intervention strategy for poor readers.

Goldstein (1976) devised a test of children's ability to analyse words into sounds and also to synthesize or blend sounds into words. He administered this test to a group of 23 4-year-olds and then divided the group into experimental and control subgroups. Over the next 13 weeks both groups received the same amount of intervention teaching about the same book. The experimental groups were taught about sounds and about letter-sound correspondence for each word in the book. The control group were taught about the names and about the order of letters in the words. At the end of this period both groups were administered a reading test. The experimental group performed significantly better on this test than the control group.

Bradley and Bryant (1983, 1985) taught children about rhyme and alliteration in a series of 40 teaching sessions spread over a two-year period when the children were between 6 and 8 years old. One group of children were shown a series of pictures of familiar objects and were taught to categorize words that had sounds in common. A second group received the same training in the first year but during the second year the teaching sessions used plastic letters to demonstrate how words that rhyme often have letters or clusters of letters in common. Two control groups were also used. A third group learnt how to categorize the pictures on conceptual criteria and a fourth group received no training at all. At the end of the two-year period all children were given standardized tests of reading and spelling. The children who had been taught to categorize words by their sound performed significantly better on the reading and spelling tests than the control groups. Between the experimental groups, the children who had learnt to categorize sounds and who had then learnt to represent these sounds with letters had reading ages of six months better than the children just taught to categorize sounds.

All of the studies discussed so far that demonstrate a beneficial effect of increasing phonological awareness have been conducted with children who have not been identified as having a reading difficulty. The question arises of whether the technique is equally effective with children who experience reading difficulties. It is quite possible that it may not be. Children with reading difficulties might, for example, have such reduced phonological sensitivity that they are impervious to the type of training that improves the performance of normal readers. We cannot therefore simply extrapolate from the results of the studies discussed above to poor readers.

Gittelman and Feingold (1983) compared two groups of poor readers. One group received a systematic phonics programme over a period of four months; the other group received the same amount of extra attention devoted to non-specific tutoring in other subjects. By the end of the intervention programme the first group had reading ages that were a mean of about twelve months ahead of the control group. The improvement was maintained in two follow-up assessments conducted two and eight months after the intervention programme had ended.

Hornsby and Miles (1980) compared three different programmes used by remedial schools for children with reading difficulties. The schools all used some version of a phonics approach – that is, they emphasized sounds and the relation between sounds and letters. The children in all programmes made reasonable progress, which suggests that the method is effective across variation in the details of its implementation. Unfortunately, the Hornsby and Miles study does not contain any comparison data from children being taught using other methods or from children who have reading difficulties but are not receiving any specialist intervention.

The evidence from intervention programmes strongly suggests that increasing awareness of the phonological structure of words and of the relation between phonological and orthographic representations is an effective technique both of teaching reading and of intervening in cases of reading difficulties. However, much of the intervention evidence leaves a lot to be desired in the way of adequate comparison groups. It is also the case that although it seems that the methods discussed work, it is difficult to pin down in a precise fashion why they work. In order to establish this, future research will need to concentrate on a more fine-grained analysis of the relative effectiveness of the components that make up an intervention programme.

It would seem then that a sensitivity to the sound structure of language is an important determinant of reading ability. The process of learning to read probably increases this sensitivity and may create an increasing gap in reading ability between children who have difficulty in representing the sound structure of the language and those who do not. Evidence that reading itself does play an important part in the development of an awareness of the sound structure of language has been provided by Morais, Cary, Alegria and Bertelson (1979). They compared awareness of sounds in literate and illiterate adults in Portugal. The tasks involved adding and subtracting sounds from words. To illustrate in English, a typical subtraction task would be to say what the word 'stand' would sound like with the 't' removed, while a typical addition task would be to say what the word 'right' would sound like with a 'b' added. Morais et al. found a clear difference between the groups. The illiterate group could only manage 21 per cent correct responses while the literate group (some of whom had only begun to learn to read) were correct on 72 per cent of the words. This is striking evidence of the fact that learning to read plays an important role in the development of phonological awareness.

Any underlying delay or inability to create phonological representations will obviously hamper the further development of the phonological awareness of language. As has been observed previously, the use of the phonological route is a crucial part of being a skilled reader because it allows unfamiliar written words to be read by working out their sound structure.

Are There Subtypes of Reading Difficulty?

One issue that has been avoided until now is whether reading difficulties can all be attributed to the same weakness in information processing or whether there are different subtypes of reading difficulty. The question does not admit of any easy answer, although it may seem that it should. Surely, it can be reasoned, it is a relatively straightforward matter to take a large number of children with a reading difficulty and by test and experimentation determine whether or not they share a common difficulty or can be subdivided into groups with different difficulties. Unfortunately, it is not straightforward. If the children chosen have the same reading age but not the same chronological age, then the older children among the group may have developed compensating strategies for processing written information and this may yield an apparent difference where none exists. Even if chronological age and reading age can both be controlled there still remains the possibility of variation on other factors, such as intelligence, yielding apparent variations on reading where none exists.

Given our present limitations in testing reading ability and the information processes associated with reading, it is unlikely that a straightforward answer can be obtained as to whether there are distinct subtypes of reading difficulty. Few studies have tackled the question in this direct fashion.

One possible alternative way to tackle the issue is to look, not to large-scale studies, but to detailed clinical studies of single cases. A number of these have been published in recent years. Do they agree on common difficulty or do they report a variety of difficulties? In general they do not report a common difficulty. However, caution must be exercised in interpreting this. The clinical case studies are often studies of the more unusual cases, which may be highly unrepresentative of the general population. An additional problem is that clinical case studies have usually been interpreted in the light of patterns of acquired dyslexia. Acquired dyslexia is the condition of a reading difficulty as a result of some brain injury in adulthood suffered by a person who was previously a competent reader. A number of different subtypes of acquired dyslexia have been described (see Ellis, 1984, for a summary). These subtypes have been used by various authors to examine cases of children with reading difficulties. However, the comparisons have turned out to be flawed in various ways.

Jorm (1979) drew attention to similarities between reading difficulties and acquired deep dyslexia. An adult suffering from deep dyslexia exhibits a range of reading errors, rather than just one single type (see the articles in Coltheart, Patterson and Marshall, 1980). Among the more important symptoms for a comparison with reading difficulties are an apparent absence of phonemic coding (evidenced by such errors as reading ape for monkey) and an almost complete inability to read non-words. These errors suggest that deep dyslexics have lost the capacity for grapheme-phoneme conversion. Jorm (1979) noted that there was a similarity between the errors that deep dyslexics make and the errors frequently reported in studies of reading difficulties (see e.g. Seymour and Porpodas, 1980; Snowling, 1980, 1981). He proposed that a common area of the brain – the inferior parietal lobule – was implicated in deep dyslexia and in developmental reading difficulties. Jorm proposed that in deep dyslexia the inferior parietal lobule had been injured, while in children with reading difficulties it had not developed fully.

Such a theory cannot easily be tested directly. However, it is possible to examine the basis on which it has been set up. How good is the comparison between deep dyslexia and reading difficulties? Baddeley, Ellis, Miles and Lewis (1982) compared the two syndromes. They found that although children with reading difficulties performed very slowly on tasks that required phonemic encoding, they nevertheless showed clear evidence of phonemic encoding unlike deep dyslexics. The children were also able to read orthographically regular non-words (albeit more slowly and less accurately than reading age or chronological age controls) whereas deep dyslexics are unable to perform this task. Baddeley et al. concluded that there is a qualitative difference between the difficulties exhibited by deep dyslexics and those exhibited by children with reading difficulties.

Two other notable case histories have been reported by Temple and Marshall (1983) and by Coltheart, Masterson, Byng, Prior and Riddoch (1983). Both reports concern 17-year-old girls with a reading age of 10 years but with different patterns of reading difficulties. Temple and Marshall described a girl, HM, with a pattern of reading that resembles that of phonological dyslexia. Phonological dyslexia is an acquired dyslexia characterized by a difficulty in forming orthographic-phonological correspondences. Phonological dyslexics have particular difficulty reading non-sense words and unfamiliar words.

Coltheart et al. studied CD, who had a reading difficulty somewhat different from that experienced by phonological dyslexics. CD had considerable difficulty reading irregular words. This is a pattern characteristic of acquired surface dyslexia, which is a condition in which the patient can use the phonological route but seems to have no direct visual access to words. For these patients irregular words pose a problem because the direct visual access route is not available to identify irregular words as such and the phonological route leads to regularization errors. The girl studied by Coltheart et al. differed from the conventional syndrome of surface dyslexia, however, in that she had difficulty pronouncing nonsense words, which is not common among surface dyslexics.

It would seem from these two studies that there are definite subtypes of developmental dyslexia. Further, in that the patterns resemble those of acquired dyslexics, it may be that the same functional areas of the brain are implicated in both acquired dyslexia and developmental reading difficulties. However, there are problems in the way of such conclusions. The subtypes of acquired dyslexia are far from uniform internally; the same symptom, within a syndrome, can have different causes in different patients. This makes the comparison of acquired dyslexia and developmental reading difficulties extremely problematic. Snowling (1983; 1987) has been particularly critical of the use of acquired dyslexia categories for cases of developmental reading difficulties. She has highlighted serious methodological and conceptual problems implicit in such comparisons. Snowling suggests that the best policy in investigating why children fail to learn to read is to continue to look for characteristics that distinguish poor readers from normal reading age-matched controls. Following this line, the key question to ask of the subjects studied by Temple and Marshall, and Coltheart et al. is whether their reading performance is different from other children with a reading age of 10 years. Put another way, are the syndromes described different from normal reading at the appropriate reading age? Neither study, unfortunately, contained any comparison data with other children who have a reading age of 10 years. In order to answer these questions Bryant and Impey (1986) tested 16 children who had a mean reading age of about 10 years and compared the errors made by this group with the results reported by Temple and Marshall and by Coltheart et al. They reported that the group as a whole showed all the symptoms reported in CD and HM and these symptoms were stronger in some children than in others. In most cases there were individuals whose scores either approached or actually exceeded those of CD and HM. In the light of this Bryant and Impey concluded that the results of Temple and Marshall and of Coltheart et al. cannot be interpreted as identifying the causes of reading difficulty. Since normal readers make the same errors as poor readers, the idea that poor readers suffer from selective functional impairment of the brain akin to that of the acquired dyslexics is undermined. Bryant and Impey also draw attention to the large individual differences among their sample of normal readers. They argue that this suggests that there are different styles of reading among normal children and that the differences in the case studies reported by Temple and Marshall and by Coltheart et al. correspond to the difficulties experienced by a child who has adopted a particular style of reading.

Thus, in so far as there are different types of readers, there will be different types of reading difficulty in that children who have adopted one reading strategy, but have difficulty in learning to read, will exhibit different problems from children who have adopted another reading strategy. The key issue in mapping from different reading strategies to different reading difficulties is how the normal range of differences is to be represented.

The model of reading presented in figure 8.3 shows two routes to decoding a word: a direct visual access route and a phonological route. Baron and Strawson (1976) have described a dimension of individual differences among adult readers, the poles of which correspond to a reliance on one or other of these routes. At one end of the dimension are readers who rely heavily on word-specific associations between a word stimulus and its meaning. At the other end are readers who rely heavily on phonological rules. Baron (1979) reported a similar effect among children. Treiman (1984) has reported that the effect applies to spelling as well as reading. Although the point about variations is important, it may be a mistake to place too much emphasis on it. Siegel, Levey and Ferris (1985) have argued that the major factor in reading difficulties is being poor at grapheme-phoneme conversions. There is also now a substantial body of evidence that early phonological awareness provides at least moderate predictions of later reading skills (Bradley and Bryant, 1978; Calfee, Lindamood and Lindamood, 1973; Fox and Routh, 1976, 1980, 1983; Jorm and Share, 1983; Rozin and Gleitman, 1977). It has also been shown that the results are relatively robust over different methods of assessing phonological awareness (Stanovich, Cunningham and Cramer, 1984).

Summary

The ability to read is a vital skill in the world in which we live. Accordingly, an account of reading development should be high on the agenda of a theory of cognitive development. In recent years considerable attention has been devoted to the reading process by cognitive scientists. Much of the effort has been devoted to studying the basic decoding processes implicated in the recognition of words. This is the first stage of under-standing reading. It is with this stage that this chapter has been concerned. The issues discussed do not cover the whole spectrum of issues that a theory of reading would have to tackle. Little has been said in this chapter about the higher order skills involved in inference and comprehension when reading a text, although some of the relevant issues have been discussed in other chapters.

The emphasis of recent theories of decoding has been on a dual route to a word's recognition. The two routes can be summed up as 'reading by eye and by ear'. The first route is simple direct visual recognition of a word. For this route, there exists a detailed process model, implemented as a computer simulation (McClelland and Rumelhart, 1981). This is one of the few models that makes detailed proposals about how the cognitive system processes information. The emphasis of the model is on parallel interacting levels of processing. At each level there are excitatory and inhibitory connections both among the elements represented at that level and to elements at other levels. The processing competition is 'won' by the elements that receive the greatest amount of excitation. These elements inhibit other competing elements so that the processing system 'settles' on an interpretation of the input.

The second route to word recognition is by orthographic-phonological conversion, which allows access to a word's meaning through the path-ways that support spoken language. This is an especially important route because it is by this route that we can sound out words we have not encountered in print before and either recognize the word as one we are already familiar with as a spoken word, or recognize that it is a new word whose meaning we do not know. Many of the difficulties that children encounter in learning to read appear to be associated with this route to word recognition. In particular, children who are poor readers seem to have greater than usual difficulties in establishing phonological represen-tations of words. There is converging evidence from a number of studies that poor readers are delayed in their acquisition of phonological codes by comparison with normal controls. This seems to be the most robust finding to have emerged from the research into the causes of reading difficulties. Other candidate causes, such as the once popular perceptual deficit theories, are now largely discredited.

From a practical point of view, the discovery that many cases of reading difficulty are caused by difficulties in establishing a phonological representation of words is of considerable importance. A number of studies with both normal and reading retarded children have shown that it is possible to intervene to increase children's awareness of the phonological structure of words. Children who have received such intervention have generally shown improved reading scores when compared with control groups of children who did not receive the same intervention.   Lastly, the question of individual differences was discussed. In recent years there have been many parallels drawn between developmental reading difficulties and acquired dyslexia. However, using the categories of acquired dyslexia to study reading difficulties is a questionable enterprise. As several authors have pointed out, children rarely display the complete failures displayed by adult patients. The variation among children who have a reading difficulty seems to reflect the natural variation that occurs among normal readers.

The reading errors made by children with reading difficulties do not reveal any abnormality of information processing; the errors are no different in kind from the errors made by younger children who have a similar reading age, although they do differ from the errors made by normal readers with the same chronological age. There is increasing support for the position that children with reading difficulties follow the same learning path as normal readers but at a much slower rate. However, this conclusion does not lessen in any way the severity of a reading difficulty; its effect on a child's learning and life can be profound, whatever the cause.

9

The Process of Cognitive Development

Levels of Cognitive Theory

In this chapter I want to return to the more general theoretical issues raised in Chapter 1 and reflect on these in the light of the content covered in the succeeding seven chapters. In doing so an attempt will be made to draw common strands together and also to identify areas of continuing weakness in our attempts to understand cognitive development.

In Chapter 1 a distinction was drawn between three levels at which cognitive theories can be articulated. Level I is the level of tasks; Level II is the level of domains; Level III is the level of the cognitive architecture: the basic principles of organization of the cognitive system. Here, I want to raise the issue of the relation between these levels. As a contrast let us consider two extreme approaches to this relation: the top-down and the bottom-up. The top-down approach postulates general principles of cognitive functioning and then applies these principles consistently across domains and also across tasks. Although domains may differ in their content, top-down theories postulate that the same organizational principles will be evident upon empirical investigation. The empirical research generated by such theories will be largely devoted to testing the predictions derived from the top-down principles. Bottom-up theories, by contrast, are constructed by beginning at the level of tasks and constructing models that explain observed performance on the tasks. This approach acknowledges the importance of task-specific strategies, about which top-down theories are often silent. But the bottom-up approach is not solely an attempt to catalogue task-specific strategies; it is also an attempt to discover empirically, principles that are general across tasks and that would constitute the basic organizational structure of cognition. In an ideal world the top-down and the bottom-up approach would converge on the same set of principles.

One or other of these approaches has guided much of the research that has been conducted on cognitive development. Piaget's theory is an example of a top-down approach in which the same organizational structure and the same mechanisms of development are postulated across domains. However, as was seen in chapters 3 and 6, careful empirical investigation has revealed more differences than similarities among domains. By contrast with Piaget's theory, the information processing framework has generated a great deal of detailed bottom-up analysis of individual tasks. This has proved to be a very productive way of understanding individual skills but it has not always added significantly to our understanding of general principles. It would seem that the considerable effort that has been expended within these two frameworks should have led by now to a greater *theoretical* understanding of cognitive development than has been achieved. The fact that it has not suggests that there may be some fundamental flaw in the way that the issue has been approached. I want to suggest that there is such a flaw and that it lies in the way that the relation between the levels of tasks, domains of related tasks, and general principles has been conceptualized.

Obviously, a theory of cognitive development must include all three levels but it is worth discussing what the relation is, or should be, between these levels. First, lower levels must be consistent with the principles of the higher levels. Thus, a theory that postulated some basic organizational principles for cognition at Level III should not have these principles violated by lower levels. This much is, I hope, obvious. However, there is a certain sting in this implication. Given that cognition covers such diverse content areas as perception, reasoning, and language it is unlikely that general principles will be powerful or plentiful. Nevertheless, there are evidently some general principles of cognition. Association between items, for example, seems to be a ubiquitous principle across domains. When the problem is approached from the other direction, from the bottom-up, there is abundant evidence for powerful principles in plenty. But they lack generality. They are not the same principles that are postulated by top-down theories. But neither are they competitors for the role of general principles. They seem to be specific to the level at which the theory operates. This has sometimes been taken to suggest that cognition is not a unitary system; that it is essentially a collection of modules that are autonomously organized to process only certain types of input (e.g., Fodor, 1983). This view has the advantage that it can allow the postulation of principles that need have no applicability beyond a certain module. However, it suffers in attempting to account for how modules achieve integration into a single cognitive system. This cannot be accounted for, by definition, by module-specific principles. Beyond a few special cases, most notably language, it is exceedingly difficult to begin to construct a module-specific developmental theory, without trivializing the issue of developmental origins by appeal to innate representations and procedures. Even for language, it was seen in chapter 7 that it is possible to construct a plausible theory of the initial origins of language structure without recourse to innate module-specific principles.

It may be that a theory of cognitive modules is an overstatement of a good case for cognitive domains. The term 'domain' is being used here to denote a collection of tasks that share a common representation system and a common set of procedures for operating on these representations to perform tasks. Thus, for example, number is a domain of cognition; so is language (whether or not it is also a module, I shall leave as an open question). On this account, chess is a domain; music also. In fact, wherever it is possible to create a specialized representation system with dedicated procedures there is a domain. Unlike modules, domains may overlap, either by having similar representations (i.e., some mapping function exists between the representations) or similar procedures. When this occurs, it is reasonable to expect that skill in one domain will correlate with skill in another.

Many who have studied cognition have come to the conclusion that the cognitive system is characterized by representations and procedures specialized for particular domains of cognition. Some domains are probably the product of our evolutionary history. Language and the perceptual systems are obvious examples. However, it is unlikely that evolution could have provided the human organism with all the specialized systems of representation that characterize normal adult cognition. Instead, it seems that evolution has provided something more useful: an ability to develop specialized systems of representation and specialized procedures to operate on these systems. Most domains seem to develop from an initial application of general-purpose processes that create structured representations, which in turn allow the development of processes dedicated to operating on those representations.

The development of the number domain discussed in chapter 6 is an example, in which associative mechanisms play a large part in setting up a number representation system and a process – counting – for operating on it. This process itself then forms the basis for the development of more specialized processes of addition and subtraction, and they in their turn facilitate the development of higher mathematical operations. The development of a powerful representation system for number is of comparatively recent origin (as outlined in chapter 6). However, once the system had been developed it was possible to pass it on by instruction with the result that a domain of mathematical expertise is much more common now than it was a few thousand years ago.

One of the points that I wish to argue in this chapter is that cognitive development can be viewed as the development of specialized domains supported by a general cognitive architecture that can create representations of salient features of the environment and then, through the operation of general cognitive mechanisms (often with tutorial guidance), construct powerful domain-specific procedures for manipulating representations. Thus, the cognitive architecture may provide only a weak basis for learning about the different content domains of cognition; enough, as it were, to get individual domains operating with some minimal functionality and to provide a common structure for cross-domain interaction. Although the role of general principles may be most evident in the initial stages of development, it is postulated that they can continue to play the role of midwife to new systems of representation throughout an individual's life.

The same arguments can be applied to tasks: Individual tasks may initially be performed without optimal efficiency because they are controlled by higher-level principles. In time, dedicated processes develop that enable them to be performed more efficiently but that have little applicability beyond the particular task. If this argument is true, it helps to explain the pervasive fragmentary theoretical structure of an information processing framework that focuses to a large extent on tasks, to which attention was drawn in chapter 1.

In this chapter I intend to work through the arguments above and consider various proposals that have been advanced about how the relation between the levels of cognitive theory can be worked out in more detail. In doing so I shall, where possible, draw on the material presented in the preceding chapters to illustrate the arguments.

The Architecture of Cognition

A Symbolic Information Processing Architecture

The architecture of cognition specifies the basic foundations that are necessary and sufficient for cognitive functioning. From a developmental perspective let us consider what an architecture of cognition ought to contain based on the evidence reviewed in the previous chapters. Since our perspective is a developmental one we shall approach the architecture by considering how it would support the most basic forms of learning that we see in infancy and proceed from there. It should be remembered that the architecture is generally considered to represent the fixed unchanging structure of cognition so we shall not necessarily expect to find changes during development in the ways that it operates.

Most traditional information processing accounts of cognition have been premised on the view that the mind is a system that constructs and manipulates symbols (Newell, 1980a; Pylyshyn, 1984). Symbols constitute the basic representational elements that are manipulated during information processing. A symbol is an *abstract* characterization of how information is represented by the brain. It is evident that the brain does not literally contain words; it simply contains neural circuits. In the symbolic model of cognition, neural circuits are the implementation hardware for symbols. It is part of the philosophy of symbol processing accounts of cognition that a theory of information processing can be constructed independently of the implementation level (Newell, 1980a; Pylyshyn, 1984).

Symbols are not themselves part of the architecture of cognition; they are the products of the architecture. Thus, it is possible that different researchers might subscribe to a common view of the architecture of cognition but differ in how they see its products, either because they address different issues or because they simply disagree on some issue of symbolic representation. In fact, there is an extremely catholic approach to the matter of symbols within the information processing framework, as Palmer (1978) has noted. In the current text a variety of types of symbolic representations have been discussed including schemas, concepts, words, numbers, and scripts. This is by no means an exhaustive list. To some extent, the variety of representations that are postulated reflects the adaptive nature of the cognitive system; to some extent it may also reflect a tendency to postulate internal representations that conveniently match external descriptions of behaviour. Scripts are probably an example of the latter; the phenomena they purport to explain are probably better explained as the result of processes rather than representations (Schank, 1983).

Symbols are only one half of what is required. The other half is the processes that manipulate symbols. Some symbol manipulation, such as the creation of associations between representations, is a result of a mechanism that can be regarded as part of the architecture of cognition. However, the cognitive system also creates a wide variety of procedures dedicated to operating on particular representations. The procedures for addition, for example, only operate on numbers.

What type of cognitive architecture is necessary to support the representations and procedures that are postulated by symbolic accounts of cognition? Most, if not all, information processing psychologists would subscribe to the view that there is a limited amount of processing that can be performed by the cognitive system at any given time. In order to explain this phenomenon various structural models of the cognitive system have been proposed. Historically, the most important of these models was Atkinson and Shiffrin's (1968) model of a limited capacity short-term memory. Contemporary theories have refined the model of simple limited capacity to a working memory that contains several components (Baddeley and Hitch, 1974). Nevertheless, the underlying assumption remains the same: that the cognitive system is inherently subject to limits in the resources that it can deploy and that tasks that cause overloading of these resources will not be completed successfully. Many of the procedures that arise for processing information can be seen as a way of seeking to optimize the uses that can be made of limited resources. Part of the process of development is learning to use these resources efficiently in various domains. Efficiency can be accomplished in a number of ways: by chunking two or more representations that co-occur regularly into a single representation; by discarding irrelevant representations; by chunking procedures together. Mechanisms such as chunking that are used to accomplish efficiency must themselves be part of the cognitive architecture. Other mechanisms that are commonly invoked to explain the derivation of rules for processing information, such as induction, must likewise be part of the architecture.

In addition to proposing a limited capacity short-term memory, Atkinson and Shiffrin (1968) also proposed a long-term memory of essentially unlimited capacity in which information is permanently stored. This constitutes the second key structural assumption of the architecture of cognition within the information processing framework. Long-term memory is essentially associative in character, although other forms of organization can be overlaid on this. Thus, an associative mechanism must be part of the cognitive architecture.

The proposal that an associative long-term store is part of the cognitive architecture fits well with the facts of infant cognition. A striking feature of infant cognition is its associative character. From birth infants are capable of forming associations between two stimuli and of learning contingent relations between associated stimuli so that the presence of one stimulus predicts for the infant the presence of the other. The infant data also suggest that information is stored in a categorical fashion. Infants are capable from birth of selectively using some stimulus dimensions as a sufficient basis for the functional equivalence of stimuli while ignoring (but not necessarily failing to detect) differences among the stimuli along other dimensions. It is possible to construct a model of the information processing that is involved in categorization along the lines of that shown in figure 9.1. In this model input is placed in working memory and a central processor then controls a process of comparison between the information in working memory and that stored in long-term memory. The processor may be innately disposed to treat some stimulus dimensions as more significant than others for purposes of comparison (and it may additionally learn further bases for selective evaluation of similarity during the course of development). If there is sufficient similarity between the input in working memory and the stored information, then the new input will be treated as equivalent to the stored information. If the stored information has an action of some sort associated with it, such as a head turn in a particular direction, then the new input will elicit that action.

The type of information processing envisaged by models such as that in figure 9.1 is heavily influenced by the digital computer in which information is stored as symbols in particular memory locations from which it is fetched as required by a central processing unit that effectively runs the system. The central processing unit carries out logical operations on the data it receives as inputs and stores the outputs either in a temporary memory or in a permanent memory. This type of model has served the analysis of human information processing well. In particular, it has been the source of many fruitful hypotheses about the human mind. The mind has been conceived as a system that represents information as symbols, processes the symbols in a serial fashion according to rules for their manipulation, and stores the results in localized slots in a long-term memory. This model of human information processing works particularly

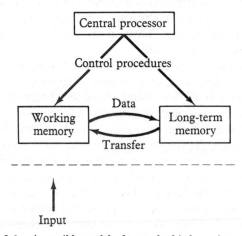

Figure 9.1 *A possible model of control of information processing.*

well for tasks that require conscious effort and thought, such as playing chess or doing arithmetic. However, the model also has obvious limitations. It does not apply equally well to tasks that require little conscious thought or effort, such as detecting an object in the environment or performing a skilled action. Even though such tasks are performed with ease, they require considerable information processing, perhaps more than the tasks that we perform more slowly and effortfully (Marr, 1982).

Human cognition is a product of the human brain, and the more that is learnt about the brain, the less like a digital computer it seems in its functional architecture. Relating the physical architecture of the brain to the architecture of cognition is a task of considerable complexity (see Churchland (1986) for a recent discussion), and one that can only be accomplished very imperfectly at present. Nevertheless, sufficient is known to suggest that revisions of standard information processing models are required. Some of these revisions have implications for the way in which the basic architecture of cognition is construed, so it is important to consider them here.

A Connectionist Architecture

The human brain consists of a very large number of neurons, which are densely interconnected. These connections are of two sorts: excitatory and inhibitory. Brain activity seems to consist of large numbers of neurons being active simultaneously sending both excitatory and inhibitory signals to other neurons. This activity has no functional parallel in standard models of information processing. However, there has been a resurgence of interest in constructing models that are inspired by the neural structure of the brain. The approach, variously called *connectionism* and *parallel distributed processing* hypothesizes (a) that information processing is a parallel rather than a serial process, with neural-like 'units' stimulating or inhibiting each other; (b) that each unit processes a fragment of the information that is considerably smaller than a symbol and is often called a *subsymbol*; and (c) that information is not stored in the conventional sense but exists as a pattern of connectivity among the units. We have already encountered an example of this type of model in the McClelland and Rumelhart (1981) account of reading considered in chapter 8.

Connectionist models pose a challenge to conventional views of information processing. However, the challenge is not necessarily one of a paradigm shift in which connectionism replaces information processing. The two views of cognition are not necessarily incompatible (Smolensky, 1988). In particular, connectionist models show most promise at present in just those areas in which symbol processing theories have been least successful, such as the structure of concepts. On the other hand, there is no reason to believe at present that connectionist models will offer a better account of those areas in which symbol processing theories have been strongest such as problem solving. However, it is not the ultimate outcome of the debate between connectionism and symbol processing that is of most interest here but the contributions that connectionist models can make to understanding the innate architecture of cognition. The major contribution that I wish to focus on is the model of distributed memory representation, from which a good deal follows that is consonant with the data discussed in earlier chapters.

In connectionist models the storage of information is not achieved by depositing a symbol in long-term memory. In order to understand how information is stored in a connectionist model it is necessary to consider how it is processed. Figure 9.2 shows a fragment of the model presented previously in figure 8.4. Connectionist models hypothesize that each input unit in a network processes only a very simple piece of information, such as a line at a particular orientation. These constitute the subsymbols out of which concepts and other higher level constructs arise. They are subsymbols because none of these features has meaning in their own right. They are meaningful only in combination with other units and it is the process of combination that is of particular interest in understanding connectionist systems.

Any unit has both excitatory and inhibitory connections with other units such that when it is activated it will send an excitatory signal to

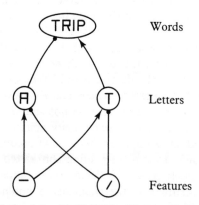

Figure 9.2 *A fragment of the McClelland and Rumelhart (1981) model shown in figure 8.4. Arrows indicate excitatory connections and dots indicate inhibitory connections.*

some other units and an inhibitory signal to still others. For any given input many units in a network will be activated simultaneously and will process their input in parallel. Each of these units will send both excitatory and inhibitory signals to other units. In particular, they will send excitatory signals to each other. According to a hypothesis originally advanced by Hebb (1949), units that are active together will have their excitatory connections strengthened and units that are not active will have their connections weakened. (When Hebb originally proposed this hypothesis the inhibitory action of neurons had not been discovered, so he did not hypothesize inhibitory connections.) Over time a network that repeatedly receives the same input will develop a group of units that respond to this input and that have strong excitatory connections among themselves. It is this dynamic configuration of units that constitutes the system's memory of the input. It is a memory in the sense that the whole configuration will respond when presented again with the input that gave rise to the configuration. However, there is no symbol that represents the input stored in memory. What is stored is a dynamically stable configuration of subsymbols.

There are several consequences that follow from this view of memory. First, the whole configuration will be activated when only some of the input units are activated. Thus, the configuration constitutes a content-addressable memory. Since human memory is content-addressable, this is a desirable feature of the model. Second, no single feature is critical for the configuration to be activated. This fits well with the data on concepts and concept development and will be discussed further below. Third, the system is stable but not unchanging. New inputs that share many features in common with a dynamically stable configuration will activate that configuration and will also activate the units that respond to the features that are not strongly connected to the configuration. This will result in a small adjustment in connection strengths following Hebb's hypothesis. Repeated presentation of new input will lead to repeated modification of the original configuration. Thus, the system learns continually, in virtue of its architecture. Fourth, the system is also associative in virtue of its architecture; different inputs are simply represented by different patterns of activation over the same network. In order to see how this is so, it is necessary to consider how several different representations with elements in common would be stored by a connectionist system.   In a connectionist network each (sub)feature is represented only once by a unit. Each unit participates in many different networks; the extent to which it will be activated will be a function of the input it receives from other units. Thus the activity of a unit will vary as a function of the context in which it occurs. However, every time a unit is activated it will attempt to activate all the other units to which it is connected. This is the basis of associativity built into the system's architecture. The extent to which other units are activated will, of course, depend on their total input in the context. Thus, a unit, a, that has strong excitatory connections with another unit b, will not always successfully activate that unit because in certain contexts b may receive stronger inhibitory than excitatory inputs. This is why, although the architecture is inherently associationist, associations do not run rampant with every input.

The Origins of Representations

In considering the origins of representations it is worth recalling briefly the major results about the infant's perceptual abilities that have been established by the literature reviewed in chapter 2. The perceptual systems are a series of highly specialized modules, which, to a large extent, have been hardwired by evolution for the initial processing of stimulus input. At birth both the visual and auditory systems are highly developed. From birth infants are capable of processing much of the stimulation that they receive through these senses. Further, there appear to be innate control mechanisms that ensure that infants attend to the type of stimulation that leads to further post-natal development. This is evident in the preference by infants for complex over simple stimuli and by the innate tendency to orientate the eyes towards the source of an auditory stimulus, both of which were discussed in chapter 2.

The perceptual systems determine what information is received by higher cognitive systems. Some of what might be considered part of these higher cognitive systems is also innately organized. Depth perception and shape constancy are examples in the visual modality as is the categorical perception of speech sounds in the auditory modality.

Recent research has done much to clarify the sensitivity of infants to the various dimensions of stimulus input. What, however, is the long-term fate of the information received? Sophisticated perceptual processing systems would be of limited evolutionary benefit if the organism could not use the information to learn about the environment. In this context learning implies that the organism construct representations of the environment, store these representations, at a later time detect similarities between new inputs and stored representations, and alter the stored representation in the light of new experience.

Probably the most fundamental requirement of an architecture in order for learning to be possible is recognition of similarity. If organisms cannot

recognize events in the environment as similar to each other then there
is no possibility of learning because present experience cannot be interpreted in the light of past experience. However, this begs a question as
to what constitutes similarity. Events are never identical in all details.
Thus, organisms must be able to tolerate differences among inputs while
categorizing them as similar. Connectionist architectures meet this
requirement and are therefore a promising foundation for the representation of information by a cognitive system that begins with no knowledge
of the world but is capable of constructing representations of the input
it receives. A connectionist architecture provides the basic framework
within which concepts can be represented and modified in the light of
new experiences. Once a sufficient stock of related concepts has been
established, these can become the basis of specialized patterns of development. Before examining this latter issue, we shall consider in more
detail the relation between a connectionist architecture and the review of
concepts presented in chapter 4.

Concepts

Recent research on concepts has established that instances of a concept
do not usually have any single defining feature that determines membership of the concept. Instead, concepts have a 'family resemblance' structure such that any instance will have some features in common with other
instances and some other features in common with an overlapping but
different set of further instances. Any given feature will be shared by
many but not by all instances of a concept. It is not difficult to see that
this cognitive description of the structure of concepts is also a description
of the structure of a connectionist network. Further, such a network
could be constructed directly from experience of the environment with the
weights between features being adjusted as a function of their frequency in
the environment.

In order to test the prediction that a connectionist network could, in
fact, learn different concepts from presentations of exemplars, McClelland
and Rumelhart (1986) presented a network with 16 feature units with
exemplars of dogs, cats, and bagels. The network was presented with 50
exemplars of each category and after each presentation the weights
between units were adjusted as a function of their activation by the
exemplars. After training the network could successfully distinguish
among the three concepts. In addition, given input of some unique part
of the concept, it could successfully recall the correct concept. Thus, the
same network of features was capable of learning different concepts. But,
of course, it was also capable of learning their similarities because if

concepts shared a feature in common it was represented by the same unit.

Concepts have prototypical structure, which means that some instances are regarded as more typical of the concept than others. This also can be readily explained by a connectionist network. Prototypicality is a function of the number of features an instance shares with other instances. In any given concept, features possessed by instances will be mutually excitatory. Thus, the more features an instance has, the more strongly will a connectionist network be activated.

One of the more interesting discoveries about prototypes is that even if the prototype is not presented in the exemplars, it will still subsequently be judged the best instance (Homa and Chambliss, 1975; Homa et al., 1973; Posner and Keele, 1968, 1970). This result has also been simulated by the connectionist network described above. In one of their simulations, McClelland and Rumelhart presented the network with distortions of a prototype. After training the network responded more strongly to the prototype than to any distortion of it.

Most of the major findings about conceptual structure can be simulated by a connectionist architecture. There is therefore some justification in regarding this type of architecture as the appropriate structure for the development of concepts. In the discussion of conceptual development in chapter 4 it was concluded that the structure of children's concepts did not differ from the structure of adult concepts, even though children might know considerably less about a particular concept than an adult. Bomba and Siqueland (1983) have shown that 3-month-old infants form concepts with a prototypic structure which is exactly what would be predicted by a connectionist architecture. On encountering objects in the world a child will represent those features of the object for which units are available. Nature has seen to it that a plentiful supply of hardwired units are available for basic perceptual recognition. This will be sufficient to allow conceptual development to begin. Objects with similar features will have a similar representation and thus will become members of the same concept because they will activate the same complete network of units (and not just the units that respond to the features that the object contains). Thus, the objects in the world will be grouped together as a function of the units that they share in common and the strength of the connections that have been established between units by experience.

The architectural foundation for concepts provided by connectionism is particularly relevant to the issue of the origin of representations discussed in chapter 3. There, it was argued that mental representations could be attributed to an infant if there was evidence that infants were capable of categorization. Not only is there such evidence, there is also an architectural theory that provides a solid foundation for the view that infants are capable of creating representations from birth. This does not mean that the infant is an intellectual genius. There are many constraints that operate to limit an infant's ability to create representations in the early months of life in particular. The infant is rarely awake for long; there are limits imposed by the perceptual systems on what information can be processed; and there is considerable post-natal brain development, which undoubtedly disrupts existing representations. This, in fact, may be the explanation for infantile amnesia: we cannot remember our early experiences because post-natal brain development has disrupted the pattern of interconnections that was established by early experience.

An implication of proposing a connectionist architecture for concepts is that recognition memory will be functional from birth, at least over short to medium term times. The evidence reviewed in chapters 2 and 4 suggests that recognition memory is a functional and robust system from birth. In this chapter the architectural principles that help explain these empirical findings have been discussed. Recognition memory is functional because the stimulus presented causes nodes that have been activated together to have their connection strength increased. When the stimulus is re-presented, the same nodes are activated but this time they are activated as an interconnected unit, which constitutes the process of recognition.

It is worth emphasizing at this stage the difference in the model of memory between a symbol processing model of cognition and a connectionist model. In a symbol processing model symbols are stored in a dedicated structure, which is usually called long term memory. In a connectionist system what is stored is the weights between connections and these are stored only in the sense that when the network is next activated its starting weights will be a function of the weights that resulted from the previous activation. (They may not be identical because weights are assumed to be subject to a decay function over time.) In a connectionist network symbols are not stored and recalled; they are recreated in the presence of appropriate cues that cause a certain pattern of activation over a network.

Object Permanence

In chapter 3 the concept of object permanence was discussed. It was concluded that infants possess object permanence from at least six months. Nevertheless, they make errors in searching for hidden objects until well into their second year. The most striking of the errors is perseverative search, which is caused when an infant several times retrieves an object hidden at a location, A, and the object is then hidden at location B. In this situation the infant will frequently search at A for the object even though he or she has observed the object being hidden at B. However, there are two sets of circumstances that significantly improve the probability of search occurring at B. The first is when search is allowed to take place immediately. Diamond (1985) showed that between 7 and 12 months of age the critical length of the delay increased steadily from 3 to 10 seconds. The second set of circumstances that improves the probability of correct search is the provision of distinctive visual cues associated with the different hiding places. The following is an entirely speculative account of how a connectionist architecture could go some way towards explaining these findings.

I shall assume that the infant's representation of where the object has been hidden controls its search behaviour. I shall also assume that the representation of the object's location is a connectionist network. On first encountering an object being hidden, a representation is created of the location where the object is hidden and a motor action is effected to search at that location. With each repeated encounter the representation network is strengthened. When an object is now hidden at a new location the representation of the new location will be assimilated by the existing network because the act of hiding will activate that network. Provided search is allowed to occur immediately, the motor response will be effected before assimilation has occurred and the search will be at the correct location. However, if search is delayed, the stronger existing representations will control the motor response and search will occur at the location where the object was previously found. Landmark cues will improve the probability of search at the correct location because the more distinct the two locations, the less successful will the existing representation be at assimilating the new.

Let us now consider the increase in the delay that can occur with age before the perseverative error occurs. This is not due to a decrease in the rate of assimilation with age (I shall assume that the rate at least remains constant) but to the maturation of attentional control procedures that select which features of the network are to control the motor behaviour. The obvious feature required is something like 'place where last hiding observed'. The attentional procedure must 'tune' the network so that search for hidden objects is carried out under the control of such a feature. The observed increase in the delay possible with age before error occurs is the result of such tuning occurring; with increasing age the motor response comes to depend less and less on the whole representation of the hidden object and more and more on one specialist representation.

Domains and the General Architecture

In this section I shall consider developmental issues in two domains of cognition, number and language. I have chosen to discuss number because it seems to me a very clear case of how specialized representations and procedures develop to create a cognitive domain. I have chosen language because it is likely to be the domain in which the debate between connectionist and symbolic approaches to cognition will rage most fiercely, just as it was in the debate between behaviourist and cognitive approaches to psychology.

Number

Number is a particularly interesting cognitive domain. There is some innate sensitivity to the property of numerosity (Starkey and Cooper, 1980; Strauss and Curtis, 1984), which is probably based on the ability to subitize small numerosities. Number reasoning such as counting and arithmetic is built on the foundation of this innate ability, but its development is not automatic – it needs the support of a general problem-solving architecture in order to establish first the mapping between count words and objects and then the development of arithmetical skills from counting.

The first major developmental issue with number is to explain how the child constructs and uses a representation system for number. The child's initial representation system is the system of count words. The development of counting shows how a simple associative system can be the basis for the development of a powerful domain of cognition. The child may initially know count words well in excess of an ability to count accurately because these words can be learnt by rote as an associative chain. Initially, the child has considerable difficulty in coordinating the words at his or her disposal and the objects in the array being counted, as Fuson (1988) has shown. The research reviewed in chapter 6 suggests that children frequently learn to coordinate count words with objects through the use of an intermediary behaviour of pointing. Pointing is recruited into this role through being used initially as a referential indicator of the object to which the count word being uttered refers. However, it then comes to serve a regulatory function of matching words with objects on a one-to-one basis. Once the child has the ability to count accurately, counting can then become the basis for the development of arithmetical skills.

Number development illustrates well some of the points made earlier in this chapter about the relation between general architectural principles and the development of domain-specific procedures. The initial counting system requires both general architectural principles of associativity in order to group number words together and a sensitivity by the information processing system to the feature of numerosity in the environment. The information processing system can encode numerosity before count words have been learnt as evidenced by research with pre-speech infants (Starkey and Cooper, 1980; Strauss and Curtis, 1984). This means that when count words are taught while drawing attention to the property of numerosity, the child will have little difficulty in inferring which property of the environment should be encoded.

The counting system encodes just one feature of the world. It is a feature that can be manipulated in certain ways that are peculiar to itself and these manipulations are represented in the procedures of arithmetic that develop out of counting. These procedures have developed to manipulate just one single domain of representation and have no applicability to other domains because the property of numerosity is only encoded in numbers. The development of the procedures to manipulate numbers requires the support of a general problem-solving architecture such as that proposed by Brown and Burton (1978), Brown and Van Lehn (1980), and Young and O'Shea (1981). Thus, the architecture of the cognitive system can be effective in creating a module of cognition based on special-purpose representations, with procedures dedicated to operating in those representations. However, the general architectural principles themselves will not necessarily be principles within the module of number itself. They are rather a scaffolding with which dedicated modules can be built.

Although procedures such as counting are specific to the domain of number, there is at least one situation in which they may give rise to procedures that can be applied more generally. That is in the discovery of conservation principles. It was observed in chapter 6 that number conservation is the earliest of the conservation skills to be acquired and that the initial ability to conserve depends either on counting or on one-to-one matching. Thus, initially, the child discovers that arrays of objects are unaffected by certain transformations, such as lengthening or shortening the array, by counting the array before and after transformation. From such domain-specific procedures the child can induce that transformation of the appearance of an amount does not affect the quantity of the amount. It seems probable that this induction is not made all at once but may be arrived at through a series of more low-level inductions, each one building on the previous: that transformations do not affect small numbers; that transformations do not affect any numbers; that transformations do not affect length; that transformations do not affect mass; that transformations do not affect any quantity. This type of developmental pattern is consistent with the sequence of conservation development that was described in chapter 6. Although this inductive sequence relies on counting for its origin, once it begins, the procedure of counting that gave rise to it becomes superfluous to conservation judgements. Furthermore, the induced principle is initially restricted to a representation of numerosity, but is then extended to be applicable to any quantitative dimension. Thus, what began as a discovery about a particular representation (number) within a particular domain, becomes the basis of a general principle applicable to a large range of representations.

Language

If any higher cognitive process has claims to be a separate module on evolutionary grounds, then language has. The arguments that language is a module whose development is largely controlled by innate cognitive principles have been discussed in chapter 7. However, the identification of these principles has proved problematic. The view that language could be acquired largely through general-purpose principles has not yet been discredited. Historically, the debate between the opposing camps has been one about the nature of the rules that are necessary to account for the syntactic structure of language and the origins of those rules. The arguments relating to these issues were reviewed in chapter 7. In recent years, the debate has been given a new twist by the claim that syntactic regularities need not be the product of rules at all. What is of particular interest about this claim in the context of the present chapter is that rules are replaced by a connectionist architecture. Although connectionist architectures might be considered as plausible models of concepts, can they be extended to higher-level representations such as syntactic regularities?

One of the major pieces of evidence that has been used to argue that cognition is rule-based is the way in which children learn the syntactic rules of language. The acquisition of the past tense by English-speaking children is a particularly interesting example. The majority of verbs form the simple past by adding -ed to the verb stem. (These are called *weak* verbs.) There is, however, a significant minority of verbs that do not form the past tense in this way. (These are called *strong* verbs.) This minority includes most of the most frequently used verbs in English (Kucera and Francis, 1967).

Many of the child's initial verbs are strong verbs. When the past tense for these verbs is learnt, the child initially learns the correct irregular form. However, later, as more weak verbs are added to the system, the child changes from using the correct past tense forms for strong verbs to an incorrect form based on the rule for weak verbs of adding *-ed* to the verb stem. Thus, a child who had previously said *did, made, came, gave, got,* and *took* will change to saying *doed, maked, comed, gived, getted,* and *taked,* as was discussed in chapter 7. The phenomenon is very striking and is observed in all children learning English.

The usual explanation of the observed sequence of development is that the child initially learns the correct form of all verbs, both strong and weak, on an item-by-item basis. As the number of verbs represented in the child's lexicon increases, the weak verbs achieve a critical majority and the child induces a rule of past-tense formation from the majority of weak verbs: form the past tense by adding *-ed* to the verb stem. This rule is then applied to all verbs and results in the over-regularizations observed.

Rumelhart and McClelland (1986) have simulated the learning of the past tense using a model with a connectionist architecture. The model is presented with linguistic input about verbs and learns to produce the past tense as its output. Initially, the model produced the correct output for all verbs, but when further examples were presented, the model began to overregularize its output of strong verbs in a way similar to children. Of particular importance is the fact that the model did this without inducing any rule about how the past tense is formed. The model could be said to behave *as if* it had learnt the rule for the past tense.

Does Rumelhart and McClelland's simulation have any relevance to the way in which children learn verbs? Or, to put it another way, is the mechanism proposed by Rumelhart and McClelland a serious alternative to the traditional accounts based on rule induction? In order to address this issue it is necessary to consider in more detail how the model works.

Before considering the model itself, it is important to point out that any simulation model must make some simplifying assumptions in order for the simulation to be practicable. The Rumelhart and McClelland model contains a number of simplifying assumptions. The most obvious simplification is that they have produced a model that is dedicated to learning the past tense without being part of a more general language processor. Because of the model's simplicity, its input is accordingly simple: it only receives verbs as input, and then it receives them in a rather special form. We shall examine these simplifications later.   For any given verb, the model is presented with both the root form of the verb and the correct past tense form. The function of the root form is to activate the model's network. It does this by activating a set of input units, which will be described below. These units in turn generate a past tense by activating a set of output units. Exactly which output units will be activated by a given input will be determined by the model's history of learning. It is the function of the past tense form to allow the model to learn what its output should be. The model's output is compared with what would be the correct output, as provided by the past tense form. If the outputs differs from the correct form then the weights between the input and the output forms are adjusted according to a formula.

The Rumelhart and McClelland model does not contain a complete simulation of the language processing that a child would have to perform in learning verbs. It contains two important simplifications of that process. The first is that it receives only verbs as input, whereas children hear verbs in the context of many other words in continuous speech. The second simplification is that both the root and the past tense forms are presented to the model as a string of phonemes. In principle, this is similar to what a child's representation might be at some intermediate point in processing the input that is heard. However, there is deliberately no attempt to capture faithfully the child's representation of words in phonemic form. Instead, Rumelhart and McClelland derived a special phonemic representation system, for the purposes of the simulation, based on a model first proposed by Wickelgren (1969). The basic idea is that each phoneme is represented not as an individual phoneme but as the middle part of a trio that also contains the preceding and succeeding phoneme that occurred. In this way each phoneme carries information about the context of other phonemes in which it occurred. This is called a 'Wickelphone' representation. The number of possible Wickelphones is very large (assuming 35 different phonemes there are over 42,875 Wickelphones). Instead of building a network of Wickelphones, Rumelhart and McClelland achieved a compact representation by representing each Wickelphone not individually but as a distributed pattern of activation over a set of 460 feature detectors, which they called Wickelfeatures. Each Wickelphone activates 16 Wickelfeatures of the network. This is the final form of the representation. The model consists of two sets of Wickelfeatures, as shown in figure 9.3. One set represents the root form of the verb and the other set represents the past tense form.

The model works as follows. It is presented with the root form of a verb and the past tense form. From the root form the model generates a past tense form, which is a function of how strongly the Wickelfeatures activated by the root form are connected to the Wickelfeatures that represent the past tense. Each output generated is compared with the correct past tense form. If there is a discrepancy between the Wickelfeatures generated as output and the Wickelfeatures that comprise the correct output then the connection strength between the input and output units is adjusted according to a formula to increase the probability of activation

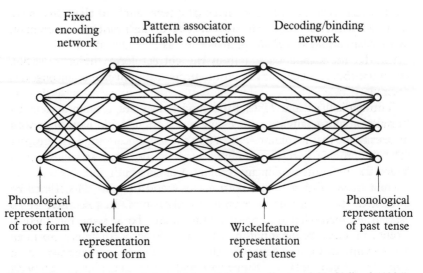

Figure 9.3   *The structure of the model used by Rumelhart and McClelland (1986) to simulate learning the past tense of verbs.*

of output units that should be activated but were not and to decrease the probability of activation of output units that should not be activated but were.

Initially all connections between the root and the past tense representations are 0. The connection strengths will change as the model learns. To simulate learning Rumelhart and McClelland first presented the model with the 10 highest frequency verbs from Kucera and Francis (1967). Eight of these verbs are, in fact, irregular. After 10 cycles of training the performance of the model was very similar to that of children in the initial stages of verb learning: it produced the correct output to a very large extent. At this point 410 medium-frequency verbs were introduced and a further 190 learning trials followed, with each trial consisting of one presentation of each of the 420 verbs. The output of the model was recorded after each trial. Finally, 86 low-frequency verbs were presented to the model and the generalization responses were recorded.

The results of these learning trials are particularly interesting. During the early phases of learning the performance of the model corresponded closely to the overregularization period of the child's learning. As the trials progress regular and irregular forms came to co-exist, as they do in the later stages of children's learning of the past tense. Rumelhart and McClelland concluded that their model 'shows, to a remarkable degree, the characteristics of young children learning the morphology of the past tense in English' (1986: p. 266) and that it provides 'a distinct alternative to the view that children learn the rules of English past-tense formation in any explicit sense' (1986: p. 267).

Clearly, the simulation is impressive and it raises a serious question about whether it is necessary to postulate that children induce unconscious or implicit rules when learning the past tense of English. Nevertheless, the simulation falls far short of showing that the conventional rule-learning account is unnecessary. We shall discuss this issue first with respect to the methodology employed in the simulation; then with respect to the representational assumptions made; and finally with respect to larger theoretical issues in the domain of language.

How should the methodology used by Rumelhart and McClelland be evaluated? It is difficult to answer this question because there is no established methodological procedure for simulations. However, there is a sense in which a simulation of a cognitive process is comparable to an experiment on a cognitive process. The purpose of an experiment on a cognitive process is to test predictions about a hypothetical process with a sample of subjects representative of a given population, employing experimental stimuli representative of a population of stimuli.

The major reason for using a sample of subjects is that the cognitive process under investigation will vary among subjects because of individual differences and because of uncontrolled effects that contribute noise to the data. In a simulation the sampling of cognitive processes (over subjects) is replaced by an explicit model of the process that is isolated and is therefore not subject to extraneous noise. This seems to me to be an entirely legitimate methodological move. Individual variability and noise have been dispelled, and therefore a model can replace the sampling of subjects. This is not to say that the model must be accepted as a legitimate model of the cognitive process but only that the procedure is methodologically sound. If the model is to be criticized it must be on theoretical rather than methodological grounds.

The model itself is only part of the process of creating a simulation. The model must be supplied with data on which it will operate. Here it seems reasonable to impose the requirement that the model receive input that is similar to what a child learning language would receive. It is clear that the input received by the Rumelhart and McClelland model differs in many respects from what a child learning English would receive. Let us consider the differences in turn.

The model receives only verbs as input. Children, on the other hand, usually hear verbs in the context of continuous speech, although they may sometimes hear isolated verbs. Thus, the general problem of identifying the verbs in continuous speech is finessed in the Rumelhart and

McClelland model. However, it is important to remember, in this context, that the model simulates only part of the cognitive process. There is no reason, in principle, why the model could not be extended to include processes that identified verbs in an input of continuous speech and then proceeded to work in the way that the rest of the model does.

The model receives its input of verbs in a representational form that is different from the input to children. The model always receives a pairing of the root and the past tense form. Children do not receive such regular pairings, although they may sometimes do so. However, there is clearly a serious discrepancy here between the input received by children and the input received by the model that cannot be resolved by in principle extensions of the model.

The model receives its learning input in two blocks, the first consisting of 10 cycles of the 10 most common verbs in Kucera and Francis (1967), and the second consisting of 190 cycles of the next 410 most frequent verbs. There are at least two issues of methodology here. The first is whether the frequencies reported by Kucera and Francis are representative of the frequencies with which verbs are heard by children. It seems unlikely, since the Kucera and Francis norms were established by sampling written text for adults. The second, and probably more substantial, issue of methodology is the manner of presentation of the verbs. Children are not suddenly introduced to hundreds of verbs at once in the environment as the model was. It would therefore be unwise to accept that the model has simulated the learning of children until it has been shown that the results obtained can be reproduced under more normal conditions of input. If we consider what is likely to have happened in the model when the second block of 410 verbs were introduced, then there is added reason for caution. Essentially, what is happening in the model is that with the sudden increase in the number of verbs on the eleventh cycle, regular forms predominate, and this dramatically changes the pattern of the mapping between the root and the past tense form such that most, if not all, Wickelfeatures in the input now have connections to the identical Wickelfeatures in the output that are stronger than any previous connection established, and most, if not all, sets of Wickelfeatures in the input strongly activate the regular -ed inflection in the output. Thus, it may be that the reproduction of the pattern of output produced by children is an artifact of the method used, and would not occur if the input received were closer to that received by children.

Let us now discuss the issues of representation raised by Rumelhart and McClelland's model. Are the assumptions about representation justifiable? At least two problems can be raised here. The first concerns the fact that the model receives only verbs as input. Let us, for the sake of argument, assume that there is a part of the cognitive system dedicated to processing only verbs. An explanation of how this system works would constitute only part of an explanation of how children learn verbs. It must also be explained how children recognize verbs in the input that they receive, such that the dedicated cognitive module receives only verbs as input. Rumelhart and McClelland do not address this issue. As was discussed in chapter 7, the issue of identifying parts of speech is by no means a trivial one for a theory of language acquisition.

The second issue concerns the phonological representation used. The input to the model consists of Wickelphones. The justification for this would, presumably, have to run along the following lines: a Wickelphone is equivalent to the representation that the cognitive system has derived at some intermediate point of information processing and is therefore a legitimate starting point to simulate the later stages of processing. It is very difficult to provide independent justification for this assumption. There is still relatively little known about how phonological information is represented by the cognitive system. A number of models attempt to encode contextual information, as Wickelgren's (1969) model does, and this aspect of the model may prove to be desirable (Klatt, 1979; Marcus, 1984). However, Wickelgren's model probably overrepresents the amount of context-sensitive coding that actually occurs; contextual information about phonemes may be restricted to within-syllable groups (Segui, 1984). In addition, there is the more general issue that Rumelhart and McClelland assume that there is a complete pattern of phoneme representation available at some intermediate stage of input. There may be, but it will have to be part of the explanation of language processing how it is derived rather than an assumption to be taken for granted. Phoneme detection is a considerable task for the linguistic system. We do not actually hear all speech elements; some must be inferred from their context of occurrence. Paradoxically, a more detailed connectionist model than that presented by Rumelhart and McClelland could provide an explanation for just this phenomenon, because connectionist models seem to be powerful in explaining how a complete pattern can be created from a fragment of the input. However, this assumes operating with a different representation of the input than the one assumed in the model of verb learning.

Pinker and Prince (1988) raise a number of general theoretical objections to the Rumelhart and McClelland model of verb learning. The criticisms are important because they highlight the grounds for debate between a connectionist approach to language and a more conventional rule-based symbolic approach. The criticisms are extensive and it is not possible to do justice to them in a summary here. Instead, I shall focus on just two issues. The first simply illustrates how the nature of what is to be explained can seem different from different perspectives. The second concerns the role of symbols in an information processing architecture, which is an issue of central importance in considering the role of connectionist models in explanations of cognition.

Pinker and Prince object that Rumelhart and McClelland have represented some properties as local to verbs that are, in fact, more general properties of the language module. The irregular forms of the past tense is a case in point. The strong verbs of English are not irregular in a random way; the verbs that will be irregular are largely predictable from their root form and their irregular past tense form is also predictable. This is so because the irregular past tense forms obey general phonological principles that hold for word inflections across all parts of speech. The assumption behind this criticism is that the irregular past tense forms are derived by the child from some more general phonological rules that already exist. This is certainly a possibility, but it is not the only one. It is also possible that the general phonological rules do not exist prior to learning the past tense of verbs and that the rules are in fact a later induction from the mappings that are formed locally while learning morphological relations in such sub-domains as past tense forms.

An objection raised by Pinker and Prince that goes deeper to the heart of the issue about the relation between connectionist and conventional symbolic models of information processing is the status of words in the Rumelhart and McClelland model. In the Rumelhart and McClelland model there is no unit for a word. Words are simply distributed patterns of representations. Pinker and Prince object that words as explicit representations play a crucial role in many linguistic phenomena. In particular, Pinker and Prince draw attention to the fact that the notion of a lexical item as something that can be operated upon by other linguistic procedures of grammar, morphology, and so forth, has no place in the model. This is certainly true, and no proposals are put forward as to how it is envisaged that a connectionist model would deal with operations performed upon lexical units. More generally, there is the issue of whether connectionist models and symbol-processing accounts are totally incompatible systems.

It has been suggested in this chapter that a connectionist architecture provides a plausible account of the formation and structure of concepts and the associative character of memory. These are important basics of a cognitive system, but there is a great deal more besides. In particular, there are the domain-specific representations and procedures that are the chief feature of cognitive development. To date there have been few attempts to explain any of these 'higher' cognitive functions using connectionist models. Theorizing about these functions is still exclusively in terms of symbolic representations and procedures that act on these representations. This division may occur for one of two major reasons. The first is that connectionist theorists have not yet had time to develop models for these phenomena. The second is that connectionist models are not applicable at higher levels of the cognitive system. It seems to me that it is one of the major issues for a theory of information processing to work out whether or not connectionist models and symbolic models can co-exist as part of a common architecture.

As an example of the fact that connectionist and symbolic models of cognition may not be incompatible, let us reconsider briefly the McClelland and Rumelhart (1981) model of reading discussed in chapter 8. The model was a forerunner of connectionist models, which contains some clear connectionist principles, but also uses symbolic representations. In the model, letters are constructed out of features that form an interconnected network along connectionist principles. Each feature unit has inputs to letter units at the next level of the hierarchy. A given feature unit will send excitatory signals to any letter unit that contains that feature. Thus, a given feature will send excitatory signals not only to the letter that contained the feature but also to any other letter that contains the same feature. However, the letters themselves are not simply a pattern of activation over a set of feature units. The individual letters are represented as units (and therefore as symbols) one level higher in the processing hierarchy. This level also forms an interconnected network along connectionist principles, which activates word units at the next highest level in the hierarchy.

It may be that such a layered approach to the architecture of cognition is a potential means to integrate symbolic and distributed representations. Each symbol is the product of a distributed representation at the next lowest level in the hierarchy. Such a system has the advantage that it combines the benefits of bottom-up activation by sensory input, together with top-down control from higher levels. In fact, these are very similar to the principles that underlie the McClelland and Rumelhart (1981) model of word recognition. Thus, a letter, for example, can be activated top-down as a symbol by a higher-level unit as well as bottom-up by activation of the features that constitute the word (but see Seidenberg and McClelland (1989) for a model that dispenses with explicit representation of symbols).

What and *How*: A Last Pass

The fundamental questions for a theory of cognitive development are *what develops?* and *how does development occur?* I have argued that what develops are representations and procedures to support tasks and domains. I have also argued that these developments can only properly be understood within the context of a theory of the architecture of cognition; it is necessary to have a theory of the architecture in order to have a theory of how development occurs. The architecture of the cognitive system does not itself change, it provides the foundation for development and change. In this chapter I have tried to discuss some of the fragments of that architecture. I have suggested that a connectionist architecture provides a solid foundation for conceptual development, both from a representational perspective and from a learning perspective. This architecture ensures that an organism continually adapts its representations as a function of its experience in its environment because the weights of connections are continually adjusted. But the adjustments are small, and thus conceptual representations change gradually rather than dramatically. This seems to fit well the natural course of development. Connectionist architectures also embody one of the major architectural mechanisms required by the cognitive system: association. However, current connectionist models are not a complete specification of a cognitive architecture, as I have attempted to indicate. Although they seem to provide a useful account of the subsymbolic architecture of cognition, they do not provide an equally useful account of symbolic representations. One of the key issues for future theories is to provide an integrated account of the subsymbolic and symbolic levels of cognition. At the symbolic level of cognition, by which I mean the level at which symbols with semantic content are manipulated, there is a compelling need for greater discussion of the mechanisms by which the cognitive system operates.

One of the clear architectural implications of the symbolic approach to information processing is the limited resources available for deliberate information processing. Much of development can be seen as the construction of efficient representations and procedures to overcome the resource limitations of the information processing system. One of the means by which this is postulated to occur is by chunking. Chunking is the mechanism by which representations and procedures that regularly occur together come to be accessed together automatically. Chunking items together is, for example, the way to overcome the limit of retaining about seven elements of information in working memory. Chunking is not particularly easy to study experimentally, and so it has not featured prominently in theories of cognitive development. However, it is commonly employed as a learning mechanism in simulations of cognitive development. In the Soar architecture (Laird, Newell and Rosenbloom, 1987; Laird, Rosenbloom and Newell, 1986; Newell, 1990), in which information processing is modelled as a production system, chunking is the single mechanism of learning employed. In Soar, productions that cooccur under certain conditions are simply chunked together. Like many symbolic simulations of learning, this method is likely to create learning that is unrealistically rapid. However, it may be possible to obtain the same effect in more realistic time by seeing chunking not as a mechanism itself, but as an outcome of the mechanism of association. Consider a set of procedures that operate in series in order to perform a task. Now assume that every time that one procedure follows another when carrying out the task, the associative link between the procedures is increased. As the link is strengthened over time, the operation of one procedure will increasingly lead to the automatic operation of the next procedure. The end result will be equivalent to what is called *chunking* but no mechanism of chunking is involved. In fact, there is no reason why a connectionist architecture could not explain the phenomenon of chunking in a suitable timescale.

One of the barriers that any novice faces in mastering a complex task without guidance is discovering which procedures are effective. It is possible to hit upon a solution but not be able to recreate the steps that led to it. Children are likely to find themselves in this situation more than most, and often face the added difficulty of not recognizing a solution when it occurs. There are two possible ways through these difficulties: monitoring one's own behaviour and guidance. The importance of monitoring has received considerable emphasis in recent theories of cognitive development. What has perhaps received less emphasis is the extent to which children fail to monitor good procedures but can easily be induced to do so simply by being told that the procedure is effective. Experiments reported in chapter 5 on memory development and chapter 6 on number development can be used to illustrate this. Keeney et al. (1967) trained children to rehearse when asked to recall. Rehearsal improved performance but the procedure was abandoned by the children after the training trials and on subsequent testing performance deteriorated to, its pre-training level. Kennedy and Miller (1976) also trained children to rehearse. They also obtained improved recall during training but this time the procedure was maintained after training. The crucial difference between the two experiments was that Kennedy and Miller provided the children with feedback that rehearsal was improving their performance, while Keeney et al did not. The children were, apparently, unable to monitor the change in performance themselves.

Michie (1984b) conducted an experiment that has similar implications. She examined the use of counting by 3- to 4-year-olds in reasoning about the relative numerosity of two arrays. She found that children rarely counted spontaneously when judging which of two rows had more although they could easily be induced to do so, and accuracy of judgement improved significantly when the children did count. If the children were given feedback on the effect of counting on performance, then they tended to maintain the procedure beyond the experimental situation. Michie concluded that young children do not deploy counting because they are not aware of its value as a strategy in number reasoning. When provided with guidance on the effectiveness of the strategy they are likely to maintain it.

Guidance is widely employed in both adult–child and child–child interaction. It can be a powerful means of learning because it focuses on only the procedures that are essential to solving the task. However, there is more to guidance than simply demonstrating how it should be done, as anyone who has tried to teach a skill to anyone else (not necessarily a child) can testify. Guidance works best when the tutor has a model of how the skill to be imparted can be decomposed into components that the learner can master individually and assemble together. Knowing what a learner can master is itself a complex task. Tackling these issues brings us to the application front of developmental theory. It is only when we understand the basic processes of development that we will have an effective application of developmental theory to issues such as learning difficulties.

References

Abramov, I., Gordon, J., Hendrickson, A., Hainline, L., Dobson, V., & La Bossiere, E. (1982). The retina of the newborn human infant. *Science, 217,* 265–7.

Abravanel, E., & Sigafoos, A. O. (1984). Exploring the presence of imitation during early infancy. *Child Development, 55,* 381–92.

Acredolo, C., & Acredolo, L. P. (1979). Identity, compensation, and conservation. *Child Development, 50.* 524–35.

Acredelo, L. P. (1978). Development of spatial orientation in infancy. *Developmental Psychology, 141,* 224–34.

Alegria, J., & Noirot, E. (1978). Neonate orientation behavior toward human voice. *International Journal of Behavioral Development, 1,* 291–312.

Allen, J. (1978). Visual acuity development in human infants up to 6 months of age. Unpublished doctoral dissertation. University of Washington.

Allport, G. W., & Postman, L. (1947). *The Psychology of Rumor.* New York: Henry Holt.

Ames, A. (1951). Visual perception and the rotating trapezoidal window. *Psychological Mongraphs, 65* (1, Whole. No. 324).

Anderson, J. R. (1983). *The Architecture of Cognition.* Cambridge, MA: Harvard University Press.

Anderson, J. R., & Bower, G. H. (1973). *Human Associative Memory.* Washington, DC: Winston.

Anderson, N. H., & Cuneo, D. O. (1978). The height and width rule in children's judgements of equality. *Journal of Experimental Psychology, 107,* 335–78.

Appel, L. F., Cooper, R. B., McCarrell, N., Sims-Knight, J., Yussen, S. R., & Flavell, J. H. (1972). The development of the distinction between perceiving and memorizing. *Child Development, 43,* 1365–81.

Aronson, E., & Rosenbloom, S. (1971). Space perception within a common auditory-visual space. *Science, 172,* 1161–3.

Aslin, R. N. (1977). Development of binocular fixation in human infants. *Journal of Experimental Child Psychology, 23,* 133–50.

Aslin, R. N., Pisoni, D. B., & Jusczyk, P. W. (1983). Auditory development and speech perception in infancy. In P. H. Mussen (Ed.), *Handbook of Child Psychology, Vol. II: Infancy and Developmental Psychobiology*. New York: Wiley.

Atkinson, J., & Braddick, O. (1976). Stereoscopic discrimination in infants. *Perception, 5*, 29–38.

Atkinson, J., Braddick, O., & Moar, K. (1977). Development of contrast sensitivity over the first 3 months of life in the human infant. *Vision Research, 17*, 1037–44.

Atkinson, R. C., & Shiffrin, R. M. (1968). Human memory: A proposed system and its control processes. In K. W. Spence & J. T. Spence (Eds), *Advances in the Psychology of Learning and Motivation, Vol. 2*. New York: Academic Press.

Atkinson, R. C., & Shiffrin, R. M. (1971). The control of short-term memory. *Scientific American, 225(2)*, 82–90.

Au, T. K., & Markman, E. M. (1987). Acquiring word meanings via linguistic contrast. *Cognitive Development, 2*, 217–36.

Backman, J. E., Mamen, M., & Ferguson, H. B. (1984). Reading level design: Conceptual and methodological issues in reading research. *Psychological Bulletin, 96*, 560–8.

Baddeley, A. D. (1976). *The Psychology of Memory*. New York: Basic Books.

Baddeley, A. D., Ellis, N. C., Miles, T. R., & Lewis, V. J. (1982). Developmental and acquired dyslexia: A comparison. *Cognition, 11*, 185–99.

Baddeley, A. D., & Hitch, G. (1974).; Working Memory. In G. H. Bower (Ed.), *Recent Advances in Learning and Motivation, Vol. 8*. New York: Academic Press.

Baggett, R. (1979). Structurally equivalent stories in movies and text and the effect of the medium on recall. *Journal of Verbal Learning and Verbal Behavior, 18*, 333–56.

Bahrick, L. E., Walker, A. S., & Neisser, U. (1981). Selective looking by infants. *Cognitive Psychology, 13*, 377–90.

Bahrick, H. P., Bahrick, P. O., & Wittlinger, R. P. (1975). Fifty Years of memory for names and faces: A cross-sectional approach. *Journal of Experimental Psychology: General, 104*, 54–75.

Baillargeon, R. (1986). Representing the existence and the location of hidden objects. *Cognition, 23*, 21–41.

Baldwin, J. M. (1895). *Mental Development in the Child and the Race: Methods and Processes*. New York: Macmillan.

Ball, W., & Tronick, E. (1971). Infant responses to impending collision: Optical and real. *Science, 171*, 818–20.

Banks, M. S. (1980). The development of visual accommodation during early infancy. *Child Development, 51*, 646–66.

Banks, M. S., & Ginsburg, A. P. (1985). Infant visual preferences: A review and new theoretical treatment. In H. W. Reese (Ed), *Advances in Child Development and Behavior, Vol. 19*. New York: Academic Press.

Banks, M. S., & Salapatek, P. (1978). Acuity and contrast sensitivity in 1-2-, and 3-month-old human infants. *Investigative Opthalmology and Visual Science, 17*, 361–5.

Banks, M. S., & Salapatek, P. (1981). Infant pattern vision: A new approach based on the contrast sensitivity function. *Journal of Experimental Child Psychology, 31*, 1–45.

Banks, M. S., & Salapatek, P. (1983). Infant visual perception. In P. H. Mussen (Ed.), *Handbook of Child Psychology, Vol II: Infancy and Developmental Psychobiology*. New York: Wiley.

Baron, J. (1979). Orthographic and word-specific mechanisms in children's reading of words. *Child Development, 50*, 60–72.

Baron, J., & Strawson, C. (1976). Use of orthographic and word-specific knowledge in reading words aloud. *Journal of Experimental Psychology: Human Perception and Performance, 2*, 386–93.

Barr, R. (1974). The effect of instruction on pupil reading strategies. *Reading Research Quarterly, 10*, 555–82.

Barrett, M. D. (1978). Lexical development and overextension in child language. *Journal of Child Language, 5*, 205–19.

Barrett, M. D. (1982). Distinguishing between prototypes: The early acquisition of the meaning of object names. In. S. A. Kuczaj (Ed.), *Language Development, Vol. 1*. New York: Springer-Verlag.

Bartlett, F. C. (1932). *Remembering*. Cambridge: Cambridge University Press.

Bates, E., & MacWhinney, B. (1982). Functionalist approaches to grammar. In E. Wanner & L. R. Gleitman (Eds), *Language Acquisition: The State of the Art*. Cambridge: Cambridge University Press.

Bechtoldt, H. P., & Hutz, C. S. (1979). Stereopsis in young infants and stereopsis in an infant with congenital esotropia. *Journal of Pediatric Opthalmology, 16*, 49–54.

Beckner, M. (1959). *The Biological Way of Thought*. New York: Columbia University Press.

Beckwith, M., & Restle, F. (1966). Processes of enumeration. *Psychological Review, 73*, 437–44.

Beilin, H. (1968). Cognitive capacities of young children. A replication. *Science, 162*, 920–21.

Belmont, J. M., & Butterfield, E. C. (1969). The relations of short-term memory to development and intelligence. In L. P. Lipsett & H. W. Reese (Eds), *Advances in Child Development and Behavior, Vol. 4*. New York: Academic Press.

Berg, W. K., & Berg, K. M. (1979). Psychophysiological development in infancy. State, sensory function, and attention. In J. D. Osofsky (Ed.). *Handbook of Infant Development*. New York: Wiley.

Berko, J. (1958). The child's learning of English morphology. *Word, 14*, 150–77.

Berliner, L., & Barbieri, M. K. (1984). The testimony of the child victim of sexual assault. *Journal of Social Issues, 40*, 125–37.

Bernard, J., & Sontag, L. W. (1947). Fetal reactivity to tonal stimulation: A preliminary report. *Journal of Genetic Psychology, 70*, 205–10.

Bertenthal, B. I., Campos, J. J., & Haith, M. M. (1980). Development of visual organization: The perception of subjective contours. *Child Development*, *51*, 1072–80.

Bertoncini, J., & Mehler, J. (1981). Syllables as units in infant perception. *Infant Behavior and Development*, *4*, 247–60.

Bever, T. G., Mehler, J., & Epstein, J. (1968). What children do in spite of what they know. *Science*, *162*, 921–4.

Biemiller, A. J. (1970). The development of the use of graphic and contextual information as children learn to read. *Reading Research Quarterly*, *6*, 75–96.

Bijou, S., & Baer, D. (1961). *Child Development: A Systematic and Empirical Theory*. New York: Apleton-Century-Crofts.

Binet, A. (1890). Perceptions d'enfants. *Revue Philosophique*, *30*, 582–611.

Binet, A., & Henri, V. (1894). La Mémoire des phrases (mémoire des idées). *L'Année Psychologique*, *1*, 24–59.

Binet, A., & Simon, T. (1905). Application des méthodes nouvelles diagnostic de niveau intellectual chez des enfants normaux et anormaux d'hospice et d'ecole primaire. *L'Année Psychologique*, *11*, 245–336.

Binet, A., & Simon, T. (1908). Le développement de l'intelligence chex les enfants. *L'Année Psychologique*, *14*, 1–94.

Bjorklund, D. F., & Jacobs, J. W. (1985). Associative and categorical processes in children's memory: The role of automaticity in the development of organization in free recall. *Journal of Experimental Child Psychology*, *39*, 599–617.

Black, M. & Chiat, S. (1981). Psycholinguistics without 'psychological reality'. *Linguistics*, *19*, 37–61.

Blakemore, C., & Van Sluyters, R. C. (1975). Innate and environmental factors in the development of the kitten's visual cortex. *Journal of Physiology*, *261*, 423–44.

Blaney, R. L., & Winograd, E. (1978). Developmental differences in children's recognition memory for faces. *Developmental Psychology*, *14*, 441–2.

Bloom, L. (1970). *Language Development: Form and Function in Emerging Grammars*. Cambridge, MA: MIT Press.

Bloom, L. M. (1973). *One Word at a Time*. The Hague: Mouton.

Bloom, L., Lightbown, D., & Hood, L. (1975). Structure and variation in child language. *Monographs of the Society for Research in Child Development*, *40*, (2, Serial No. 160).

Bomba, P. C., & Siqueland, E. R. (1983). The nature and structure of infant form categories. *Journal of Experimental Child Psychology*, *35*, 295–328.

Borkowski, J. G., Levers, S., & Gruenenfelder, T. M. (1976). Transfer of mediational strategies in children: The role of activity and awareness during strategy acquisition. *Child Development*, *47*, 779–86.

Borstelmann, L. J. (1983). Children before psychology: Ideas about children from antiquity to the late 1800s. In P. H. Mussen (Ed.), *Handbook of Child Psychology. Vol. I: History, Theory, and Methods*. New York: Wiley.

Bower, G. H., Black, J. B., & Turner, T. J. (1979). Scripts in memory for text. *Cognitive Psychology*, *11*, 177–220.

Bower, T. G. R. (1966). The visual world of infants. *Scientific American*, *215(6)*, 80–92.

Bower, T. G. R. (1967). The development of object-permanence: Some studies of existence constancy. *Perception and Psychophysics*, *2*, 411–18.

Bower, T. G. R. (1974). *Development in Infancy*. San Francisco: W. H. Freeman.

Bower, T. G. R., Broughton, J. M., & Moore, M. K. (1970a). Demonstration of intention in the reaching behaviour of neonate humans. *Nature*, *228*, 679–81.

Bower, T. G. R., Broughton, J. M., & Moore, M. K. (1970b). The co-ordination of vision and tactual input in infancy. *Perception and Psychophysics*, *8*, 51–3.

Bower, T. G. R., Broughton, J. M. & Moore, M. K. (1971a). Development of the object concept as manifested in the tracking behaviour of infants between 7 and 20 weeks of age. *Journal of Experimental Child Psychology*, *11*, 182–93.

Bower, T. G. R., Broughton, J. M., & Moore, M. K. (1971b). Infant responses to approaching objects: An indication of response to distal variables. *Perception and Psychophysics*, *9*, 193–96.

Bower, T. G. R., & Patterson, J. G. (1973). The separation of place, movement and object in the world of the infant. *Journal of Experimental Child Psychology*, *15*, 161–8.

Bower, T. G. R., & Wishart, J. G. (1972). The effects of motor skill on object permanence. *Cognition*, *1*, 165–71.

Bowerman, M. (1973). *Early Syntactic Development: A Cross-Linguistic Study with Special Reference to Finnish*. Cambridge: Cambridge University Press.

Bowerman, M. (1985). What shapes children's grammars? In D. I. Slobin (Ed.), *The Crosslinguistic Study of Language Acquisition. Vol. 2: Theoretical Issues*. Hillsdale, NJ: Erlbaum.

Bowerman, M. (1987). Commentary: Mechanisms of language acquisition. In B. MacWhinney (Ed.), *Mechanisms of Language Acqusition*. Hillsdale, NJ: Erlbaum.

Braddick, O., Atkinson, J., French, J., & Howland, H. C. (1979). A photorefractive study of infant accommodation. *Vision Research*, *19*, 1319–30.

Bradley, L., & Bryant, P. (1978). Difficulties in auditory organisation as a possible cause of reading backwardness. *Nature*, *271*, 746–7.

Bradley, L., & Bryant, P. (1983). Categorising sounds and learning to read: a causal connexion. *Nature*, *301*, 419–21.

Bradley, L., & Bryant, P. (1985). *Rhyme and Reason in Reading and Spelling*. Ann Arbor, MI: University of Michigan Press.

Braine, M. D. S. (1963). The ontogeny of English phrase structure: The first phase. *Language*, *39*, 1–13.

Braine, M. D. S. (1976). Children's first word combinations. *Monographs of the Society for Research in Child Development*, *41*, (1, Serial No. 164).

Brainerd, C. J. (1973). Judgements and explanations as criteria for the presence of cognitive structures. *Psychological Bulletin*, *79*, 172–9.

Brainerd, C. J. (1977). Feedback, rule knowledge, and conservation learning. *Child Development*, *48*, 404–11.

Brainerd, C. J. (1978a). *Piaget's Theory of Intelligence*. Englewood Cliffs, NJ: Prentice-Hall.

Brainerd, C. J. (1978b). The stage question in cognitive-developmental theory. *Behavioral and Brain Sciences, 1*, 173–82.

Brainerd, C. J., & Hooper, F. H. (1975). A methodological analysis of developmental studies of identity conservation and equivalence conservation. *Psychological Bulletin, 82*, 725–37.

Bremner, J. G. (1978a). Spatial errors made by infants: inadequate spatial cues or evidence for egocentrism. *British Journal of Psychology, 69*, 77–84.

Bremner, J. G. (1978b). Egocentric versus allocentric coding in nine-month-old infants: factors influencing the choice of code. *Developmental Psychology, 14*, 346–55.

Brennan, W., Ames, E. W., & Moore, R. W. (1966). Age differences in infants' attention to patterns of difference complexities. *Science, 151*, 354–6.

Bresnan, J., & Kaplan, R. M. (1982). Introduction: Grammars as mental representations of language. In J. Bresnan (Ed.), *The Mental Representation of Grammatical Relations*. Cambridge, MA: MIT Press.

Broadbent, D. E. (1958). *Perception and Communication*. London: Pergamon Press.

Brown, A. L. (1980). Metacognitive development and reading. In R. J. Spiro, B. Bruce, & W. Brewer (Ed.), *Theoretical Issues in Reading Comprehension*. Hillsdale, NJ: Erlbaum.

Brown, A. L., Bransford, J. D., Ferrara, R. A., & Campione, J. C. (1983). Learning, remembering, and understanding. In P. H. Mussen (Ed.), *Handbook of Child Psychology, Vol. 3: Cognitive Development*. New York: Wiley.

Brown, A. L., & Campione, J. C. (1972). Recognition memory of perceptually similar pictures in preschool children. *Journal of Experimental Child Psychology, 95*, 55–62.

Brown, A. L., & Day, J. D. (1983). Macrorules for summarizing text: The development of expertise. *Journal of Verbal Learning and Verbal Behavior, 22*, 1–14.

Brown, A. L., & Scott, M. S. (1971). Recognition memory for pictures in preschool children. *Journal of Experimental Child Psychology, 11*, 401–12.

Brown, A. L., & Smiley, S. S. (1977). Rating the importance of structural units of prose passages: A problem of metacognitive development. *Child Development, 48*, 1–8.

Brown, A. L., & Smiley, S. S. (1978). The development of strategies for studying texts. *Child Development, 49*, 1076–88.

Brown, A. L., Smiley, S. S., & Lawton, S. C. (1978). The effects of experience on the selection of suitable retrieval cues for studying texts. *Child Development, 49*, 829–35.

Brown, J. S., & Burton, R. R. (1978). Diagnostic models for procedural bugs in basic mathematical skills. *Cognitive Science, 2*, 155–92.

Brown, J. S., Van Lehn, K. (1980). Repair theory: A generative theory of bugs in procedural skills. *Cognitive Science, 4*, 379–426.

Brown, R. (1957). Linguistic determinism and the part of speech. *Journal of Abnormal and Social Psychology*, *55*, 1–5.

Brown, R. (1958). How shall a thing be called? *Psychological Review*, *65*, 14–21.

Brown, R. (1973a). *A First Language*. Cambridge, MA: Harvard University Press.

Brown, R. (1973b). Development of the first language in the human species. *American Psychologist*, *28*, 97–106.

Brown, R., & Bellugi, U. (1964). Three processe in the acquisition of syntax. *Harvard Educational Review*, *34*, 133–51.

Brown, R., & Fraser, C. (1963). The acquisition of syntax. In C. Cofer & B. Musgrave (Eds), *Verbal Behavior and Learning: Problems and Processes*. New York: McGraw-Hill.

Bruner, J. S. (1966). On the conservation of liquids. In J. S. Bruner, R. R. Olver, P. M. Greenfield, et al. *Studies in Cognitive Growth*. New York: Wiley.

Bruner, J. S., Goodnow, J., & Austin, G. A. (1956). *A Study of Thinking*. New York: Wiley.

Bruner, J. S., & Koslowski, B. (1972). Visually preadapted constituents of manipulatory action. *Perception*, *1*, 3–14.

Bruner, J. S., Olver, R. R., Greenfield, P. M., et al. (1966). *Studies in Cognitive Growth*. New York: Wiley.

Bryant, P., & Bradley, L. (1985). *Children's Reading Problems*. Oxford: Blackwell.

Bryant, P., & Goswami, U. (1986). Strengths and weaknesses of reading level design: A comment on Backman, Mamen, and Ferguson. *Psychological Bulletin*, *100*, 101–3.

Bryant, P., & Impey, L. (1986). The similarities between normal readers and developmental and acquired dyslexics. *Cognition*, *24*, 121–37.

Bryant, P., Jones, P., Claxton, V., & Perkins, J. (1972). Recognition of shapes across modalities by infants. *Nature*, *240*, 303–4.

Butterfield, E., & Siperstein, G. N. (1972). Influence of contingent auditory stimulation upon non-nutritive suckle. In J. Bosma (Ed.), *Third Symposium on Oral Sensation and Perception: The Mouth of the Infant*. Springfield, IL: Charles C. Thomas.

Butterworth, G. (1975). Object identity in infancy: The interaction of spatial location codes in determining search errors. *Child Development*, *46*, 866–70.

Butterworth, G. (1977). Object disappearance and error in Paiget's stage IV task. *Journal of Experimental Child Psychology*, *23*, 391–401.

Butterworth, G., & Castillo, M. (1976). Co-ordination of auditory and visual proprioception in newborn human infants. *Perception*, *5*, 155–60.

Butterworth, G., Jarrett, N. & Hicks, L. (1982). Spatio-temporal identity in infancy: perceptual competence or conceptual deficit. *Developmental Psychology*, *18*, 435–49.

Bybee, J. L., & Slobin, D. I. (1982). Rules and schemas in the development and use of the English past tense. *Language*, *58*, 265–89.

Byrne, B., & Shea, P. (1979). Semantic and phonetic memory codes in beginning readers. *Memory and Cognition*, *7*, 333–8.

Cairns, R. B. (1983). The emergence of developmental psychology. In P. H. Mussen (Ed.), *Handbook of Child Psychology, Vol. I: History, Theory, and Methods*. New York: Wiley.

Calfee, R., Lindamood, P., & Lindamood, C. (1973). Acoustic-phonetic skills and reading: Kindergarten through twelfth grade. *Journal of Educational Psychology, 64*, 293–8.

Calhoun, L. G. (1971). Number conservation in very young children: The effect of age and mode of responding. *Child Development, 42*, 561–72.

Callanan, M. A., & Markman, E. M. (1982). Principles of organization in young children's natural language hierarchies. *Child Development, 53*, 1093–101.

Campos, J. J., Hiatt, S., Ramsay, D., Henderson, C., & Svejda, M. (1978). The emergence of fear on the visual cliff. In M. Lewis & L. A. Rosenblum (Eds), *The Development of Affect, Vol. 1*. New York: Plenum.

Campos, J., Langer, A., & Krowitz, A. (1970). Cardiac responses on the visual cliff in prelocomotor human infants. *Science, 170*, 195–6.

Carey, S. (1985). *Conceptual Change in Childhood*. Cambridge, MA: MIT Press.

Carey, S., & Bartlett, E., (1978). Acquiring a single new world. *Papers and Reports on Child Language Development, 15*, 17–29.

Carey, S., & Diamond, R. (1977). From piecemeal to configurational representation of faces. *Science, 195*, 312–14.

Carey, S., Diamond, R., & Woods, B. (1980). Development of face recognition – a maturational component? *Developmental Psychology, 16*, 257–69.

Caron, A. J., Caron, R. F., & Carlson, V. R. (1979). Infant perception of the invariant shape of an object varying in slant. *Child Development, 50*, 716–21.

Case, R., Kurland, M., & Goldberg, J. (1982). Operational efficiency and the growth of short-term memory span. *Journal of Experimental Child Psychology, 33*, 386–404.

Cavanaugh, J. C., & Borkowski, J. G. (1979). The metamemory–memory 'connection': Effects of strategy training and transfer. *Journal of General Psychology, 101*, 161–74.

Cavanaugh, J. C., & Borkowski, J. G. (1980). Searching for metamemory-memory connections: A developmental study. *Developmental Psychology, 16*, 441–53.

Cavanaugh, J. C., & Perlmutter, M. (1982). Metamemory: A critical examination. *Child Development, 53*, 11–28.

Cazden, C. B. (1968). The acquisition of noun and verb inflections. *Child Development, 39*, 433–48.

Ceci, S. J., Ross, D. F., & Toglia, M. P. (1987). Suggestibility of children's memory: Psycholegal implications. *Journal of Experimental Psychology: General, 116*. 38–49.

Chance, J. E., & Goldstein, A. G. (1984). Face-recognition memory: Implications for children's eyewitness testimony; *Journal of Social Issues, 40*, 69–85.

Chance, J. E., Turner, A. L., & Goldstein, A. G. (1982). Development of differential recognition for own- and other-race faces. *Journal of Psychology, 112*, 29–37.

Chi, M. T. H. (1976). Short-term memory limitations in children: Capacity or processing deficits? *Memory and Cognition, 4,* 559–72.

Chi, M. T. H. (1977). Age differences in memory span. *Journal of Experimental Child Psychology, 23,* 266–81.

Chi, M. T. H. (1978). Knowledge structures and memory development. In R.S. Siegler (Ed.), *Children's Thinking: What Develops?* Hillsdale, NJ: Erlbaum.

Chi, M. T. H., Glaser, R., & Rees, E. (1982). Expertise in problem solving. In R. J. Sternberg (Ed.), *Advances in the Psychology of Human Intelligence, Vol. 1.* Hillsdale, NJ: Erlbaum.

Chi, M. T. H., & Koeske, R. D. (1983). Network representation of a child's dinosaur knowledge. *Developmental Psychology, 19,* 29–39.

Chomsky, N. (1957). *Syntactic Structures.* The Hague: Mouton.

Chomsky, N. (1959). Review of 'Verbal Behavior' by B. F. Skinner. *Language. 35,* 26–58.

Chomsky, N. (1965). *Aspects of the Theory of Syntax.* Cambridge, MA: MIT Press.

Chomsky, N. (1968). *Language and Mind.* New York: Harcourt, Brace, & World.

Chomsky, N. (1980). Rules and representations. *Behavioral and Brain Sciences, 3,* 1–61.

Chromiak, W., & Weisberg, R. W. (1981). The role of the object concept in visual tracking: Child-like errors in adults. *Journal of Experimental Child Psychology, 32,* 531–43.

Churchland, P. S. (1986). *Neurophilosophy: Towards a Unified Science of the Mind/Brain.* Cambridge, MA: MIT Press.

Clark, E. V. (1973). What's in a word? On the child's acquisition of semantics in his first language. In T. E. Moore (Ed.), *Cognitive Development and the Acquisition of Language.* New York: Academic Press.

Clark, E. V. (1983). Meanings and concepts. In P. H. Mussen (Ed.), *Handbook of Child Psychology, Vol. III: Cognitive Development.* New York: Wiley.

Clark, E. V. (1987). The principle of contrast: A constraint on language acquistion. In B. MacWhinney (Ed.), *Mechanisms of Language Acquisition.* Hillsdale, NJ: Erlbaum.

Clifton, R. K., Morrongiello, B. A., Kulig, J. W., & Dowd, J. M. (1981). Newborns' orientation toward sound: Possible implications for cortical development. *Child Development, 53,* 833–8.

Clifton, R. K., & Nelson, M. N. (1976). Developmental study of habituation in infants: The importance of paradigm, response system, and state. In T. J. Tighe and R. N. Leaton (Eds), *Habituation: Perspectives from Child Development, Animal Behavior, and Neurophysiology.* Hillsdale, NJ: Erlbaum.

Cohen, L. B., DeLoache, J. S., & Pearl, R. A. (1977). An examination of interference effects in infants' memory for faces. *Child Development, 48,* 88–96.

Cohen, R. L., & Harnick, M. A. (1980). The susceptibility of child witnesses to suggestion. *Law and Human Behavior, 4,* 201–10.

Collins, A. M., & Loftus, E. F. (1975). A spreading activation theory of semantic processing. *Psychologicial Review*, *82*, 407–28.

Collins, A. M., & Quillian, M. R. (1969). Retrieval time from semantic memory. *Journal of Verbal Learning and Verbal Behavior*, *8*, 240–7.

Collis, G. M. (1977). Visual co-orientation and maternal speech. In H. R. Schaffer (Ed.), *Studies in Mother-Infant Interaction*. London: Academic Press.

Collis, G. M., & Schaffer, H. R. (1975). Synchronization of visual attention in mother-infant pairs. *Journal of Child Psychology and Psychiatry*, *16*, 315–20.

Coltheart, M., Masterson, J., Byng, S., Prior, M., & Riddoch, J. (1983). Surface dyslexia. *Quarterly Journal of Experimental Psychology*, *35*, 469–95.

Coltheart, M., Patterson, K. E., & Marshall, J. C. (Eds), (1980). *Deep Dyslexia*. London: Routledge & Kegan Paul.

Condry, S. M., Halton, M., & Neisser, U. (1977). Infant sensitivity to audiovisual discrepancy: A failure to replicate. *Bulletin of the Psychonomic Society*, *9*, 431–2.

Cook, T. D., & Campbell, D. T. (1979). *Quasi-Experimentation: Design and Analysis Issues for Field Settings*. Chicago, Ill.: Rand McNally.

Conrad, R. (1964). Acoustic confusion in immediate memory. *British Journal of Psychology*, *55*, 75–84.

Conrad, R. (1971). The chronology of the development of covert speech in children. *Developmental Psychology*, *5*, 398–405.

Coren, S., Porac, C., & Ward, L. M. (1978). *Sensation and Perception*. New York: Academic Press.

Corman, H. H., & Escalona, S. K. (1969). Stages of sensorimotor development: A replication study. *Merrill-Palmer Quarterly*, *15*, 351–61.

Cornell, E. H. (1979). The effects of cue reliability on infants' manual search. *Journal of Experimental Child Psychology*, *28*, 81–91.

Corsale, K. (1978). Factors affecting children's use of organization in recall. Unpublished doctoral dissertation. University of North Carolina at Chapel Hill.

Corsale, K., & Ornstein, P. A. (1980). Developmental changes in children's use of semantic information in recall. *Journal of Experimental Child Psychology*, *30*, 231–45.

Crassini, B., & Broerse, J. (1980). Auditory visual integration in neonates: A signal detection analysis. *Journal of Experimental Child Psychology*, *29*, 144–55.

Critchley, M. (1970). *The Dyslexic Child*. London: Heinemann.

Cross, J. F., Cross, J., & Daly, J. (1971). Sex, race, age and beauty as factors in recognition of faces. *Perception and Psychophysics*, *10*, 393–6.

Curcio, F., Kattef, E., Levine, D., & Robbins, O. (1977). Compensation and susceptibility to conservation training. *Developmental Psychology*, *7*, 259–65.

Davies, G. (1989). Children as witnesses. In A. M. Colman & J. G. Beaumont (Eds), *Psychology Survey 7*. Leicester: British Psychological Society.

Day, R. H., & McKenzie, B. E. (1973). Perceptual shape constancy in early infancy. *Perception*, *2*, 315–20.

Day, R. H., & McKenzie, B. E. (1977). Constancies in the perceptual world of the infant. In W. Epstein (Ed.), *Stability and Constancy in Visual Perception: Mechanisms and Processes*. New York: Wiley.

Day, R. H., & McKenzie, B. E. (1981). Infant perception of the invariant size of approaching and receding objects. *Developmental Psychology*, *17*, 670–7.

DeCasper, A. J., & Fifer, W. P. (1980). Of human bonding: Newborns prefer their mothers' voices. *Science*, *208*, 1174–6.

De Loache, J. (1987). Rapid change in the symbolic functioning of very young children. *Science*, *238*, 1556–7.

Dent, H., & Stephenson, G. M. (1979). Identification evidence: Experimental investigations of factors affecting the reliability of juvenile and adult witnesses. In D. P. Farrington, K. Hawkins, & S. M. Lloyd-Bostock (Eds), *Psychology, Law, and Legal Processes*. Atlantic Highlands: NJ: Humanities Press.

Derrington, A. M., & Fuchs, A. F. (1981). The development of spatial-frequency selectivity in kitten striate cortex. *Journal of Physiology*, *316*, 1–10.

Diamond, A. (1985). Development of the ability to use recall to guide action, as indicated by infants' performance on AB. *Child Development*, *56*, 868–83.

Diamond, R., & Carey, S. (1977). Developmental changes in the representation of faces. *Journal of Experimental Child Psychology*, *23*, 1–22.

Dockrell, J. (1981). The child's acquisition of unfamiliar words: An experimental study. Unpublished doctoral dissertation. University of Stirling.

Dockrell, J., & Campbell, R. (1986). Lexical acquisition strategies in the pre-school child. In S. A. Kuczaj & M. D. Barrett (Eds), *The Development of Word Meaning*. New York: Springer-Verlag.

Dockrell, J., & McShane, J. (1990). Young children's use of phrase-structure and inflectional information in form-class assignments of novel nouns and verbs. *First Language*, **10**, 127–40.

Dodd, B. (1979). Lip reading in infants: Attention to speech presented in and out-of-synchrony. *Cognitive Psychology*, *11*, 478–84.

Dodwell, P. C., Muir, D., & Di Franco, D. (1976). Responses of infants to visually presented objects. *Science*, *194*, 209–11.

Donaldson, M. (1978). *Children's Minds*. London: Fontana.

Duncan, E. M., Whitney, P., & Kunen, S. (1982). Integration of visual and verbal information in children's memories. *Child Development*, *53*, 1215–23.

Ebbinghaus, H. (1885). *Memory: A Contribution to Experimental Psychology*. (Trans. by M. Ruyer & C. E. Bussenius). New York: Teacher's College Press, 1913.

Egan, D., Pittner, M., & Goldstein, A. G. (1977). Eyewitness identification: Photographs vs. live models. *Law and Human Behavior*, *1*, 199–206.

Eimas, P. D. (1974). Auditory and linguistic processing of cues for place of articulation by infants. *Perception and Psychophysics*, *16*, 513–21.

Eimas, P. D. (1975). Auditory and phonetic coding of the cues for speech: Discrimination of the [r - l] distinction by young infants. *Perception and Psychophysics*, *18*, 341–7.

Eimas, P. D., Miller, J. L., & Jusczyk, P. W. (1987). On infant speech perception and the acquisition of language. In S. Harnad (Ed.), *Categorical Perception*. Cambridge: Cambridge University Press.

Eimas, P. D., Siqueland, E. R., Jusczyk, P., & Vigorito, J. (1971). Speech perception in infants. *Science, 171*, 303–6.

Elkind, D. (1967). Piaget's conservation problems. *Child Development, 38*, 15–27.

Elkind, D., & Schoenfeld, E. (1972). Identity and equivalence conservation at two age levels. *Developmental Psychology, 6*, 529–33.

Ellis, A. W. (1984). *Reading, Writing and Dyslexia: A Cognitive Analysis*. Hillsdale, NJ: Erlbaum.

Ellis, N. C., & Miles, T. R. (1978). Visual information processing in dyslexic children. In M. M. Gruneberg, P. E. Morris, & R. N. Sykes (Eds), *Practical Aspects of Memory*. London: Academic Press.

Ellis, N. C., & Miles, T. R. (1981). A lexical encoding deficiency 1: Experimental evidence. In G. Th. Pavlidis & T. R. Miles (Eds), *Dyslexia Research and its Applications to Education*. London: Wiley.

Engel, R., & Young, N. B. (1969). Calibrated pure tone audiograms in normal neonates based on evoked electroencephalographic responses. *Neuropaediatrie, 1*, 149–60.

Ericsson, K. A., & Simon, H. A. (1980). Verbal reports as data. *Psychological Review, 87*, 215–51.

Ericsson, K. A., & Simon, H. A. (1984). *Protocol Analysis: Verbal Reports as Data*. Cambridge, MA: MIT Press.

Ervin, S. (1964). Imitation and structural change in children's language. In E. Lenneberg (Ed.) *New Directions in the Study of Language*. Cambridge, MA: MIT Press.

Fagan, J. F. (1972). Infants' recognition memory for faces. *Journal of Experimental Child Psychology, 14*, 453–76.

Fagan, J. F. (1973). Infants' delayed recognition memory and forgetting. *Journal of Experimental Child Psychology, 16*, 424–50.

Fagan, J. F. (1977). Infant recognition memory: Studies in forgetting. *Child Development, 48*, 68–78.

Fantz, R. L. (1958). Pattern vision in young infants. *Psychological Research, 8*, 43–7.

Fantz, R. L. (1961). The origin of form perception. *Scientific American, 204(5)*, 66–72.

Fantz, R. L. (1963). Pattern vision in newborn infants. *Science, 140*, 296–7.

Fantz, R. L., Fagan, J. F., & Miranda, S. B. (1975). Early visual selectivity. In L. B. Cohen & P. Salapatek (Eds). *Infant Perception: From Sensation to Cognition. Vol. 1: Basic Visual Processes*. New York: Academic Press.

Fantz, R. L., Ordy, J. M., & Udelf, M. S. (1962). Maturation of pattern vision in infants during the first six months. *Journal of Comparative and Physiological Psychology, 55*, 907–17.

Fernald, A., & Simon, T. (1984). Expanded intonation contours in mothers' speech to newborns. *Developmental Psychology, 20*, 104–13.

Field, I. M., Woodson, R., Greenberg, R., & Cohen, D. (1982). Discrimination and imitation of facial expressions by neonates. *Science, 218,* 179–81.

Field, J. (1977). Coordination of vision and prehension in young infants. *Child Development, 48,* 97–103.

Field, J., Muir, D., Pilon, R., Sinclair, M., & Dodwell, P. (1980). Infants' orientation to lateral sounds from birth to three months. *Child Development, 50,* 295–8.

Fillmore, C. (1968). The case for case. In E. Bach & R. Harms (Eds), *Universals in Linguistic Theory.* New York: Holt, Rinehart, & Winston.

Flavell, J. H. (1963). *The Developmental Psychology of Jean Piaget.* Princeton, NJ: Van Nostrand.

Flavell, J. H. (1971). First discussant's comments: What is memory development the development of? *Human Development, 14,* 272–8.

Flavell, J. H. (1972). An analysis of cognitive developmental sequences. *Genetic Psychology Monographs, 86,* 279–350.

Flavell, J. H., Beach, D. R., & Chinsky, J. M. (1966). Spontaneous verbal rehearsal in a memory task as a function of age. *Child Development, 37,* 283–99.

Flavell, J. H., Friedrichs, A. G., & Hoyt, J. D. (1970). Developmental changes in meorization processes. *Cognitive Psychology, 1,* 324–40.

Flavell, J. H., & Wellman, H. M. (1977). Metamemory. In R. V. Kail & J. W. Hagen (Eds), *Perspectives on the Development of Memory and Cognition.* Hillsdale, NJ: Erlbaum.

Flegg, G. (1983). *Numbers: Their History and Meaning.* London: Penguin.

Flin, R. H. (1980). Age effects in children's memory for unfamiliar faces. *Developmental Psychology, 16,* 373–4.

Fodor, J. A. (1983). *The Modularity of Mind.* Cambridge, MA: MIT/Bradford Books.

Fodor, J. A., Bever, T. G., & Garrett, M. F. (1974). *The Psychology of Language: An Introduction to Psycholinguistics and Generative Grammar.* New York: McGraw-Hill.

Fodor, J. A., & Pylyshyn, Z. W. (1981). How direct is visual perception? Some reflections on Gibson's 'Ecological Approach'. *Cognition, 9,* 139–96.

Fox, B., & Routh, D. (1976). Phonemic analysis and synthesis as word attack skills. *Journal of Educational Psychology, 68,* 70–4.

Fox, B., & Routh, D. (1980). Phonemic analysis and severe reading disability. *Journal of Psycholinguistic Research, 9,* 115–19.

Fox, B., & Routh, D. (1983). Reading disability, phonemic analysis, and dysphonic spelling: A follow-up study. *Journal of Clinical Child Psychology, 12,* 28–32.

Fox, R., Aslin, R. N., Shea, S. L., & Dumais, S. T. (1980). Stereopsis in human infants. *Science, 207,* 323–4.

Frankel, M. T., & Rollins, H. A. (1985). Associative and categorical hypotheses of organization in the free recall of adults and children. *Journal of Experimental Child Psychology, 40,* 304–18.

Friedman, S. (1972a). Habituation and recovery of visual response in the alert human newborn. *Journal of Experimental Child Psychology*, *13*, 339–49.

Friedman, S. (1972b). Newborn visual attention to repeated exposure of redundant vs. 'novel' targets. *Perceptions and Psychophysics*, *12*, 291–4.

Friedman, S., Bruno, L. A., & Vietze, P. (1974). Newborn habituation to visual stimuli: A sex difference in novelty detection. *Journal of Experimental Child Psychology*, *18*, 242–51.

Friedman, S., & Carpenter, G. C. (1971). Visual response decrement as a function of age of human newborn. *Child Development*, *42*, 1967–73.

Frith, U. (1985). Beneath the surface of developmental dyslexia. In K. E. Patterson, J. C. Marshall, & M. Coltheart (Eds), *Surface Dyslexia: Neuropsychological and Cognitive Studies of Phonological Reading*. Hillsdale, NJ: Erlbaum.

Frith, U., & Frith, C. D. (1980). Relationships between reading and spelling. In J. F. Kavanagh & R. L. Venezky (Eds), *Orthography, Reading and Dyslexia*. Baltimore, MD: University Park Press.

Fundudis, T., Kolvin, I., & Garside, R. F. (1979). *Speech Retarded and Deaf Children: Their Psychological Development*. London: Academic Press.

Furrow, D., Nelson, K. & Benedict, H. (1979). Mother's speech to children and syntactic development: Some simple relationships. *Journal of Child Language*, *6*, 423–42.

Fuson, K. C. (1982). An analysis of counting-on solution procedures in addition. In T. P. Carpenter, J. M. Moser, & T. A. Romberg (Eds), *Addition and Subtraction: A Cognitive Perspective*. Hillside, NJ: Erlbaum.

Fuson, K. C. (1988). *Children's Counting and Concepts of Number*. New York: Springer-Verlag.

Fuson, K. C., Richards, J., & Briars, D. J. (1982). The acquisition and elaboration of the number word sequence. In C. J. Brainerd (Ed.), *Progress in Cognitive Development Research: Vol. 1. Children's Logical and Mathematical Cognition*. New York: Springer-Verlag.

Fuson, K. C. & Hall, J. W. (1983). The acquisition of early number word meanings. In H. Ginsburg (Ed.) *The Development of Children's Mathematical Thinking*, New York: Academic Press.

Gagne, R. M. (1968). Contributions of learning to human development. *Psychological Review*, *75*, 177–91.

Ganon, E. C., & Swartz, K. B. (1980). Perception of internal elements of compound figures by one-month-old infants. *Journal of Experimental Child Psychology*, *30*, 159–70.

Gardner, H. (1985). *The Mind's New Science*. New York: Basic Books.

Gardner, J. & Gardner, H. (1970). A note on selective imitation by a 6-week-old infant. *Child Development*, *41*, 1209–13.

Garner, W. R. (1974). *The Processing of Information and Structure*. Potomac, MD: Erlbaum.

Garnica, O. K. (1977). Some prosodic and paralinguistic features of speech to young children. In C. E. Snow & C. A. Ferguson (Eds), *Talking to Children.* Cambridge: Cambridge University Press.

Gathercole, V. C. (1987). The contrastive hypothesis for the acquisition of word meaning: a reconsideration of the theory. *Journal of Child Language, 14,* 493–531.

Gelb, I. J. (1963). *A Study of Writing (2nd ed.).* Chicago: University of Chicago Press.

Gelman, R. (1972a). The nature and development of early number concepts,. In H. W. Reese (Ed.), *Advances in Child Development and Behavior, Vol. 7.* New York: Academic Press.

Gelman, R. (1972b). Logical capacity of very young children: Number invariance rules. *Child Development, 43,* 75–90.

Gelman, R. & Baillargeon, R. (1983). A review of some Piagetian concepts. In P. H. Mussen (Ed.), *Handbook of Child Psychology, Vol. III: Cognitive Development.* New York: Wiley.

Gelman, R., & Gallistel, C. R. (1978). *The Child's Understanding of Number.* Cambridge, MA: Harvard University Press.

Gelman, R., & Weinberg, D. (1972). The relation between liquid conservation and compensation. *Child Development, 43,* 371–83.

Gelman, S. A., & Markman, E. M. (1986). Categories and induction in young children. *Cognition, 23,* 183–208.

Gelman, S. A., & Taylor, M. (1984). How two-year-old children interpret proper and common names for unfamiliar objects. *Child Development, 55,* 1535–40.

Gentner, D. (1982). Why nouns are learned before verbs: Linguistic relativity vs. natural partitioning. In S. A. Kuczaj (Ed.), *Language Development: Syntax and Semantics.* Hillsdale, NJ: Erlbaum.

Gibson, E. J. & Spelke, E. S. (1983). The development of perception. In P. H. Mussen (Ed.), *Handbook of Child Psychology, Vol. III: Cognitive Development.* New York: Wiley.

Gibson, E. J., & Walk, R. D. (1960). The 'visual cliff'. *Scientific American, 202(4),* 64–71.

Gibson, J. J. (1950). *The Perception of the Visual World.* Boston, MA.: Houghton Mifflin.

Gibson, J. J. (1966). *The Senses Considered as Perceptual Systems.* Boston, MA.: Houghton Mifflin.

Gibson, J. J. (1979). *The Ecological Approach to Visual Perception.* Boston, MA.: Houghton Mifflin.

Gittelman, R., & Feingold, I. (1983). Children with reading disorders - I: Efficacy of reading remediation. *Journal of Child Psychology and Psychiatry, 24,* 167–92.

Gleitman, L. R. & Rozin, P. (1977). The structure and acquisition of reading 1: Relations between orthographies and the structure of language. In A.S. Reber & D. L. Scarborough (Eds), *Toward a Psychology of Reading.* Hillsdale, NJ: Erlbaum.

Gleitman, L. R., & Wanner, E. (1982). Language acquisition: the state of the state of the art. In E. Wanner & L. R. Gleitman (Eds), *Language Acquisition: The State of the Art.* Cambridge: Cambridge University Press.

Gold, E. M. (1967). Language identification in the limit. *Information and Control, 10,* 447–74.

Goldberg, S. (1976). Visual tracking and existence constancy in five-month-old infants. *Journal of Experimental Child Psychology, 22,* 478–91.

Goldfield, E. C., & Dickerson, D. J. (1981). Keeping track of locations during movements in 8- to 10-month-old infants. *Journal of Experimental Child Psychology, 32,* 48–64.

Goldstein, D. M. (1976). Cognitive-linguistic functioning and learning to read in preschoolers. *Journal of Educational Psychology, 68,* 680–8.

Golinkoff, R. M. (1982). The case for semantic relations: Evidence from the verbal and non-verbal domains. *Journal of Child Language, 8,* 413–37.

Goodman, G. S. (1984a). Children's testimony in historical perspective. *Journal of Social Issues, 40,* 9–31.

Goodman, G. S. (1984b). The child witness: conclusions and future directions for research and legal practice. *Journal of Social Issues, 40,* 157–75.

Gordon, F. R., & Yonas, A. (1976). Sensitivity to binocular depth information in infancy. *Journal of Experimental Child Psychology, 22,* 413–22.

Gottfried, A. W., Rose, S. A., & Bridger, W. H. (1977). Cross-modal transfer in human infants. *Child Development, 48,* 118–23.

Graesser, A. C., Woll, S. B., Kowalski, D. J., & Smith, D. A. (1980). Memory for typical and atypical actions in scripted activities. *Journal of Experimental Psychology: Human Learning and Memory, 6,* 503–15.

Graham, F. K., & Clifton, R. K. (1966). Heart-rate change as a component of the orienting response. *Psychological Bulletin, 65,* 305–20.

Granrud, C. E., & Yonas, A. (1984). Infants' perception of pictorially specified interposition. *Journal of Experimental Child Psychology, 37,* 500–11.

Granrud, G. E., Yonas, A., & Petterson, L. (1984). A comparison of monocular and binocular depth perception in 5- and 7-month-old infants. *Journal of Experimental Child Psychology, 38,* 19–32.

Gratch, G. (1972). A study of the relative dominance of vision and touch in six-month-old infants. *Child Development, 43,* 615–23.

Gratch, G., Appel, K. J., Evans, W. F., LeCompte, G. K., & Wright, N. A. (1974). Piaget's stage IV object concept error: Evidence of forgetting or object conception? *Child Development, 45,* 71–7.

Greenberg, D. J., & Blue, S. Z. (1975). Visual complexity in infancy: Contour or numerosity? *Child Development, 46,* 357–63.

Greeno, J. G., Riley, M. S., & Gelman, R. (1984). Conceptual competence and children's counting. *Cognitive Psychology, 16,* 94–143.

Grimwade, J. C., Walker, D. W., Bartlett, M., Gordon, S., & Wood, C. (1971). Human fetal heart rate change and movement in response to sound and vibration. *American Journal of Obstetrics and Gynecology, 109,* 86–90.

Groen, G. J., & Parkman, J. M. (1972). A chronometric analysis of simple addition. *Psychological Review, 79*, 329–43.

Groen, G. J., & Poll, M. (1983). Subtraction and the solution of open sentence problems. *Journal of Experimental Child Psychology, 16*, 292–302.

Groen, G. J., & Resnick, L. B. (1977). Can pre-school children invent addition algorithms? *Journal of Educational Psychology, 69*, 645–52.

Hainline, L. (1978). Developmental changes in visual scanning of face and non face patterns by infants. *Journal of Experimental Child Psychology, 25*, 90–115.

Haith, M. M. (1980). *Rules that Babies Look by: The Organisation of Newborn Visual Activity.* Hillsdale, NJ: Erlbaum.

Haith, M. M., Bergman, T., & Moore, M. J. (1977). Eye contact and face scanning in early infancy. *Science, 198*, 853–5.

Hamel, B. R. (1971). On the conservation of liquids. *Human Development, 14*, 39–46.

Halliday, M. A. K. (1975). *Learning How to Mean,* London: Edward Arnold.

Haroutunian, S. (1983). *Equilibrium in the Balance: A Study of Psychological Explanation.* New York: Springer-Verlag.

Harris, B. (1979). Whatever happened to little Albert? *American Psychologist, 34*, 151–60.

Harris, P. L. (1973). Perseverative errors in search by young infants. *Child Development, 44*, 28–33.

Harris, P. L. (1983). Infant Cognition. In P. H. Mussen (Ed.), *Handbook of Child Psychology. Vol. II: Infancy and Development Psychobiology.* New York: Wiley.

Hasher, L., & Zacks, R. T. (1979). Automatic and effortful processes in memory. *Journal of Experimental Psychology: General, 108*, 356–88.

Hayes, L. A., & Watson, J. S. (1981). Neonatal imitation: Fact or artifact? *Developmental Psychology, 17*, 655–60.

Haynes, H., White, B. L., & Held, R. (1965) Visual accommodation in human infants. *Science, 148*, 528–30.

Hebb, D. O. (1949). *The Organization of Behavior.* New York: Wiley.

Hecox, K. (1975). Electro-physiological correlates of human auditory development. In L. B. Cohen & P. Salapatek (Eds).; *Infant Perception: From Sensation to Cognition. Vol. 2.* New York: Academic Press.

Hecox, K. (1984). Auditory psychophysics. In P. Salapatek & L. B. Cohen (Eds), *Handbook of Infant Perception.* New York: Academic Press.

Hecox, K., & Galambos, R. (1974). Brainstem auditory evoked responses in human infants and adults. *Archives of Otolaryngology, 99*, 30–33.

Hershenson, M. (1964). Visual discrimination in the human newborn. *Journal of Comparative and Physiological Psychology, 43*, 112–22.

Hillenbrand, J. (1984). Speech-perception by infants: Categorization based on nasal consonant place of articulation. *Journal of the Acoustical Society of America, 75*, 1613–22.

Hinshelwood, J. (1917). *Congenital Word Blindness.* London: H. K. Lewis.

Hochberg, J. E. (1962). Nativism and empiricism in perception. In L. Postman (Ed.), *Psychology in the Making*. New York: Knopf.

Hoff-Ginsberg, E., & Shatz, M. (1982). Linguistic input and the child's acquisition of language. *Psychological Bulletin*, *92*, 3–26.

Hofsten, C. von, (1982). Eye-hand coordination in the newborn. *Developmental Psychology*, *18*, 450–61.

Holland, J. H., Holyoak, K. J., Nisbett, R. E., & Thagard, P. R. (1986). *Induction: Processes of Inference, Learning, and Discovery*. Cambridge, MA: MIT Press.

Holmes, D. R., & McKeever, W. F. (1979). Material specific serial memory deficit in adolescent dyslexics. *Cortex*, *15*, 51–62.

Homa, D., & Chambliss, D. (1975). The relative contributions of common and distinctive information on the abstraction from ill-defined categories. *Journal of Experimental Psychology: Human Learning and Memory*, *1*, 351–9.

Homa, D., Cross, J., Cornell, D., Goldman, D., & Schwartz, S. (1973). Prototype abstraction and classification of new instances as a function of number of instances defining the prototype. *Journal of Experimental Psychology*, *101*, 116–22.

Horton, M. S., & Markman, E. M. (1980). Developmental differences in the acquisition of basic and superordinate categories. *Child Development*, *51*, 708–19.

Hornsby, B., & Miles, T. (1980). The effects of a dyslexia-centred teaching programme. *British Journal of Educational Psychology*, *50*, 236–42.

Huddleston, R. (1976). *An Introduction to English Transformational Syntax*. London: Longman.

Hull, C. L. (1920). Quantitative aspects of the evolution of concepts. *Psychological Monographs*, *28*, Whole No. 123.

Hunt, T. D. (1975). Early number 'conservation' and experimenter expectancy. *Child Development*, *46*, 984–7.

Huttenlocher, J., & Burke, D. (1976). Why does memory span increase with age? *Cognitive Psychology*, *8*, 1–31.

Inhelder, B., & Piaget, J. (1955). *The Growth of Logical Thinking from Childhood to Adolescence*. (Trans. by A. Parsons & S. Milgram.) London: Routledge & Kegan Paul, 1958.

Inhelder, B. & Piaget, J. (1959). *The Early Growth of Logical Thinking in the Child*. (Trans. by E. A. Lunzer & D. Papert.) London: Routledge & Kegan Paul, 1964.

Inhelder, B., Sinclair, H., & Bovet, M. (1974). *Learning and the Development of Cognition*. London: Routledge & Kegan Paul.

Jackendoff, R. (1977). $\bar{X}$ *Syntax: A Study of Phrase Structure*. Cambridge, MA: MIT Press.

Jackendoff, R. (1983). *Semantics and Cognition*. Cambridge, MA: MIT Press.

Jacobs, J. (1887). Experiments on prehension. *Mind*, *12*, 75–9.

Jacobson, S. W. (1979). Matching behavior in the young infant. *Child Development*, *50*, 425–30.

James, W. (1890). *Principles of Psychology* (2 vols). New York: Holt.

Johnson-Laird, P. N., & Wason, P. C. (1977). Conceptual thinking: Introduction. In P. N. Johnson-Laird & P. C. Wason (Eds), *Thinking: Readings in Cognitive Science*. Cambridge: Cambridge University Press.

Johnston, R. S. (1982). Phonological coding in dyslexic readers. *British Journal of Psychology, 73*, 455–60.

Jorm, A. F. (1979). The cognitive and neurological basis of developmental dyslexia: A theoretical framework and review. *Cognition, 7*, 19–32.

Jorm, A. F. (1983). Specific reading retardation and working memory: A review. *British Journal of Psychology, 74*, 311–42.

Jorm, A. F., & Share, D. (1983). Phonological recoding and reading acquisition. *Applied Psycholinguistics, 4*, 103–47.

Julesz, B. (1960). Binocular depth perception of computer generated patterns. *Bell System Technical Journal, 39*, 1125–62.

Julesz, B. (1965). Texture and visual perception, *Scientific American, 212(2)*, 38–48.

Jusczyk, P. W. (1977). Perception of syllable-final stop consonants by two-month-old infants. *Perception and Psychophysics, 21*, 450–4.

Jusczyk, P. W. (1985). On characterizing the development of speech perception. In J. Mehler & R. Fox (Eds), *Neonate Cognition: Beyond the Blooming Buzzing Confusion*. Hillsdale, NJ: Erlbaum.

Jusczyk, P. W., & Thompson, E. (1978). Perception of a phonetic contrast in multisyllabic utterances by two-month-old infants. *Perception and Psychophysics, 23*, 105–9.

Just, M. A. & Carpenter, P. A. (1980). A theory of reading from eye fixations to comprehension. *Psychological Review, 87*. 329–54.

Kail, R. (1990). *The Development of Memory in Children*. (3rd. ed.). New York: Freeman.

Kaitz, M., Meschulach-Sarfaty, O., Auerbach, J., & Eidelman, A. (1988). A re-examination of newborns' ability to imitate facial expressions. *Developmental Psychology, 24*, 3–7.

Kaplan, R. M., & Bresnan, J. (1982). Lexical-functional grammar: A formal system for grammatical representation. In J. Bresnan (Ed.), *The Mental Representation of Grammatical Relations*. Cambridge, MA: MIT Press.

Karmel, B. Z. (1969). The effect of age, complexity, and amount of contour on pattern preferences in infants. *Journal of Experimental Child Psychology, 7*, 339–54.

Karmel, B. Z., & Maisel, E. B. (1975). A neuronal activity model for infant visual attention. In L. B. Cohen & P. Salapatek (Eds), *Infant Perception: From Sensation to Cognition. Vol. 1*. New York: Academic Press.

Karmiloff-Smith, A. (1986). Stage/structure versus phase/process in modelling linguistic and cognitive development. In I. Levin (Ed.), *Stage and Structure*. Norwood, NJ: Ablex.

Karz, N., Baker, E., & Macnamara, J. (1974). What's in a name? A study of how children learn common and proper names. *Child Development, 45*, 469–73.

Kaufmann, R., Maland, J., & Yonas, A. (1981). Sensitivity of 5- and 7-month-old infants to pictorial depth information. *Journal of Experimental Child Psychology*, *32*, 162–8.

Kay, D. A., & Anglin, J. M. (1982). Overextension and underextension in the child's expressive and receptive speech. *Journal of Child Language*, *9*, 83–98.

Kaye, K. (1982). *The Mental and Social Life of Babies*. Chicago: University of Chicago Press.

Keenan, E. L. (1976). Towards a universal definition of 'subject'. In C. Li (Ed.), *Subject and Topic*. New York: Academic Press.

Keeney, T. J., Cannizzo, S. R., & Flavell, J. H. (1967). Spontaneous and induced verbal rehearsal in a recall task. *Child Development*, *38*, 953–66.

Kellman, P. J., & Spelke, E. S. (1983). Perception of partly occluded objects in infancy. *Cognitive Psychology*, *15*, 483–524.

Kelly, M., Scholnick, E. K., Travers, S. H., & Johnson, J. W. (1976). Relations among memory, memory appraisal, and memory strategies. *Child Development*, *47*, 648–59.

Kendler, T. S. (1961). Development of mediating responses in children. In J. C. Wright & J. Kagan (Eds), Basic cognitive processes in children. *Monographs of the Society for Research on Child Development*, *28*, (2), 33–52.

Kennedy, B. A., & Miller, D. J. (1976). Persistent use of verbal rehearsal as a function of information about its value. *Child Development*, *47*, 566–9.

Kessen, W. (1984). Introduction: The end of the age of development. In R. J. Sternberg (Ed.), *Mechanisms of Cognitive Development*. New York: W. H. Freeman.

King, M. A., & Yuille, J. C. (1987). Suggestibility and the child witness. In S. J. Ceci, M. P. Toglia, & D. F. Ross (Eds) *Children's Eyewitness Testimony* New York: Springer-Verlag.

Kintsch, W. (1974). *The Representation of Meaning in Memory*. Hillsdale, NJ: Erlbaum.

Kintsch, W., & van Dijk, T. A. (1978). Toward a model of text comprehension and production. *Psychological Review*, *85*, 363–94.

Klahr, D., & Wallace, J. G. (1975). *Cognitive Development: An Information Processing View*. Hillsdale, NJ: Erlbaum.

Klatt, D. H. (1979). Speech perception: A model of acoustic-phonetic analysis and lexical access. *Journal of Phonetics*, *7*, 279–312.

Klatzky, R. L. (1984). *Memory and Awareness*. San Francisco: W. H. Freeman.

Koepke, J. E., Hamm, M., & Legerstee, M. (1983). Neonatal imitation: Two failures to replicate. *Infant Behavior and Development*, *6*, 97–102.

Kreutzer, M. A., Leonard, C., & Flavell, J. H. (1975). An interview study of children's knowledge about memory. *Monographs of the Society for Research in Child Development*, *40* (1, Serial No. 159).

Kramer, J., Hill, K., & Cohen, L. (1975). Infant's development of object permanence: A refined methodology and new evidence of Piaget's hypothesized ordinality. *Child Development*, *46*, 149–55.

Krech, D., Crutchfield, R. S., & Livson, N. (1969). *Elements of Psychology, (2nd ed.).* New York: Knopf.

Kucera, H., & Francis, W. (1967). *Computational Analysis of Present-Day American English.* Providence, RI: Brown University Press.

Kuczaj, S. A. (1977). The acquisition of regular and irregular past tense forms. *Journal of Verbal Learning and Verbal Behavior, 16,* 589–600.

Kuffler, S. W., Nicholls, J. G., & Martin, A. R. (1984). *From Neuron to Brain: A Cellular Approach to the Function of the Nervous System.* 2nd ed. Sunderland, MA: Sinauer.

Kuhl, P. K. (1979). Speech perception in early infancy: Perceptual constancy for spectrally dissimilar vowel categories. *Journal of the Acoustical Society of America, 66,* 1668–79.

Kuhl, P. K. (1983). The perception of auditory equivalence classes for speech in early infancy. *Infant Behavior and Development, 6,* 263–85.

Kuhl, P. K., & Miller, J. D. (1975). Speech perception by the chinchilla: Voiced-voiceless distinction in alveolar-plosive consonants. *Science, 190,* 69–72.

Kuhl, P. K., & Miller, J. D. (1978). Speech perception by the chinchilla: Identification functions for synthetic VOT stimuli. *Journal of the Acoustical Society of America, 63,* 905–17.

Kuhl, P. K., & Padden, D. M. (1982). Enhanced discriminability at the phonetic boundaries for the voicing feature in macaques. *Perception and Psychophysics, 32,* 542–50.

Kuhl, P. K., & Padden, D. M. (1983). Enhanced discriminability at the phonetic boundaries for the place feature in macaques. *Journal of the Acoustical Society of America, 73,* 1003–10.

Lachman, R., Lachman, J. L., & Butterfield, E. C. (1979). *Cognitive Psychology and Information Processing: An Introduction.* Hillsdale, NJ: Erlbaum.

Laird, J. E., Newell, A., & Rosenbloom, P. S. (1987). Saor: An architecture for general intelligence. *Artificial Intelligence, 33,* 1–64.

Laird, J. E., Rosebloom, P. S., & Newell, A. (1986). Chunking in Soar: The anatomy of a general learning mechanism. *Machine Learning,1,* 11–46.

Lange, G. (1978). Organization-related processes in children's recall. In P. A. Ornstein (Ed.), *Memory Development in Children.* Hillsdale, NJ: Erlbaum.

Larsen, G. Y., & Flavell, J. H. (1970). Verbal factors in compensation performance and the relation between conservation and compensation. *Child Development, 41,* 965–77.

Lasky, R. E., Syrdal-Lasky, A., & Klein, R. E. (1975). VOT discrimination by four- to six-and-a-half-month-old infants from Spanish environments. *Journal of Experimental Child Psychology, 20,* 215–25.

Leahy, R. L. (1976). Development of preferences and processes of visual scanning in the human infant during the first 3 months of life. *Developmental Psychology, 12,* 250–4.

Leopold, W. (1939–49). *Speech Development of a Bilingual Child. Vol. 1: Vocabulary Growth in the First Two Years. Vol. 2: Sound Learning in the First Two*

Years. Vol. 3: Grammar and General Problems in the First Two years. Vol. 4: Diary from Age Two. Evanston. IL.: Northwestern University Press.

Lewis, M. M. (1936). *Infant Speech.* London: Routledge & Kegan Paul.

Liberman, A M., Cooper, F. S., Shankweiler, D. P., & Studdert-Kennedy, M. (1967). Perception of the speech code. *Psychological Review, 74,* 431–61.

Liberman, I. Y., Mann, U. S., Shankweiler, D., & Werfelman, D. (1982). Children's memory for recurring linguistic and non-linguistic material in relation to reading ability. *Cortex, 18,* 367–75.

Lightfoot, D. (1982). *Tha Language Lottery: Toward a Biology of Grammars.* Cambridge, MA: MIT Press.

Locke, J. (1690). *An Essay Concerning Human Understanding.* New York: Dover Publications, 1959.

Loftus, E. F., & Davies, G. M. (1984). Distortions in the memory of children. *Journal of Social Issues, 40,* 51–67.

Lundberg, I., Olofsson, A., & Wall, S. (1981). Reading and spelling skills in the first school years predicted from phonemic awareness skills in kindergarten. *Scandanavian Journal of Psychology, 21,* 159–73.

Lyons, J. (1977a). *Semantics, Vol. I.* Cambridge: Cambridge University Press.

Lyons, J. (1977b). *Semantics, Vol. II.* Cambridge: Cambridge University Press.

McCall, R. B., Kennedy, C. B., & Dodds, C. (1977). The interfering effect of distracting stimuli on the infant's memory. *Child Development, 48,* 79–87.

McClelland, J. L. (1979). On the time relation of mental processes: An examination of systems of processes in cascade. *Psychological Review, 86,* 287–330.

McClelland, J. L. (1986). The programmable blackboard model of reading. In J. L. McClelland & D. E. Rumelhart (Eds), *Parallel Distributed Processing: Explorations in the Microstructure of Cognition. Vol. 2: Psychological and Biological Models.* Cambridge, MA: MIT Press.

McClelland, J. L., & Rumelhart, D. E. (1981). An interactive activation model of context effects in letter perception: Part 1. An account of basic findings. *Psychological Review, 88,* 375–407.

McClelland, J. L., & Rumelhart, D. E. (1986). A distributed model of human learning and memory. In J. L. McClelland & D. E. Rumelhart (Eds), *Parallel Distributed Processing: Explorations in the Microstructure of Cognition. Vol. 2: Psychological and Biological Models.* Cambridge, MA: MIT Press.

McDonnell, P. M. (1978). Patterns of eye-hand co-ordination in the first year of life. *Canadian Journal of Psychology, 33,* 253–67.

McGarrigle, J., & Donaldson, M. (1975). Conservation accidents. *Cognition, 3,* 341–50.

McGraw, M. B. (1943). *The Neuromuscular Maturation of the Human Infant.* New York: Columbia University Press.

McGurk, H., & Lewis, M. M. (1974). Space perception in early infancy: Perception within a common auditory-visual space? *Science, 186,* 649–50.

McGurk, H., Turnure, C., & Creighton, S. J. (1977). Auditory-visual co-ordination of neonates. *Child Development, 48,* 138–43.

McKenzie, B. E., & Day, R. H. (1972). Distance as a determinant of visual fixation in early infancy. *Science*, *178*, 1108–10.

McKenzie, B. E., & Day, R. H. (1976). Infant's attention to stationary and moving objects at different distances. *Australian Journal of Psychology*, *28*, 45–51.

McKenzie, B., & Over, R. (1983). Young infants fail to imitate facial and manual getures. *Infant Behavior and Development*, *6*, 85–95.

McKenzie, B. E., Tootell, H. E., & Day, R. H. (1980). Development of visual size constancy during the first year of human infancy. *Developmental Psychology*, *16*, 163–74.

McShane, J. (1979). The development of naming. *Linguistics*, *17*, 879–905.

McShane, J. (1980). *Learning to Talk*. Cambridge: Cambridge University Press.

McShane, J., & Dockrell, J. (1983). Lexical and grammatical development. In B. Butterworth (Ed.), *Speech Production. Vol. 2*. London: Academic Press.

McShane, J., & Morrison, D. L. (1983). How young children pour equal quantities: A case of pseudo-compensation. *Journal of Experimental Child Psychology*, *35*, 21–9.

McShane, J., & Morrison, D. L. (1985). Are young children's judgements of liquid inequality rule guided or stimulus driven? *British Journal of Development Psychology*, *3*, 57–63.

McShane, J., & Whittaker, S. (1983). The role of symbolic thought in language development. In D. R. Rogers & J. A. Sloboda (Eds), *The Acquisition of Symbolic Skills*. New York: Plenum Press.

McShane, J., Whittaker, S., & Dockrell, J. (1986). Verbs and Time. In S. A. Kuczaj & M. D. Barrett (Eds), *The Development of Word Meaning*. New York: Springer-Verlag.

Mackworth, N. H., & Bruner, J. S. (1970). How adults and children search and recognize pictures. *Human Development*, *13*, 149–77.

Macnamara, J. (1972). Cognitive basis of language learning in infants. *Psychological Review*, *79*, 1–13.

MacWhinney, B. (1978). Processing a first language: The acquisition of morphophonology. *Monographs of the Society for Research in Child Development*, *43*, (1–2, Serial No. 174).

Mandler, J. M. (1978). A code in the node: The use of a story schema in retrieval. *Discourse Processes*, *1*, 14–35.

Mandler, J. M. (1983). Representation. In P. H. Mussen (Ed.), *Handbook of Child Psychology, Vol. III: Cognitive Development*. New York: Wiley.

Mandler, J. M., & De Forest, M. (1979). Is there more than one way to recall a story? *Child Development*, *50*, 886–9.

Mandler, J. M., & Johnson, N. S. (1977). Remembrance of things parsed: Story structure and recall. *Cognitive Psychology*, *9*, 111–51.

Mandler, J. M., & Murphy, C. (1983). Subjective judgements of script structures. *Journal of Experimental Psychology: Learning, Memory, and Cognition*, *9*, 534–43.

Mandler, J. M., Scribner, S., Cole, M., & De Forest, M. (1980). Cross-cultural invariance in story recall. *Child Development*, *51*, 19–26.

Mann, V. A., Liberman, I. Y.,& Shankweiler, D. (1980). Children's memory for sentences and word strings in relation to reading ability. *Memory and Cognition*, *8*, 329–35.

Maratsos, M. (1979). How to get from words to sentences. In D. Aaronson & R. Rieber (Eds), *Perspectives in Psycholinguistics*. Hillsdale, NJ: Erlbaum.

Maratsos, M. (1982). The child's construction of grammatical categories. In E. Wanner & L. R. Gleitman (Eds), *Language Acquisition: The State of the Art*. Cambridge: Cambridge University Press.

Maratsos, M. (1983). Some current issues in the study of the acquisition of grammar. In P. H. Mussen (Ed.), *Handbook of Child Psychology, Vol. III: Cognitive Development*. New York: Wiley.

Maratsos, M. P. & Chalkley, M. A. (1980). The internal language of children's syntax: The ontogenesis and representation of syntactic categories. In. K. E. Nelson (Ed.), *Children's Language, Vol. 2*. New York: Gardner Press.

Marcus, S. M. (1984). Recognizing speech: On the mapping from sound to word. In H. Bouma & D. G. Bouwhuis (Eds), *Attention and Performance X*. Hillsdale, NJ: Erlbaum.

Marg, E., Freeman, D. N., Peltzman, P., & Goldstein, P. J. (1976). Visual acuity development in infants: Evoked potential measurements. *Investigative Opthalmology*, *15*, 150–3.

Marin, B. V., Holmes, D. L., Guth, M., & Kovac, P. (1979). The potential of children as eyewitnesses: A comparison of children and adults on eyewitness tasks. *Law and Human Behavior*, *3*, 295–305.

Mark, L. S., Shankweiler, D., Liberman, I. Y., & Fowler, C. A. (1977). Phonetic recoding and reading difficulty in beginning readers. *Memory and Cognition*, *5*, 623–9.

Markman, E. M. (1979). Realizing that you don't understand: Elementary school children's awareness of inconsistencies. *Child Development*, *50*, 643–55.

Markman, E. M. (1985). Why superordinate category terms can be mass nouns. *Cognition*, *19*, 311–53.

Markman, E. M. (1989). *Categorization and Naming in Children*. Cambridge, MA: MIT/Bradford Books.

Markman, E. M., & Wachtel, G. F. (1988). Children's use of mutual exclusivity to constrain the meanings of words. *Cognitive Psychology*, *20*, 121–57.

Marr, D. (1982). *Vision: A Computational Investigation into the Human Representation and Processing of Visual Information*. San Francisco: W. H. Freeman.

Marsh, G., Friedman, M., Welch, V., & Desberg, P. (1981). A cognitive-developmental theory of reading acquisition. In G. E. Mackinnon & T. G. Waller (Eds), *Reading Research: Advances in Theory and Practice*. New York: Academic Press.

Marshall, J. C., & Newcombe, F. (1973). Patterns of paralexia: A psycholinguistic approach. *Journal of Psycholinguistic Research*, *2*, 175–99.

Martin, R. M. (1975). Effects of familiar and complex stimuli on infant attention. *Development Psychology*, *11*, 178–85.

Mason, M., & Katz, L. (1976). Visual processing on nonlinguistic strings: Redundancy effects and reading disability. *Journal of Experimental Psychology: General*, *105*, 338–48.

Masur, E. F., McIntyre, C. W., & Flavell, J. H. (1973). Developmental changes in apportionment of study time among items in a multitrial free recall task. *Journal of Experimental Child Psychology*, *15*, 237–46.

Maurer, D. (1975). Infant visual perception: Methods of study. In L. B. Cohen & P. Salapatek (Eds), *Infant Perception: From Sensation to Cognition. Vol. 1: Basic Visual Processes*. New York: Academic Press.

Maurer, D., & Salapatek, P. (1976). Developmental changes in the scanning of faces by young infants. *Child Development*, *47*, 523–7.

Medin, D. L. (1983). Structural principles in categorization. In T. J. Tighe & B. E. Shepp (Eds), *Perception, Cognition, and Development*: Interactional Analyses. Hillsdale, NJ: Erlbaum.

Mehler, J., & Bever, T. (1967). Cognitive capacity of very young children. *Science*, *158*, 141–2.

Meicler, M., & Gratch, G. (1980). Do five-month-olds show object conception in Paiget's sense? *Infant Behavior and Development*, *3*, 265–82.

Meltzoff, A. N., & Moore, M. K. (1977). Imitation of facial and manual gestures by human neonates. *Science*, *198*, 75–8.

Meltzoff, A. N., & Moore, M. K. (1983). Newborn infants imitate adult facial gestures. *Child Development*, *54*, 702–9.

Meltzoff, A. N., & Moore, M. K. (1985). Cognitive foundations and social functions of imitation and intermodal representation in infancy. In J. Mehler & R. Fox (Eds), *Neonate Cognition: Beyond the Blooming Buzzing Confusion*. Hillsdale, NJ: Erlbaum.

Mendelson, M., & Haith, M. M. (1976). The relation between audition and vision in the human newborn. *Monographs of the Society for Research in Child Development*, *41*, 1–61.

Menn, L. (1982). Development of articulatory, phonetic, and phonological capabilities. In B. Butterworth (Ed.), *Language Production. Vol. 2: Development, Writing and Other Language Processes*. London: Academic Press.

Merriman, W. E. (1986a). How children learn the reference of concrete nouns: A critique of current hypotheses. In S. A. Kuczaj & M. D. Barrett (Eds), *The Development of Word Meaning*. New York: Springer-Verlag.

Merriman, W. E. (1986b). Some reasons for the occurrence and eventual correction of children's naming errors. *Child Development*, *57*, 942–51.

Mervis, C. B., & Crisafi, M. A. (1982). Order of acquisition of subordinate, basic, and superordinate level categories. *Child Development*, *53*, 258–66.

Michie, S. (1984a). Number understanding in preschool children. *British Journal of Educational Psychology*, *54*, 245–53.

Michie, S. (1984b). Why preschoolers are reluctant to count spontaneously. *British Journal of Developmental Psychology*, , 347–58.

Michotte, A. (1955). Perception and cognition. *Acta Psychologica, 11*, 69–91.

Milewski, A. E. (1976). Infants' discrimination of internal and external pattern elements. *Journal of Experimental Child Psychology, 22*, 229–46.

Milewski, A. E. (1978). Young infants' visual processing of internal and adjacent shapes. *Infant Behavior and Development, 1*, 359–71.

Miller, G. A. (1956). The magical number seven, plus or minus two: Some limits on our capacity for processing information. *Psychological Review, 63*, 81–97.

Minsky, M. A. (1975). A framework for representing knowledge. In P. Winston (Ed.), *The Psychology of Computer Vision*. New York: McGraw-Hill.

Moely, B. E., Olson, F. A., Halwes, T. G., & Flavell, J. H. (1969). Production deficiency in young children's clustered recall. *Developmental Psychology, 1*, 26–34.

Moore, M. K., Borton, R., & Darby, B. L. (1978). Visual tracking in young infants: Evidence for object identity or object permanence? *Journal of Experimental Child Psychology, 25*, 183–98.

Morais, J., Cary, L., Alegria, J. & Bertelson, P. (1979). Does awareness of speech as a sequence of phones arise spontaneously? *Cognition, 7*, 323–31.

Morrison, F. J., & Manis, F. R. (1982). Cognitive processes and reading ability: A critique and proposal. In C. J. Brainerd & M. Presley (Eds), *Verbal Processes in Children: Progress in Cognitive Development Research*. New York: Springer-Verlag.

Morton, J. (1969). Interaction of information in word recognition. *Psychological Review, 76*, 165–78.

Morton, J. (1979). Facilitation in word recognition: Experiments causing change in the logogen model. In P. A. Kolers, M. E. Wrolstad, & H. Bowma (Eds), *Processing of Visible Language*. New York: Plenum.

Morton, J. (1982). Disintegrating the lexicon: An information processing approach. In J. Mehler, E. C. T. Walker, & M. Garrett (Eds), *Perspectives on Mental Representation*. Hillsdale, NJ: Erlbaum.

Moynahan, E. D. (1973). The development of knowledge concerning the effect of categorization upon free recall. *Child Development, 44*, 238–46.

Muir, D., Abraham, W., Forbes, F., & Harris, L. (1979). The ontogenesis of an auditory localisation response from birth to four months of age. *Canadian Journal of Psychology, 33*, 320–33.

Muir, D., & Field, J. (1979). Newborn infants orient to sounds. *Child Development, 50*, 431–6.

Muller, A. A. & Aslin, R. N. (1978). Visual tracking as an index of the object concept. *Infant Behavior and Development, 1*, 309–19.

Murphy, C. M., & Messer, D. J. (1977). Mothers, infants and pointing: a study of gesture. In H. R. Schaffer (Ed.), *Studies in mother-infant interaction*. London: Academic Press.

Murphy, G. L., & Medin, D. L. (1985). The role of theories in conceptual coherence. *Psychological Review, 92*, 289–316.

Murray, F. B., & Johnson, P. C. (1969). Reversibility in nonconservation of weight. *Psychonomic Science, 16*, 285–6.

Mussen, P. H., (Ed.), (1983). *Handbook of Child Psychology, Vol, I: History, Theory, and Methods, Vol. II: Infancy and Developmental Psychobiology. Vol. III: Cognitive Development. Vol. IV: Socialization, Personality, and Social Development*. New York: Wiley.

Neilson, I., Dockrell, J., & McKenchnie, J. (1983a). Does repetition of the question influence children's performance in conservation tests? *British Journal of Developmental Psychology, 1*, 163–74.

Neilson, I., Dockrell, J., & McKechnie, J. (1983b). Justifying conservation: A reply to McGarrigle and Donaldson. *Cognition, 15*, 277–91.

Neisser, U. (1976). *Cognition and Reality*. San Francisco: W. H. Freeman.

Nelson, K. (1971). Accommodation of visual-tracking patterns in human infants to object movement patterns. *Journal of Experimental Child Psychology, 12*, 182–96.

Nelson, K. (1973). Structure and strategy in learning to talk. *Monographs of the Society for Research in Child Development, 38*, (1–2, Serial No. 149).

Nelson, K. (1978a). How young children represent knowledge of their world in and out of language. In R. S. Siegler (Ed.), *Children's Thinking: What Develops?* Hillsdale, NJ: Erlbaum.

Nelson, K. (1978b). Semantic Development and the development of semantic memory. In. K. E. Nelson (Ed.), *Children's Language*. New York: Gardner.

Nelson, K. (1985). *Making Sense: The Acquisition of Shared Meaning*. New York: Academic Press.

Nelson, K., Fivush, R., Hudson, J., & Lucariello, J. (1983). Scripts and the development of memory. In M. Chi (ed.), *What is Memory Development the Development of?* Basel: S. Karger.

Nelson, K. & Gruendel, J. M. (1981). Generalized event representation: Basic building blocks of cognitive development. In A. L. Brown & M. Lamb (Eds), *Advances in Developmental Psychology, Vol. 1*. Hillsdale, NJ: Erlbaum.

Newcombe, N. E., Rogoff, B., & Kagan, J. (1977). Developmental changes in recognition memory for pictures of objects and scenes. *Developmental Psychology, 13*, 337–41.

Newell, A. (1973). You can't play 20 questions with nature and win. In W. G. Chase (Ed.), *Visual Information Processing*. New York: Academic Press.

Newell, A. (1980a). Physical symbol systems. *Cognitive Science, 4*, 135–83.

Newell, A. (1980b). Reasoning, problem solving, and decision processes: The problem space as a fundamental category. In R. S. Nickerson (Ed.), *Attention and Performance VIII*. Hillsdale, NJ: Erlbaum.

Newell, A. (1990). *Unified Theories of Cognition*. Cambridge, MA: Harvard University Press.

Newell, A., Shaw, J. C., & Simon, H. A. (1958). Elements of a theory of human problem solving. *Psychological Review, 65*, 151–66.

Newell, A., & Simon, H. A. (1972). *Human Problem Solving*. Englewood Cliffs, NJ: Prentice Hall.

Newmeyer, F. J. (1980). *Linguistic Theory in America*. New York: Academic Press.

Newport, E. L., Gleitman, H., & Gleitman, L. R. (1977). Mother I'd rather do it myself: Some effects and non-effects of maternal speech style. In C. E. Snow & C. A. Ferguson (Eds), *Talking to Children*. Cambridge: Cambridge University Press.

Ninio, A. (1980). Ostensive definition in vocabulary teaching. *Journal of Child Language*, 7, 565–73.

Ninio, A., & Bruner, J. (1978). The achievement and antecedents of labelling. *Journal of Child Language*, 5, 1–15.

Olson, G. M., & Sherman, T. (1983). Attention, learning, and memory in infants. In. P. H. Mussen (Ed.), *Handbook of Child Psychology, Vol. II: Infancy and Developmental Psychobiology*. New York: Wiley.

Olson, G. M. & Strauss, M. S. (1984). The development of infant memory. In M. Moscovitch (Ed.), *Infant Memory*. New York: Plenum.

Olson, R. K., Kliegel, R., Davidson, B. J., & Davies, S. E. (1984). Development of phonetic memory in disabled and normal readers. *Journal of Experimental Child Psychology*, 37, 187–206.

Ornstein, P. A., & Corsale, K. (1979). Organizational factors in children's memory. In C. R. Puff (Ed.), *Memory Organization and Structure*. New York: Academic Press.

Ornstein, P. A., Naus, M. J., & Liberty, C. (1975). Rehearsal and organizational processes in children's memory. *Child Development*, 46, 818–30.

Ornstein, P. A., Naus, M. J., & Stone, B. P. (1977). Rehearsal training and developmental differences in memory. *Developmental Psychology*, 13, 15–24.

Orton, S. T. (1937). *Reading, Writing and Speech Problems in Children*. New York: Norton.

Palmer, S. E. (1978). Fundamental aspects of cognitive representation. In E. Rosch & B. B. Lloyd (Eds), *Cognition and Categorization*. Hillsdale, NJ: Erlbaum.

Parmelee, A. H. (1974). Ontogeny of sleep patterns and associated periodicities in infants. In F. Falkner, N. Kretchmer, & E. Rossi (Eds), *Modern Problems in Peadiatrics: Vol. 13*. Basel: S. Karger.

Parmelee, A. H., & Stern, E. (1972). Development of state in infants. In C. D. Clemente, D. P. Purpura, & F. E. Mayer (Eds), *Sleep and the Maturing Nervous System*. New York: Academic Press.

Patterson, K. E., & Baddeley, A. D. (1977). When face recognition fails. *Journal of Experimental Psychology: Human Learning and Memory*, 3, 406–17.

Patterson, K. E., & Marcel, A. J. (1977). Aphasia, dyslexia and the phonological coding of written words. *Quarterly Journal of Experimental Psychology*, 29, 307–18.

Patterson, K. E. & Morton, J. (1985). From orthography to phonology: An attempt at an old interpretation. In K. E. Patterson, J. C. Marshall, & M. Coltheart (Eds), *Surface Dyslexia: Neuropsychological and Cognitive Studies of Phonological Reading*. Hillsdale, NJ: Erlbaum.

Pavlov, I. P. (1927). *Conditioned Reflexes*. (Trans. by G. V. Anrep.) Oxford: Oxford University Press.

Perret-Clermont, A. N. (1980). *Social Interaction and Cognitive Development in Children.* London: Academic Press.

Petrig, B., Julesz, B., Kropfl, W., Baumgartner, G., & Anliker, M. (1981). Development of stereopsis and cortical binocularity in human infants: Electrophysiological evidence. *Science, 213,* 1402–5.

Pettigrew, J. D. (1974). The effect of visual experience on the development of stimulus specificity by kitten cortical neurones. *Journal of Physiology, 237,* 49–74.

Piaget, J. (1923). *The Language and Thought of the Child.* (Trans. by M.Gabain.) London: Routledge & Kegan Paul, 1926.

Piaget, J. (1924). *Judgement and Reasoning in the Child.* (trans. by M. Warden.) London: Routledge & Kegan Paul, 1926.

Piaget, J. (1926). *The Child's Conception of the World.* (Trans. by J. & A. Tomlinson.) London: Routledge & Kegan Paul, 1929.

Piaget, J. (1927). *The Child's Conception of Physical Causality.* (Trans. by M. Gabain.) London: Routledge & Kegan Paul, 1930.

Paiget, J. (1932). *The Moral Judgement of the Child.* (Trans. by M. Gabain.) London: Routledge & Kegan Paul, 1932.

Piaget, J. (1936a). *The Origins of Intelligence in the Child.* (Trans. by M. Cook.) London: Routledge & Kegan Paul, 1952.

Piaget, J. (1936b). *The Contruction of Reality in the Child.* (Trans. by M. Cook.) London: Routledge & Kegan Paul, 1955.

Piaget, J. (1941). *The Child's Conception of Number.* (Trans. by C. Gattegno & F. M. Hodgson.) London: Routledge & Kegan Paul, 1952.

Piaget, J. (1945). *Play, Dreams and Imitation in Childhood.* (Trans. by C. Gattegno & F. M. Hodgson.) London. Heinemann, 1951.

Piaget, J. (1946a). *The Child's Conception of Time.* (Trans. by A. J. Pomerans.) London: Routledge & Kegan Paul, 1969.

Piaget, J. (1946b). *The Child's Conception of Movement and Speed.* (Trans. by G. E. T. Holloway & M. J. Mackenzie.) London: Routledge & Kegan Paul, 1970.

Piaget, J. (1960). The general problems of the psychological development of the child. In S. M. Tanner & B. Inhelder (Eds), *Discussions on Child Development, Vol. 4.* London: Tavistock.

Piaget, J. (1964). Development and learning, In R. E. Ripple & V. N. Rockcastle (Eds), *Piaget Rediscovered.* Ithaca, NY: Cornell University Press.

Piaget, J. (1965). *Insights and Illusions of Philosophy.* (Trans. by W. Mays.) London: Routledge & Kegan Paul, 1972.

Piaget, J. (1967a). *Biology and Knowledge.* (Trans. by B. Walsh.) Edinburgh: Edinburgh University Press, 1971.

Piaget, J. (1967b). Cognitions and conservation: Two views. Review of 'Studies in Cognitive Growth' by J. S. Bruner, R. R. Olver, P. M. Greenfield, et al. *Contemporary Psychology, 12,* 530–2.

Piaget, J. (1968). Quantification, conservation and nativism. *Science, 162,* 976–9.

Piaget, J. (1970). Piaget's theory. In P. H. Mussen (Ed.), *Carmichael's Manual of Child Psychology, Vol. 1.* New York: Wiley. Reprinted in P. H. Mussen (Ed.), *handbook of Child Psychology, Vol. I: History Theory, and Methods.* New York: Wiley, 1984.

Piaget, J. (1974). *Experiments and Contradiction.* (Trans. by D. Coltman.) Chicago: University of Chicago Press, 1980.

Piaget, J., & Inhelder, B. (1941). *Le Développement des Quantités Physiques chez l'Enfant.* Neuchâtel: Delachaux & Niestlé.

Pinker, S. (1984). *Language Learnability and Language Development.* Cambridge, MA: Harvard University Press.

Pinker, S. (1987). The bootstrapping problem in language acquisiton. In B. MacWhinney (Ed.), *Mechanisms of Language Acquisition.* Hillsdale, NJ: Erlbaum.

Pinker, S., & Prince, A. (1988). On language and connectionism: Analysis of a parallel distributed processing model of language acquisition. *Cognition, 28,* 73–193.

Pirchio, M., Spinelli, D., Fiorentini, A., & Maffei, L. (1978). Infant contrast sensitivity evaluated by evoked potentials. *Brain Research, 141,* 179–84.

Posner, M. I. (1969). Abstraction and the process of recognition. In G. H. Bower & J. T. Spence (Eds), *The Psychology of Learning and Motivation. Vol. 3.* New York: Academic Press.

Posner, M. I., & Keele, S. W. (1968). On the genesis of abstract ideas. *Journal of Experimental Psychology, 77,* 353–63.

Posner, M. I., & Keele, S. W. (1970). Retention of abstract ideas. *Journal of Experimental Psychology, 83,* 304–8.

Prechtl, H. F. R. (1974). Continuity and change in early neural development. In H. F. R. Prechtl (Ed.), *Continuity of Neural Function from Prenatal to Postnatal Life.* Oxford: Blackwell.

Price, D. W. W. (1983). The development of children's comprehension of recurring episodes. Unpublished doctoral dissertation. University of Denver.

Pylyshyn, Z. W. (1984). *Computation and Cognition.* Cambridge, MA: MIT Press.

Querleu, D., & Renard, K. (1981). Les perceptions and auditives du foetus humain. *Médicine et Hygiène, 39,* 2102–10.

Quine, W. V. O. (1960). *Word and Object.* Cambridge, MA: MIT Press.

Quinn, P. C., & Eimas, P. D. (1986). On categorization in early infancy. *Merrill-Palmer Quarterly, 32,* 331–63.

Rader, N., Bausano, M., & Richards, J. E. (1980). On the nature of the visual cliff avoidance response in human infants. *Child Development, 51,* 61–8.

Rader, N., & Stern, J. D. (1982). Visually elicited reaching in neonates. *Child Development, 53,* 1004–7.

Ramsay, D. S. & Campos, J. J. (1978). The onset of representation and entry into Stage VI of object permanence development. *Developmental Psychology, 14,* 79–86.

Ratner, H. H., Smith, B. S., & Dion, S. A. (1986). Development of memory for events. *Journal of Experimental Child Psychology, 41,* 411–28.

Reese, H. W. (1962). Verbal mediation as a function of age level. *Psychological Review, 59,* 502–9.

Repp, B. H. (1983). Categorical perception: Issues, methods, findings. In NJ Lass (Ed.), *Speech and Language: Advances in Basic Research and Practice, Vol. 10.* New York: Academic Press.

Resnick, L. B. (1983). A developmental theory of number understanding. In H. P. Ginsburg (Ed.), *The Development of Mathematical Thinking.* New York: Academic Press.

Resnick, L. B. (1986). The development of mathematical intuition. In M. Perlmutter (Ed.), *Minnesota Symposia on Child Psychology, Vol. 19: Perspectives on Intellectual Development.* Hillsdale, NJ: Erlbaum.

Resnick, L. B., & Ford, W. W. (1981). *The Psychology of Mathematics for Instruction.* Hillsdale, NJ: Erlbaum.

Ricciuti, H. (1965). Object grouping and selective ordering behavior in infants 12-24 months old. *Merrill-Palmer Quarterly, 11,* 129–48.

Richards, J. E., & Rader, N. (1981). Crawling-onset age predicts visual cliff avoidance in infants. *Journal of Experimental Psychology, Human Perception and Performance, 7,* 382–7.

Richards, M. M. (1979). Sorting out what's in a word from what's not: Evaluating Clark's semantic features acquisition theory. *Journal of Experimental Child Psychology, 27,* 1–47.

Ringel, B. A., & Springer, C. J. (1980). On knowing how well one is remembering: The persistence of strategy use during transfer. *Journal of Experimental Child Psychology, 29,* 322–33.

Rips, L. J., Shoben, E. J., & Smith, E. E. (1973). Semantic distance and the verification of semantic relations. *Journal of Verbal Learning and Verbal Behavior, 12,* 1–20.

Rosch, E. (1973). On the internal structure of perceptual and semantic categories. In T. E. Moore (Ed.), *Cognitive Development and the Acquisition of Language.* New York: Academic Press.

Rosch, E. (1978). Principles of categorization. In E. Rosch & B. B. Lloyd (Eds), *Cognition and Categorization.* Hillsdale, NJ: Erlbaum.

Rosch, E., & Mervis, C. B. (1975). Family resemblances: Studies in the internal structure of categories. *Cognitive Psychology, 7,* 573–605.

Rosch, E., Mervis, C., Gray, W., Johnson, D., & Boyes-Braem, P. (1976). Basic objects in natural categories. *Cognitive Psychology, 8,* 382–439.

Rose, S. A., & Blank, M. (1974). The potency of context in children's cognition: An illustration through conservation. *Child Development, 45,* 499–502.

Rose, S. A., Gottfried, A. W., & Bridger, W. H. (1983). Infants' cross-modal transfer from solid objects to their graphic representations. *Child Development, 54,* 686–94.

Ross, G. S. (1980). Categorization in 1- to 2-year-olds. *Developmental Psychology, 16,* 391–6.

Rotman, B. (1977). *Jean Piaget: Psychologist of the Real.* Hassocks, Sussex: Harvester.

Rovee-Collier, C. (1984). The ontogeny of learning and memory in human infancy. In R. Kail & N. E. Spear (Eds), *Comparative Perspectives on the Development of Memory.* Hillsdale, NJ: Erlbaum.

Rozin, P., & Gleitman, L. (1977). The structure and acquisition of reading. II. The reading process and the acquisition of the alphabetic principle. In A. S. Reber & D. L. Scarborough (Eds), *Toward a Psychology of Reading.* Hillsdale, NJ: Erlbaum.

Rubenstein, J. (1976). Concordance of visual and manipulative responsiveness to novel and familiar stimuli: A function of test procedures or prior experience? *Child Development, 47,* 1197–9.

Ruff, H. A. (1976). The co-ordination of manipulation and visual fixation: A response to Schaffer (1975). *Child Development, 47,* 868–71.

Ruff, H. A. (1978). Infant recognition of the invariant form of objects. *Child Development, 49,* 293–306.

Ruff, H. A., & Halton, A. (1978). Is there directed reaching in the human neonate? *Developmental Psychology, 14,* 425–6.

Rumelhart, D. E. (1975). Notes on a schema for stories. In D. G. Bobrow & A. Collins (Eds), *Representation and Understanding: Studies in Cognitive Science.* New York: Academic Press.

Rumelhart, D. E. (1977). Toward an interactive model of reading. In S. Dornic (Ed.), *Attention and Performance, VI.* Hillsdale, NJ: Erlbaum.

Rumelhart, D. E., & McClelland, J. L. (1982). An interactive activation model of context effects in letter perception: Part 2. The contextual enhancement effect and some tests and extensions of the model. *Psychological Review, 98,* 60–94.

Rumelhart, D. E., & McClelland, J. R. (1986). On learning the past tenses of English verbs. In J. L. McClelland & D. E. Rumelhart (Eds), *Parallel Distributed Processing: Explorations in the Microstructure of Cognition, Vol. 2: Psychological and Biological Models.* Cambridge, MA: MIT Press.

Rumelhart, D. E., Smolensky, P., McClelland, J. L., & Hinton, G. E. (1986). Schemata and sequential thought processes in PDP models. In J. L. McClelland & D. E. Rumelhart (Eds), *Parallel Distributed Processing: Explorations in the Microstructure of Cognition. Vol. 2: Psychological and Biological Models.* Cambridge, MA: MIT Press.

Russell, B. (1912). *The Problems of Philosophy.* London: Williams & Norgate.

Salapatek, P. (1975). Pattern perception in early infancy. In L. B. Cohen & P. Salapatek (Eds), *Infant Perception: From Sensation to Cognition. Vol. 1: Basic Visual Processes.* New York: Academic Press.

Salapatek, P., & Kessen, W. (1966). Visual scanning of triangles by the human newborn. *Journal of Experimental Child Psychology, 3,* 155–67.

Salapatek, P., & Kessen, W. (1973). Prolonged investigation of triangles by the human newborn. *Journal of Experimental Child Psychology, 15,* 22–9.

Salatas, H., & Flavell, J. H. (1976). Behavioral and metamnemonic indicators of strategic behavior under remember instructions in first grade. *Child Development, 47,* 81–9.

Saxe, G. B., & Kaplan, R. (1981). Gesture in early counting: A developmental analysis. *Perceptual and Motor Skills, 53,* 851–4.

Saywitz, K. J. (1987). Children's testimony: Age-related patterns of memory errors. In S. J. Ceci, M. P. Toglia, & D. F. Ross (Eds) *Children's Eyewitness Testimony.* New York: Springer-Verlag.

Scaife, M., & Bruner, J. (1975). The capacity for joint visual attention in the infant. *Nature, 253,* 265–6.

Scarr, S., & Salapatek, P. (1970). Patterns of fear development during infancy. *Merrill-Palmer Quarterly, 16,* 53–90.

Schank, R. C. (1983). *Dynamic Memory: A Theory of Reminding and Learning in Computers and People.* New York: Cambridge University Press.

Schank, R. C., & Abelson, R. (1977a). *Scripts, Plans, Goals, and Understanding.* Hillsdale, NJ: Erlbaum.

Schank, R. C., & Abelson, R. P. (1977b). Scripts, plans, and knowledge. In P. N. Johnson-Laird & P. C. Wason (Eds), *Thinking: Readings in Cognitive Science.* Cambridge: Cambridge University Press.

Schlesinger, I. M. (1971). Production of utterances and language acquisition. In D. I. Slobin (Ed.), *The Ontogenesis of Grammar.* New York: Academic Press.

Schneider, W., & Shiffrin, R. M. (1977). Controlled and automatic human information processing: I. Detection, search, and attention. *Psychological Review, 84,* 1–66.

Schulman-Galambos, C., & Galambos, R. (1979). Brain stem evoked response audiometry in newborn hearing screening. *Archives of Otolaryngology, 105,* 86–90.

Schwartz, A, Campos, J., & Baisel, E. (1973). The visual cliff: Cardiac and behavioral correlates on the deep and shallow sides at five and nine months of age. *Journal of Experimental Child Psychology, 15,* 86–99.

Scibetla, J. J., Rosen, M. G., Hochberg, C. J., & Chik, L. (1971). Human fetal brain responses to sound during labour. *American Journal of Obstetrics and Gynecology, 109,* 82–5.

Sears, R. R. (1975). Your ancients revisited: A history of child development. In E. M. Hetherington (Ed.), *Review of Child Development Research, Vol. 5.* Chicago: University of Chicago Press.

Segui, J. (1984). The syllable: A basic perceptual unit in speech processing? In H. Bouma & D. G. Bouwhuis (Eds), *Attention and Performance X.* Hillsdale, NJ: Erlbaum.

Secada, W. G., Fuson, K. C., & Hall, J. W. (1983). The transition from counting-all to counting-on in addition. *Journal for Research in Mathematics Education, 14,* 47–57.

Seidenberg. M. S., & McClelland, J. L. (1989). A distributed, developmental model of word recognition and naming. *Psychological Review, 96.* 523–68.

Seymour, P. H. K. (1986). *Cognitive Analysis of Dyslexia.* London: Routledge & Kegan Paul.

Seymour, P. H. K., & Porpodas, C. D. (1980). Lexical and non-lexical processing of spelling in developmental dyslexia. In U. Frith (Ed.), *Cognitive Processes in Spelling.* London: Academic Press.

Shankweiler, D., Liberman, I. Y., Mark, L. S., Fowler, C. A., & Fischer, F. W., (1979). The speech code and learning to read. *Journal of Experimental Psychology: Human Learning and Memory, 5,* 531–45.

Shannon, C. E. (1948). A mathematical theory of communication. *Bell System Technical Journal, 27,* 379–423, 623–56.

Shepard, R. N. (1967). Recognition memory for words, sentences and pictures. *Journal of Verbal Learning and Verbal Behavior, 6,* 156–63.

Shiffrin, R. M., & Dumais, S. T. (1981). The development of automatism. In J. R. Anderson (Ed.), *Cognitive Skills and Their Acquisition.* Hillsdale, NJ: Erlbaum.

Shiffrin, R. M., & Schneider, W. (1977). Controlled and automatic human information processing: II. Perceptual learning, automatic attending, and a general theory. *Psychological Review, 84,* 127–90.

Siegel, L. S., Levey, P., & Ferris, H. (1985). Subtypes of developmental dyslexia: Do they exist? In F. J. Morrison, C. Lord, & D. P. Keating (Eds), *Applied Developmental Psychology, Vol. 2,* New York: Academic Press.

Siegler, R. S. (1976). Three aspects of cognitive development. *Cognitive Psychology, 4,* 481–520.

Siegler, R. S. (1981). Developmental sequences between and within concepts. *Monographs of the Society for Research in Child Development, 46* (2, Serial No. 189).

Siegler, R. S. (1983). Information processing approaches to development. In P. H. Mussen (Ed.), *Handbook of Child Psychology, Vol. 1 History, Theory, and Methods.* New York: Wiley.

Siegler, R. S. (1984). Encoding and combination as sources of cognitive variation. In R. J. Sternberg (Ed.), *Mechanisms of Cognitive Development.* New York: W. H. Freeman.

Simonoux, K., & Decarie, T. G. (1979). Cognition and perception in the object concept. *Canadian Journal of Psychology, 33,* 396–407.

Sinnott, J. M., Pisoni, D. B., & Aslin, R. N. (1983). A comparison of pure tone auditory thresholds in infants and adults. *Infant Behavior and Development, 6,* 3–17.

Siqueland, E. R., & DeLucia, C. A. (1969). Visual reinforcement of non-nutritive sucking in human infants. *Science, 165,* 1144–6.

Skinner, B. F. (1957). *Verbal Behavior.* New York: Appleton-Century-Crofts.

Slater, A. M., & Morison, V. (1985). Shape constancy and slant perception at birth. *Perception, 14,* 337–44.

Slater, A. M., Morison, V., & Rose, D. (1982). Visual memory at birth. *British Journal of Developmental Psychology, 3,* 211–20.

Slobin, D. I. (1966). Comments on McNeill's 'Developmental psycholinguisitics'. In F. Smith & G. A. Miller (Eds), *The Genesis of Language: A Psycholinguistic Approach.* Cambridge, MA: MIT Press.

Slobin, D. I. (1970). Universals of grammatical development in children. In G. B. Flores d'Arcais & W. J. M. Levelt (Eds), *Advances in Psycholinguistics.* Amsterdam: North-Holland.

Slobin, D. I. (1973). Cognitive prerequisites for the development of grammar. In C. A. Ferguson & D. I. Slobin (Eds), *Studies of Child Language Development.* New York: Holt, Rinehart & Winston.

Slobin, D. I. (1981). The origins of of grammatical encoding of events. In W.

Deutsch (Ed.), *The Child's Construction of Language.* London: Academic Press.

Slobin, D. I. (1985). Crosslinguistic evidence for the language-making capacity. In D. I. Slobin (Ed.), *The Crosslinguistic Study of Language Acquisition, Vol. 2: Theoretical Issues.* Hillsdale, NJ: Erlbaum.

Smith, E. E., & Medin, D. L. (1981). *Categories and Concepts.* Cambridge, MA: Harvard University Press.

Smolensky, P. (1988). On the proper treatment of connectionism. *Behavioral and Brain Sciences, 11,* 1–74.

Snow, C. E., & Ferguson, C. A. (Eds), (1977). *Talking to Children.* Cambridge: Cambridge University Press.

Snowling, M. J. (1980). The development of grapheme-phoneme correspondences in normal and dyslexic readers. *Journal of Experimental Child Psychology, 29,* 294–305.

Snowling, M. J. (1981). Phonemic deficits in developmental dyslexia. *Psychological Research, 1981,* 219–34.

Snowling, M. J. (1983). The comparison of acquired and developmental disorders of reading. *Cognition, 14,* 105–18.

Snowling, M. J. (1987). *Dyslexia: A Cognitive Developmental Perspective.* Oxford: Blackwell.

Sokal, R. R. (1974). Classification: Purposes, principles, progress, prospects. *Science, 185,* 1115–23.

Sokol, S. (1978). Measurement of infant visual-acuity from pattern reversal evoked-potentials. *Vision Research, 18,* 33–9.

Spear, N. E. (1984). Ecologically determined dispositions control the ontogeny of learning and memory. In R. Kail & N. E. Spear (Eds), *Comparative Perspectives on the Development of Memory.* Hillsdale, NJ: Erlbaum.

Spelke, E. S. (1976). Infants' intermodal perception of events. *Cognitive Psychology, 8,* 553–60.

Spelke, E. S. (1979). Perceiving bimodally specified events in infancy. *Development Psychology, 15,* 626–36.

Spelke, E. S. (1981). The infants' acquisition of knowledge of bimodally specified events. *Journal of Experimental Child Psychology, 31,* 279–99.

Stanley, G. (1978). Eye movements in dyslexic children. In G. Stanley & K. Walsh (Eds), *Brain Impairment: Proceedings of the 1977 Brain Impairment Workshop.* Victoria: Dominion Press.

Stanovich, K. E., Cunningham, A. E., & Cramer, B. B. (1984). Assessing phonological awareness in kindergarten children: Issues of task comparability. *Journal of Experimental Child Psychology, 38,* 175–90.

Stanovich, K. E., Nathan, R. G., & Zolman, J. E. (1988). The developmental lag hypothesis in reading: Longitudinal and matched reading-level comparisons. *Child Development, 59,* 71–86.

Starkey, D. (1981). The origins of concept formation: Object sorting and object preference in early infancy. *Child Development, 52,* 489–97.

Starkey, P., & Cooper, R. G. (1980). Perception of numbers by human infants. *Science, 210,* 1033–5.

Stein, N. L., & Glenn, C. G. (1979). An analysis of story comprehension in elementary school children. In R. O. Freedle (Ed.), *Discourse Processing: Advances in Research and Theory, Vol. 2.* Norwood, NJ: Ablex.

Sternberg, R. J., (Ed.), (1984). *Mechanisms of Cognitive Development.* New York: W. H. Freeman.

Sternberg, S. (1969). The discovery of processing stages. Extensions of Donder's method. *Acta Psychologica, 30,* 276–315.

Stevens, K. N., & Blumstein, S. E. (1981). The search for invariant acoustic correlates of phonetic features. In P. D. Eimas & J. L. Miller (Eds), *Perspectives on the Study of Speech.* Hillsdale, NJ: Erlbaum.

Strauss, M. S. & Cohen, L. B. (1980). Infant immediate and delayed memory for perceptual dimensions. Paper presented at the International Conference on Infant Studies.

Strauss, M. S., Curtis, L. E. (1984). Development of numerical concepts in infants. In C. Sophian (Ed.) *Origins of Cognitive Skills.* Hillsdale, NJ: Erlbaum.

Streeter, L. A. (1976). Language perception of 2-month-old infants show effects of both innate mechanisms and experience. *Nature, 259,* 39–41.

Sugarman, S. (1981). The cognitive basis of classification in very young children: An analysis of object ordering trends. *Child Development, 52,* 1172–8.

Suzuki, T., & Ogiba, Y. (1961). Conditioned orientation reflex audiometry. *Archives of Otolaryngology, 74,* 192–8.

Svenson, O. (1975). Analysis of time required by children for simple additions. *Acta Psychologica, 39,* 289–302.

Svenson, O., & Hedenborg, M. L. (1979). Strategies used by children when solving simple subtractions. *Acta Psychologica, 43,* 1–13.

Svenson, O., Hedenborg, M. & Lingman, L. (1976). On children's heuristics for solving simple additions. *Scandinavian Journal for Educational Research, 20,* 161–73.

Taguchi, K., Picton, T. W., Orpin, J. A., & Goodman, W. S. (1969). Evoked response audiometry in newborn infants. *Acta Oto-Laryngologica* (Supplement), *252,* 5–17.

Temple, C. (1985). Surface dyslexia: variations within a syndrome. In K. E. Patterson, J. C. Marshall, & M. Coltheart (Eds), *Surface Dyslexia: Neuropsychological and Cognitive Studies of Phonological Reading,* Hillsdale, NJ: Erlbaum.

Temple, C., & Marshall, J. (1983). A case study of developmental phonological dyslexia. *British Journal of Psychology, 74,* 517–33.

Thieman, T. J., & Brewer, W. F. (1978). Alfred Binet on memory for ideas. *Genetic Psychology Monographs, 97,* 243–64.

Thomas, H. (1973). Unfolding the baby's mind: The infant's selection of visual stimuli. *Psychological Review, 80,* 468–88.

Thomson, J. R., & Chapman, R. S. (1977). Who is 'Daddy' revisited: The status of two-year-olds' overextended words in use and comprehension. *Journal of Child Language*, *4*, 359–75.

Thorndike, E. L. (1922). *The Psychology of Arithmetic*. New York: Macmillan.

Tinbergen, N. (1951). *A Study of Instinct*, Oxford: Oxford University Press.

Torrey, J. W. (1979). Reading that comes naturally: The early reader. In T. G. Waller & G. E. Mackinnon (Eds), *Reading Research: Advances in Theory and Practice, Vol. 1*. New York: Academic Press.

Touwen, B. (1976). *Neurological Development in Infancy*. London: Spastics International & Heinemann.

Trehub, S. A. (1976). The discrimination of foreign speech contrasts by infants and adults. *Child Development*, *47*, 466–72.

Trehub, S. E., Schneider, B. A., & Endman, M. (1980). Developmental changes in infant's sensitivity to octave-band noises. *Journal of Experimental Child Psychology*, *29*, 282–93.

Treiman, R. (1984). Individual differences among children in spelling and reading styles. *Journal of Experimental Child Psychology*, *37*, 463–77.

Tulving, E. (1972). Episodic and semantic memory. In E. Tulving & W. Donaldson (Eds), *Organization of Memory*. New York: Academic Press.

Turing, A. M. (1936). On computable numbers, with an application to the Entscheidungsproblem. *Proceedings of the London Mathematical Society*, (Series 2), *42*, 230–65.

Ullman, S. (1980). Against direct perception. *Behavioral and Brain Sciences*, *3*, 373–81.

Uzgiris, I. C. (1972). Patterns of vocal and gestural imitation in infants. In F. Monks, W. Hartup, & J. de Wit (Eds), *Determinants of Behavioral Development*, New York: Academic Press.

Uzgiris, I. & Hunt, J. McV. (1975). *Assessment in Infancy: Ordinal Scales of Psychological Development*. Urbana,: Ill. University of Illinois Press.

Vellutino, F. R. (1979). *Dyslexia: Theory and Research*. Cambridge, MA: MIT Press.

Vellutino, F. R. (1987). Dyslexia. *Scientific American*, *256(3)*, 20–7.

Vellutino, F. R., Pruzek, R. M., Steger, J. A., & Meshoulam, U. (1973). Immediate visual recall in poor and normal readers as a function of orthographic-linguistic familiarity. *Cortex*, *9*, 370–86.

Vinter, A. (1986). The role of movement in eliciting early imitations. *Child Development*, *57*, 66–71.

Vygotsky, L. (1934). *Thought and Language*. (Trans. by E. Hanfman & G. Vakar.) Cambridge, MA: MIT Press, 1962.

Walk, R. D., & Gibson, E. J. (1961). A comparative and analytical study of visual depth perception. *Psychological Monographs*, *75*, (15, Whole No. 519).

Walker, D. W., Grimwade, J. C., & Wood, C. (1971). Intrauterine noise: A component of the fetal environment. *American Journal of Obstetrics and Gynecology*, *109*, 91–5.

Walkerdine, V., & Sinha, C. (1978). The internal triangle: language, reasoning, and the social context. In I. Markova (Ed.), *The Social Context of Language.* New York: Wiley.

Wallace, I., Klahr, D., & Bluff, K. (1987). A self-modifying production system model of cognitive development. In D. Klahr, P. Langley, & D. Neches (Eds), *Production System Models of Learning and Development.* Cambridge, MA: MIT Press.

Watson, J. B., & Rayner, R. A. (1920). Conditional emotional reactions. *Journal of Experimental Psychology, 3,* 1–14.

Wellman, H. M., Ritter, K., & Flavell, J. H. (1975). Deliberate memory behavior in the delayed reactions of very young children. *Developmental Psychology, 11,* 780–7.

Wells, G. L., Turtle, J. W., & Luus, C. A. E. (1989). The perceived credibility of child eyewitnesses: What happens when they use their own words? In S. J. Ceci, D. F. Ross, & M. P. Toglia (Eds) *Perspectives on Children's Testimony.* New York: Springer-Verlag.

Werker, J. F., & Tees, R. C. (1984). Cross-language speech perception: Evidence for perceptual reorganization during the first year of life. *Infant Behavior and Development, 7,* 49–63.

Wertheimer, M. (1961). Psycho-motor co-ordination of auditory-visual space at birth. *Science, 134,* 1692–6.

White, B., Castle, R., & Held, R. (1964). Observations on the development of visually directed reaching. *Child Development, 35.* 349–64.

Whittaker, S. (1983). The development of memory in 3- to 6-year-olds: Learning how to learn. Unpublished doctoral dissertation. University of St. Andrews.

Wickelgren, W. A. (1969). Context-sensitive coding, associative memory, and serial order in (speech) behavior. *Psychological Review, 76,* 1–15.

Willoughby, R. H., & Trachy, S. (1971). Conservation of number in very young children: a failure to replicate Mehler and Bever. *Merrill-Palmer Quarterly, 17,* 205–9.

Wittgenstein, L. (1953). *Philosophical Investigations.* (Trans. by. G. E. M. Anscombe). Oxford: Blackwell.

Wohlwill, J. F. (1960). Developmental studies of perception. *Psychological Bulletin, 57,* 249–88.

Wohlwill, J. F. (1970). The age variable in psychological research. *Psychological Review, 77,* 49–64.

Wohlwill, J. F. (1973). *The Study of Behavioral Development.* New York: Academic Press.

Woods, S. S., Resnick, L. B., & Groen, G. J. (1975). An experimental test of five process models for subtraction. *Journal of Educational Psychology, 67,* 17–21.

Yarmey, A. D. (1979). *The Psychology of Eyewitness Testimony.* New York: Free Press.

Yonas, A., Bechtold, A. G., Frankel, D., Gordon, F. R., McRoberts, G., Norcia, A., & Sternfels, S. (1977). Development of sensitivity to information for impending collision. *Perception and Psychophysics, 21.* 97–104.

Yonas, A., Cleaves, W., & Pettersen, L. (1978). Development of sensitivity to pictoral depth. *Science, 200*, 77–9.

Yonas, A., & Granrud, C. E. (1985). Development of visual space perception in young infants. In J. Mehler & R. Fox (Eds), *Neonate Cognition: Beyond the Blooming Buzzing Confusion*. Hillsdale, NJ: Erlbaum.

Yonas, A., Granrud, C. E., & Pettersen, L. (1985). Infants' sensitivity to relative size information for distance. *Developmental Psychology, 21*, 161–7.

Yonas, A., Oberg, C., & Norcia, A. (1978). Development of sensitivity to binocular information for the approach of an object. *Developmental Psychology, 14*, 147–52.

Yonas, A., Pettersen, L., & Granrud, C. E. (1982). Infants' sensitivity to familiar size as information for distance. *Child Development, 53*, 1285–90.

Young, R. M. (1976). *Seriation By Children: An Artificial Intelligence Analysis of a Piagetian Task*. Basel: Birkhauser.

Young, R. M., & O'Shea, T. (1981). Errors in children's subtraction. *Cognitive Science, 5*, 153–77.

Younger, B. A., & Cohen, L. B. (1983). Infant perception of correlations among attributes. *Child Development, 54*, 858–67.

Yussen, S. R. (1974). Determinants of visual attention and recall in observational learning by preschoolers and second graders. *Developmental Psychology, 10*, 93–100.

Yussen, S. R., Levin, J. R., Berman, L., & Palm, J. (1979). Developmental changes in the awareness of memory benefits associated with different types of picture organization. *Developmental Psychology, 15*, 447–9.

Yussen, S. R., & Levy, V. M. (1975). Developmental changes in predicting one's own span of short-term memory. *Journal of Experimental Child Psychology, 19*, 502–8.

Yussen, S. R., Matthews, S. R. II, Buss, R. R., & Kane, P. T. (1980). Developmental change in judging important and critical elements of stories. *Developmental Psychology, 16*, 213–19.

Zaragoza, M. S. (1987). Memory, suggestibility, and eyewitness testimony in children and adults. In S. J. Ceci, M. P. Toglia, & D. F. Ross (Eds) *Children's Eyewitness Testimony*. New York: Springer-Verlag.

Subject Index

Name Index